THE HORIZON
HISTORY

AMERICAN HERITAGE PUBLISHING CO., INC., New York

OF RUSSIA

BY THE EDITORS OF **HORIZON MAGAZINE**

EDITOR IN CHARGE **WENDY BUEHR**

AUTHOR **IAN GREY**

HORIZON
BOOK DIVISION

EDITORIAL DIRECTOR
Richard M. Ketchum

GENERAL EDITOR
Alvin M. Josephy, Jr.

Staff for this Book

EDITOR
Wendy Buehr

ART DIRECTOR
Emma Landau

MANAGING EDITOR
Kaari I. Ward

PICTURE EDITORS
Mary Leverty
Emese Wood, *Assistant*

ASSOCIATE EDITOR
Angela Hill

CONTRIBUTING EDITORS
Margot Brill
Mary Durant
Thomas Froncek

RESEARCHER
Gay Sherry

ASSISTANT EDITOR
Roxanne Wehrhan

EUROPEAN BUREAU
Gertrudis Feliu, *Chief*

CONSULTANT
S. Frederick Starr
Assistant Professor of History, Princeton University

AMERICAN HERITAGE
PUBLISHING CO., INC.

PRESIDENT
James Parton

EDITORIAL COMMITTEE
Joseph J. Thorndike, *Chairman*
Oliver Jensen
Alvin M. Josephy, Jr.
Richard M. Ketchum

EDITORIAL ART DIRECTOR
Murray Belsky

PUBLISHER, HORIZON MAGAZINE
Paul Gottlieb

Horizon Magazine is published quarterly by American Heritage Publishing Co., Inc., 551 Fifth Avenue, N.Y., N.Y. 10017. Printed in the United States of America. Library of Congress Catalog Card Number: 76-117351. Standard Book Numbers: Regular Edition 8281-0098-5; Deluxe Edition 8281-0099-3; Boxed Edition 8281-0102-7.

Published simultaneously in Canada by Fitzhenry & Whiteside Limited.

ABOVE: *The diamond- and ruby-studded Order of Victory—the highest Soviet decoration awarded military heroes—recalls tsarist extravagance. Its medallion depicts the Kremlin's Spassky Tower.*
Soviet Life

HALF-TITLE PAGE: *An enticing siren, carved in wood by a contemporary peasant craftsman, perpetuates the ancient Russian folk myth of the bird damsels who lured Volga boatmen to their doom.*
Soviet Life

TITLE PAGE: *In the early 1700's Peter the Great abandoned xenophobic Moscow and forged the new capital of St. Petersburg on the Gulf of Finland. The city became a "window on the West," a point of contact with the modern world. This mid-nineteenth-century view captures the metropolis at the height of its neoclassical grandeur.*
Russia Illustrated

Modern Russia, a rich commingling of cultures and races, is the product of centuries of migration, conquest, and peaceful assimilation across the vast Eurasian plain. Although Slavs predominate, accounting for more than two thirds of the 242 million population, over 130 peoples have shared in shaping the country that Winston Churchill described as "a riddle wrapped in a mystery inside an enigma." A glimpse of a few of the many faces of the U.S.S.R. is given on these and the next six pages: below, Leningraders celebrating opening day of school; pages 8-9, a surgeon and the Party chairman of a factory; pages 10-11, from left to right, an Uzbek merchant, a Kirgiz student, a Yakutsk reindeer herder, a Pskov machinist, a Tadzhik artisan, Moscow railroad workers, a Kiev policewoman, and a Ukrainian peasant; pages 12-13, a soldier and a ribbon-bedecked Heroine of Soviet Labor.

The People

HAMENT CORPORA

Roots of Old Russia

The history of Russia is an epic of unending struggle to settle the Eurasian plain, an area of nearly nine million square miles, the largest extent of land on the earth's surface. The growth of the Russian nation is also the story of extraordinary tenacity and endurance of peoples who have suffered invasion, calamity, and hardship in every century on a scale experienced by few other countries. A generally harsh climate, a terrain that has no effective natural barriers to obstruct migrations and invasions, and a network of mighty rivers have inspired and directed events.

Toward the end of the ice age, some fifteen thousand years ago, when the glaciers that covered northern Europe began to recede, belts of vegetation evolved that would determine man's future habitation. Within the Arctic Circle the tundra, a bleak zone of mosses and lichens, is covered with snow and ice for most of the year. South of the tundra is the taiga, a vast belt of dense coniferous forests, broken only by peat bogs, which extends from Finland eastward for four thousand miles to the Bering Sea. This zone was rich in fur-bearing animals—among them squirrel, wolf, ermine, sable,

The Great Goddess, a pre-Christian deity revered by the nomadic tribes of Russia, is seated on her throne and holds a "scepter" representing the tree of life. The detail is from a fifth-century B.C. felt wall hanging found in a chieftain's tomb in Siberia.

fox, marten, bear—whose pelts would become the economic foundation of the first Russian state.

The zone of mixed pine, fir, and birch forests came next as a roughly triangular wedge stretching eastward from the Baltic and Poland and narrowing gradually into a finger, touching the Ural Mountains. This was a region of dense forests and poor soils, but it had advantages that made it the cradle of the Russian nation. It is the region of the great network of rivers, principal among them the Don, Volga, Dvina, Dnieper, Dniester, which were of tremendous commercial, military, and political significance in Russia's history.

The mixed forests merged imperceptibly into the steppe, from the Russian word for "lowland," a sparsely wooded grassland. This belt extended from the Carpathian Mountains, rising between modern-day Czechoslovakia and Poland, to the Altai Mountains, bordering Mongolia. Between this belt and the Black Sea stretched the true steppe, the zone of *chernaya zemlya*, or "black earth," that would, over the centuries, become Russia's agricultural heartland. Still farther south lay the semideserts of central Asia.

The conflict between forest and steppe zones, between insular and expansive social organization, has been a major factor in the development of the Russian state. The extremes of weather have also played a part. Over most of the plain a continental climate prevails. The upsurge of life in spring

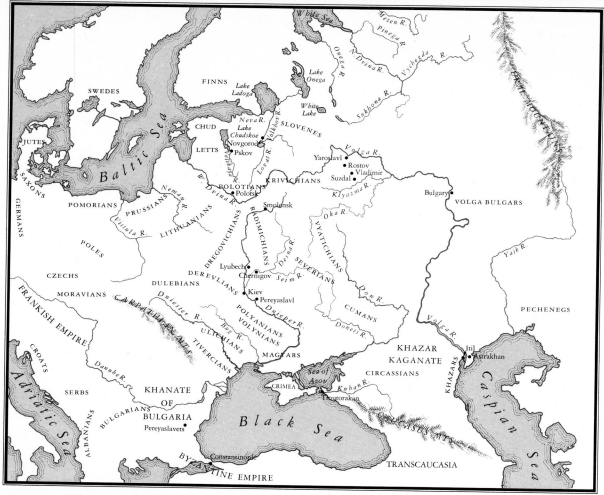

The dispersion of the Slavs, a process hurried by recurrent nomadic invasions, was all but complete when the first Russian state began to form. This map shows the ninth-century location of the numerous tribes that comprised the East Slavs, progenitors of modern Russians; the West Slavs, who peopled Poland and Czechoslovakia; and the South Slavs, who established themselves in the Balkans.

and the sudden heat of summer contrast with the savage cold of winter. The people inhabiting this principal area of settlement early became inured to these sharp changes in weather and developed great stamina and hardiness. The climate has also contributed to, or even dictated, the tempo of Russian life and the pattern of Russia's history—in which periods of quiescence have given way to furious outbursts of activity.

Another physical factor of great importance is the terrain of the Eurasian plain—flat, broken only by a low north-south range of eroded hills, rising little more than a thousand five hundred feet above the plain, known as the Ural Mountains. Though traditionally ascribed the role of barrier between Europe and Asia, the Urals are readily penetrable, with numerous low passes that have proved strategically indefensible for Russia. Lastly, there are the navigable rivers, principally flowing north and south, but with sufficient east-west courses to lace the plain. These rivers, plus easy portages, enabled the Russians and their invaders to travel great distances, even through the forest lands, for purposes of trade and war; though none led directly to open oceans, they did have links with such major seas as the Baltic, the Black, and the Caspian. The flatness of the plain and the system of waterways have given a sense of unity and have promoted acceptance of central authority in Russia, in contrast with western Europe, where numerous natural barriers encouraged the growth of small sovereign states.

By the time of the Neolithic period in Russia (around 3000 B.C.), the Indo-European peoples of the forests and steppelands were already developing distinctively different ways of life. Hunting and fishing were the chief occupations in the north, whereas the warmer climate and black soil in the south encouraged agriculture and cattle herding. During the Bronze Age (2000–1000 B.C.) the people of the steppes continued to develop more rapidly; but the northerners, too, were beginning to keep cattle and to cultivate the land.

Around 1000 B.C. the Cimmerians, generally designated an Aryan people, became the first to rule rather than simply occupy south Russia. About 700 B.C., however, the Scythians displaced them as lords of the steppelands. They were the first of the great waves of nomadic peoples who swept from Asia through Turkistan along the road south of the Urals and into the steppes. The origins of the nomads and the reasons for their surging westward migrations are not certain. Droughts, overpopulation, and the uprise of tribes in new strength were certainly some of the factors, but some historians attribute the beginning of history's great Völkerwanderung, which continued until the thirteenth century, to China's intensified campaign against the barbarian peoples harassing their borders.

The Asiatic nomads were horsemen and sturdy, savage

Brilliant burial ornaments offer many clues to the life of Scythian nomads. Left, chieftains share a cup of blood-steeped wine to seal an oath of fealty. Below, two warriors seek comfort beneath a tree, where they are met by a woman, perhaps the Great Goddess.

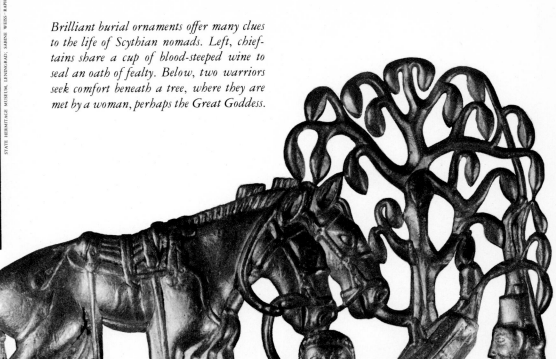

warriors. They herded cattle, sheep, and goats, and were constantly on the move to new pastures, their simple possessions being carried in covered wagons in which they also slept. Meat was their main diet, supplemented by kumiss, a fermented drink made from mare's milk. They spent lengthy periods in the saddle watching over their herds; and on raids or campaigns they could ride great distances. The short, double-curved bow was their weapon, and in war or on hunting expeditions they could shoot their bronze-tipped arrows with deadly accuracy for several hundred feet. They imposed their bondage over defeated enemies, but allowed them to continue cultivating the land while they levied tribute.

The Scythians were masters of the steppelands at the time when the Greeks established colonies on the northern shores of the Black Sea. Lively trade relations developed between them, with the nomads assimilating elements of Greek culture. But about 200 B.C. the Scythians were swept away by the Sarmatians, an Iranian people who dominated the steppes for some four centuries, levying tribute and actively participating in the rich commerce of the region. In turn the Sarmatians were conquered by the Goths, a Germanic tribe that, deflected from migrating into parts of southern Europe by the Romans, descended upon south Russia. Though the Goths were not horsemen, they quickly learned the art of fighting in the saddle and thus were able to conquer the steppes; but their rule was cut short around A.D. 370 by the Huns. This Asiatic horde, primarily a military force, invaded European Russia, driving the Goths westward and into conflict with the Roman empire. The Huns established a vast empire, extending from the Volga to the Danube, and they spread terror throughout Europe as they moved inexorably westward. Attila (c. 406–53), their greatest leader, made his headquarters in the Hungarian plains, exacting tribute from Rome, Constantinople, and numerous lesser states. The "Scourge of God," as Attila was called, was poised to conquer Europe when he suddenly died in 453, and the empire of the Huns promptly disintegrated. Succeeding waves of Asian nomads—the Avars; Khazars; Bulgars; Magyars; Pechenegs, or Patzinaks; Cumans, or Polovtsi; Mongols; Turks; and Tatars—came over a period of a thousand years. The steppelands of southern Russia were like a great highway along which nomadic hordes fought for dominion and for the rich trade between China and Europe, only to be crushed or pushed farther to the west by a new tribe.

In the midst of these movements of peoples across the great plain, the Slavic tribes emerged. Their origins are not known; in the first century A.D. the Roman historian Tacitus wrote of them as the Veneti, or Wends, who were then settled in the basin of the Vistula River and the region of the upper Dnieper—roughly equivalent to the areas of eastern

With small, maneuverable vessels such as those depicted in the twelfth-century manuscript opposite, the Varangians were able to cross the Baltic and penetrate northern Russia. Once on land, they plunged into deep forests where the perils multiplied: in the bronze plaque above left, which decorated a seventh-century casket, two well-armed soldiers cast a weather eye; in the companion plaque at right, a bare-chested figure confronts a fabulous monster he has just collared.

Poland and Belorussia today. He noted that, unlike the nomadic Sarmatians, they traveled on foot and lived in settlements. Already they were spreading out, colonizing westward toward the Carpathians and across the Danube, and northward and eastward into the forest zones. In the course of these colonizing movements, which lasted several centuries, the Slavic tribes became divided into three distinct groups: the West Slavs of the Vistula basin who became the Poles and Czechs; the South Slavs who settled in the Balkans; and the East Slavs who were divided into a number of *ulus*, or tribes. These last, the Derevlians, the Polyanians, the Volhynians, the Dulebians, the Dregovichians, the Polotians, the Slovenes, the Severians, the Krivichians, the Radimichians, the Vyatichians, the Ulichians, and the Tivercians, were to provide the dominant stock of the Russian nation. During the seventh, eighth, and ninth centuries A.D. the East Slavs pushed back the numerous Finnish tribes and the Letts and Lithuanians, who occupied the lands to the north.

The main area, inhabited by the East Slavs, lay in the zone of dark, almost impenetrable forests. The nomads did not occupy this region; they needed the freedom and space of the steppes, over which they could range on their horses. But the Slavs were also drawn southward along the river routes, seeking a share in the lively trade controlled by their Khazar neighbors. In the seventh and eighth centuries the

Khazars ruled the steppes from their capital of Itil (supposed to be near modern Astrakhan) on the lower Volga, exacting customs duties from the steady stream of commercial caravans and boats that passed through its crossroads stronghold. The Slavs paid tribute to the Khazars, but became increasingly involved in this trade, sending goods and slaves, mainly the fair-haired Finns so much in demand in the slave markets of the Mediterranean. Their early cities of Pskov on the Velikaya River, Novgorod on the Volkhov, Polotsk on the Dvina, and Smolensk and Kiev on the Dnieper flourished while the trade routes were secure; but in the tenth century the power of the Khazars began to weaken, and they were challenged by the nomadic Pechenegs. Slavic merchants found that peaceful passage along the great river highways could no longer be taken for granted and that they had to contend with the new menace from the north, the Varangians, as the Slavs called the Vikings, who appeared along the river routes in the eighth century.

The Varangians, mostly of Danish and Swedish origin, were adventurers, traders, and freebooters. Highly skilled as seamen and warriors, they made dangerous foes. Just as Britain and other parts of western Europe had learned to dread the Northmen's sudden destructive raids, so the Slavs feared these eastern incursions waged on a far greater scale. The Varangians pressed south by way of the Neva, Volkhov,

Lovat, Dnieper, Donets, and Don rivers to the Black Sea, and by the Northern Dvina and Volga to the Caspian Sea. Though they had come to plunder, the prosperous trade along these routes made them stay. The rivers that they controlled first were probably the Donets and Don, to the Sea of Azov, whence they hoped to open trade to Asia.

Often the local communities hired Varangian bands to defend their towns, for the Slavs recognized the superior leadership, organization, and great energy of these professional warriors. The Varangians themselves were soon taking over the commercial towns and raiding the surrounding countryside. They began to settle along the river highways, intermarrying with the Slavs, adopting their language and customs, and gradually merging completely with them.

The Varangians were to play an important part—historians dispute whether it was dominant or subsidiary—in the formation of Kievan Rus, the first Russian state. Moreover, they probably gave to Russia and its people the name by which they have been known for over a thousand years. Across the vast plain the Varangians early became known as *Rus* or *Rhos*, possibly from the Finnish word for "rowers," and from this the name of Russia is derived.

By tradition the year A.D. 862 marks the beginning of Russia's history, for in this year the Varangian prince Rurik, who established the first Russian ruling dynasty, arrived in Novgorod. The most important source of information on these early years is the *Primary Chronicle*, set down by monks in the eleventh century to record, according to oral tradition, the events of the past. Unfortunately, as with so many Russian historical documents, the original perished, and its text survives only in the fifteenth-century *Book of Annals (Povest Vremennykh Let)* in which it was copied. The monks who made the copies sometimes edited and embellished them, introducing errors. Often they confused fact and legend. Although unreliable and incomplete, the *Chronicle* nevertheless recorded the flow of history in these early centuries.

According to the *Chronicle*, the Slavic people of Novgorod had rebelled against the Varangians, who were demanding payment of heavy tribute, and had driven them from the city. But they soon found themselves divided by rivalries that threatened to reduce the city and its extensive trade to chaos. In desperation they called on the Varangians to return so that Novgorod could once again have order and defense. Sometime around 862 Rurik, most probably a Danish feudal lord, came with his warrior band to Novgorod in response to the pleas. He was accompanied by two lieutenants, possibly his brothers, Askold and Dir; but they promptly moved on to Kiev, nearly six hundred miles to the south, where they established the foundation of the Russian state.

This version of the beginnings of modern Russia has been

A pantheon of pagan gods and sacred symbols worshiped by the Slavs and by invading Varangians, from left to right: the carved stone head of an ancient Slavic idol unearthed from a burial mound near Moscow; a four-sided, four-faced obelisk, the whole over eight feet tall, believed to be the Slavic war god Svantovit, whose attributes included a sword and a white horse; a seventh-century bronze clasp from the Ukraine, perpetuating an ancient siren motif that combined female and bird forms; a bronze figure of the phallic deity Frey, Norse god of fertility; a bronze Thor, Scandinavian thunder god.

strongly impugned as a romantic legend, and the very existence of Rurik and his brothers has been questioned. Certainly a Russian state arose in some form long before the record of the *Chronicle* begins. The fact that an army large enough to attempt the capture of Constantinople in 360 was reported by a Greek chronicler provides evidence that the East Slavs had attained a degree of political organization.

Kiev's location, below the convergence of three branches of the Dnieper and close to the northern edge of the steppelands, was vastly superior to that of Novgorod. Kiev became the advance depot, where goods from Novgorod, Smolensk, and the other northern towns were assembled and made ready for shipment to the Black Sea and to Constantinople. The tenth-century Byzantine Emperor Constantine VII, or Porphyrogenitus, has left a detailed description of this annual ingathering of Kievan exports. Beginning in November, the prince and his retinue set out to visit all the Slavic subjects who owed him tribute,—everyone paying in the goods of his region. The tour ended around April, by which time boatbuilders had completed a new flotilla of cargo boats, each hollowed from a huge tree trunk in the manner of a log canoe, and had floated them downstream after the spring thaw. In Kiev the boats were fitted out with oarlocks, and then loaded. Sometime in June, accompanied by a Varangian military escort and numerous independent merchants bent on their own business, the prince's fleet ventured upon the dangerous voyage south. In addition to natural dangers, including portage around the seven rapids of the lower Dnieper, ships and men were exposed to attack by the Pechenegs and other nomads. The defense of this trade route, in fact, had provided a strong incentive for the Slavs to unite; and it was primarily for this reason that they had been ready to accept the Varangians.

From Kiev, Askold and Dir imposed their rule over the Pechenegs and the neighboring Slavs, making the city the base from which the trade route, and later the steppelands, were defended against nomadic invaders. In 879 Oleg, another Varangian and Rurik's successor, came from Novgorod and murdered Askold and Dir. Oleg was evidently an energetic ruler, and he lives in legend as the "Wise One" (*Veschi*). During his reign he established authority over both the northern and southern tribes, thus achieving for the first time a degree of unity along the main river roads to Byzantium.

The highpoint of Oleg's thirty-three-year rule was his ambitious attack on Constantinople in 907. The *Primary Chronicle* relates the event: "With [his] entire force, Oleg sallied forth by horse and by ship, and the number of his vessels was two thousand. He arrived before Tsar'grad [Constantinople], but the Greeks fortified the strait and closed up the city. Oleg disembarked upon the shore, and ordered his

In an eleventh-century Byzantine manuscript Princess Olga of Kiev, widow of Igor, is pictured at the emperor's court in Constantinople, where she was royally welcomed about 957 as Russia's first Christian ruler.

As the story is told in the Russian chronicles, Olga received a proposal of marriage from the Byzantine emperor, which she declined; and with his gifts of "gold, silver, silks, and various vases," returned to Kiev.

The legendary creation of Slavic letters, a medium by which Christianity was exported to the pagans, is celebrated in the miniature at center. The scholar-saint at far right is Methodius, who, with his brother Cyril, devised the Cyrillic alphabet to translate Byzantium's sacred books into Slavonic. The small Kievan tax tally on wood (above) used Slavonic to more worldly ends: it reads, "three grivna collected."

soldiery to beach the ships. . . . The Russes inflicted many . . . woes upon the Greeks after the usual manner of soldiers. Oleg commanded his warriors to make wheels which they attached to the ships, and when the wind was favorable, they spread the sails and bore down upon the city from the open country. When the Greeks beheld this, they were afraid, and sending messengers to Oleg, they implored him not to destroy the city and offered to submit such tribute as he should desire. . . . Oleg demanded that they pay tribute for his two thousand ships at the rate of twelve *grivna* [silver coins] per man, with forty men reckoned to a ship."

These matters apparently settled to Oleg's satisfaction, his deputies then imposed a trade agreement on the Byzantines. The Greeks were forced to offer generous terms. "Oleg gave orders that sails of brocade should be made for the Russes and silken ones for the Slavs, and his demand was satisfied. The Russes hung their shields upon the gates as a sign of victory, and Oleg then departed. . . . The Russes unfurled their sails of brocade and the Slavs their sails of silk, but the wind tore them. Then the Slavs said, 'Let us keep our canvas ones; silken sails are not made for the Slavs.' So Oleg came to Kiev, bearing palls, gold, fruit, and wine, along with every sort of adornment."

In opening the fabled markets of Byzantium to his people, Oleg had established the basis for the growth of Kiev

and its ascendancy during the next three centuries of Russian history. In 912 Oleg died, and Igor, presumably the son or grandson of Rurik, succeeded as grand prince. The chroniclers described Igor as ruthless and greedy, but, like Oleg, he was also an effective leader. He put down a rebellion among the Derevlian Slavs and then repelled another invasion by the Pechenegs. He made extensive preparations for campaigns in Anatolia (in present-day Turkey) and Transcaucasia (Georgia, Azerbaidzhan, and Armenia), which proved to be costly failures. He was not deterred, and eager for fame and the prizes of conquest, he hired Varangian and Pecheneg troops to strengthen his own army for another attack on Byzantium in 944. However, envoys from Constantinople met him and the representatives of numerous other Rus princes and merchants on the banks of the Danube, with presents and offers of generous trade concessions as the basis of a peace. As related in the *Primary Chronicle*, Igor agreed in the name of "all the people of the land of Rus, by whom is ordained the renewal of the former peace to the confusion of the devil, who hates peace and loves discord." In 945 this second Russo-Byzantine treaty was signed. Igor did not live to enjoy its benefits. He went with a small retinue to exact a second tribute from the Derevlians, but this time they were ready to resist. According to the *Chronicle*, the Derevlians said to their Prince Mal: "If a wolf comes among the sheep,

24

he will take away the whole flock one by one, unless he be killed." The Derevlians then set upon Igor and his retainers, slaughtering them to a man.

As Svyatoslav, Igor's son, was only a boy, his mother, Princess Olga, acted as regent. A native of Pskov and a Slav, despite her Scandinavian name, she was "the wisest of women." The chronicler relates that when Igor's murderers came to Kiev to offer her in marriage to Prince Mal, she proved herself a crafty statesman, replying, "Your proposal is pleasing to me; indeed, my husband cannot rise again from the dead. But I desire to honor you tomorrow in the presence of my people. Return now to your boat, and remain there with an aspect of arrogance. I shall send for you on the morrow, and you shall say, 'We will not ride on horses nor go on foot; carry us in our boat.'"

Olga then commanded some of her retainers to dig a large ditch within the castle and sent others to escort the Derevlians. According to her instructions, the unwary envoys demanded to be carried to the castle in their boats. The Kievans, apprised of Olga's scheme, behaved in a convincingly servile manner and hoisted the vessels as if to honor the conquerors. "The [Derevlians] sat on the cross-benches in great robes, puffed up with pride. They thus were borne into the court before Olga, and when the men had brought the Derevlians in, they dropped them into the trench along with

the boat. Olga bent over and inquired whether they found the honor to their taste. They answered that it was worse than the death of Igor.' She then commanded that they should be buried alive."

Following Olga's revenge against her husband's enemy, she abandoned her pagan beliefs to embrace Christianity, a decision that would account in part for the especially enthusiastic treatment she received from the monk-chroniclers. This happened either in 955 in Kiev or three years later when she visited Constantinople. She was, however, an able woman. She introduced reforms in the general administration of the country, and by dividing the land into tax-paying districts, each with an agent responsible for collecting and paying taxes and tribute to Kiev, she eliminated the need for annual winter expeditions by the ruler to collect levies from subject princes.

The imperial city of Constantinople was the main goal of Kievan merchants, and the magnificence of the city was famed among the Slavs. Contact with Byzantium had, moreover, induced some Russians to become Christians, but they were not numerous. The conversion of Princess Olga was therefore a significant event. Her baptism was sponsored by the Emperor Constantine, and Olga took the name of Helen in honor of his empress. Her example did not inspire the Christianization of the whole nation, however, and her own

25

The baptism shown below, pictured in a medieval Bulgarian chronicle, marks the symbolic beginning of Christianized Russia in 988. Vladimir of Kiev, the sponsor, was also the first Russian ruler to mint coins like that at right. His murdered sons, Boris and Gleb, depicted in the icon opposite, were the first native saints.

son, Svyatoslav, rejected her attempts to convert him.

Svyatoslav I began his rule in 962 and at once showed himself to be a leader of tremendous vitality, well able to direct the dynamic expansionism that was characteristic of the young state. His first objective was to extend the control of Kievan Rus eastward, over the Don River basin and the Azov region, and then over the Volga River trade route to the Caspian Sea. In effect, this meant linking Kievan Rus with Tmutorakan Rus, the small commercial state and Varangian outpost on the straits between the Sea of Azov and the Black Sea. He had first to conquer the neighboring steppelands. He attacked and defeated the great Khazar khanate and sacked Itil on the lower Volga. Next, since he was determined to control the whole course of the Volga, he conquered the Volga Bulgars, a Turkic people who dominated the upper Volga region from their capital at Bolgary. He extended his authority over the lower Don basin, and in the Kuban region the Circassians swore allegiance to him.

Svyatoslav then turned westward against the powerful Bulgarian tsardom in the valley of the Danube. He was encouraged in this enterprise by the Byzantines and even helped with subsidies and troops, for the Bulgarians had become a dangerous threat to Byzantium. In 967 he conquered northern Bulgaria and made the city of Pereyaslavets his headquarters. In desperation the Bulgarian tsar appealed

to the Pechenegs to attack in the rear, and they promptly laid siege to Kiev. Svyatoslav hastened to his capital and repelled the Pechenegs, but he longed to return to the Danubian basin. In 969 he declared to his mother and his chief retainers: "I do not care to remain in Kiev, but should prefer to live in Pereyaslavets on the Danube since that is the center of my realm, where all riches are concentrated; gold, silks, wines, and various fruits from Greece, silver and horses from Hungary and Bohemia, and from Rus furs, wax, honey and slaves." Returning to Bulgaria, he found that the Bulgarians had now settled their differences with the Greeks and formed an alliance. He suffered several defeats at the hands of their combined forces, and finally in July, 971, he signed a treaty with the Byzantine Emperor John Zimisces, abandoning his claims to Bulgaria.

At this time Svyatoslav had a meeting with Zimisces and a Greek historian, Leo Diaconus, who was present, described the occasion: "The Emperor arrived at the bank of the Danube on horseback, wearing golden armor, accompanied by a large retinue of horsemen in brilliant attire. Svyatoslav crossed the river in a kind of Scythian boat; he handled the oar in the same way as his men. His appearance was as follows: he was of medium height—neither too tall, nor too short; he had bushy brows, blue eyes, and was snubnosed; he shaved his beard but wore a long and bushy

With the adoption of Christianity came foreign commerce, culture, and alliances. Yaroslav the Wise, seen offering the model of the Church of the Saviour in the thirteenth-century fresco at right, wanted to make his Kievan capital the rival of Constantinople. St. Sofia (left), its original design masked by later additions, was his most munificent architectural gift to the city. As a Christian ruler, Yaroslav was also able to arrange marriages for three of his four daughters portrayed at far right, in a St. Sofia mural, to the kings of France, Norway, and Hungary.

mustache. His head was shaven except for a lock of hair on one side as a sign of the nobility of his clan; his neck was thick, his shoulders broad; and his whole stature pretty fine. He seemed gloomy and savage. On one of his ears hung a golden earring adorned with two pearls with a ruby set between them. His white garments were not distinguishable from those of his men except for cleanness."

On his journey back to Kiev from this meeting, however, the Pechenegs attacked the Russian party. Svyatoslav, in the ninth year of his rule, was killed. The prince of the Pechenegs, following nomadic custom, had the Russian's skull overlaid with gold, and used it as a drinking cup.

Then, for a time, Kievan Rus was divided between the three sons of Svyatoslav: Oleg ruled over the Derevlians; Yaropolk over Kiev; and Vladimir over Novgorod. It was an uneasy period of fratricidal strife and treachery, from which Vladimir, who showed himself to be ruthless, emerged as grand prince with Kiev as his city. He at once revived most of his father's ambitious policies. He reasserted Kievan authority in the Azov region and took vigorous action to expand Russian trade in the west. He captured a number of important towns from the Poles in the western Ukraine. In the northwest he defeated the Lithuanian tribes on the upper reaches of the Neman River. He was an active prince and a conqueror; but he is renowned in Russian history for his

conversion to the faith of Christian Europe.

In the tenth century many peoples abandoned their pagan gods and adopted one of the monotheistic beliefs. The Volga Bulgars adopted Islam in 922, the Danubian Bulgars having already become Christian; the Khazars had adopted Judaism about 865; Poland, Hungary, Denmark, and Norway converted to Roman Christianity in the second half of the tenth century. Kievan Rus was ready.

Grand Prince Vladimir approached the matter methodically. He sent envoys to inquire into Islam, Judaism, and Eastern and Roman Christianity. He studied their reports and listened to preachers expounding the virtues of each faith. According to the *Primary Chronicle*, however, he was impressed most of all by the fervent description of Orthodox worship given by his envoys on their return from Constantinople. They had attended divine service in the Cathedral of St. Sofia and had been so transported by its magnificence that, so they said, "we knew not whether we were in heaven or on earth." A further reason for embracing Orthodox Christianity, advanced by Vladimir's advisers, was: "If the Greek faith were evil, it would not have been adopted by your grandmother Olga, who was wiser than all men."

The cultural, commercial, and military prestige of Byzantium stood so high among the Russians that it was perhaps inevitable that they should have taken their religion from

Constantinople. To them the imperial city was the bastion of civilization. Immediate political considerations also played an important part. At this time the young Byzantine Emperor Basil II was eager for friendly relations with the Kievan grand prince. He urgently needed Russian support to defend Constantinople against a provincial uprising in Anatolia. Early in 988 Basil's envoys reached Kiev, bringing the offer of marriage with his sister, Princess Anna, in return for a detachment of Varangian troops in Kiev's service. His proposal, of course, involved Vladimir's conversion.

Members of the imperial family were called Porphyrogenetes, or "born in the purple." They did not marry foreigners, and proposals of marriage from European royal families were loftily rejected. Vladimir was keenly aware of the honor and the great prestige that he would gain for himself and the Rurikide dynasty by this marriage. He accepted without delay and was baptized in Kiev in February, 988. Moreover, he promptly fulfilled his part of the bargain by sending a force of six thousand Varangians, who were to play a leading part in the defeat of Byzantium's enemies. (Some years earlier Vladimir, in a less generous mood, had reportedly sent a retinue to Greece in an effort to cleanse Kiev of the most unruly of these adventurers. He had recommended to the Greek emperor: "Do not keep many of them in your city, or else they will cause you such harm as they have done here. Scatter them therefore in various localities, and do not let a single one return this way.")

Basil appeared reluctant, however, to send his sister to Kiev. Negotiations regarding the degree of autonomy to be accorded the Russian Church further complicated matters; Vladimir was not prepared to accept the political control that could follow upon conversion. Finally, in 989, angered by the slowness of the Greeks to honor the marriage arrangement, Vladimir launched a campaign against the Crimea, then part of the Byzantine empire. He intended in this way to bring pressure to bear upon the emperor and also to gain control over the episcopal sees in the peninsula. In July his troops captured the important town of Kherson. This event apparently convinced the emperor that he could no longer evade the marriage. Princess Anna was dispatched to Kherson, where she was at once married to Vladimir, and he then returned the captured town to the emperor as "the bridegroom's gift." In the spring of 990 Vladimir arrived with his bride in Kiev, bringing with him several priests from the Crimea as well as icons, sacred vessels, and relics of saints captured during his peninsular campaign.

Vladimir next sent instructions to Novgorod and other towns that all people must be baptized without delay. He ordered the destruction of pagan temples and idols, and forbade the heathen priests and magicians to practice their ar-

Warriors set out from twelfth-century Kiev to overtake and vanquish the pillaging Cumans. The event is pictured in the Radziwill Chronicle, a fifteenth-century manuscript compiled by monks in the principality of Vladimir-Suzdal.

cane ceremonies. In Kiev the statue of Perun, the god of thunder and lightning who had been the chief deity, was tied to the tail of a horse and dragged ignominiously into the Dnieper. Other idols, raised in worship of the forces of nature, suffered similar fate. The people were bewildered; their familiar gods were being destroyed, but they understood nothing of the new faith that they were ordered to embrace. In many places they rebelled against the destruction of their idols, but their rebellions were put down. Christian churches were hastily built. In 990 the erection of Kiev's Cathedral of the Dormition of the Holy Virgin was begun in stone, and six years later it was completed. Such churches, giving solid physical form to the new religion, made acceptance easier; but the old pagan rites persisted.

Vladimir took his new faith very seriously. Practical considerations aside, his conversion was evidently sincere, as his works demonstrated. The chronicler recorded: "He invited each beggar and poor man to come to the Prince's palace, and receive whatever he needed, both food and drink, and money from the treasury. With the thought that the weak and the sick could not easily reach his palace, he arranged that wagons should be brought in, and after having them loaded with bread, meat, fish, various vegetables, mead in casks, and *kvas*, he ordered them driven out through the city. The drivers were under instruction to call out, 'Where is

there a poor man or a beggar who cannot walk?' To such they distributed according to their necessities."

Vladimir had been noted for his love of war, his ruthlessness, and his pleasure in women. Before his conversion he was said to have had eight hundred concubines living in three large harems and also seven wives. The monks who compiled the *Primary Chronicle* were undoubtedly eager to portray him as a sinful man who changed his ways completely after conversion, and to promote veneration of their first Christian ruler, they may well have exaggerated the transformation. Vladimir nevertheless appeared to undergo a complete change of heart: the warlike, sensual heathen was in his later years judged a saintly ruler; in the thirteenth century he was canonized.

The conversion of the Russian people to the Christianity of the Eastern Church was one of the most significant events in Russian history. Although imposed upon the people, who clung for many years to their heathen creeds, the Orthodox faith was to sink deep roots in Russian society. It gradually permeated their lives and helped to shape their history, their culture, and their national character. The immediate result was to bring closer relations with Christian Europe. The dynasty of Rurik would be linked by the end of the eleventh century with the ruling families of France, England, Hungary, Poland, Bohemia, and the Scandinavian countries.

Kievan Rus belonged to the European comity of nations, and no one questioned its membership. But in later centuries the fact that the Russians had embraced Eastern Christianity was to be one of the factors alienating them from the Roman Catholic West. It would contribute to their isolation from the mainstream of Western development and to the division of Europe into east and west.

The death of Vladimir in 1015 was followed by more savage fratricidal struggles for power. He had evidently intended that Boris, his son by his Byzantine wife Anna, should succeed him as grand prince. Boris was returning from a campaign against the rebellious Pechenegs when he learned of his father's death and also of the seizure of Kiev by Svyatopolk, his half brother. As an earnest Christian, however, he refused to fight against his own brother. He sent away his army and retinue, and quietly awaited assassins sent by Svyatopolk, who killed him and also his brother, Gleb.

Yaroslav of Novgorod alone among Vladimir's sons was ready to stand against the treacherous Svyatopolk. He had the full support of the Novgorodtsi, who had long resented the primacy of Kiev. Indeed, the war between the two brothers, lasting four years (1015–19), was a struggle between the two cities. Yaroslav finally defeated Svyatopolk, but then found himself challenged by yet another brother, Mstislav. Their struggle ended in an agreement to divide the country into two parts; Yaroslav took the lands west of the Dnieper, and although Kiev was in his territory, he continued to reside in Novgorod; Mstislav, ruling over the lands east of the Dnieper, made Chernigov, one hundred thirty miles northeast of Kiev, his capital. In 1036, while on a hunting expedition, Mstislav died. As he left no heir, Yaroslav became grand prince, moving to Kiev—whence he ruled over the whole of Russia, save the small eastern enclave of Polotsk.

The reign of Yaroslav the Wise (called the Lawgiver), from 1036 to 1054, carried Kiev to the zenith of its power and prestige. He established that the patriarchate of Constantinople would ordain the metropolitan of Kiev as the head of the Russian Church, thus making Kiev the ecclesiastical as well as the political capital of Russia. Byzantine influence remained strong, and taking Constantinople as the paragon, he was active in developing Kiev as an imperial city. He engaged Greek masters to build a cathedral, dedicated to Saint Sofia, and also a new citadel, known as the Golden Gate. He was tireless in erecting new buildings. By the end of his reign Kiev had become a beautiful city, and in size and wealth one of the greatest in Europe. It had advanced as a center of civilization and trade far beyond most of the cities in the West. Foreign visitors reported that it rivaled Constantinople.

Kiev also developed as a center of learning. This was

ARMOURY OF THE KREMLIN, MOSCOW; NOVOSTI

closely connected with the founding of new monasteries, of which the Monastery of the Caves became renowned for the sanctity and the learning of its monks. But Yaroslav himself contributed directly to this interest in learning. He "applied himself to books and read them continually day and night. He assembled many scribes to translate from the Greek into Slavic. He caused many books to be written and collected. . . . Thus Yaroslav . . . was a lover of books and, as he had many written, he deposited them in the Church of St. Sofia." Historians have disputed his authorship of even part of the *Pravda Russkaya* ("Russian truth"), the code of laws; but the legend reflects the spirit of learning and justice that evidently marked his reign.

It is certain that this first Russian code of laws was compiled under his sponsorship and that its rules derived in part from the tribal common law of the day and in part from Byzantine law—itself evolved out of Roman law. Only two peace treaties concluded between the Russians and the Byzantines in the tenth century predate the *Pravda Russkaya* as written Russian law.

Yaroslav's eighteen decrees tell us much about the nature of life in the Kievan Rus of his day: blood revenge was customary, though the grand prince reserved the right to limit those permitted to take it. Article One of Yaroslav's *Pravda* declares: "If a man kills a man [the following relatives of

the murdered man may avenge him]: the brother is to avenge his brother; the son, his father; or the father, his son; and the son of the brother [of the murdered man] or the son of his sister, [their respective uncle]. If there is no avenger, [the murderer pays] 40 *grivna*. . . ." Lesser offenses were generally dealt with by fining the guilty. A number of articles deal with payment for physical injury: "If anyone hits another with a club, or a rod, or a fist, or a bowl, or a [drinking] horn, or the butt [of a tool or of a vessel], and [the offender] evades being hit . . . he has to pay 12 *grivna*. . . . If a finger is cut off, 3 *grivna*. . . . And for the mustache, 12 *grivna*; and for the beard, 12 *grivna*." Eight articles deal with crimes against property. "If a slave runs away . . . and [the man who conceals that slave] does not declare him for three days, and [the owner] discovers him on the third day, he . . . receives his slave back and 3 *grivna* for the offense. . . . If anyone rides another's horse without asking the owner's permission, he has to pay 3 *grivna*." From these simple, sometimes harsh, beginnings would evolve Russia's legal code; evidence that the state was growing quickly is suggested by the fact that Yaroslav's sons would soon find it necessary to greatly enlarge its jurisdictions.

Sensing the approach of his own death, Yaroslav called his five sons together to proclaim his will. The *Primary Chronicle* quotes him: "My sons, I am about to quit this

Life in a medieval Russian city was controlled by three factors: the Church, the government, and the necessity of repeated wars. The twelfth-century silver chalice at left was given to the Cathedral of the Transfiguration in Pereyaslavl by Yury Dolgoruky, prince of Vladimir-Suzdal. The fourteenth-century woodcut at center shows citizens being summoned by bell to the veche, *a representative town meeting. The iron and silver helmet at right, bearing the figure of Archangel Michael, patron saint of warriors, was found at the site of a battle fought in 1216 between the sons of Prince Vsevolod III over rights.*

world. Love one another, since ye are brothers by one father and mother. If ye abide in amity with one another, God will dwell among you, and will subject your enemies to you, and ye will live at peace. But if ye dwell in envy and dissension, quarreling with one another, then ye will perish. . . . The throne of Kiev I bequeath to my eldest son, your brother Izyaslav. Heed him as ye have heeded me, that he may take my place among you. To Svyatoslav I give Chernigov, to Vsevolod Pereyaslav, to Igor the city of Vladimir, and to Vyacheslav Smolensk." However fanciful this account of Yaroslav's remarks to his sons, the account is held by most historians to explain the ranking of city-states that were affected at this time. Kiev was to continue as the great principality; with the death of its prince, lesser princes would move up one step, the prince of Chernigov occupying Kiev and so on. The system was generally observed in the breach. Bitter dissensions soon broke out. The three elder sons formed a triumvirate, but they were unable to impose order. Meanwhile the Pechenegs had ceased to be a danger. The Turkic Cumans had taken their place and were now harassing the Russians, shutting off their trade routes to the south. Their rise marked the beginning of a time of hardships for Kievan Rus. Of the year 1093 the chronicler reported: "Our own native land has fallen prey to torment; some of our compatriots are led into servitude, others are slain, and

some are even delivered up to vengeance and endure a bitter death. Some tremble as they cast their eyes upon the slain, and others perish of hunger and thirst." They sacked Kiev, leading away slaves—who "made their painful way naked and barefoot, upon feet torn with thorns, toward an unknown land and barbarous races."

Among the Russians discontent had been mounting over rivalries for the succession. The period of stability and good government that they had known under the wise rule of Yaroslav made them all the more impatient of the conflicts between his sons. The Grand Prince Izyaslav fled to Poland following the second conflict with his brothers, leaving Kiev to Svyatoslav, but not before the city had twice been victim to fratricidal strife. The princely system, as it had developed in Kievan Rus, provided that the first duty of the grand prince was to maintain order and defend the country. But the struggles for power were now promoting internal disorder and weakening the defenses of the country against their Asiatic enemies. In an attempt to regulate the succession and to avoid further rivalries, the numerous princes of the Rurikide dynasty met together at Lyubech in 1097; but they merely agreed that the system of patrimonial succession should be confirmed. This agreement not only failed to ensure that struggles for power would be avoided in future, but it also encouraged the trend toward princes asserting their independence as rulers in their own principalities and thus promoted the dismemberment of Kievan Rus.

On the death of Svyatopolk II in 1113, the people of Kiev acted. The *veche*, medieval Russia's traditional citizen parliament, held an emergency meeting and agreed to offer the throne to Vladimir Monomakh, prince of the southern city of Pereyaslavl and a son of Vsevolod by his Greek wife (hence the surname Monomakh). This was contrary to the Lyubech agreement, in accordance with which the son of Svyatopolk should succeed. In making the decision the citizens of Kiev had not consulted the metropolitan or the leading men of the deceased grand prince's retinue. To select the ruler in this way was unprecedented, and Yaroslav's grandson, fearing the armed opposition of the other princes of the Rurikide dynasty, refused to go to Kiev. On learning of his decision, the people began rioting in the city. The Church leaders and the upper class generally became alarmed and sent an urgent message to Vladimir: "Come, O Prince, to Kiev; and if you do not come, know that much evil will befall. . . ." Recognizing the danger that revolution would overtake Kiev and the whole country if he did not accept the throne, Vladimir went to the city, where he was acclaimed by the metropolitan and the people.

Vladimir Monomakh was a remarkable man. Generous, kind, and just, he has been called the exemplar of the old Russian prince. The ideals he pursued were love of God and of fellow man. He cared for the poor, promoted education, and by all accounts led a blameless life. His "Instruction to his Children" is a model for liberal, responsible leadership. He directs, in part: "Whenever you speak, whether it be a bad or a good word, swear not by the Lord, nor make the sign of the cross, for there is no need. If you have occasion to kiss the cross with your brothers or with anyone else, first inquire your heart whether you will keep the promise, then kiss it. . . . Honor the elders as your father, and the younger ones as your brothers. . . . If you start out to a war, be not slack, depend not upon your generals, nor abandon yourselves to drinking and eating and sleeping. . . . Whenever you travel over your lands, permit not the servants, neither your own, nor a stranger's, to do any damage in the villages, or in the fields, that they may not curse you. Whencesoever you go, and wherever you stay, give the destitute to eat and to drink. Above all honor the stranger, whensoever he may come, whether he be a commoner, a nobleman or an ambassador. . . . Call on the sick, go to funerals, for we are all mortal, and pass not by a man without greeting him. . . . But the main thing is that you should keep the fear of the Lord higher than anything else. . . . Whatever good you know, do not forget it, and what you do not know, learn it. . . . Let not the sun find you in bed. . . ."

Vladimir contributed much to the glorification of Kiev. He also sought to ensure stability within the state, organizing effective defenses against nomadic invaders from the east; but he was unable to arrest Kiev's decline.

Kievan Rus had become vast in extent, stretching from a frontier about one hundred miles south of the city to the Arctic Ocean. But it had never been more than a loose federation of principalities. The family of Rurik had grown numerous. As many as sixty-four principalities could be counted at one stage in the twelfth century. Singly and in groups, they struggled for power. The rule of Kiev, far to the south, had depended on the trade with Byzantium and the strength of individual grand princes. Increasingly the princes to the north had shown reluctance to acknowledge the supremacy of Kiev. But throughout the country the practice of dividing and subdividing principalities to provide an independent *udel*, or estate, for each son of each prince had led to fragmentation of principalities and the creation of countless petty princes who could survive only by expanding their lands at the expense of their neighbors. Rivalries among the numerous members of the Monomakh clan over the succession and the control of the great trade routes had further intensified the princely anarchy, inhibiting the growth of a sense of nationhood among the Russians. They could not put aside their rivalries even for the purpose of common defense. The great empire of the Khazars had long ceased to serve as an eastern shield, and sweeping across the Eurasian plain, the Pechenegs, the Cumans, and other nomadic tribes came in increasingly frequent waves. While united under a strong prince, the Russians had managed to defend their lands; but now they were unable to beat off those invasions. Moreover, the Germanic tribes were beginning to move eastward, driving the Lithuanians and Letts before them and presenting another challenge.

Migration to the north had already begun to drain the strength of Kiev. Novgorod had built up a great commercial empire, extending to the Arctic Ocean and east to the Urals. It offered security and opportunity to the Russians, weary of the princely feuds and nomadic attacks in the south. Many Russians made their way into Galicia and to Belorussia, which were later to come under the rule of Poland-Lithuania. But the most important wave of migration was to the northeast, the dense forest lands of the upper Volga and its tributaries. Here, in the second half of the twelfth century, the foremost prince was Monomakh's grandson, Andrei Bogolyubsky of the central Russian principality of Rostov-Suzdal. An able and energetic ruler, he expanded his lands and built as his capital the city of Vladimir on the Klyazma River, some one hundred twenty miles east of the site that would later become Moscow. In March, 1169, his army captured Kiev and laid waste the proud city, which never recovered from this savage blow. The center of the Russian state had moved to the forests of the northeast; but before the Russians could develop further toward nationhood, they were overwhelmed by the calamitous Mongol invasion.

Russia took from Byzantium the concept of a church state ruled by God-appointed autocrats, here exemplified by the Byzantine emperor John VI, enthroned at a priestly council called in Constantinople in 1351 to sanction his imperial views on a theological controversy.

The Divine City

When Constantine moved his capital from Rome to Byzantium in 330, he took with him the glory and grandeur of the Christian world. The emperor chose to found his "Second Rome" at the crossroads of East-West trade on the straits of the Bosporus, the link to Asia. Thus, in addition to exercising spiritual and political power over much of the known world, Constantinople (whose hieratic being is personified in the fifth-century ivory at left) could also hold a virtual monopoly over the traffic in such precious stuffs as silks, gold, wines, gems, and slaves. The most powerful men and institutions were the city's patrons, and though the Russians had not yet developed appetites for some of the refinements of civilization, they were lured southward in search of plunder. Constantinople's defenses held against repeated attacks early in the tenth century; Byzantine military technology, especially an incendiary substance known as Greek fire, left the marauders as envious as they were frightened. Only through an agreement made in 945 were the Russians accorded trading courtesies on condition that they live by the local laws during their visits. Subsequently, annual convoys of princes and merchants arrived, bearing furs, hides, honey, wax, and other rough goods. The foreigners were quartered in a suburb across the harbor (the central city and outlying district is shown in the fifteenth-century map opposite) and allowed to enter "through one gate in groups of fifty without weapons. . . . An officer of [the Byzantine] government shall guard them. . . . When the Russes depart hence, they shall receive from us as many provisions as they require for the journey." Under such peaceable arrangements Byzantium became the principle source of Russian wealth and, ultimately, its culture, for the commerce in Christianity soon surpassed all other imports. Vladimir's decision in 988 to embrace Eastern Orthodoxy, reached after considering all the major religions, was momentous. His rejection of the Western Church effectively divided Russia from its Slavic neighbors, creating some of the circumstances that would feed centuries of Russian-Polish wars. And it would deny the Russian people not only the aide of Catholic kingdoms when the Mongol hordes struck, but also the cultural stimulation of the Renaissance. On the positive side, Kiev's Christianized princes had gained a powerful political mentor. The Greek concept of government—that the emperor was God's vicar on earth and the custodian of an indivisible authority transmitted from father to son—superseded the ancient rule of elected tribal leaders. And lastly, the adoption of Eastern Christianity—mystical and magnificent—brought with it artistic traditions perfectly suited to glorifying the nascent Russian civilization.

NEWLY CHRISTIANIZED RUSSIA *was a learning civilization, and the arts, as the mise en scène of spiritual conversion, were thrust into Byzantine prominence. The new ideal in the arts was opulence, to make life on earth the mirror image of heaven; it could produce such splendor as the jeweled cross (above), ordered by Emperor Justin II in the sixth century, and the studded enamel and gold icon of Archangel Michael (opposite), the work of a tenth- or eleventh-century Greek. With memories of the magnificence they had left behind and an official instructional on the iconography of the Church as their guide, Byzantium's missionary-craftsmen set forth to recreate the ethos of their revered Constantinople in the rude and rugged setting of medieval Russia.*

A DESCRIPTION OF CONSTANTINOPLE
by Benjamin of Tudela

Rabbi Benjamin ben Jonah, a wandering Jew from Tudela, Spain, visited Constantinople in 1161. He recorded his impressions of the city's cosmopolitan aura and splendor in his diary.

The circumference of the city of Constantinople is eighteen miles; half of it is surrounded by the sea, and half by land, and it is situated upon two arms of the sea, one coming from the sea of Russia, and one from the sea of Sepharad. . . . It is a busy city, and merchants come to it from every country by sea or land, and there is none like it in the world except Bagdad, the great city of Islam. In Constantinople is the church of Santa Sophia, and the seat of the Pope of the Greeks, since the Greeks do not obey the Pope of Rome. There are also churches according to the number of the days of the year. A quantity of wealth beyond telling is brought hither year by year as tribute from the two islands and the castles and villages which are there. And the like of this wealth is not to be found in any other church in the world. And in this church there are pillars of gold and silver, and lamps of silver and gold more than a man can count. Close to the walls of the palace is also a place of amusement belonging to the king, which is called the Hippodrome, and every year on the anniversary of the birth of Jesus the king gives a great entertainment there. And in that place men from all the races of the world come before the king and queen with jugglery and without jugglery, and they introduce lions, leopards, bears, and wild asses, and they engage them in combat with one another; and the same thing is done with birds. No entertainment like this is to be found in any other land.

This King Emanuel [Manuel I, the emperor] built a great palace for the seat of his government upon the sea-coast, in addition to the palaces which his fathers built, and he called its name Blachernae. He overlaid its columns and walls with gold and silver, and engraved thereon representations of the battles before his day and of his own combats. He also set up a throne of gold and of precious stones, and a golden crown was suspended by a gold chain over the throne, so arranged that he might sit thereunder. It was inlaid with jewels of priceless value, and at night time no lights were required, for every one could see by the light which the stones gave forth. Countless other buildings are to be met with in the city. From every part of the empire of Greece tribute is brought here every year, and they fill strongholds with garments of silk, purple, and gold. Like unto these storehouses and this wealth, there is nothing in the whole world to be found. It is said that the tribute of the city amounts every year to 20,000 gold pieces, derived both from the rents of shops and markets, and from the tribute of merchants who enter by sea or land.

The Greek inhabitants are very rich in gold and precious stones, and they go clothed in garments of silk with gold embroidery, and they ride horses, and look like princes. Indeed, the land is very rich in all cloth stuffs, and in bread, meat, and wine.

Wealth like that of Constantinople is not to be found in the whole world. Here also are men learned in all the books of the Greeks, and they eat and drink every man under his vine and his fig-tree.

They hire from amongst all nations warriors called Loazim (Barbarians) to fight . . . for the natives are not warlike, but are as women who have no strength to fight.

PRINCE VLADIMIR'S CONVERSION TO CHRISTIANITY
from the Primary Chronicle

In 987 Vladimir sent ten envoys out to help him choose a religion. Their discoveries, and Vladimir's decision to follow the Greeks' faith, are described in this passage from Russian lore.

The envoys reported: "When we journeyed among the Bulgarians, we beheld how they worship in their temple, called a mosque, while they stand ungirt. The Bulgarian bows, sits down, looks hither and thither like one possessed, and there is no happiness among them, but instead only sorrow and a dreadful stench. Their religion is not good. Then we went among the Germans, and saw them performing many ceremonies in their temples; but we beheld no glory there. Then we went on to Greece, and the Greeks led us to the edifices where they worship their God, and we knew not whether we were in heaven or on earth. For on earth there is no such splendor or such beauty, and we are at a loss how to describe it. We know only that God dwells there among men, and their service is fairer than the ceremonies of other nations. For we cannot forget that beauty. Every man, after tasting something sweet, is afterward unwilling to accept that which is bitter, and therefore we cannot dwell longer here." . . . Vladimir then inquired where they should all accept baptism, and they replied that the decision rested with him. . . .

When the people were baptized, they returned each to his own abode. Vladimir, rejoicing that he and his subjects now knew God himself, looked up to heaven and said: "O God, who has created heaven and earth, look down, I beseech thee, on this thy new people, and grant them, O Lord, to know thee as the true God, even as the other Christian nations have known thee. Confirm in them the true and unalterable faith, and aid me, O Lord, against the hostile adversary, so that, hoping in thee and in thy might, I may overcome his malice." Having spoken thus, he ordained that churches should be built and established where pagan idols had previously stood. . . . He began to found churches and to assign priests throughout the cities, and to invite the people to accept baptism in all the cities and towns. . . . Vladimir was enlightened . . . and his country with him.

Sensuous line and sumptuous materials—the essence of Byzantine architecture—are distilled in this medieval reliquary.

Divided and Conquered

Prospects for a strong, well-defended Russian state had died with the collapse of Kiev. Andrei Bogolyubsky, a grandson of Vladimir Monomakh and architect of this latest defeat, transferred the center of power to his own principality of Vladimir-Suzdal in central Russia (a small settlement with the Finnish name of "Moskva" was established about this time along the southern border of the principality). Prince Andrei then attempted to put down the last remaining challenge, Novgorod, the northern merchant city that had been autonomous since 1136. According to the Novgorodian Chronicle, miraculous intercession saved the city. "There were only four hundred men of Novgorod against seven thousand soldiers from Suzdal, but God helped the Novgorodians, and the Suzdalians suffered thirteen hundred casualties, while Novgorod lost only fifteen men. . . ." After several months had passed, Andrei Bogolyubsky's troops returned, this time strengthened by soldiers from a number of other principalities. "But the people of Novgorod were firmly behind their leader, Prince Roman, and their *posadnik* [mayor] Yakun. And so they built fortifications about the city. On Sunday

The fifteenth-century icon depicts legendary events in Novgorod's defense against its rival, Vladimir-Suzdal, in 1169. The outnumbered Novgorodsti brandish their miraculous icon of the Virgin of the Sign, who, according to tradition, invoked God's aid to save them.

[Prince Andrei's emissaries] came to Novgorod to negotiate, and these negotiations lasted three days. On the fourth day, Wednesday, February 25th . . . the Suzdalians attacked the city and fought the entire day. Only toward evening did Prince Roman, who was still very young, and the troops of Novgorod manage to defeat the army of Suzdal with the help of the holy cross, the Holy Virgin, and the prayers of . . . Bishop Elias. Many Suzdalians were massacred, many were taken prisoner, while the remainder escaped only with great difficulty. And the price of Suzdalian prisoners fell to two *nogatas* [a coin of small value]."

The political situation among Russia's princes gradually evolved into a balance of minor powers. Kiev's last claim to dominance—its special relationship with the seat of Orthodoxy—dissolved with Constantinople's fall to the crusaders of the Latin Church in 1204.

This decline of the Kievan state and the fragmentation of Russian land into numerous warring principalities, none capable of leading a united defense, coincided with the climactic last westward drive of Asiatic hordes, led by the Mongols. Through military and economic vassalage they were able to halt abruptly Russia's groping toward nationhood for almost two hundred years.

Early in the thirteenth century the scattered tribes of the Mongolian desert—a mixture of Mongol, Alan, and

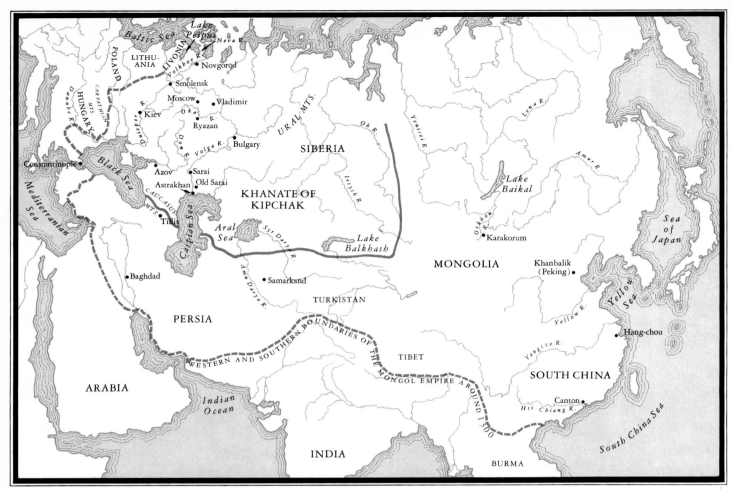

Genghis Khan's dreams of world conquest were pursued with such vigor by his heirs that by 1300 the Mongol empire spanned the Eurasian continent from the Sea of Japan to the Carpathian Mountains. The Russian principalities, which had met their first taste of Mongol devastation in 1237, thenceforth became part of the khanate of Kipchak, the huge domain of the Golden Horde.

Turkic peoples—were united into a single fighting army. Responding to historical forces that are yet to be fully understood, they drove across the Eurasian plain, following the paths of so many other Asian incursions, and threatened to change the course of Christendom.

The leader who organized and led the nomads in their great conquest of Asia was Temujin. He had been a minor chieftain whose success in a series of intertribal wars on the vast steppe region of northern Mongolia had united first his clan, then his tribe, and finally the majority of tribes—of which the Mongols were but one—in his support. A *kuriltai*, or great assembly of chieftains, in 1206 had proclaimed him not just the "Supreme Khan" but the "Genghis Khan," meaning the "all-encompassing lord." Thenceforth his authority was understood to derive from "the Eternal Blue Sky," as the Mongols called their god.

Genghis Khan ruled over a people of extraordinary hardihood and ferocity. The Mongols were tent-dwelling nomads whose horses were their constant companions. Mongol boys learned to ride almost from birth, and at the age of three they began handling the bow and arrow, which was the main weapon in hunting and in war. Their small sturdy horses were, like their riders, capable of feats of great endurance. Unlike Western horses, Mongol ponies were highly self-sufficient, requiring no special hay or fodder and able to find

enough food even under the snow cover. The Mongols took care of their horses, which were readily rounded up in herds of ten thousand or more, allowing them regular periods of rest; and on campaigns each warrior was followed by as many as twenty remounts. To their horses they owed the mobility that allowed them their favorite tactic of striking suddenly and unexpectedly against their enemies. Furthermore, the Mongols were more skilled in war than earlier nomad hordes, and they were undeterred by forest lands.

The Mongol nation numbered only one million people at the time of the empire's greatest extent. Within the empire, Turks and other nomadic tribes were far more numerous, serving mainly in the lower ranks of the armies. (The hordes that swept across Russia, under the minority rule of Mongols, were predominantly Turkic and were generally known as Tatars, derived from the European name for all the peoples east of the Dnieper.) Among them the authority of Genghis and of his law commanded unquestioning obedience. The Great Yasa, compiled in the main by Genghis, was the written code of Mongol custom and law, laying down strict rules of conduct in all areas of public life—international law, internal administration, the military, criminal law, civil and commercial law. With few exceptions, offenses were punishable by death. This was the sentence for serious breaches of military efficiency and discipline, for possessing a stolen

Genghis Khan's son and successor, Ogadai, is shown be-low in a later copy of a thirteenth-century Chinese por-trait. The 1310 Persian miniature at right depicts Gen-ghis Khan's grandson, Batu, who founded the Golden Horde, which held sway over Russia until the 1400's.

horse without being able to pay the fine, for gluttony, for hiding a runaway slave or prisoner and preventing his or her recapture, for urinating into water or inside a tent. Persons of royal rank enjoyed no exemption from the law, except to the extent that they received a "bloodless" execution by being put inside a carpet or rug and then clubbed to death, for to spill a man's blood was to drain away his soul.

The functioning of the military state was set forth mainly in the Yasa's Statute of Bound Service, which imposed the duty of life service on all subjects, women as well as men. Every man was bound to the position or task to which he was appointed. Desertion carried the summary punishment of death. The Army Statute, which organized the Mongol armies in units of ten, was explicit: "The fighting men are to be conscripted from men who are twenty years old and up-wards. There shall be a captain to every ten, and a captain to every hundred, and a captain to every thousand, and a cap-tain to every ten thousand. . . . No man of any thousand, or hundred, or ten in which he hath been counted shall depart to another place; if he doth he shall be killed and also the captain who received him." Even in the far-off khanates, which the Mongols eventually established, the Great Yasa was known and revered much as the Magna Charta, of about the same time, was regarded in England. It provided the legal foundation of the Great Khan's power and the means

to administer the immense Mongol-Tatar empire from the remote capital, which he established at Karakorum.

In 1215 Genghis Khan captured Yenching (modern Pe-king) and northern China; he went on to subdue Korea and Turkistan, and to raid Persia and northern India. The fa-mous *tuq*, or standard, of Genghis—a pole surmounted by nine white yak's tails that was always carried into battle when the Great Khan was present—had become an object of divine significance to the Mongols and of dread to their prey.

After taking Turkistan, gateway to Europe, Genghis Khan sent a detachment of horsemen to reconnoiter the lands far-ther to the west. In 1223 this force advanced south to the Caspian Sea and north into the Caucasus, finally invading the territory of the Cumans, a Turkic people settled in the region of the lower Volga. The khans of the Cumans called on the Russian princes to help them. "Today the Tatars have seized our land," they declared. "Tomorrow they will take yours." Heeding their call for aid, Prince Mstislav of Galicia and a few lesser princes marched with their troops to rescue their neighbor. In the battle on the banks of the Kalka River, at the northeastern end of the Sea of Azov, the Cumans and their allies suffered disastrous defeat. Few escaped with their lives, though Mstislav and two other captured princes were saved for special treatment.

Chivalry required that enemies of high rank be executed

45

The yak-plumed headgear of the warrior (above) marks him as a Mongol general. The figure opposite bears the lance and saber of a trooper.

"bloodlessly"—according to the same rules as Mongol chieftains—so another expedient was devised. The vanquished were laid on the ground and covered with boards, upon which the Mongol officers sat for their victory banquet. The Russians were crushed to death.

Apparently satisfied with their foray, the conquerors vanished from southern Russia as suddenly and as mysteriously as they had appeared. "We do not know whence these evil Tatars came upon us, nor whither they have betaken themselves again; only God knows," wrote a chronicler. Most historians attribute their departure to political changes in Mongolia.

Genghis Khan died in 1227 while on a military campaign against a Tibetan tribe. As his eldest son and heir, Juji, had died earlier, Genghis Khan's son Ogadai was chosen to rule in Karakorum as Chief Khan. However, Genghis directed that the administration of the empire was to be divided among all his sons, each receiving a vast *ulus*, or regional khanate, a portion of the empire's troops, and the income of that area over which they ruled.

Juji's original share was to have been the khanate of Kipchak—the region west of the Irtysh River and the Aral Sea —most of which was still unconquered. It was left to his son, Batu, to complete the mission. In 1236 Batu, with the blessing of Ogadai, led a strong army westward. The Mongols advanced by way of the Caspian Gate and then northwestward. They took Bulgary, the capital of the Volga Bulgars, and making their way through the forests around Penza and Tambov, they reached the principality of Ryazan. The northern winter had already closed in, but Batu's forces, some fifty thousand strong, were accustomed to harsh conditions. The snow-covered frozen lakes and riverbeds served as highways for their mounts.

The Russians were in no position to defend themselves. Kievan Rus was in decline, and the newer principalities, like Vladimir-Suzdal, had not yet developed the strength to withstand such foes as the Mongols. For five days Ryazan was under siege, and on December 21, 1237, the town fell to the enemy. A chronicler described the ferocity of the Mongols: "The prince with his mother, wife, sons, the boyars and inhabitants, without regard to age or sex, were slaughtered with the savage cruelty of Mongol revenge; some were impaled or had nails or splinters of wood driven under their finger nails. Priests were roasted alive and nuns and maidens were ravished in the churches before their relatives. No eye remained open to weep for the dead." Similar stories were repeated wherever the Mongols ranged. The invaders believed that their Great Khan was directed by God to conquer and rule the world. Resistance to his will was resistance to the will of God and must be punished by death. It was a

The painting at left shows Batu's army (in conical hats) fighting the Hungarians (in visored helmets) on a Danubian bridge in 1241. The Mongols eventually triumphed by bombarding them with rocks, arrows, and burning naphtha.

simple principle and the Mongols applied it ruthlessly.

By February, 1238, fourteen towns had fallen to their fury. The whole principality of Vladimir-Suzdal had been devastated. They then advanced into the territory of Novgorod. They were some sixty miles from the city itself, when suddenly they turned south and Novgorod was spared. The dense forests and extensive morasses had become almost impassable in the early thaw, and Batu decided to return with his warriors to the steppes, occupied then by the Pechenegs. On their way south they laid siege to the town of Kozelsk, which resisted bravely for seven weeks. The Mongols were so infuriated by this delay that on taking the town they butchered all that they found alive, citizens and animals alike. The blood was so deep in the streets, so the chronicler relates, that children drowned before they could be slain.

During 1239 Batu allowed his men to rest in the Azov region, but in the following year he resumed his westward advance. His horsemen laid waste the cities of Pereyaslavl and Chernigov. They then sent envoys to Kiev, demanding the submission of the city. Unwisely, the governor had the envoys put to death. Kiev was now doomed. At the beginning of December, 1240, Batu's troops surrounded the city and after a few days of siege took it by storm. The carnage that followed was fearful. Six years later John of Plano Carpini, sent by Pope Innocent IV as his envoy to the Great Khan of

Karakorum, passed through Kiev; he wrote that "we found an innumerable multitude of men's skulls and bones, lying upon the earth," and he could count only two hundred houses standing in what had been a vast and magnificent city, larger than any city in western Europe.

The Mongols pressed farther westward, and then divided into three armies. One advanced into Poland; the central army, commanded by Batu, invaded Hungary; the third army moved along the Carpathian Mountains into southern Hungary. The Mongols were intent on punishing King Béla of Hungary because he had granted asylum to the khan of the Cumans and two hundred thousand of his men, women, and children who had fled westward in 1238. Batu had sent warnings, which Béla had ignored. Now the Mongols overran the whole of Hungary, while the northern army laid waste Poland, Lithuania, and East Prussia. They were poised to conquer the rest of Europe, when suddenly in the spring of 1242 couriers brought news that the Great Khan Ogadai was dead. Batu withdrew his armies, wishing to devote all his energies to gathering support as Ogadai's successor. Western Europe was thus spared the Mongol devastation, which, had it spread to the Atlantic, would have had an incalculable impact on the history of Europe and of the world.

Ogadai had ruined his health, as he frankly admitted, by continued indulgence in wine and women. Sensing death

47

CATHEDRAL OF THE ARCHANGEL MICHAEL, MOSCOW; NOVOSTI

KUNSTHISTORISCHES
MUSEUM, VIENNA

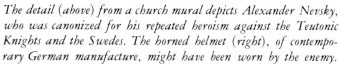

The detail (above) from a church mural depicts Alexander Nevsky, who was canonized for his repeated heroism against the Teutonic Knights and the Swedes. The horned helmet (right), of contemporary German manufacture, might have been worn by the enemy.

approaching, the khan appointed his favorite grandson as successor. But Ogadai's widow, who acted as regent during the boy's minority, intrigued to procure the election of her own son, Kuyuk, although this was strongly opposed by Batu and many other Mongol leaders.

Batu had established his headquarters at Sarai, some sixty-five miles north of Astrakhan on the lower Volga. It was little more than a city of tents, for the khan of the Kipchaks remained a nomad at heart; but the splendor of his court became legendary among the princes of his realm. Batu's Golden Horde (from the Tatar *altūn ordū*) also impressed John of Plano Carpini, who wrote: "Batu lives with considerable magnificence, having door-keepers and all officials just like their Emperor. He even sits raised up as if on a throne with one of his wives. . . . He has large and very beautiful tents of linen which used to belong to the King of Hungary. . . . drinks are placed in gold and silver vessels. Neither Batu nor any other Tatar prince ever drinks, especially in public, without there being singing and guitar-playing for them. . . ." Though Batu owed allegiance to the Great Khan, he now refused to visit Karakorum and to pay homage to Kuyuk. The Golden Horde remained a province of the Mongol-Tatar empire, but Batu and his successors thenceforth administered the khanate with a large measure of independence, particularly in its relations with Russia.

It was directly to Sarai that the Russian princes perforce paid tribute. The terror and destruction wrought by the Tatar invasion had left the Russians stupefied and brought their national life to a standstill. Decades passed before they began to recover, for the Mongol yoke lay heavy on them. In certain regions, mainly in western Ukraine, the Mongols took over the administration from the Russian princes and ruled directly; in other regions they set up their own officials alongside the Russians and exercised direct supervision. In most parts of Russia, however, the khan allowed the local Russian princes to administer as before.

Before the Mongol invasions, a distinctly Russian system of landholding and agricultural production had emerged. Feudalism as it was known in western Europe had not yet taken hold; with vast areas of Russia still open to settlement, no one but the slave was legally held to the acreage on which he was born. Land was organized rather loosely in the hands of four principal classes. First came the grand princes and lesser nobility, Russia's proliferating royal family. Beginning sometime in the tenth or eleventh century the princes turned from creating wealth through plunder and tribute to producing wealth from the land. Yaroslav's decision to divide Kievan Rus into five portions, one for each of his sons, can be taken as the formal beginning of the appanage system, by which titles and estates passed from generation to generation.

Conrad von Thüringen, grand master of the Teutonic Knights, is depicted in the thirteenth-century tomb relief at left. His family shield (above), which he was required to exchange for the order's white robes and shield, rejoined him by tradition only at his death.

Ranking below the appanage princes, and coming somewhat later to land ownership, was the class of boyars, who were roughly equivalent to the barons and knights of Europe. The boyars were an outgrowth of the Varangian *druzhina*, the prince's retinue, made up of a mixture of Scandinavian and native Slavic leaders whose lands were secured by conquest, colonization, or outright princely gift. In the tradition of adventurers, the boyars were free to shift allegiance from one prince to another as it suited their own interests. Initially, no contract, either formal or by custom, held the boyar in vassalage to the prince, nor did a change of loyalty affect his title to his land. Service was not a condition of ownership, and land passed from father to son.

The Church formed the third and still later developing class of landlords, its right to tenure and administration independent of the princes established by Byzantine precedent. Church lands were acquired either by colonization in unclaimed lands or by donations from princes who might receive in exchange the prayers of the Church.

The fourth and most elusive of definition was the peasant majority. Conditions varied from one principality to another, depending on local custom and the power of the prince. Prior to the development of boyars' estates, a peasant held the land by virtue of having wrested it from the wilderness. This he usually accomplished as a member of a commune—

a gathering of a few family units, itself an outgrowth of the more primitive Slavic tribal family. The peasant was technically a free man and remained so until the reign of Alexei in the middle of the seventeenth century, though the intervening centuries brought an accumulation of legislation that would progressively limit his right to exercise this freedom. With the growing power of the various landlord classes, however, peasants living in the more settled areas of Russia were put under obligations, the most common being *obrok*, quitrent or payment in kind for land use, and *barshchina*, payment in contracted days of labor on the owner's estate. Only the *kholopy*, or "slaves," a motley assortment of prisoners and indebted poor, were entirely excluded from landholding during the period of Mongol domination.

As the khans of the Golden Horde were interested in the conquered lands only as a source of revenue and troops, they were content to allow the continuation of this political structure. The appanage princes had to acknowledge that they were the khan's vassals and that they recognized the overall suzerainty of the Great Khan of Karakorum. They could hold their positions only upon receiving the khan's *yarlyk*, or patent to rule; often they had first to journey to Sarai to prostrate themselves before him. On occasion they even went to Mongolia to make their obeisances. Moreover, they had to refer to the khan for resolution of major disputes with

49

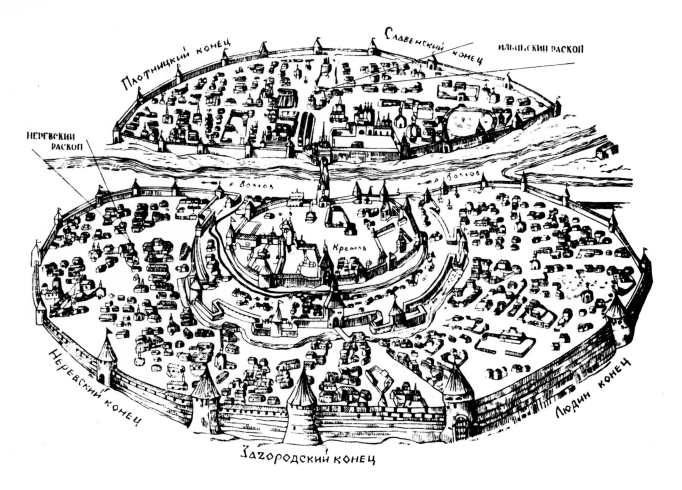

The Volkhov divided Novgorod's commercial side (top) from the St. Sofia quarter (bottom).

other princes and to justify themselves against any serious charges, competing among one another for the khan's recognition with gifts, promises to increase their payments of tribute, and mutual denunciations.

Prompt action was taken in each newly conquered country to promote a census of the population so that the amount of tax to be levied and the number of recruits for the army to be taken could be assessed. Mongol officials were appointed to collect and to enroll recruits. Delays in making payments to the tax collector, or producing men, or rebellion of any kind were punished with extreme ferocity. Nevertheless, driven beyond endurance by Mongol demands, the Russians sometimes rebelled. No fewer than forty-eight Mongol-Tatar raids took place during the period of the domination of the Golden Horde, and some of these expeditions had the purpose of suppressing uprisings among the Russians. Gradually, however, the khan's grip on his vassal states relaxed. Early in the fourteenth century it became the practice to allow the Russian princes to collect taxes on behalf of the Horde, and the tax collectors and other officials were withdrawn. The Russian lands once again became autonomous, though they continued to acknowledge the suzerainty of the khan. However, internal rivalries, much like those that had fractured the Russian principalities, were weakening the Golden Horde, which was ceasing to dis-

play the bold confidence of conquerors. In the fourteenth and early fifteenth centuries the khan's direct rule came to be limited to the middle and lower Volga, the Don, and the steppelands as far west as the Dnieper.

The impact of the Mongol invasion and occupation on Russia's social and cultural fortunes was largely negative, halting progress and introducing a number of harsh customs. In such evil practices as flogging, torture, and mutilation, the seclusion of women of the upper classes in the *terem,* or the women's quarters, the cringing servility of inferiors, and the arrogant superiority and often brutality of seniors toward them, the Mongols probably left their mark. Evidence that the invaders made any enduring, positive impression is slight. The Russian historians S. M. Solovyev and V. O. Klyuchevsky considered that it was not of major importance: Russia had embraced Orthodox Christianity and the political ideas of Byzantium two centuries before the coming of the Mongols, and its development was too deeply rooted in Byzantine soil to be greatly changed. Further, the Mongol conception of the Great Khan's absolute power was, in practice, close to the Byzantine theory of the divine authority of the emperor, and, indeed, the Mongol and Byzantine concepts might well have merged in the minds of the Russian princes.

Only the Orthodox Church flourished. The religion of the Mongols was a primitive Shamanism in which the seer and

The round-domed Cathedral of St. Sofia, built in 1045–52 within Novgorod's kremlin, served as
the center of the city's political, social, and cultural life as well as the seat of its religious activities.

Novgorod's influential merchant families, such as the Kuzmins who commissioned this icon in 1467, amassed their wealth through trade with the Hanse cities. Painted four years before their city's fall to Moscow, this detail shows three generations of Kuzmins praying for divine intercession.

medicine man, the shaman, acted as the intermediary with the spirit world. He made known the will of Tengri, the great god who ruled over all the spirits in heaven. This form of worship could readily accommodate many faiths, and the Mongols showed a tolerance toward other religions, which Christian Churches would have done well to emulate. The Mongols were familiar with Nestorian Christianity, a heretical sect for which Nestorius, patriarch of Constantinople, was deposed in the fifth century, and certain clans had embraced Nestorianism. Though the Great Khan, after considering Buddhism, Christianity, and Judaism, had finally in the fourteenth century decided to adopt Islam as the faith of the Mongols, they continued to show a generous tolerance toward the Christians.

The Russian Orthodox Church, in fact, enjoyed a privileged position throughout the period of the Mongol yoke. All Christians were guaranteed freedom of worship. The extensive lands owned by the Church were protected and exempt from all taxes, and the labor on Church estates was not liable to recruitment into the khan's armies. Metropolitans, bishops, and other senior clerical appointments were confirmed by the *yarlyk*, but this assertion of the khan's authority apparently involved no interference by the Mongols in Church affairs.

Under this protection the Church grew in strength. Its influence among the people deepened, for it fostered a sense of unity during these dark times. Both the black, or monastic, clergy and the white clergy, which ministered to the secular world and was permitted to marry, shared in this proselytizing role. Moreover, the Church preserved the Byzantine political heritage, especially the theory of the divine nature of the secular power. In accordance with this tradition, the support that the Church gave to the emerging grand princes of Moscow was to be of importance in bringing the country under Moscow's rule.

The Orthodox Church was also strengthened in being undisturbed by the challenge of other ideas and influences. Kievan Rus had maintained regular contact with the countries to the south and west. Russian merchants had brought by the great trade routes news of the arts and cultures, as well as the merchandise, of these foreign lands. But the Mongol occupation had isolated the Russians almost completely. The great ferment of ideas in the West, leading to the Renaissance, the Reformation, the explorations, and the scientific discoveries, did not touch them. The Orthodox Church encouraged their natural conservatism and inculcated the idea of spiritual and cultural self-sufficiency among them. Indeed, this isolation, which was to contribute notably to Russia's backwardness in the coming centuries, was to be one of the most disastrous results of Mongol domination.

The German miniature at left shows Hanseatic merchants in the teeming port of Hamburg. The escutcheon (above) adorned one of their factories at Lübeck, a leading Baltic outpost, where they exchanged woolens, metalware, and other staples for goods such as furs, wax, and honey.

Only the remote, northern republic of Novgorod had managed to escape the devastation of Batu's westward advance in 1238. The city, standing on the banks of the Volkhov River, three miles to the north of Lake Ilmen, in a region of lakes, rivers, and marshes, had built up a commercial empire "from the Varangians to the Greeks," as they described it. "Lord Novgorod the Great," the Novgorodtsi's title for their republic, had been one of the first centers of Russian civilization. Beginning with Prince Oleg's rule in the last years of the ninth century, it had acknowledged the primacy of Kiev; but as the power and prestige of "the mother of Russian cities" declined, Novgorod had asserted anew its independence. In 1136 its citizens had taken counsel together and promptly expelled the prince appointed by Kiev on the complaints that he had shown no care for the common people, that he had tried to use the city as a means to his own advancement, and that he had been both indecisive and cowardly in battle. The city concentrated its efforts on commerce, especially its connections with the Hanseatic trading ports of the Baltic, avoiding most of the internecine strife that had wracked the other principalities. "Lord Novgorod" showed the same pragmatism in dealings with the khan.

The Novgorodian Chronicle relates that their prince, Alexander Nevsky, son of Yaroslav I of Vladimir, had recognized the futility of opposition and had directed his people to render tribute. In the year 1259 "the Prince rode down from the [palace] and the accursed Tatars with him. . . . And the accursed ones began to ride through the streets, writing down the Christian houses; because for our sins God has brought wild beasts out of the desert to eat the flesh of the strong, and to drink the blood of the *Boyars.*" Nevsky also made frequent journeys of homage to the khan of the Golden Horde, at least once to distant Karakorum, and had won the trust of the Mongols. But a further reason, which was perhaps of overriding importance in gaining the khan's favor, was that Mongol policy stimulated Baltic trade, for international commerce was the source of the Golden Horde's prosperity. While Kiev lay in ruins, Novgorod's trade in the Baltic, and south by the river road to the Caspian Sea, continued to flourish, and the people—hundred thousand strong in its heyday—to prosper. Confident in their wealth and power, the citizens asked arrogantly: "Who can stand against God and Great Novgorod?"

Novgorod was unique in claiming the right to choose its own prince; it allowed him only limited authority, in effect keeping him as titular head of state with certain judicial and military functions. The real power emanated from the *veche* —an unwieldy but relatively democratic assembly of male citizens—and its more select, more operative council of notables, which functioned on a day-to-day basis in the run-

Moscow's Grand Prince Ivan I (shown at court in the sixteenth-century miniature above) gained the epithet "Money-bag" for his diligence as the khan's tax collector. Aside from a tithe, property assessments were levied upon all classes but the clergy. City merchants paid according to the value of goods sold, and rural people according to the amount

of land tilled plus the number of workers and plows in use. Convinced that keeping his contract with Muscovy's overlords was the best way to discourage the khan's meddling in internal affairs, Ivan could be harsh in gathering the tribute. Above right, his agents punish a recalcitrant boyar while a wary public watch.

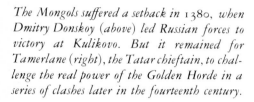

The Mongols suffered a setback in 1380, when Dmitry Donskoy (above) led Russian forces to victory at Kulikovo. But it remained for Tamerlane (right), the Tatar chieftain, to challenge the real power of the Golden Horde in a series of clashes later in the fourteenth century.

ning of the city's business, be it taxation, legislation, commercial controls, or the like. Participation in the *veche* was by class—groups of boyars, merchants, artisans, and the poorer people—with the aristocratic element generally dominant by virtue of its close ties with the council. Conflicts within the assembly were often violent—a unanimous vote was required to pass any decision—and meetings broke up in disorder. Nevertheless, they managed to elect their *posadnik*, or mayor, and *tysyatsky*, or commander of the troops. The *veche* also nominated the archbishop, who played an influential part in the secular affairs of the republic. Both council and *veche* had existed in Kievan Rus as advisory institutions; but in Novgorod they represented an impressive, if short-lived, experiment in genuine democratic government.

Prince Alexander was one prince who seems to have enjoyed the good will of his electors. He had an equally successful record in dealing with the armed threat from the West. While the Russian lands were falling under Mongol-Tatar occupation, powerful forces were putting pressure upon the Western principalities. In 1240 Alexander routed the Swedes on the banks of the Neva River, thereby gaining for himself the name "Nevsky" and for the Novgorodtsi an outlet to the Baltic. Two German military religious orders, whose conquests were directed at the extension of Roman Catholicism among the pagan Letts and Livonians of the

Baltic, were also major threats. First to be organized were the Teutonic Knights, an army of noblemen that had come into existence as a hospital order during the third crusade. Beginning in the thirteenth century they took over lands roughly equivalent to later-day Prussia. At this time a second order, the Livonian Knights, was founded by the bishop of the Baltic city of Riga. The two united in 1237 and five years later marched on Novgorod. They were met on the frozen Lake Peipus, near Pskov, and defeated in the Battle on Ice, thus halting for a time the German drive eastward.

The Knights continued, however, to harass the pagan Letts and Lithuanians, who were forced to reach out in the only direction left them: eastward toward their weakened neighbor Russia. The Mongols had laid waste Lithuania in 1258, but had then withdrawn and not returned. The Lithuanians had recovered quickly, and not long afterward, under their great military leader Gedimin the Conqueror (1316–41), they succeeded in occupying most of west and southwest Russia, including Kiev. Though technically it now lay outside the sphere of Russia proper, this new "grand princedom of Lithuania and Russia" would rival the strongest all-Russian principality for decades to come. Olgierd, the son and successor of Gedimin, eventually defeated Novgorod in 1346, thereafter subduing the sister city of Pskov, expelling the Tatars from southwest Russia, and taking the Crimea.

Sergius of Radonezh is seen supervising the fencing of the Troitsa Monastery (which he founded north of Moscow in 1337) in this miniature from a later account of his life. Saint Sergius was a key figure in the monastic revival and unification of Russia in the 1300's.

Meanwhile, Moscow was growing from an insignificant settlement into the matrix and capital of the nation. Of this dramatic and unexpected development in Russia's history a Muscovite would write in the seventeenth century: "What man could have divined that Moscow would become a great realm?" The chronicle relates that in 1147 Prince Yury Dolgoruky of Vladimir-Suzdal sent a message to his ally, Prince Svyatoslav of Novgorod-Seversk: "Come to me, brother, in Moscow! Be my guest in Moscow!" It is not certain that the town was then on its present site. Prince Yury founded the town of Moscow nine years later by building wooden walls around the high ground between the Moskva River and its tributary, the Neglinnaya, and thus created the first kremlin, or fortress. It soon became the seat of a family of minor princes under the hegemony of Vladimir-Suzdal. In 1238 the Mongols destroyed Moscow and laid waste the surrounding territory. About 1283 Daniel, son of Alexander Nevsky, acquired the principality and became the first of a regular line of Muscovite rulers. The rise of Moscow had begun.

Among Moscow's neighbors, Tver, Vladimir-Suzdal, Ryazan, and Novgorod were more powerful and seemed stronger contenders for leadership of the nation; but Moscow had important advantages. It stood in the region of the upper Volga and Oka rivers, at the center of the system of waterways extending over the whole of European Russia.

Tver shared this advantage to some extent, but Moscow was at the hub. This was a position of tremendous importance for trade and even more for defense. Moscow enjoyed greater security from attacks by Mongols and other enemies. As a refuge and a center of trade, the new city attracted boyars, merchants, and peasants from every principality, all of whom added to its wealth and power.

Another important factor in Moscow's development was the ability of its rulers. They do not emerge as individuals from the shadowed distance of history; but all were careful stewards of their principality—enterprising, ruthless, and tenacious. They acquired new lands and power by treaty, trickery, purchase, and as a last resort by force. In a century and a half their principality would grow from some five hundred to more than fifteen thousand square miles.

Ivan I (1328–41), called Kalita, or Moneybag, the first of the great "collectors of the Russian land," was, like his grandfather Alexander Nevsky, scrupulously subservient to the Golden Horde. His reward was to obtain the khan's assent to his assuming the title of grand prince and also to the removal of the seat of the metropolitan of all Russia from Vladimir to Moscow, an event of paramount importance to Moscow's later claims of supreme authority.

Ivan I strengthened his city by erecting new walls around it. He built the Cathedral of the Assumption and other churches in stone. The merchant quarter, the *kitai gorod*, expanded rapidly as trade revived. Terrible fires destroyed large areas of the city, but houses were quickly replaced, and Moscow continued to grow.

Ivan I was succeeded by Simeon the Proud, who died twelve years later in a plague that devastated Moscow. He was, in turn, succeeded by his brother, Ivan II, a man whose principal contribution to Russian history seems to have been the fathering of the future Dmitry Donskoy, who became grand prince of Moscow in 1363. Under Prince Dmitry's reign Moscow took advantage of the waning power of the Golden Horde to extend its influence over less powerful principalities. Generous gifts to Mamai, the khan of the Golden Horde, put an end to Dmitry's most serious competitor, Prince Mikhail of Tver; Dmitry's patent was confirmed and Mikhail's claims to the throne ignored for several years. Then, with Moscow's power growing at an alarming rate, Mamai reversed his earlier grant and sent an army against Moscow in 1380.

Dmitry was well prepared. He had rebuilt the Kremlin walls in stone, adding battlements, towers, and iron gates. He had secured by treaty the promise of support troops from other principalities. He had introduced firearms on a limited scale. Dmitry won enduring fame by launching the first counterattack against the dreaded Mongol enemy. The heroic battle of Kulikovo, fought on the banks of the river Don (hence Dmitry's surname "Donskoy") ended with the Russians inflicting a major defeat on the Golden Horde. The news was greeted with great rejoicing in Moscow, though the Russians had lost nearly half their men in the struggle. It inspired all Russians with a new spirit of independence. The battle was not decisive, however, and it brought retribution. In 1382 the Mongols, this time led by the Khan Tokhtamysh, laid siege to Moscow. For three days and nights they made furious attacks on the city, but they could not breach the stone walls. The khan then gained entry by offering to discuss peace terms. Once inside the city, his warriors began to slaughter the people—"until their arms wearied and their swords became blunt." Recording these events the chronicler lamented that "until then the city of Moscow had been large and wonderful to look at, crowded as she was with people, filled with wealth and glory . . . and now all at once all of her beauty perished and her glory disappeared. Nothing could be seen but smoking ruins and bare earth and heaps of corpses." More than twenty thousand victims were buried. With extraordinary vitality, however, Moscow soon revived, and within a few years had been restored to its former power.

In the reign of Dmitry's son, Vasily I, Moscow was threatened with an attack by Tamerlane, the Turkic conqueror who had, by a feat of historical revisionism, claimed to be a descendant of Genghis Khan. In 1395, following his successful campaign against his rivals, the doubting Tokhtamysh and the Golden Horde, Tamerlane advanced from the south to within two hundred miles of Moscow, but then turned aside, apparently convinced that another siege would be too costly to his own troops. The city was saved, the people said, because of the miraculous intervention of the icon of Our Lady of Vladimir.

Though the Tatars would continue to be a major factor in Muscovite history for another half century, the balance of power was shifting to the Lithuanian front. Ladislas Jagello, son of the Lithuanian grand duke who had brought parts of western Russia under his suzerainty, ascended the Lithuanian throne in 1377. During the Jagello era, which his reign inaugurated, the prince conceived a dynastic union with his former enemy, Poland, through marriage to Jadwiga, heiress to that throne. Jagello thus became sovereign of the federated states of Poland and Lithuania, the latter under the vassal rule of his cousin. Husband and wife shared an ambition to control a still larger portion of Russia. Jagello's conversion to Roman Catholicism, which was part of the marriage treaty, made this imperial plan all the more dangerous to Muscovite security. With Smolensk's fall to the Lithuanians in 1404, almost all the lands on the right bank of the Dnieper were brought under dynastically-united Polish and Lithuanian rule.

Only a matter as crucial to all Slavic peoples as the defeat of the Teutonic Knights held them in a brief state of peace. In 1410 the combined Polish and Lithuanian forces met the German forces at Tannenberg. Their grand master, many of their officers, and a devastating number of knights fell in the bloody clash. The eastward drive of the German Knights was effectively halted for all time, but the Polish and Lithuanian drives received new impetus.

The reign of Vasily I ended in 1425. His son and successor, Vasily II, ascended the Muscovite throne against strong opposition from a powerful boyar faction; the first twenty-five years of his long reign were largely devoted to suppressing these rivals, a feat achieved only after he had himself been blinded. Events outside of Muscovy would be of more lasting significance: the Golden Horde was losing large parts of its territory to the breakaway khanates of Crimea and Kazan; and the Ottoman Turks were threatening the very existence of the Greek Orthodox Church. In a desperate move to defend itself from total destruction, the Eastern clergy had sought help in Rome, at the price of recognizing the supremacy of the pope. Moscow was represented at the Council of Florence, which met in 1439, by the Russian Metropolitan Isadore. Acting on his own initiative, Isadore committed Russian Orthodoxy to the bargain. Upon his return he was deposed and arrested, and Moscow formally severed its ties with Byzantium. When Constantinople, the capital of Eastern Orthodoxy, fell to the Turks in 1453, no Russian was surprised. It was God's retribution to the duplicitous Greeks. Holy Russia would find its own way.

As the nomadic life of Genghis Khan's subjects did not encourage development of artists, history has had to rely on the idealizations of later generations for images of the Mongol chief. The portrait of the khan is a detail from a sixteenth-century Persian genealogy.

The Mongol Masters

"They were terrible to look at and indescribable, with large heads like a buffalo's, narrow eyes like a fledgling's, a snub nose like a cat's, projecting snouts like a dog's, narrow loins like an ant's, short legs like a hog's, and by nature with no beards at all. With a lion's strength they have voices more shrill than an eagle. They appear where least expected. . . . Their [women's] broad faces are plastered with a poisonous mixture of gum. They give birth to children like snakes and eat like wolves. Death does not appear among them, for they survive for three hundred years." This beastly report, delivered in 1271 by the Armenian monk Grigor of Akanc, confirmed the worst fears of Westerners, who had come to regard the Mongols as superhuman. Indeed, the exaggerated reputation that accompanied the hordes, following their first descent upon Russia in 1223, was among their strongest weapons. Eyewitnesses told of whole cities surrendering to a handful of warriors. (The Persian miniature above shows Mongol cavalrymen in typical leather armor; opposite, one of their methods of dispatching prisoners and their horses.) Then, too, the Mongols, and the Turkic tribes they assimilated along the way, went at their warfare with uncommon zest. Genghis Khan exulted that "man's highest joy is in victory: to conquer one's enemies, to pursue them, to deprive them of their possessions, to make their beloved weep, to ride on their horses, and to embrace their daughters and wives." His armies, and those of his sons and successors, were organized into peerless fighting machines of extraordinary mobility and total dedication; their chieftains were thought to be invested with supernatural authority. Russia suffered the most of the lands conquered, for its contacts with Western civilization were impaired for nearly two centuries, and the Golden Horde—that branch of the empire that immediately controlled Russia's destiny—had little to teach the vanquished. Cultural imperialism played no part in Mongol dreams of world conquest; with no real homeland of their own, no cities in which to develop arts and sciences, they brought "neither algebra nor Aristotle," as Alexander Pushkin was to lament. To the Mongols' credit, they did succeed in reopening the ancient overland route to China; the Pax Mongolica, which was imposed upon the lawless peoples of the steppes, guaranteed friendly merchants and envoys safe passage (monks shuttled back and forth carrying a prolonged written debate between the pope and the Great Khan as to who should send tribute to whom). And in Russia the Mongol presence was enough to force the shattered remnants of princely authority to cease squabbling and to discover a common cause: the building of a unified Russian state.

AN ANCIENT LEGEND *seeking to trace the origins of the Mongols told of two families, the sole survivors of the wars with the Tatars and Chinese, who fled to a mountain fastness—where they multiplied and learned to make iron weapons. In the Persian miniature opposite, the descendants are seen packing to return to the plain and their nomadic life. However, historians attribute the upsurge of Mongol energy to Genghis Khan's unification of the tribes. Regarded by his people as immortal, the son of the Eternal Blue Sky, the Great Khan was given an impressive funeral celebration (above) when he died in 1227.*

THE COURT AT KARAKORUM
by *William of Rubruck*

Sent by Louis IX of France to "preach the work of God," Friar William walked across the steppes to the court of Mangu Khan. His reception in 1253 is described in this excerpt.

Near the entrance was a bench with some cosmos on it, and they made the interpreter stand near this while we were made to sit on a stool in front of the ladies. The whole dwelling was completely covered inside with cloth of gold and in the middle in a little hearth was a fire of twigs and roots of wormwood, which grows to a great size there, and also the dung of oxen. The Chan was sitting on a couch wearing a speckled and shiny fur like seal-skin. He is a flat-nosed man of medium height, about forty-five years old; a young wife was sitting next to him and a grown-up daughter, who was very ugly, Cirina by name, was sitting on a couch behind them with some little children. . . .

Then the Chan had them ask us whether we would like to drink wine or *terracina*, that is rice wine, or caracosmos, that is clear mares' milk, or *bal*, that is mead made from honey, for these are the four drinks they use in winter. I replied: "Sir, we are not men seeking our desire in drink; whatever pleases you satisfies us." Then he had some of the rice drink brought for us, it is clear and tastes like white wine; out of respect to him we sipped it for a short time. . . .

Then I spoke: ". . . You are a man to whom God has given great dominion on earth, we therefore beg Your Puissance to grant us leave to stay in your country to carry out the service to God on behalf of you, your wives and your children. We have neither gold nor silver nor precious stones which we could present to you; we have but ourselves and we offer ourselves to serve God and pray to Him for you. . . ."

Then the Chan began to reply: "Just as the sun spreads its rays in all directions, so my power and the power of Baatu is spread everywhere. Therefore we have no need of your gold or silver." Up to this point I understood my interpreter but beyond this I could not grasp a single complete sentence which showed me clearly that he was drunk. And Mangu Chan himself appeared to me intoxicated. He ended however by saying, so it seemed to me, that he was not pleased that we had gone to Sartach first, rather than to him. . . . I begged him not to be offended at what I had said about gold and silver, for I had said it not because he had need of or desired such things, but rather because we would gladly have honored him with both temporal and spiritual gifts.

OF THEIR WORSHIP
by *John of Plano Carpini*

With Christendom threatened, Pope Innocent IV dispatched the author, a Franciscan, to inform the khan of God's displeasure. A portion of his report, made in 1247, follows.

They believe in one God, and they believe that He is the maker of all things visible, and invisible; and that it is He who is the giver of the good things of this world as well as the hardships; they do not, however, worship Him with prayers or praises or any kind of ceremony. Their belief in God does not prevent them from having idols of felt. . . .

Although they have no law concerning the doing of what is right or the avoidance of sin, nevertheless there are certain traditional things, invented by them or their ancestors, which they say are sins; for example, to stick a knife into a fire, or even in any way to touch fire with a knife, or to extract meat from the cauldron with a knife, or to chop with an axe near a fire; for they believe that, if these things were done, the fire would be beheaded; likewise to lean on a whip with which a horse is lashed, for they do not use spurs: also to touch arrows with a whip; again to catch or kill young birds, to strike a horse with a bridle; also to break a bone with another bone, to pour out upon the ground milk or any kind of drink or food; to pass water inside a dwelling. If a man does this on purpose he is put to death, otherwise he has to pay a large sum of money to the soothsayer, who purifies him and has the dwelling and its contents carried between two fires; but before this purification has been carried out no one dare enter the dwelling or take away anything from it: again, if anyone takes a morsel and, unable to swallow it, spits it out of his mouth, a hole is made under the dwelling and he is dragged out by that hole and without any mercy put to death; also if a man treads on the threshold of a dwelling belonging to any chief he is put to death in the same way. . . .

On the other hand, to kill men, to invade the countries of other people, to take the property of others in any unlawful way, to commit fornication, to revile other men, to act contrary to the prohibitions and commandments of God, is considered no sin by them. . . .

When anyone is sick past cure, they put a spear there and wind black felt round it and from then onwards no outsider dares to enter within the bounds of his dwellings. When the death agony begins almost everybody leaves him. . . .

The relatives of the dead man and all those living in his dwellings have to be purified by fire. This purification is performed in the following manner: they make two fires and they put two spears near the fires, with a rope fastened on to the top of them, on to which they tie strips of buckram; under this rope and its ribbons and between the two fires pass men, animals and dwellings. And there are two women, one this side, the other that, who sprinkle water and recite incantations. If any carts break down there, or if anything falls to the ground on that spot, the enchanters get it. If anyone is killed by a thunderbolt, all the people living in his dwellings have to pass through the fires in the manner described; no one touches his tent, his bed, cart, felt, clothes or any other such things as he had; but they are spurned by all as unclean.

The political center of the empire was the court of the Great Khan. It was moved in 1267 from remote Karakorum to Khanbalik in newly conquered China, where such creature comforts as silk underwear began to
temper Mongol barbarism. The elegant enthronement below is part of the investiture ceremony of a new khan.

TOPKAPI PALACE MUSEUM, ISTANBUL; ARA GULER

BIBLIOTHÈQUE NATIONALE, SERVICE PHOTOGRAPHIQUE

TOPKAPI PALACE MUSEUM, ISTANBUL; ARA GULER

THE POLYGAMOUS WARRIOR, *despite the hardships of his life, rarely left his large family far behind. Each man was followed by his wives and concubines, who cared and cooked for him in* yurts *(small tents made of greased and ornamented felt stretched over wooden frames) that were pitched in family clusters in the camp, as shown in the Persian miniature top left. The first wife was usually acquired by formal marriage (the festive procession at bottom left is a bridal party). Subsequent mates were inherited upon the death of a father or brothers, or gathered as the booty of war—one such prize is shown being delivered to Genghis Khan (above).*

67

SPIRITUAL LIFE *was entrusted to the care of shamans, priests who mediated between mortals and the host of daemons, who inhabited earth and sky and all that lay between. These spirits, like the brutish creature opposite, were believed to be capable of extreme violence when left untended, and only the shamans were equipped to interpret and satisfy their pleasures. The miniature above shows two shamans performing a ritual dance.*

OVERLEAF: *Mongol troops are shown preparing to storm Baghdad in 1258, a massacre that reportedly left more than 800,000 dead. Such devastating victories were won with sophisticated military techniques: typically, bowmen would drive their enemy to seek safety in a city, seal them off within a hastily built stockade, then advance catapults, battering rams, javelin throwers, and other siege engines toward the fortified inner city.*

THE MONGOL TERROR

OF WAR AND BATTLE ARRAY
by John of Plano Carpini

To the armies of Christianity, as yet unschooled in military science, Carpini's estimate of the heathens' forces must have been terrifying. Following is his examination of Mongol discipline.

Chingis Chan [Genghis Khan] ordained that the army should be organized in such a way that over ten men should be set one man and he is what we call a captain of ten. . . . When they are in battle, if one or two or three or even more out of a group of ten run away, all are put to death; and if a whole group of ten flees, the rest of the group of a hundred are all put to death, if they do not flee too. In a word, unless they retreat in a body, all who take flight are put to death. Likewise if one or two or more go forward boldly to the fight, then the rest of the ten are put to death if they do not follow. . . .

When they are going to make war, they send ahead an advance guard and these carry nothing with them but their tents, horses and arms. They seize no plunder, burn no houses and slaughter no animals; they only wound and kill men or, if they can do nothing else, put them to flight. They much prefer, however, to kill than to put to flight. The army follows after them, taking everything they come across, and they take prisoner or kill any inhabitants who are to be found. . . .

It should be known that when they come in sight of the enemy they attack at once, each one shooting three or four arrows at their adversaries; if they see that they are not going to be able to defeat them, they retire, going back to their own line. They do this as a blind to make the enemy follow them as far as the places where they have prepared ambushes. . . . Similarly if they see that they are opposed by a large army, they sometimes turn aside and, putting a day's or two days' journey between them, they attack and pillage another part of the country and they kill men and destroy and lay waste the land. If they perceive that they cannot even do this, then they retreat for some ten or twelve days and stay in a safe place until the army of the enemy has disbanded, whereupon they come secretly and ravage the whole land.

SATAN'S SWARM
by Matthew Paris

The convulsions caused the civilized world by the Mongol "locusts" are vividly described in this Englishman's Chronica Majora *of 1259. Here Paris finds God's reason even in disaster.*

That the joys of mortal man be not enduring, nor worldly happiness long lasting without lamentations . . . the countless army of Tatars, broke loose from its mountain-environed home, and, piercing the solid rocks [of the Caucasus] poured forth like devils. . . . they have razed cities, cut down forests, overthrown fortresses, pulled up vines, destroyed gardens, killed townspeople and peasants. If perchance they have spared any suppliants, they have forced them, reduced to the lowest condition of slavery, to fight in the foremost ranks against their own neighbors. . . . they have misused their captives as they have their mares. For they are inhuman and beastly, rather monsters than men, thirsting for and drinking blood, tearing and devouring the flesh of dogs and men, dressed in ox-hides, armed with plates of iron, short and stout, thickset, strong, invincible, indefatigable, their backs unprotected, their breasts covered with armor; drinking with delight the pure blood of their flocks, with big, strong horses, which eat branches and even trees, and which they have to mount by the help of three steps on account of the shortness of their thighs. They are without human laws, know no comforts, are more ferocious than lions or bears, have boats made of ox-hides which ten or twelve of them own in common; they are able to swim or manage a boat, so that they can cross the largest and swiftest rivers without let or hindrance, drinking turbid and muddy water when blood fails them [as a beverage]. They have one-edged swords and daggers, are wonderful archers, spare neither age, nor sex, nor condition.

THE TALE OF THE DESTRUCTION OF RYAZAN

The carnage committed by Batu Khan provided a dramatic subject for Russia's oral historians. Even centuries later they could command a rapt audience for this 1237 tragedy.

On the dawn of the sixth day the pagan warriors began to storm the city, some with firebrands, some with battering rams, and others with countless scaling ladders for ascending the walls of the city. And they took the city of Ryazan on the 21st day of December. And the Tatars came to the Cathedral of the Assumption of the Blessed Virgin, and they cut to pieces the Great Princess Agrippina, her daughters-in-law, and other princesses. They burned to death the bishops and the priests and put the torch to the holy church. . . . And the churches of God were destroyed, and much blood was spilled on the holy altars. And not one man remained alive in the city. All were dead. All had drunk the same bitter cup to the dregs. And there was not even anyone to mourn the dead.

Remnants of the once-powerful Golden Horde, the khanates of Crimea, Kazan, and Astrakhan, were further weakened through internal wars. Opposite, forces of one khan capture another on the shores of the Black Sea.

3

Rise of Muscovy

Ivan III, the chief architect of Russia's unification, ascended the throne of Moscow in 1462. At the time of his accession Moscow had not yet established its supremacy. The Russian peoples were not yet united, and many were under foreign rule. The Smolensk region—embracing Belorussia, or White Russia—and most of present-day Ukraine had been conquered by Lithuania. Eastern Galicia had been annexed by Poland; and Carpatho-Russia was part of Hungary. The steppes, extending southward from Ryazan and Tula to the Caspian and Black seas, continued to be dominated by the Tatars; although their former unity was dissolving, they still managed to prevent Russians from settling this fertile region. Among the principalities of eastern Russia, four—Yaroslavl, Ryazan, Rostov, and Tver—were independent. Also, the city-state of Novgorod, with its great empire stretching across northern Russia, and the smaller city-states of Pskov and Vyatka, remained outside the authority of Moscow.

During Ivan's childhood Muscovy had been wracked by savage internal struggles for power. Ivan had been constantly at his father's side, gaining invaluable experience in the arts

Ivan IV, shown opposite in a contemporary icon, was the first grand prince to be crowned tsar. Ivan the Terrible is remembered as the classic Russian tyrant because of the ruthless methods by which he destroyed his enemies and established Muscovite absolutism.

of war and government. Vasily II had his son proclaimed grand prince and co-ruler in 1449; and on the death of the old man in 1462, Ivan held sole authority.

The Italian traveler Ambrogio Contarini, who visited Moscow about 1499, wrote that the grand prince was tall, thin, and handsome. Though less barbaric and cruel than many contemporary rulers, he was not an attractive sovereign. He commanded the loyalty and respect of his subjects, but not their love. He was too reserved and suspicious, probably as a result of the terrors of his childhood; and, it was said, he could be so forbidding that on occasion women fainted on coming face to face with him. By nature he was immensely ambitious, but also cautious and practical. He possessed the broad vision of a statesman, combined with extraordinary patience and tenacity. He has left the impression of a man who throughout his long reign was master of himself, of his principality, and of the great developments that he directed.

The goal toward which Ivan worked was nothing less than the formation of the Russian nation, centralized upon the throne of Moscow and ruled by an autocrat. The nation he envisaged would not be limited to Great Russia—the upper Volga-Oka region, of which Moscow was the center—but would embrace all lands occupied by Orthodox Russians; Ivan insisted that "since olden times from our ancient

forebears they have been part of our patrimony." This policy meant war with the Tatars and Lithuanians, and the subjugation of Novgorod and the independent principalities. Ivan devoted the forty-three years of his reign to patient planning, tortuous diplomacy; and he waged major wars on several fronts in pursuit of his objective.

Soon after ascending the throne Ivan began devising action against the khanate of Kazan, one of the four independent states that occupied lands once held by the Golden Horde. Kazan's capital, some four hundred miles directly east of Moscow, placed the Tatars within easy striking distance, and their control over a section of the Volga threatened a major part of Muscovy's trade. In 1467, 1468, and again in the following year his armies invaded the khanate; but in spite of these repeated efforts, he failed to capture Kazan. His campaigns had the effect, however, of diminishing the zest of the Tatars for attacking Muscovy; they recognized that they could no longer raid and plunder with impunity.

The next Tatar threat came in 1479. Ivan found himself challenged by Ahmad, the new khan of the Golden Horde. Ahmad prided himself on his direct descent from Genghis Khan through Genghis' eldest son, Juji. He was determined to restore the khan's suzerainty over Muscovy and to collect the tribute. According to tradition, Ahmad sent his envoys to Moscow with his demands, and Ivan spat publicly on the

khan's badge of office when it was proffered and threw it to the ground. This incident was said to have happened in 1480, the year generally taken to mark the end of the Mongol yoke over the Russians.

Khan Ahmad's plans to invade Muscovy were constantly jeopardized and delayed by the bitter enmity between his followers and the Tatars of the Crimea. In 1465 the Crimean Khan Haji-Girei had routed Ahmad's armies on the Don, where they were massing to advance on Moscow. In 1472 Ahmad mounted another invasion of Muscovy with which Casimir, grand prince of Lithuania, was to coordinate his attacks from the west. The Lithuanian support did not materialize, however, and Ahmad's army was forced to withdraw.

At this stage Ivan sent envoys to Mengli-Girei—who had succeeded his father Haji-Girei as khan of the Crimean Tatars—proposing an alliance against the Golden Horde and Lithuania. This approach did not bear fruit for some five years: in April, 1480, Ivan and Mengli-Girei agreed on an offensive pact against Lithuania and a defensive alliance against the Golden Horde. As Ivan had no intention of invading Ahmad's vast realm, and every intention of waging war against Lithuania sometime in the future, he was well satisfied. The alliance was timely, for a new joint campaign against Muscovy was being prepared by Ahmad and Casimir. Ahmad invaded Muscovy, but retreated when once again the

The efforts of Ivan III (far left) to elevate the majesty of his throne led to a political marriage with the Byzantine Princess Zoe. Her dowry, which the couple is seen accepting from Pope Sixtus IV in the Italian fresco at center, included the right to adopt the Byzantine two-headed eagle (above) as the tsar's royal coat of arms.

OVERLEAF: *The* Tree of the Russian Nation, *bearing several generations of Church and state leaders, is shown flourishing in the earthly paradise of Moscow's Kremlin. The gardeners depicted in a detail of the 1668 allegory are Ivan Kalita and the Metropolitan Peter, the first prince of the Church to take up residence there.*

expected Lithuanian support did not appear. The following year Siberian and Nogai Tatars captured Sarai, the capital of the Golden Horde, and murdered Ahmad.

In the midst of his complex diplomacy, his wars with the Tatars, and his longer-term plans against Lithuania, Ivan did not overlook the three city-states of Novgorod, Pskov, and Vyatka. Their continued independence stood as an obstacle to the unification of Russia under Moscow's rule. Pskov and Vyatka were important, but Novgorod far exceeded them in extent, riches, and significance.

Obsessed with wealth and independence, the Novgorodtsi had watched with misgiving the growth of Muscovy's power. The upper classes, including the boyars, favored alliance with Lithuania to secure their city-state against Muscovite encroachment. The lower classes wanted good relations with Moscow because they were dependent on its fertile lands for a cheap and plentiful food supply.

During the first half of the fifteenth century the Lithuanians had made strenuous but unsuccessful efforts to annex Novgorod; then, plagued by internal conflicts, Prince Svidrigaylo of Lithuania signed an "eternal peace" with the Novgorodtsi. At this stage Muscovite pressure revived. In 1456 Vasily II sent a small force, which routed the Novgorod cavalry and imposed limits on the autonomy of the city, restricting the power of the *veche* to issue charters without

princely permission and demanding extradition of political enemies seeking asylum from Moscow. The Novgorodtsi became restless and increasingly rebellious. Finally, the boyar party secured agreement within the *veche* for alliance with Lithuania's Grand Prince Casimir, and renouncing their ties with Muscovy, which had by now passed to Ivan, they signed the treaty in February, 1471.

Ivan acted promptly. Three armies set out from Moscow in June, 1471. The Novgorodtsi were divided among themselves and now in serious difficulties. Casimir was involved in Czech and Hungarian disputes, and was further prevented from sending help by the Livonian Knights, who declined to allow his army to pass through their lands. Pskov sided with Moscow. In the month-long campaign that followed, the Novgorodtsi suffered heavy casualties and finally complete defeat. Ivan was lenient, however, allowing them to retain nominal independence. He spent the winter of 1475 in the city amid demonstrations of loyalty.

Soon after his departure, however, new conflicts erupted between the pro-Muscovite party of the middle and lower classes, and the pro-Lithuanian party of the upper classes. In March, 1477, a small mission, apparently unauthorized by the *veche*, traveled to Moscow to offer the Muscovite grand prince full sovereignty over the city and its possessions. Without delay Ivan sent his envoys to announce that he ac-

77

STATE TRETYAKOV GALLERY, MOSCOW

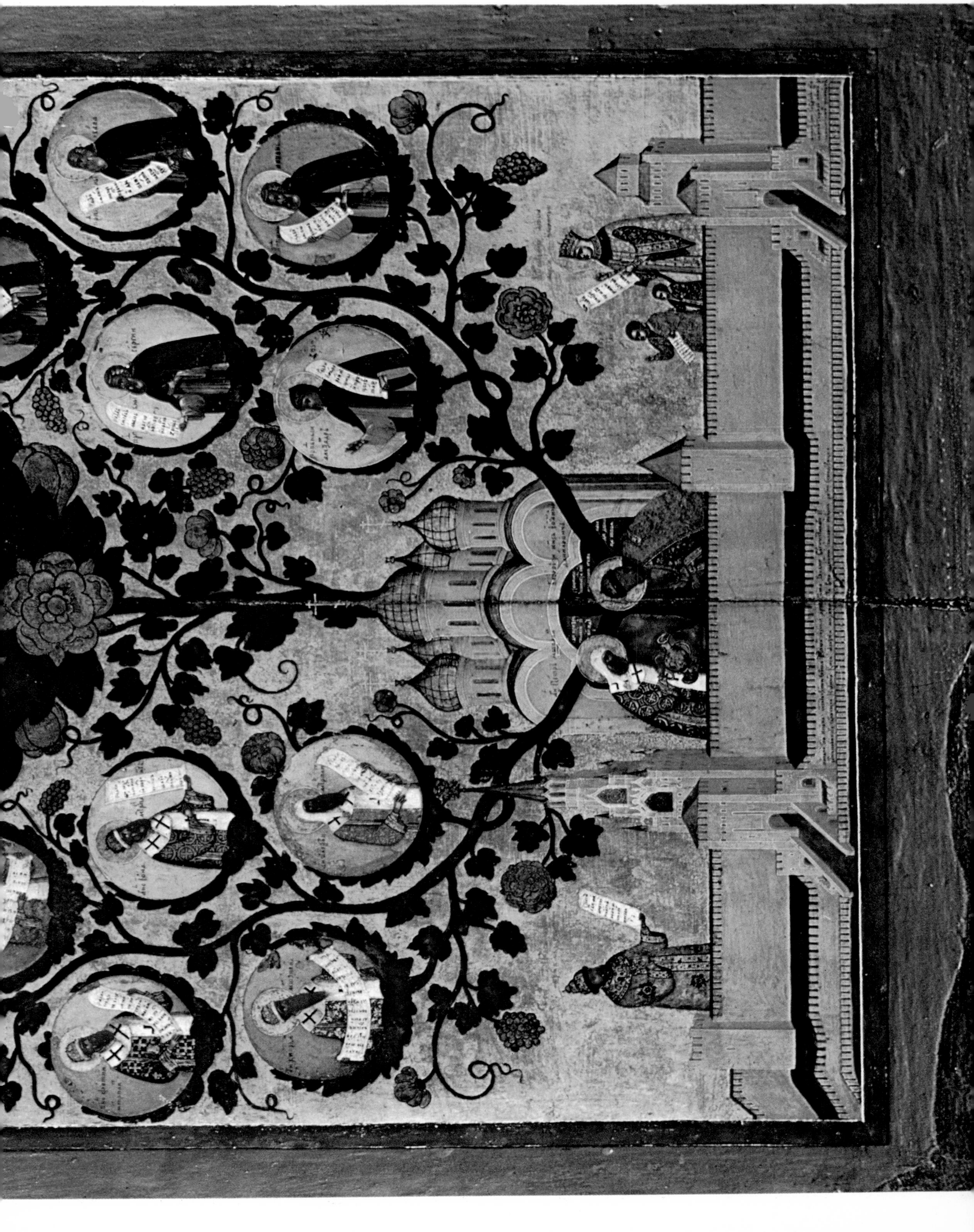

The palace of Kolomenskoye, shown above in an engraving done shortly before its demolition in 1768, was a favorite royal retreat near Moscow. Begun in the 1300's by Ivan Kalita, it was progressively enlarged, becoming in the process a lexicon of Muscovite wooden architectural styles.

cepted the proffered sovereignty; he used the more elevated title of *gosudar*, or "sovereign," in place of the traditional *gospodin*, then meaning "lord." It was just the beginning of Ivan's plan to enlarge his titles along with his authority.

Novgorod was in an uproar. Many boyars and merchants again pressed for alliance with Lithuania. They held Ivan's envoys for six weeks before sending them back with the message that the city would recognize Ivan only as their *gospodin*.

In response to this personal affront, Ivan sent a declaration of war on September 30, 1477; and nine days later his armies marched. The Novgorodtsi manned their defenses and refused to surrender. In November Ivan surrounded the city, intending to starve the people into submission. He did not have long to wait. In December Novgorod capitulated, and its citizens swore allegiance to him as *gosudar*. Ivan now put an end to Novgorod's independence. He abolished the *veche* and took away the treasured symbol of the city's freedom: the bell that was used to summon citizens to meetings of the *veche*. He annexed Novgorod's eastern dependencies; and the territories left in the city's possession had to pay heavy tribute. In October, 1479, a group that was seeking Lithuanian aid was discovered; Ivan had one hundred boyars executed, the archbishop imprisoned, and many rebellious citizens deported to other parts of Muscovy. Novgorodtsi continued to cherish memories of their city's

independence, and although trouble sometimes arose, they were no longer able to challenge the authority of Moscow.

Pskov, the small, strongly fortified city-state to the west of Novgorod, had developed its own defenses and resources, and its people were generally more self-reliant than the Novgorodtsi. But Pskov was in an exposed position. The Teutonic Knights were on its western frontiers and the Lithuanians to the southwest. Often Pskov was compelled to seek the help of Moscow against their attacks, in return for which they backed some of Muscovy's plans for aggrandizement.

About the middle of the fifteenth century the Knights began planning a new eastward drive, directed against Pskov and Novgorod. Their objectives were set aside when they became involved in war with Poland. In 1480, however, they marched on Pskov. The people appealed urgently to Moscow, and Ivan at once sent an army to invade Livonia, laying waste the land as far as Dorpat (Tartu) and compelling the Knights to give up their campaign.

Ivan attached great importance to Pskov as a defensive outpost on the northwestern frontier. Unlike the Novgorodsti, the Pskovsti were reliable and did not threaten alliance with his enemies. When in 1501 Walter von Plettenberg, later the grand master of the Teutonic order, made an agreement with the Lithuanian grand prince for a joint attack

The 1551 miniature above depicts roofers at work on one of the gilt domes of the Uspensky Cathedral (left). The church, located in the Kremlin, was built in 1475–79 by Fioravanti, an Italian architect summoned to Moscow by Ivan III. It was the place where all later tsars were crowned.

on Pskov and the surrounding lands, Ivan again sent a strong army, which devastated large areas of Livonia in retaliation. Ivan took no steps, however, to annex Pskov or to curtail its independence; and it was left to his successor, Vasily III, to incorporate the city-state into Muscovy.

By contrast, Vyatka presented an immediate threat to Muscovy. This small city-state to the northeast of Moscow embraced the upper reaches of the Vyatka River and had as its capital the town of Khlynov. The Vyatkans were wild, arrogant horsemen; they were akin to the Tatars—who had briefly occupied their land—in outlook and in their disruptive effect on neighboring Russian states. But, more than their predatory raids, the danger that they would join forces with the Tatars against Muscovy disturbed Ivan. Vasily II had sent two expeditions against the republic, and in 1460 the Vyatkans had been forced, as a chronicler recorded, to "bow submission to the grand prince, according to his entire will, as is fitting to a sovereign." But when Ivan called on them to support his campaign against the Tatars of Kazan, they not only refused, but declared their neutrality. Finally, in 1489, Ivan sent a strong army, which compelled the Vyatkans to capitulate. He then eliminated the rebellious republic: all the people of Vyatka were resettled near Moscow, their leader executed, and loyal Muscovites sent to manage the abandoned lands—perhaps the first time in

Russian history that a forced resettlement of a whole people was undertaken by the government.

Ivan's long-term plan for war against Lithuania was drawing nearer. He had always made it clear that he considered the lands annexed by Lithuania in the previous century to be part of his patrimony and that he would recover them. But first he had had to ensure his Swedish frontiers against attack.

With Novgorod under Ivan's sovereignty, Muscovy had become a Baltic power, and Ivan was determined to secure his access to the Gulf of Finland. The Swedes were equally determined to control the Neva River, which flows from Lake Ladoga into the Gulf of Finland and which provided the natural route between central Russia and the Baltic Sea. In 1492 Ivan built the fortress town of Ivangorod on the Narva River; it was located some ten miles from the mouth of the river, on the opposite bank from the great Livonian trading town of Narva. In 1495 and 1496 he mounted three invasions of Swedish Finland. Distracted by internal strife, the Swedes finally sued for peace in March, 1497. With this peace and with an alliance with Denmark, Sweden's chief enemy, Ivan was ready to take on Lithuania.

The annexation of Novgorod had given Muscovy a common frontier with Lithuania. Russian bands began invading the border region, instigated and even organized by Moscow. This border warfare greatly encouraged the Russo-

ALTERA LEGATIONE A FERDINANDO IMPERA-
TORE TVNC ARCHIDVCE MISSVS AD MOSCVM,
ILLE ME TALI REMISIT VESTE.

The sketch of Vasily III (left) is taken from a 1560 edition of von Herberstein's Description. *As ambassador of the Holy Roman emperor, he twice visited Moscow during the grand prince's reign and brought back lively and authentic accounts of Muscovy. He reported that Vasily "in the control which he exercises over his people easily surpasses all the rulers of the entire world." Vasily's drive to extend Russia's western boundaries was arrested with his defeat by the Poles at the battle of Orsha. The clash occurred in 1514 on the banks of the Dnieper. A detail of a painting of the event, by a contemporary Polish artist, appears opposite.*

Lithuanian nobles in eastern Lithuania, who were Orthodox and angered by Lithuania's affirmation of the Council of Florence. Many nobles seceded to Moscow, taking with them, in accordance with the custom of the time, their hereditary estates and retainers.

Alexander, who succeeded as grand prince of Lithuania on the death of Casimir in 1492, was at that time young, inexperienced, and insecure. He offered to negotiate a peace with Muscovy that would be confirmed upon his marriage to Ivan's daughter, Elena. By the treaty, which was finally signed in 1494, Ivan acquired important territories, especially the principality of Vyazma; from Vyazma he could readily advance against Lithuanian-held Smolensk, the key to the conquest of the northwestern region.

The marriage took place only after bitter wrangling over safeguards for Elena's Orthodox faith. Muscovite fear and suspicion of Roman Catholic subversion were so intense that a contract had to be drawn, and Alexander himself had to swear formally that her Orthodoxy would be secure from pressure of every kind. Indeed, it would seem that Ivan was already planning to make his daughter's freedom of worship a pretext for renewing the war.

Elena was to prove a disappointing agent. Although given in marriage to a man whom she had never seen, she evidently learned to respect and even love him. She refused to spy on

Alexander or seek to influence him, as required by her father. She denied that she was under Catholic pressure and went so far as to protest vehemently against Muscovite aggression. In 1501 Alexander also became king of Poland, and Elena was exposed to the bigotry of the Poles, who had little of the Lithuanians' tolerance. Nevertheless, she remained steadfast in her Orthodoxy.

By 1499 Ivan was ready to embark on the next stage of territorial expansion. The Kazan and Nogai Tatars were at peace with Moscow. Mengli-Girei and the Crimean Tatars were his firm ally, ready at all times to attack Lithuania and Poland; and the Turkish sultan, although not bound by any alliance with Muscovy, was inclined to support Muscovy in order to maintain the profitable trade.

In the spring of 1499 Ivan seized on a report from Vilna, the capital of Lithuania, alleging that Elena and all Orthodox believers in Lithuania were under severe pressure to embrace the Uniat Church. He magnified the allegations and interpreted Alexander's conciliatory replies to his protests as evidence of Lithuania's weakness. In the summer of 1500 his armies marched, and after three years of war, an armistice conceded to Moscow the vast territories along the upper Oka River as well as most of the Chernigov-Sever region, including Chernigov and eighteen other major towns.

The failure of his armies to capture Smolensk and Kiev

VERA·DE

SERENISSIMO
POTENTISSIMOQVE REGIAE
Domino Sigismundo Augusto, Regi Poloniæ,
Magno Duci Lythuaniæ, Russiæ, Prussiæ, Mas
soviæ, Samogitiæque, etc. Domino et hæredi, Do-
mino suo Clementissimo.

Grodno, a Russian settlement in the twelfth century, was one of the Lithuanian cities that the Muscovite tsars regarded as part of their patrimony. This bird's-eye view of the flourishing trade center shows the city as it appeared in 1568, prior to the union of Poland and Lithuania. Dominating the high ground, from left to right, are the palace, churches, houses, the royal stables, and a lone victim dangling from the gallows. At center, soldiers, some of them on horseback, cross over the Neman River. At bottom, two important leaders— each with an army behind him —embrace at left, while a caravan approaches from the right.

rankled Ivan. But with Smolensk now only some thirty miles from his frontier, and Kiev readily accessible from his new territories on the Desna River, he considered both towns to be practically in his hands. He saw the war of 1500–1503 as an important stage in the recovery of the lands he regarded as his patrimony; but both Ivan and Alexander died before they could enter the next phase.

In unifying the Russian lands, Ivan had faced another hard problem: limiting the powers of his brothers and other appanage princes. Their principalities were in some respects like independent states, over which the grand prince had no direct jurisdiction. He could claim the loyalty and obedience of the appanage princes only in matters beyond their frontiers, especially in Muscovy's relations with foreign rulers. By devious and often ruthless methods Ivan reduced them to feudal princes owing service to him as their lord.

At the same time the government and administration of Muscovy were developing rapidly under the pressure of territorial expansion. The main executive organ was the *boyarskaya duma*, the council of boyars, and through it the boyars stood firm in their customary right to take part in the government of the country. Cherishing memories of the time when their forebears were sovereign princes or untitled boyars who freely served the lord of their choosing, the duma jealously guarded its hereditary privileges. Many boyars possessed

patrimonial estates (*votchina*), which they regarded as sacrosanct and which even Ivan III hesitated to touch. They were resentful, moreover, of the new class of gentry who were coming into being and whose estates, or *pomestie*, were held as a reward for military service.

The boyars struggled to retain their hereditary rights through such cumbersome and destructive institutions as the *mestnichestvo*, a hierarchal system whereby no boyar could be required to discharge an official duty or hold an appointment that was inferior to any duty or office held at any time by a member of his family. Meticulous records were kept in the *Razryadnaya Kniga*, the official journal of court proceedings begun in 1462; and it was referred to constantly. The *mestnichestvo* shackled the grand prince in making appointments and intensified boyar rivalries.

Another fundamental change in the character of Russian society at this time was the shift of population from urban concentrations to more widely scattered rural settlements. Russian cities had declined as a result of the Mongol invasion and occupation. Muscovite merchants and artisans were never to develop into the influential classes that played an important role in Kiev and Novgorod. More than ninety-five per cent of the population was rural, and the peasant was still nominally a free man. The *trudovoe pravo*, or toiler's right, gave him title to the land he worked while he worked it.

Though technically free to move on whenever he wished, the peasant could leave only after paying taxes and after the harvest had been gathered in for that year.

The right to move was carefully defined in Ivan's *sudebnik*, the first Muscovite law code, promulgated in 1497. Gradually, however, the peasant's freedom became more restricted: it was accepted that he could not move until he had paid his debts in full; and as taxes mounted, especially as a result of increasing military needs, he fell into arrears and was burdened by a double indebtedness. This situation was soon to give way to the evil institution of serfdom.

Ivan's acquisition of lands, and now his growing control over his subjects' independence, was accompanied by a major effort to elevate the dignity and prestige of the principality so that it would be beyond challenge by neighboring princes. A major step was his marriage with a member of the imperial family of Byzantium.

Ivan's first wife, Maria, the sister of the grand prince of Tver, died in 1467. She had borne him a son, whom Ivan had recognized as his successor. The grand prince was only twenty-seven years old at the time of Maria's death, but in spite of pressures to marry again, he showed no haste to seek a new bride.

In February, 1469, however, a proposal came from an unexpected quarter. Pope Paul II offered him the hand of his ward, Zoe Palaeologus. She was the niece of Constantine XI, the last Byzantine emperor, who had died in 1453 on the walls of Constantinople fighting against the Turks, and the daughter of Thomas Palaeologus, who had taken refuge in Rome, where he died. After the latter's death, the pope had taken the children into his care. To supervise their upbringing, he appointed Cardinal Bessarion, a Greek scholar and convert to the Church of Rome who had always worked zealously to bring about the union of the Eastern and Western Churches.

At the Council of Florence, which met in 1439, the metropolitan of Moscow had accepted on behalf of the Russian Orthodox the reunion of the churches. The Russians, bitterly hostile to Rome, were horrified. On the metropolitan's return to Moscow, he was deposed by a Russian synod and had to flee for his life. But in Rome acceptance of the Union of Florence by the Russians remained an urgent objective.

The pope had two purposes in proposing this marriage. First, he was confident that Zoe, who had been converted and had accepted the decision of the Union of Florence, would further the cause of the Roman Church in Muscovy. Second, he was anxiously seeking allies against the Ottoman Turks, whose capture of Constantinople and advance into southeastern Europe alarmed Latin Christendom. In Rome it was believed that Ivan would be a strong and active ally

Ivan IV's defeat of the Tatars at Kazan inspired this icon, glorifying the victories of Russia's Church Militant. The Heavenly City (left) alludes to Moscow, and Sodom burning (right) to Kazan. The middle row of war-

against the Turks and that Zoe would work assiduously for the pope's policies.

Ivan seized upon the proposal. The prestige of the Byzantine emperors stood high among the Russians. Constantinople had been for them the capital of the world, and its capture by the infidel Turks was little less than a catastrophe. Marriage with the niece of the last emperor would not only enhance his dignity, but would also imply the direct succession of the grand prince and Moscow to the emperor and Constantinople.

Ivan nevertheless acted with caution. A Roman Catholic princess in their midst might ignite afresh the antipapist fury that had gripped the Russians three decades earlier. He consulted earnestly with the metropolitan and with the boyars. He then sent to Rome a certain Gian-Battista della Volpe, an Italian who, among other duties, was in charge of the mint. Volpe had discussions with the pope, with Cardinal Bessarion, and with Zoe, whose portrait he then bore back to Moscow. In January, 1472, three years after negotiations had opened, Ivan sent Volpe to Rome again, this time to conclude the arrangements. On the first of June, in a solemn ceremony in which Volpe acted as proxy for Ivan, Zoe and Ivan were formally engaged. Later in the month Zoe, accompanied by Cardinal Bonumbre, the papal legate, and by

an impressive suite, set out for her new country.

Zoe probably left Rome without sorrow. She had been an orphan, dependent on the charity of the pope, and she had never been allowed to forget it. Cardinal Bessarion had reminded her incessantly to be grateful to her benefactors: she must think of herself as a pauper, not as the daughter of an imperial family! (But Zoe never forgot that she was a Byzantine princess: even after twenty-six years in Muscovy, she would inscribe herself on a work of embroidery as "Princess of Constantinople.")

Zoe and her party traveled by way of Germany and the Baltic. The Turkish conquest of Byzantium and the Balkans prevented them from taking direct route to Moscow. As the party passed through Pskov and Novgorod, the people noted with approval that Zoe stopped to worship in their churches and reverence their holy icons. However, the conduct of Cardinal Bonumbre disturbed them. Robed in purple, he was preceded by an attendant bearing the Latin cross, which the Orthodox feared as a wicked heresy. As the entourage neared Moscow, a crisis threatened. The metropolitan and many boyars vowed they would leave the city if Bonumbre profaned it with his crucifix. A delegation from Muscovy convinced the cardinal that the cross was not to be uncovered within the city walls.

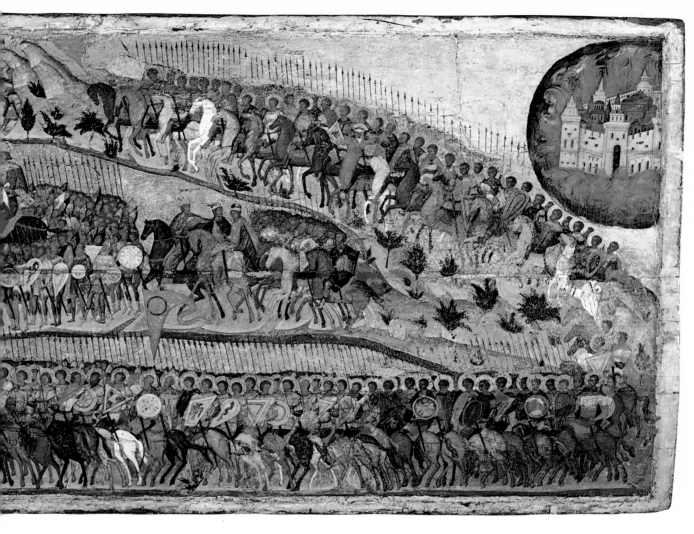

riors is led by Archangel Michael, riding a winged steed. Ivan, astride a gray horse, and Vladimir Mono-makh, bearing a cross, follow. Dmitry Donskoy heads the top row of riders; Alexander Nevsky those at bottom.

On November 12, 1472, Zoe entered Moscow. On the same day she was received into the Orthodox Church, re-baptized with the name of "Sofia," and married to Ivan according to the Orthodox ceremony. She evidently abandoned Roman Catholicism without qualms, and she was to show no interest in reviving the Union of Florence. The cardinal, distressed and bewildered, stayed in the background. Having once witnessed the fanaticism of the Orthodox Russians, he confined himself to urging the grand prince to march against the Turks. In this, too, he had no success, and he returned to Rome a saddened man.

Sofia was described by an Italian princess who visited Moscow in 1472 as beautiful, whereas a Florentine poet, present at the same meeting, considered her to be grossly fat. Whatever the lady's physical attributes, she was highly intelligent and remarkably adaptable. Though she had come from the most cosmopolitan city in Europe to one of the most barbarous, she apparently settled down quickly and without complaint. She even held her own court. Ambrogio Contarini wrote that he called on her and that "she treated me with great kindness and courtesy, and entreated me earnestly to recommend her to my Illustrious Seignory [the pope]." Well-educated by the standards of the time and fluent in several languages, her abilities must have seemed formi-dable to the illiterate Muscovite boyars and their wives, who lived shut away in the semi-Oriental seclusion of the *terem*.

Many Russians, while paying their respects to Sofia, must have remained deeply suspicious. Ivan III's son by his first wife, known as Ivan Molodoy ("the Young"), particularly resented his stepmother, for the children she had by the tsar might displace him in the succession. Contarini recorded in 1476 that the youth was "not in great favor, on account of his bad conduct," adding, "I might mention other things, but it would take too long."

Sofia bore Ivan one daughter and six sons, of whom Vasily was the eldest. Meanwhile, Ivan Molodoy had married a Moldavian princess, Elena Stepanova, who in 1483 gave birth to a son, Dmitry, yet another claimant to the throne.

The extent of Sofia's influence on Ivan III and his policies, and on the course of Russia's history, has long been debated. The enemies of her son and grandson blamed her for their misfortunes and reviled her as the sinister "Greek sorceress." The renowned Russian historians S. M. Solovyev and V. O. Klyuchevsky, while acknowledging that she contributed significantly to the transformation of the Muscovite court and the development of Moscow, point out that most of Ivan's policies had been formulated before she arrived. One recent historian has even asserted that "her main impact on

*This map of Ivan IV's Muscovy, executed in 1562 by the Flemish cartographer Abraham Ortelius,
draws its dubious geography from the travel diaries of the Elizabethan envoy Anthony Jenkinson.*

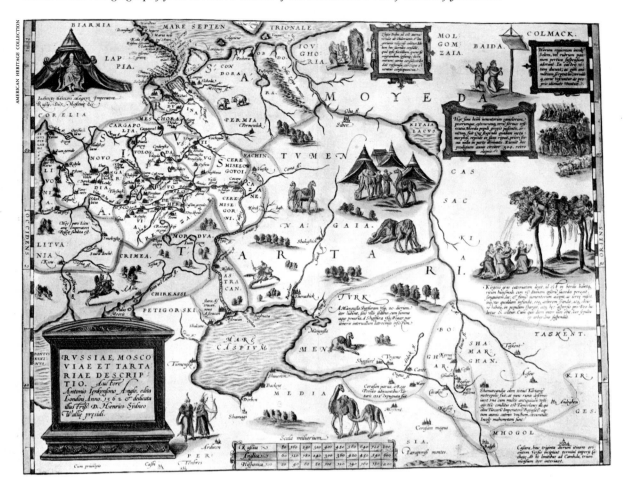

the course of Russian history was made by the fact of her giving birth to the man who was destined to become the father of Ivan the Terrible.''

The city that greeted the new bride was vast and sprawling, built almost entirely of timber; even the streets were made of logs, bound side by side. In the bitter cold of winter, when simple stoves were burning in every house, and in summer, when the wood became tinder-dry, outbreaks of fire were commonplace.

Four years earlier, in 1468, a serious fire had leveled a large part of the city; and in 1469 nearly all the buildings within the Kremlin walls burned to the ground. The Cathedral of the Dormition (Uspensky Sobor) was among those buildings destroyed. Two Russian masters were engaged to erect a new cathedral, but building on this scale was beyond their experience, and in the course of erection the cathedral collapsed.

It was probably on the suggestion of Sofia that Ivan decided to invite building masters from Italy. His agents approached several well-known masters, but only one, Ridolfo Fioravanti, was persuaded to go. He began work on the cathedral in 1475 and completed it four years later. Like many Renaissance figures, Fioravanti was skilled in several fields, and while in Muscovy he cast cannon and bells, minted coins, and performed other services for the grand prince.

Ivan's agents traveled to Italy, Venice, and Vienna to engage more masters. The Kremlin walls were enlarged and strengthened, and two other main cathedrals in the Kremlin, the Arkhangelsky and the Blagoveshchensky, were rebuilt on a grander scale. In 1487 Ivan commissioned two Italians, Pietro Antonio Solario and Marco Ruffo, to build him a palace of stone; and four years later the Granovitaya, or Faceted Palace, was completed. Boyars and rich merchants joined in the ceaseless building, erecting mansions of stone. Moscow was indeed becoming a capital worthy of the grand prince.

Ivan began also to adopt grandiose titles and formal court ceremonial, which reflected his conception of the significance and power of the office. Far from being merely exercises in pomp and ceremony, the panoply expressed the outlook of the ruler of an emerging nation. At the time of his accession his title of "grand prince" indicated that he was merely the senior and ruling prince of Moscow. Many princes at his court considered themselves his equal in birth and not without some claim to the throne, though they grudgingly acknowledged his seniority.

Since negotiating marriage for his daughter, Elena, Ivan had used the title of "sovereign of all Russia" in foreign affairs, but after 1480 he began referring to himself as "tsar of all Russia," sometimes adding *samoderzhets*, the Russian equivalent of the Byzantine "autocrat." The title of "tsar," a Slavic form of the Latin *caesar*, merely signified a ruler who owed

Herberstein's report included illustrations of the Muscovite fighter. The men at left he judged excellent archers, but too heavily clothed and armed for hand-to-hand combat. He marveled at the way Russians traveled on sleds and skiis (right).

no allegiance and paid no tribute to another state. Soon, however, his title became more elevated. "Ivan, by the grace of God, sovereign of all Russia" reflected the new religious basis of his power. The Russian Church had traditionally supported the princes of Moscow in their unification of Russian lands under one rule. But Ivan's new title reflected the Byzantine concept of the God-given authority of the autocrat. Indeed, as he had hoped, his marriage with Sofia enabled him to surround his throne with the aura of Byzantium, and he was astute in introducing imperial trappings to give it permanence.

A legend was created that the twelfth-century Kievan prince Vladimir Monomakh had been crowned with the fur-brimmed hat of the Emperor Constantine, his maternal grandfather. The *shapka Monomakha* was thereafter always used as the coronation crown of the Russian tsars. Also, in the late 1490's, the double-headed eagle, the imperial Byzantine emblem, began to appear on royal seals, and it soon became established as the insignia of tsarist Russia. This was added to the already-established concept of Moscow as the Third Rome, an idea that had arisen after the fall of Constantinople in 1453. Its clearest expression was contained in a letter from Philotheus, a monk of Pskov, to Ivan's son Vasily. He wrote: "I wish to add a few words on the present Orthodox Empire of our ruler; he is on the earth the

sole Emperor [tsar] of the Christians, the leader of the Apostolic Church which stands no longer in Rome or in Constantinople, but in the blessed city of Moscow. She alone shines in the whole world briter than the sun. . . . All Christian Empires are fallen and in their stead stands alone the Empire of our ruler in accordance with the prophetical books. Two Romes have fallen, but the third stands, and a fourth there will not be."

Family rivalry over the succession to the throne clouded Ivan's last years. His heir, Ivan Molodoy, died in 1490, leaving Dmitry, the tsar's grandson, and Vasily, the tsar's son by Sofia, as claimants, for the Muscovite law of succession was far from established. The prolonged power struggle between Dmitry and Vasily became all the more complex and bitter because of the strong characters of the mothers concerned and because of the rival boyar and Church groups that rallied behind them. According to a chronicle, Vasily and his mother Sofia conspired to murder Dmitry, to sack the treasuries in the northern provinces of Vologda and Belozersk, and to establish a center of rebellion. Discovering the plot, Ivan placed Vasily under arrest and had six supporters beheaded on the ice of the Moskva River. From this time the grand prince lived "in great vigilance" with Sofia, especially as she was rumored to be experimenting with witchcraft and poisonous herbs. Ivan proclaimed Dmitry his heir and crowned him in

The Virgin of Vladimir (left), probably painted by a Byzantine artist in the 1100's, is Russia's most revered icon. According to legend, it protected Moscow from invasion on three occasions. Moscow's Cathedral of St. Basil (opposite), whose oriental splendor has dominated Red Square for over four hundred years, was built by two native architects for Ivan IV —to commemorate his victories over the Tatars. A spectacular example of medieval Russian architecture, it was constructed of white stuccoed brick and stone. Its dazzling polychrome decoration dates from the 1600's, when the cupolas were tiled.

Moscow on February 4, 1498. Ivan later had second thoughts, however, and Vasily was restored to favor in March, 1499; and in April, 1502, Dmitry and his mother, Elena Stepanova, were arrested and disgraced. Elena died in 1504, probably by murder; Dmitry died in prison in 1509.

The reign of Ivan III ended on October 27, 1505, and Vasily succeeded to the throne of Muscovy, surprisingly without dispute. He was to prove an energetic autocrat surpassing even his father in decisiveness. Vasily found himself faced with new difficulties. The khanates of Kazan and of the Crimea were now threatening Muscovy's power. He sent troops in 1506 to assert his authority, but they suffered two serious defeats. The khan of Kazan, Mohammed Ahmin, was succeeded in 1521 by Sahib Girei, brother of Mengli-Girei of the Crimea, and the two khanates prepared to act together against Muscovy.

Mengli-Girei had been Ivan's chief ally against Lithuania and the Golden Horde. But the Horde had disintegrated, and Ivan's territorial gains from Lithuania had brought Muscovy's frontiers close to the Crimea. The fact that the lands that Mengli-Girei's troops had once raided at will were now part of Muscovy was no deterrent to continued forays. Personal relations with the Muscovite grand prince had also deteriorated. Unlike Ivan, who had cultivated the khan's goodwill and sent rich presents each year, Vasily refused to send gifts, maintaining that this was tantamount to paying tribute, as in the days when the great khan was the suzerain.

Mengli-Girei carried his new drive further by forming an alliance in 1512 with Sigismund I, Alexander's successor as grand prince of Lithuania and king of Poland. This meant that the Crimean Tatars could not invade the territories of their new ally, but were free to make frequent and damaging raids into Muscovy. In 1521 Mohammed-Girei, son and successor of Mengli, led a large-scale army to the outskirts of Moscow. The Muscovites crowded into the city, seeking refuge, and thousands died from disease in the overcrowding. The city was saved only by bribing the khan with gifts of treasure, whereupon he withdrew his troops.

For Vasily, however, Lithuania was still the chief enemy. An armistice in 1503 had been the only confirmation of Ivan's gains from Lithuania. Both countries recognized that renewal of the war was inevitable. In 1514 Vasily launched a massive attack on Lithuania, with the immediate purpose of taking Smolensk. He won his objective, but about a month later his army suffered a disastrous defeat at the city of Orsha. During the eight years that followed, the Lithuanians made attempts to recover Smolensk, but Vasily doggedly held the town. When in 1522 he concluded a five-year armistice with King Sigismund, Smolensk and its surroundings remained under the rule of the Muscovite state.

The problem of the succession faced Vasily as it had faced his father and grandfather before him. Ivan III had brought under his own rule all the appanage principalities granted earlier. Despite consolidation, princely rivalries survived. Though Ivan had bequeathed almost the whole of Muscovy to Vasily, he nevertheless felt compelled to grant small patrimonies to his four other sons, enjoining them to obey their eldest brother in all things.

Since Muscovy was surrounded by enemies, Vasily felt a strong grand prince was needed. He regarded his brothers with great suspicion. His wife, Solomoniya Saburova, was barren; and in 1525—with the approval of the Metropolitan Daniel, but against the opposition of other churchmen and some boyars—he forced his wife to enter the Church, the equivalent of divorce. Soon afterward he married Princess Elena Glinskaya. She bore him two sons; the first, born on August 25, 1530, was christened Ivan. In 1533 Vasily fell mortally ill. Twenty-eight years of relative stability in Muscovy were at an end.

Vasily's son was three years old when he ascended the throne as Ivan IV. He would become one of the most complex characters in Russian history, extending the personal power of the ruler to a degree far exceeding anything known before. One of the many English envoys who came to Muscovy during his reign observed of the mature Ivan that, "being a man of high spirit and subtle in his kind, meaning to reduce his government into a more strict form, began by degrees to clip off [the nobility's] greatness and to bring it down to a less proportion till in the end he made them not only his vassals but his *kholopy*, that is, his very villains. . . . So that now they hold their authorities, lands, lives, and all at the emperor's pleasures, as the rest do." Ivan IV created the concept and the actuality of Russia as a nation.

A tormented man who on occasion attained the grandeur of King Lear, he made a tremendous impression on Russia and Europe in his time, and as man and autocrat he has remained vividly alive for Russians of later generations. To his people Ivan would become known as *Grozny*, meaning "the Dread," or "the Awe-inspiring," an epithet that has since been incorrectly translated as "the Terrible." Anthony Jenkinson, an Englishman who visited Moscow several times, wrote: "I think no prince in Christendom is more feared of his own than he is, nor better loved."

The princes and boyars saw the accession of a minor and the regency of Elena, the young widow of Vasily III, as an opportunity to re-establish their position of privilege. Elena dealt firmly with princely sedition and managed to keep Muscovy's enemies at bay. But in April, 1538, after only five years as regent, she suddenly died. She had not been ill, and Sigmund von Herberstein recounts in his *Description of Mos-*

Peasants used primitive tools to wrest a meager living from nature. The plowman above prepares the ground for spring sowing with his sokha, *a light wooden plow with iron-tipped shares, used for breaking up shallow topsoil. Sickle-wielding reapers harvest rye in the detail (right) from a 1680 fresco.*

cow and Muscovy the widespread rumor that she had been poisoned by political enemies.

During the next ten years the boyars dominated Muscovy. Powerful boyar families, including the Shuisky and the Belsky, struggled for power and reduced the country to anarchy. The Shuisky treated Ivan with contempt, and the boy was terrified that they would kill him or cast him and his younger brother into prison. He burned with hatred of the boyars and waited impatiently to assert the power that was his birthright and to wreak vengeance on all who had filled his childhood with terror. He was only thirteen years old when he suddenly ordered the arrest of Prince Andrei Shuisky, the most hated among the boyars. According to one chronicler, Ivan had him thrown to a pack of hounds, which tore the boyar limb from limb. From this time the boyars began to live in fear of him.

Three years later, at the age of sixteen, Ivan dramatically announced his decision to take a wife. But first, he declared, he would "assume the titles of our ancestors . . . and our kinsman, Grand Prince Vladimir Vsevolodovich Monomakh." His coronation, in 1547, was an occasion without precedent, for he was crowned tsar, not grand prince, thereby formalizing a concept of rule only hinted at by his grandfather, Ivan III.

In his search for a wife, court officials traveled through the country calling on princes and boyars to bring their daughters to certain towns for examination. Maidens who were selected for their comeliness, piety, and good character were then brought to Moscow for the tsar's final selection. According to Herberstein, Vasily III had had assembled one thousand five hundred of the most beautiful maidens in the land when he chose his first wife; and Ivan probably made his selection from a similar gathering. However, nothing is known of the occasion that led to Ivan's choosing Anastasia, daughter of a deceased court official whose Prussian ancestors had migrated to Muscovy in the fourteenth century. The family was to give Russia the Romanov dynasty.

The boyars expressed horror that the tsar should choose a wife of such humble origins. Ivan's grandfather had married a Byzantine princess, and his mother had come of a noble family. He was, however, well pleased with his bride, and although he was to take another six wives, he cherished her memory until the end of his life.

After their marriage Ivan and Anastasia withdrew to the revered Troitsa Monastery, where they passed a week in prayer at the tomb of St. Sergius. Such piety was part of the way of life of the Muscovites, and especially of the ruling family, and Ivan entered into it fervently. Anastasia herself was devout, and he responded with respect and gentle affection.

However, she seems not to have been able to control

Ivan's unpredictable behavior. Soon after the marriage he exhibited advance indications of his appetite for cruelty. According to a chronicler, seventy citizens of Pskov came before him in the village of Ostrovka, bringing complaints against their *nastavnik*, the tsar's appointed local governor. Ivan was furious, regarding their presence as an act of sedition. He had hot wine poured over their heads, and their hair and beards were singed with fire. He then ordered them to strip naked and lie on the floor. They obeyed, expecting to be executed. But at this moment Ivan's attention was diverted at the news that a large bell had fallen in Moscow, and he forgot about the execution.

Fires were commonplace in Moscow, but in 1547 they were disastrous, and much of the city, including many Kremlin buildings, were burned to the ground. The people were homeless and desperate, and readily believed the rumors that the Glinsky, the tsar's kinsmen and counselors, had caused the fires by witchcraft. They ran through the city killing supporters of the family. Ivan had many of the rioters seized and summarily executed. But he recognized that popular anger was directed not only against the Glinsky but also, in some degree, against himself. As a result, he replaced the Glinsky with counselors outside the aristocracy.

The events of these months brought about a striking transformation in Ivan. Many believed that a miracle had taken place. Three centuries later the historian Nikolai Karamzin wrote that "for the correction of Ivan it was necessary that Moscow should be consumed by fire," and then that the strange and powerful priest named Sylvester should suddenly appear before him.

Stern, devout, and as forbidding as an Old Testament prophet, Sylvester was typical of the fanatic churchmen who have influenced the Russian throne. He scourged the young tsar with stories of miracles and of punishments, and on February 27, 1549, before his subjects assembled in the Red Square, Ivan publicly confessed his sins and proclaimed a new era of Christian love and justice. This momentous occasion was also of political importance, for it constituted the first *zemsky sobor*, or assembly of the land, attended by representatives of all classes of the people except the peasantry. The assembly met again on the following day, when a series of major reforms was announced.

It is evident, however, that in the beginning this and other consultative bodies were rarely more than instruments for ratifying the autocrats' policies. Giles Fletcher described a combined meeting of the boyars and the sacred council that he attended: "The emperour causeth to be summoned such of his nobilitie as himselfe thinketh meete. . . . The poynts [to be discussed] being opened, the patriarch with his cleargie men have the prerogative to be first asked their vote, or opin-

ion, what they thinke. . . . Whereto they answere . . . to this effect:—'That the emperour and his councell are of great wisdome, and experience, touching the pollicies and publike affaires of the realme, and farre better able to judge what is profitable for the common wealth. . . . That insteade of their advise, they will aide them with their prayers. . . .' "

In the next eleven years, guided by Sylvester and Alexei Adashev, an able court official, and a band of supporters known as the Chosen Council, he introduced major reforms, including a new legal code, and had the Church fathers meet to draw up the *Stoglav* (Hundred Chapters), defining the relationship of the Church and state in matters of spiritual, social, and legal supremacy. Perhaps most important was the decision to limit the further acquisition of lands by the Church, except with royal permission.

Foremost in Ivan's mind was the continuing need to secure Muscovy from attack by the Tatars. Ivan's grandfather had established his independence from the Golden Horde, but the Kazan Tatars had continued to prey upon the young nation. (At one time some hundred thousand Muscovites were held prisoner in the khanate, and the slave markets of the Mediterranean were amply supplied with fair Slavs whom the Tatars had carried off.) Moreover, Russia's colonizing drive eastward was gathering momentum, and the khanate of Kazan barred the way to the tsar's national ambitions.

Ivan saw the conquest of Kazan as a glorious crusade that would earn him renown as the tsar-liberator who had crushed the Moslems and planted the Cross in Asia. In 1552 his armies conquered Kazan. It was an event of the greatest significance, for it marked the beginning of Russia's offensive against the Asiatic hordes. All Muscovites celebrated the victory jubilantly, and their reverence for their young tsar was unbounded. More than Dmitry Donskoy and Alexander Nevsky, who had been paragons of courage and Christian virtue for the Russians, Ivan was from this time exalted in the popular imagination. Moreover, this decisive victory over a traditional enemy brought to birth a popular sense of nationhood, which economic, political, racial, and religious unity alone could not give.

The conquest of the khanate of Astrakhan, extending Moscow's rule over the whole of the Volga basin, followed in 1556. The colonization of the fertile, black soil lands, watered by tributaries of the Volga and the Don, and of the vast region beyond the Urals, could begin.

Ivan's triumphs had given him confidence and had fired his ambition to establish Muscovy among the great powers of the world. His respect for Sylvester, Adashev, and other members of the Chosen Council was unimpaired, but he was no longer dominated by them. A conflict of wills between him and Sylvester in particular began to develop. But sud-

In 1576 Ivan sent the envoys, shown in this contemporary engraving, to the Regensburg court of Emperor Maximilian II, whose aid he sought against Poland-Lithuania. The richly garbed ambassadors leading the procession are followed by less pretentious boyars bearing furs and precious gifts for their esteemed host.

denly the young tsar's high spirits were shattered.

In March, 1553, Ivan was seized with a severe fever. His condition was deteriorating very rapidly, and believing himself near death, he called upon the boyars to swear allegiance to his son, Dmitry, who was only a few months old. He was grieved to find that many boyars were unwilling to swear the oath to his dynasty, preferring Prince Vladimir Staritsky, his cousin. Sylvester and other members of the Chosen Council exerted strong influence against the succession of Tsarevich Dmitry, fearing the prospect of Anastasia's regency.

For some weeks Ivan was tormented by anxiety for his wife and son, who would surely be killed by the boyars after his death. Then his condition became so critical that last rites were administered; but, unexpectedly, he soon after began to regain his strength.

He was never to forget the experience of these weeks. He did not punish or even show anger toward those who had sought to betray him and his family; but his apparent mildness masked mistrust and deep hostility toward his boyars. Meanwhile, he concentrated on further reforms. He instituted a system of central *prikazy*, or ministries, of commerce, taxation, treasury, land management, military organization, and the like, making Moscow even more indisputably the capital and administrative center of the nation. Local government was concentrated in the hands of the *starosta*, or sheriff,

who was elected and had wide powers to maintain order and collect taxes. A start was made on dismantling the *kormlenie*, the system of "feeding" whereby officials lived off what they could collect—by whatever means they chose—from the people under their jurisdiction. The increase in the national revenue and the greater efficiency in administration were important at this time when military commitments at home and abroad were heavy.

Ivan was especially concerned with army reforms. He issued *ukazy*, or decrees, redefining the obligation of military service. Every landowner, whether his claim was hereditary or through government tenure, had to serve personally in the army and to furnish for each prescribed unit of land an armed soldier with mount and adequate supplies. Further, Ivan established artillery companies and a force called the Streltsy, or musketeers, equipped with handguns, sabers, and halberds. Strictly applied, these measures brought a marked strengthening of the tsar's army.

The reforms bore most heavily, however, upon the peasantry. The payment of taxes, military service, the demands of their landowners, and the constant struggle to wrest a living burdened the peasants. In ever-growing numbers they fled to the east and to the south. Muscovy could not afford to lose men on such a scale. Special measures were introduced to halt this migration and to recover runaway peasants.

95

Instinctively the Russian people were stretching out toward their natural frontiers. With Kazan conquered, no real barriers stood against trade and colonization eastward. But Russia's growing strength only served to increase the opposition of Sweden, the Teutonic Knights, Lithuania, and Poland toward Russian expansion westward.

However, Ivan was determined to assert his claim to Russian lands held by his western enemies and to revive Baltic trade. The tsardom was, he knew, backward compared with European countries—especially in arms production and the science of waging war. It was essential to Muscovy's growth that it master the latest technological ideas if it was to achieve the greatness Ivan envisaged.

An unexpected event in 1553 had strengthened Ivan's resolve. An English sea captain, Richard Chancellor, had brought his merchant ship by way of the extreme northern route into the White Sea, thus demonstrating that the Baltic was not the only route for trade with the rest of Europe. Ivan showed great favor to Chancellor, who, for his part, was impressed by the magnificence of his audience. In the outer chamber, where he waited, so he wrote, "sat one hundred or more gentlemen, all in cloth of gold very sumptuous and from there I came into the Council Chamber, where sat the Duke himself with his nobles which were a fair company: they sat around the chamber on high, yet so that he himself

sat much higher than any of his nobles in a chair of gilt, and in a garment of beaten gold, with an imperial crown upon his head and a staff of crystal and gold in his right hand and his other hand leaning on the chair."

Ivan granted extensive trading privileges to the Muscovy Company, which was incorporated by royal charter in London in 1554. He was soon to find, however, that the English merchants took full advantage of their privileged position, while yielding little in return. He was eager to engage skilled craftsmen and to purchase arms from England. His requests embarrassed Queen Elizabeth I, who was under pressure from Russia's neighbors to prevent advanced military weapons and industrial techniques from reaching the sleeping giant. In response she sent an architect, a doctor, and an apothecary.

Ivan bitterly resented the embargo efforts. Ever since his capture of Kazan he had been preparing for war against Livonia. In 1558 his army took the important river town of Narva. In the following year his forces advanced farther into Livonia, but the events of 1558–59 were to prove only the beginning of a twenty-five-year war with Lithuania-Poland.

In these Westernizing objectives Ivan came into conflict with Sylvester and many among his boyars still bent on a religious crusade against their Moslem neighbors to the south. Afire with crusading zeal, the priest urged the tsar to

Ivan, whose reign saw the canonization of over forty new saints, is shown on his throne with worshipers before him in the contemporary print opposite. The seventeenth-century icon at right pictures Saint Basil the Blessed, one of Russia's most popular saints, going nude to Moscow and begging for charity in the name of the Saviour. He was one of the many Holy Fools, spiritual ascetics who went barefoot, eschewed bodily comforts, ate little, and voluntarily accepted the role of a fool in order to further the teachings of Christ and to make critical remarks and prophetic utterances before even the most powerful.

conquer the Crimea as he had conquered Kazan and Astrakhan. But Ivan recognized the tremendous obstacles and the danger that it would certainly involve him in war with the Turkish empire, then reaching the zenith of its power. History was to endorse the wisdom of Ivan's decision. More than two centuries were to pass before Russia was able to put down the troublesome Tatars of the Crimea.

The year 1560 marked the beginning of Ivan's unfettered personal rule. By this time Ivan's absolute power was established. His complete faith in the divine source of his authority was shared fully by the Russian people. As he himself wrote: "By the grace of God and with the blessing of our forefathers and fathers, as we were born to rule, so have we grown up and ascended the throne by the bidding of God."

Some historians have described 1560, with bold oversimplification, as the year of his dramatic transformation in character, when the usually devout and dedicated tsar suddenly became a savage tyrant. He was always given to extremes of conduct, but in this year two events freed him from the main restraining influences in his life. The first was the removal of his chief advisers: Sylvester was sent to the Solovetsky Monastery; Adashev was banished to Livonia, where he reportedly died. Ivan had never forgiven them for their hostility toward his wife, Anastasia, during his illness, and they had ceased to be trusted friends. The second event was the

death of Anastasia on August 7. In thirteen years of marriage she had borne him six children, of whom only two, Tsarevichi Ivan and Fedor, had survived. He cut short court mourning after one week and promptly took another wife, the first in a succession of a half dozen. He then gave himself up to debauchery and launched a purge, directed first against all who had supported Sylvester and Adashev.

Among the few subjects who were prepared to question Ivan's decisions or protest against the mounting terror was Prince Andrei Kurbsky. He came of an illustrious family that had always served the grand princes of Moscow with exemplary loyalty. As a young prince, Andrei had distinguished himself in command of troops. Highly educated and advanced in outlook beyond others at court, he enjoyed Ivan's confidence; and a brilliant career seemed to lie before him. In 1564, however, he suffered an ignominious defeat at Polish hands, and fearing the tsar's anger, he defected to Lithuania. From there he wrote four letters to the tsar, protesting in plain language Ivan's iron-fisted rule. In one he asked, "Wherefore, O tsar, have you destroyed the strong [and] spilled their victorious holy blood in the churches of God during sacerdotal ceremonies, and stained the thresholds of the churches with the blood of martyrs?"

Kurbsky's writings provoked two illuminating replies from Ivan, who was a brilliant disputant. Describing himself

In this woodcut Ivan holds a human head atop his lance as he leads a band of condemned subjects to their executioners. The henchmen at left appear to be dividing newly seized spoils.

as God's "humble scepter-bearer," Ivan wrote that "by the will of God and the blessing of our ancestors and parents were we born in the realm, were brought up there and enthroned, taking . . . what belonged to us. . . . Tortures and persecutions and deaths in many forms we have devised against no one. As to treasons and magic, it is true, such dogs everywhere suffer capital punishment. . . ." His stinging answers reveal his intimate knowledge of the history of his own country and his acquaintance with the history of Greece, Rome, Byzantium, and Persia. For Ivan, history was not the chronicle of long-dead events; it was the vital record of rulers and people in the past. But the dominant influence in his letters was the Bible, and many passages in their stark, minatory style resound like passages from the Old Testament.

Kurbsky's defection and his invectives deepened the tsar's conviction that the boyar aristocracy were meditating treason against him and the nation. Ivan's reaction was the more violent because he saw such treason against a God-appointed tsar as amounting to apostasy. He ordered the arrest and summary execution of all who aroused his mistrust. He became still more savage and arbitrary in his conduct. Finally he devised a bizarre plan to give himself and his family security against his enemies.

In December, 1564, the people of Moscow were alarmed to see the tsar with his family, his treasure, and personal goods borne from the Kremlin in a convoy of sledges. His purpose and destination were a mystery. Then, after several weeks, he sent two messages to the city from Alexandrovskaya, some sixty miles to the northeast. The first message was addressed to the metropolitan of Moscow. In it he complained of the treason of the boyars and of the unworthy conduct of the Church in condoning their wrongdoings. "Not wishing," he wrote, "to endure your treachery, we with great pity in our heart have quitted the tsardom and have gone wherever God may lead us." The second message was addressed to the people, and absolving them of all blame, it assured them of his favor and love.

Ivan's statements caused panic in the city. No disaster could appall the Muscovites as much as the loss of their tsar. Boyars and churchmen shared in the general alarm. A mission to the tsar, made up of churchmen, boyars, and state officials, set out at once for Alexandrovskaya to petition him to return to his throne. Ivan received them and finally acceded to their humble prayers, but he made two conditions. The first was that he should be free to punish all whom he considered to be traitors without intercessions by the Church or pleas for mercy. The second condition, bewildering to everyone, involved the setting up of a separate civil and military domain in the central and northern parts of Muscovy as the *oprichnina*, virtually an independent state

Ivan's tragic murder of his son and heir, Ivan Ivanovich, in 1581, is the subject of this painting by Ilya Repin, the greatest of the nineteenth-century Russian realists. Here, the grief-stricken tsar, who usually vented his uncontrollable wrath on Muscovy's long-suffering populace, desperately clutches the dying tsarevich.

within the tsardom, maintained and ruled by Ivan, not as tsar, but as personal proprietor. The remainder—the border provinces to the west and south—were designated the *zemshchina*, or "rule of country," meaning that they would be administered as before by the boyars; he made it clear, however, that he considered the *zemshchina* to be a region of potential traitors.

The *oprichniky*, or special guards, were chosen personally by Ivan, and were beyond the law. They wore uniforms of black and carried at their saddles the emblems of a broom and a dog's head, signifying that they would sweep and hound treason from the realm. They were, in effect, a political security force—eventually six thousand strong—charged not only with guarding the tsar but also with destroying his enemies and in particular the boyars. Ivan believed that Kurbsky and the boyars were plotting to introduce into Muscovy the conditions that applied in Poland, where the landowning magnates and gentry had reduced the king to impotence. He was determined that Muscovy would never be crippled in the same way.

Like most security forces, the *oprichniky* quickly became instruments of terror. For seven years they ranged through the country, plundering and murdering on the pretext of uprooting treachery, and they acted with special fury against the boyars and their retainers. Many of the large patrimonial

estates were seized by the tsar and the owners executed. Their lands systematically transferred to their persecutors. Indeed, Ivan's activities had the important effect of increasing greatly the extent of the *pomestie*, the lands held on service tenure. It was a necessary development for the maintenance of the growing class of serving gentry on whom the tsar and the government were depending to fill the upper ranks of the army and the administration.

On other occasions Ivan was known to punish a whole city. Learning of a rumor that the people of Novgorod were preparing to defect in a body to Lithuania, he acted without seeking confirmation. Accompanied by his son, Tsarevich Ivan, he led his troops into the city and ordered a massacre. At the end of five weeks, some sixty thousand men, women, and children died, many of them by torture. Novgorod never fully recovered from his assault.

At the same time Ivan continued to wage war with Livonia. The capture of Polotsk in 1563 and then the Muscovite advance almost to Vilna, the capital, had convinced Ivan that complete victory was within his grasp. The Lithuanians felt that they were facing defeat, and their ambassadors arrived in Moscow in May, 1566, to propose peace. Their terms, which included the surrender to Muscovy of the lands taken by the tsar's forces, were tempting. Ivan summoned the *zemsky sobor* to consider whether to accept the

99

Lithuanian terms or to continue the war. Almost to a man the representatives urged that peace be concluded only after the whole of Livonia had been conquered.

It was already clear that Lithuania alone could not stand against the might of Muscovy. The Poles feared that they, too, would be threatened if the Muscovites defeated the Lithuanians and occupied Livonia. Finally, in 1569, the Polish and Lithuanian *seims*, or assemblies, meeting in Lublin, agreed to merge the two states. This at once brought Poland into the war. Ivan's military success nevertheless continued until 1572, when Sigismund II died and was succeeded three years later by the Hungarian Prince Stefan Batory, an outstanding military commander.

The Muscovite armies then began to suffer serious reverses. Batory recaptured Polotsk and Velikie Luki in 1579. From these two vantage points he threatened the approaches to Moscow. In 1581 Batory's advance was halted at Pskov, which withstood heavy bombardment and refused to surrender. Finally, Ivan appealed to Pope Gregory XIII. A papal nuncio mediated, and in January, 1582, Batory, whose forces were already exhausted, concluded a ten-year armistice with Ivan. By its terms Ivan ceded the whole of his Livonian and Lithuanian gains to Poland-Lithuania. It meant the total failure of his Western policy. The Baltic Sea remained firmly closed, and Russia had to wait for more than a century for Peter the Great to achieve what Ivan had won and then lost.

Ivan found some consolation for this failure in the recent acquisition of vast Siberian territories, conquered by the Stroganovs in 1581. The Stroganov family had come originally from Novgorod and had developed a mighty commercial empire of salt mines, iron mines, fur trading, and farming northeast of Moscow. In 1558 Ivan had granted to Grigory Stroganov a section of the virgin lands along the banks of the Kama River and its tributaries, south of the Perm region, with rights to establish their own independent province. In response to subsequent petitions Ivan extended their powers to the lands beyond the Urals in the region of the Irtysh, Ob, and Tobol rivers.

The rapid eastward expansion of the Russians aroused the hostility of local tribes—especially the Tatars of the Siberian khanate. The Stroganovs had maintained a small frontier force against raids, but now they began raising a private army, relying mainly on Cossacks. Hunters, freebooters, and robbers, the Cossacks of the Don, Dnieper, and Volga were mainly Slavic in origin, but had acquired a considerable admixture of Tatar and other races (the Kazaks, whose name they appropriated, were a Turkic tribe). As a free frontier force they could be useful to Moscow when attacking the Tatars and Turks, but they often plundered Moscow's trade routes. In the 1570's Ivan had sent troops to disperse the Cossack bands who were disrupting trade on the Volga. One band of Cossacks, eight hundred forty strong and led by their ataman, or chief, Ermak Timofeev, fled northward and in the spring of 1579 entered the service of the Stroganovs. Two years later Ermak, his Cossack band reinforced by some three hundred mercenaries, was sent on across the Urals on an expedition against Kuchum, the Siberian khan, and fighting against heavy odds he conquered the khanate.

At this news the people of Moscow gathered in the Kremlin, shouting, "God has bestowed a new tsardom on Russia!" Ivan himself was jubilant. After he had granted lands to the Stroganovs, his interest in Siberia had become keen. He had even established a Siberian ministry to oversee the colonization of this vast region. He acknowledged the services of the Stroganovs and rewarded them handsomely with further grants of land.

Also coincident with Ivan's Lithuanian losses was a renewed effort to forge an alliance with Elizabeth of England. Some ten years earlier she had rejected his proposals for an alliance, while assuring him in response to his inquiry that he would always be able to claim asylum in England if he found it necessary to flee from Muscovy.

In September, 1582, his ambassador, Fedor Pisemsky, again presented to Elizabeth his proposals for an alliance. Ivan added a curious request: he wanted an English bride, although he had recently married for the seventh time, and his choice had fallen upon the queen's cousin, Lady Mary Hastings. Negotiations continued, with Ivan pressing his proposals, but the two sovereigns had reached no conclusion when on March 18, 1584, Ivan died.

The failure of his campaigns in the west and, even more, anxiety over the succession to the throne clouded the last years of Ivan's reign. In 1581, while embittered by the losses to Poland-Lithuania and distressed by the threat to Pskov, personal tragedy suddenly overwhelmed him. Tsarevich Ivan, his elder son by Anastasia, his first wife, was then twenty-seven years old and had become his closest companion. All recognized that he would be a strong and able tsar. As Ivan waited impatiently for news from Pskov, the tsarevich made some remark that angered him. He erupted in fury, and raising the iron-tipped staff that he always carried, struck his son on the head. Four days later the tsarevich died. Ivan was overcome by grief and remorse. He could think only of retiring to a monastery and spending his remaining days in prayer and repentance. However, he was prevailed upon finally to continue his responsibilities as tsar; but he knew that in killing his son he had destroyed the last link with the ancient house of Rurik.

Early in March, 1584, when he believed that death was approaching, Ivan made his testament. Left with no option, he named Tsarevich Fedor as his successor to the throne, and to guide him he appointed a special council, composed of the leading boyars of the tsardom. To the young Tsarevich Dmitry, his third son by his seventh wife, he bequeathed the town of Uglich and its environs.

Muscovites of all classes were stunned by the news of the death of their tsar. They were also filled with forebodings.

In medieval Russia Orthodoxy and Slavic paganism often coexisted in a double faith (dvoeverie). Reformers, like the iconoclasts at work in this eighteenth-century illumination, taught that a heaven on earth could be achieved only after idolatry had been driven out.

Church and State

When Joseph Sanin, founder of the Volokolamsk Monastery, declared that "if the sovereign is like to all men as regards his human nature, he is like to God as regards his power," he was invoking one of the basic tenets of Muscovite Church-state relations. It was a covenant that had been reached not without some crises for Orthodoxy. Powerful minorities had been at work ever since Russia's conversion in 988 to keep the Church out of politics, to emphasize the ascetic spirit of Christianity rather than the magnificence of its rituals. The rapid growth of monasteries, especially in the sparsely populated northern reaches of Russia's principalities, had been, in part, an effort of the more selfless elements of the clergy to remove themselves from the many temptations that came their way. Such a man was Saint Cyril of Belozersk, shown in the portrait icon at left. Among the first to condemn the accumulation of monastic lands and properties, this fourteenth-century abbot prepared the way for spiritual revolt in the next century. Nils Sorsky, who had established a hermetic community near Belozersk, argued that the Church's task was to pray rigorously for others and to teach by example from a posture of worldly detachment, and not, as one of his disciples wrote, "to look into the hands of the rich, fawn slavishly, flatter . . . to get some little village" from those seeking spiritual favors. Sorsky also rejected the authority of the state in matters of individual conscience or the right of the clergy to banish or imprison those of heretical beliefs. "It should only try to influence with persuasion and prayer." The Possessors, or Josephites, led by Joseph of Volokolamsk, held a sharply divergent view of their proper relationship to the secular world. They regarded the Church as an institution with strong social obligations—among them preserving the order and authority of the state, which was, through the tsars, invested with a holy identity. Caring for the sick, giving alms to the poor, and preparing boys for high ecclesiastical office required a large, authoritarian organization. (The manuscript illumination opposite depicts a sixteenth-century monastery classroom where pupils are learning their letters.) It was further argued that men of noble birth, presumed to exercise the greater influence on common men, could not be enticed into the service of a propertyless Church. At a council held in 1503 the Josephite majority firmly rejected Nils Sorsky's challenge. The conflict, which would be taken up again, was yet another indication that Russia's spiritual life was becoming government policy—that the state was to be the true religion.

103

THE POKROVSKY CONVENT *in Suzdal is a typical example of the walled, self-sufficient monastic communities of medieval Russia. Founded in 1364, it assumed its present form in the 1500's, when the Church owned at least one third of Russia's cultivated land and many monasteries had become so rich that their worldly concerns overshadowed their religious life. Their holdings might include over one hundred villages, vast tracts of farm and forest land, saltworks, brickyards, and mills, as well as several thousand peasants bound in service.*

THE TRAVELS OF MACARIUS
by Paul of Aleppo

In his mid-seventeenth-century journey through Russia, Paul, archdeacon of Aleppo, kept a colorful travel diary in his native Arabic. Here he describes the life-style in an affluent monastery.

The road from Moscow to this convent is more difficult than . . . any other road in Muscovy; for it is all forests, valleys, mud, clay, and roots of trees; in short, it is a road not to be traveled, but in winter, during the frost. . . .

When we drew near to the lake of the convent, there came out to meet us the Abbot and the rest of the Monks, both the chiefs and their attendants, on horseback. . . . Then they made us embark in a large boat with twelve oars; and rowed us on the lake, or rather large sea, swelling with waves. . . . After an hour's time, we landed in the island, and approached the gate of the new wooden wall. At this moment the Abbot came out, accompanied by the rest of the Clergy and the Deacons, in their copes of the richest materials; and drew up before our master, in front of the gate, which they had adorned, with its arch, in tapestry. They had also strewed the ground all over with fine sand. The Abbot then opened his mouth, and made a long and grand exordium in praise of our Lord the Patriarch. . . . At the conclusion, he bowed to our master, and received his blessing, as they did all, and so, preceding us to the court of the convent, they took us up into the church . . . where we assisted at Mass; and did not leave till near the evening, whilst we were all the time fasting. . . . [After Matins, the following evening.] Then we went to look round this island, and were astonished at the smoothness and neatness of the convent walls. We saw the large stone church; which they have built this summer, with more than three hundred workmen. It is handsomer, larger, and higher than the Sobor Church in Moscow. After laying on the roof, they dug round it vast foundations for cellars and caves, to contain eatables and liquors, and for cells, &c. They had at this time piled up more than five hundred thousand bricks for the continuation of the walls. At present, the convent treasury is of wood; and the Emperor has given them two hundred janissaries for its protection. The Patriarch has sent also of late, for the use of the monastery, several pieces of cannon, muskets, gunpowder, and a quantity of coats of mail. Likewise, from the delight he takes in it, he has sent, and had brought for it from the country of the Franks, a large chandelier of brass, of a beautiful yellow, and of the size of a large tree; ornamented with flowers, birds, and other wonders, exceeding description; its price, nine hundred dinars. He has also lately purchased for it about sixty villages, with their inhabitants, for sixty thousand dinars, and attached them to the convent; besides many farms which belonged to the Patriarchal See, religious houses, messuages, and eighty lakes full of salt. It is said that he is laying out in the building of this convent more than a million of money. He has attached to it one hundred and eighty lakes for fish. The Abbot computed that the annual surplus income of the convent is upwards of ten thousand dinars.

A LETTER TO THE ST. CYRIL MONASTERY
from Ivan IV

In sixteenth-century Russia it was common for offending nobles to be imprisoned in wealthy monasteries. Here the tsar chastises the brothers on White Lake for indulging their charges.

In my youth, when we were at Saint Cyril, if dinner happened to be late, and if the intendant [visitor] asked for a sterlet or any other fish of the cellarer, he would reply, "I have no orders about it; I have only prepared what I was ordered. Now it is night, and I can give you nothing; I fear the sovereign, but I fear God more." See what was the severity of the rule. They fulfilled the word of the prophet: "Speak the truth, and have no shame before the Tsar." To-day my boyar Sheremetief reigns in his cell like a Tsar; my boyar Khabarof pays him visits with the monks. They drink as though they were of the world. Is it a wedding? a baptism?

TRIALS OF A DISSENTER
by Archpriest Avvakum

In his autobiography, completed in 1682, one of the most zealous Old Believers describes a life of struggle. Exiled repeatedly for his intransigence, he never wavered, as told below.

Then I arrived in Moscow and the Tsar received me joyfully, as if I were an angel of God. . . . He ordered that I should be given lodgings in a monastery in the Kremlin; when he passed my house, he would bow to me, saying: "Bless me and pray for me." . . . And all the boyars did as much. . . .

How should one not pity such a Tsar and such boyars? Yes, indeed, they are to be pitied. See how good they were, offering me parishes to choose from, and even suggesting that I should become confessor to the Tsar, if only I would consent to be reunited to them. I counted all this as dung. . . .

They saw that I was not going to be reconciled with them. So the Tsar ordered Rodion Streshnev to persuade me to be silent. And I did so, in order to please him. He was the God-established Tsar, and good to me. I hoped he would advance little by little. . . .

Then I saw that "it availed nothing" in the Church, "but that rather a tumult was made," and so I began once more to grumble. I wrote a long letter to the Tsar, asking him to re-establish the old ways of piety, to defend our common mother, Holy Church, against heresy, and to place on the patriarchal throne an Orthodox pastor instead of the wolf and apostate Nicon, scoundrel and heretic. . . .

From that time on the Tsar was hostile towards me. He did not like my speaking again. He wanted me to be silent, but this did not suit me. And the bishops sprang on me like goats. They wanted to exile me once more from Moscow, for many came to me in Christ's name, and, when they had heard the truth, gave up attending their mendacious services. The Tsar reprimanded me: "The bishops complain of you, they say you have emptied the churches. You shall be exiled once more."

In this sixteenth-century icon the notoriously sinful monks of the period lose their foothold on paradise.

CHURCH SLAVONIC, *a formal language closely related to the Russian vernacular, was from the beginning the medium by which the Scriptures were communicated to the people. Native texts came to be regarded as intrinsically holy; when in the sixteenth century the purist minority condemned the error-filled translations as "blaspheming God . . . instead of glorifying Him," and called for corrections based on the Greek and Latin originals, conservatives reacted as if the faith itself were under attack. Examples of manuscripts produced in Russia are these pages from the Gospel of Saint Matthew (above), and from a 1628 calendar (right), showing the saints' days to be celebrated in January.*

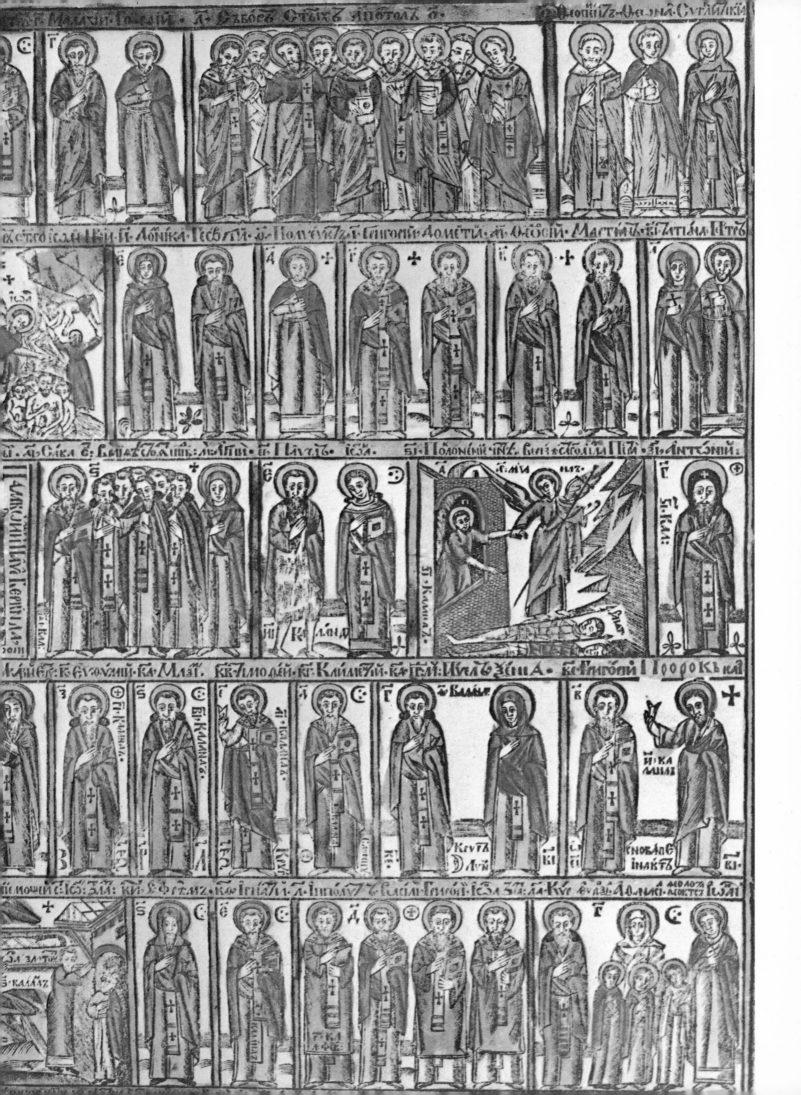

110

THE PATRON SAINTS *canonized by the Russian Church included many direct descendants of pagan deities, a practical policy devised to ensure native loyalties. Paraskeva Pyatnitsa, shown in the sixteenth-century wooden sculpture at right, replaced the Slavonic goddess Mokosh, arranger of weddings, as patron of brides and happy marriages. She was also protector of fishermen and commerce—her name means "Friday," market day in medieval Russia. Another venerated saint was Nikolai of Mozhaish, who in the 1534 wooden sculpture opposite clasps a model of a fortified city in one hand; the other once held a sword. Images of the saint, who was generally depicted as a builder and guardian of border strongholds, were usually found in settlements along the frontier.*

113

DEFENSE OF RUSSIAN ORTHODOXY *was entrusted symbol-*
ically to the warrior-saint Demetrius, depicted opposite
with the richly-robed Tsarevich Dmitry, one of Ivan IV's
sons. In reality, however, it was a succession of councils that
determined the political direction of the national Church
by legislating on such questions as dogma, ritual, heresy,
and the canonization of new saints. As early as the mid-
1300's, men like the Metropolitan Alexei, portrayed at
right in the splendid ecclesiastical robes of his office, used
the councils as a platform to press for close cooperation
with the tsars. What had been only an informal policy,
however, became official after the 1439 Council of Flor-
ence, at which the Greek and Latin Churches accepted
reunion. (The bronze panel above depicts the Greeks sail-
ing from Byzantium and arriving in Italy to attend the
conference.) Nine years later a synod of Russian bishops
deposed their Greek Metropolitan Isadore, declaring him a
"maleficent, crafty, and mercenary man" for his treason-
ous surrender to the Roman pope. Without consulting the
patriarch of Constantinople, traditionally the figure who
appointed the Russian metropolitan, the churchmen chose
one of their own as successor. Thenceforth the Church was
nominally independent, the better to serve the tsar's purposes.

GOD AND THE TSAR

FEDOR'S CORONATION
by Sir Jerome Horsey

Horsey, a British commercial agent, also acted as Elizabeth I's envoy. The following account of the 1584 coronation stresses the close relationship between Church and state.

The Emperor comming out of his palace, there went before him the metropolitan, archbishops, bishops, and chiefest monkes and clergie men, with very rich copes and priestes garments upon them, carrying pictures of our ladie, &c., with the Emperors angell, banners, censers, and many other such ceremonious things, singing all the way. The Emperor, with his nobilitie, in order entred the church named Blaveshina or Blessednes, where prayers and service were used according to the maner of their church. That done, they went thence to the church called Michael the Archangell, and there also used the like prayers and service; and from thence to our Lady church, Prechista, being their cathedrall church. In the middest thereof was a chair of majestie placed, wherein his auncestors used to sit at such extraordinarie times. His robes were then changed, and most rich and unvaluable garments put on him. Being placed in this princely seate, his nobility standing round about him in their degres, his imperiall crowne was set upon his head by the metropolitan, his scepter, globe, in his right hand, his sword of justice in his left, of great riches; his six crownes also, by which he holdeth his kingdomes, were set before him. . . . Then the metropolitan read openly a booke of small volume, with exhortations to the Emperor to minister true justice, and injoy with tranquilitie the crowne of his auncestors. . . .

Thus at last the Emperor came to the great church doore, and the people cried, "God save our Emperor Pheodor Ivanowich of al Russia!" His horse was there ready, most richly adorned with a covering of imbrodered pearle and precious stones, saddle and all furniture agreeable to it, reported to be worth 300,000 markes sterling. There was a bridge made of 150 fadome in length, three maner of waies, three foote above ground, and two fadome broad, for him to goe from one church to the other, with his princes and nobles, from the presse of the people, which were in number infinite, and some at that time pressed to death with the throng. As the Emperor returned out of the churches they were spred under foot with cloth of gold, the porches of the churches with red velvet, the bridges with scarlet, and stammell cloth from one church to another. And as soone as the Emperor was passed by, the cloth of gold, velvet and scarlet, was cut, and taken of those that could come by it; every man desirous to have a piece, to reserve it for a monument. Silver and gold coyne, then mynted of purpose, was cast among the people in great quantitie. . . . This solemnitie and triumph lasted a whole weeke, wherin many royall pastimes were shewed and used. . . .

The conclusion of the Emperors coronation was a peale of ordinance . . . being 170 great pieces of brasse of all sorts. . . .

A LETTER TO PRINCE ANDREI KURBSKY
from Ivan IV

Kurbsky, who fled to Lithuania rather than live under Ivan's harsh rule, wrote several letters to the tsar. Ivan's reply to the query "Think you yourself immortal?" follows.

The autocracy, by God's will, had its origin in Grand Prince Vladimir, who had enlightened all Russia through the holy baptism, and the great Tsar Vladimir Monomakh, who had received memorable honors from the Greeks, and the valiant great Tsar Alexander Nevsky, who had obtained a great victory over the godless Germans, and the praiseworthy great Tsar Dmitry, who had obtained a great victory over the sons of Hagar [literally "bastards"] beyond the Don, then it passed to the avenger of wrongs, our ancestor, the great Tsar Ivan, the gatherer of the Russian land from among the ancestral possessions, and to our father of blessed memory, the great Tsar Vasily until it reached us, the humble scepter-bearer of the Russian empire.

But we praise God for the great favor he has shown me in not permitting my right hand to become stained by the blood of my race: for we have not snatched the realm from anyone, but by the will of God and the blessing of our ancestors and parents, were we born in the realm, were brought up there and enthroned, taking, by the will of God and the blessing of our ancestors and parents, what belonged to us, and not seizing that which was not ours. . . .

We have never spilled blood in the churches. As for the victorious, saintly blood—there has none appeared in our land, as far as we know. *The thresholds of the churches:* as far as our means and intelligence permit and our subjects are eager to serve us, the churches of the Lord are resplendent with all kinds of adornments, and through the gifts which we have offered since your satanic domination, not only the thresholds and pavements, but even the antechambers shine with ornaments, so that all the strangers may see them. We do not stain the thresholds of the churches with any blood, and there are no martyrs of faith with us nowadays. . . . Tortures and persecutions and deaths in many forms we have devised against no one. As to treasons and magic, it is true, such dogs everywhere suffer capital punishment.

THE VICAR OF MUSCOVY
by Sigmund von Herberstein

Austria's ambassador to the court of Basil II in 1517 and again in 1526 wrote an objective but critical account of Russia. He was astounded by the people's submission to the tsar.

The Grand-duke exercises his power over both clergy and laymen, both property and life. None of his councillors has ever dared to gainsay his lord's opinion. One and all agree that their lord's will is the will of God, hence what the prince does is divinely inspired. Thus they call their prince God's *klyuchnik* or key-bearer, in the sense of chamberlain, and only regard him as the fulfiller of God's purpose. So when someone pleads for a prisoner he will say: "What God orders will take place without your plea." And when one asks about something to which there is no proper answer, they say: "God knows and the Grand-duke."

A solemn Orthodox holiday begins when the patriarch blesses the tsar on a dais before St. Basil's Cathedral.

OLEARIUS, *Voyages*, 1662

Time of Troubles

Fedor became tsar, but his succession was at once disputed. The Nagoy, the family of Ivan's seventh wife, claimed the throne for Tsarevich Dmitry, who was then only two years old; but this conspiracy was quickly scotched. The majority of boyars, supporting Fedor, sanctioned the arrest of the whole family, which was then sent under close guard to Dmitry's appanage principality of Uglich.

Nevertheless, the people of Moscow continued to be restless; they feared that boyar factions would struggle for power, as had happened during Ivan's childhood. Moreover, such evidence of political weakness would prompt the Poles, Lithuanians, and Swedes, as well as the Tatars, to invade Muscovy. At the instigation of the Church and the boyars, couriers rode to all parts of the country summoning leading men to Moscow. On May 4, 1584, the metropolitan, bishops, abbots, boyars, and senior serving gentry met in the Kremlin. The assembly begged Fedor to confirm his intention to rule. Reluctantly he agreed, and his coronation was appointed to take place on May 31, the earliest possible date, for all hoped that the magnificent formal ceremony of

The mysterious death of Tsarevich Dmitry in 1591 led to wild speculation regarding the circumstances—and generated several pretenders to the throne. A contemporary painting illustrates one version of the story: that Dmitry was murdered by the boyars.

crowning the tsar would begin an era of stability.

Tsar Fedor, then twenty-seven, bore no resemblance to his dynamic father. As Giles Fletcher, Queen Elizabeth's envoy to the Russian court, reported: "The emperour . . . is for his person of a meane stature, somewhat lowe and grosse, of a sallowe complexion, and inclining to the dropsie, hawke nosed, unsteady in his pase by reason of some weakness of his lims, heavie and unactive, yet commonly smiling almost to a laughter." Exceedingly devout, he seemed wholly unsuited to the office of autocrat. The succession of this *molchalnik*, or monk, as his father had dubbed him, merely aggravated the general anxiety over the future of the nation.

The question was who would ultimately exercise power on Fedor's behalf. Prince Ivan Mstislavsky and Prince Ivan Shuisky, the most senior titled boyars of Muscovy, and boyar Nikita Romanov, Fedor's elderly uncle, were presumed to be influential. They were, however, suspect among the Muscovites, who feared rule by the boyars.

Less clear was the position of Boris Godunov, who had been a close favorite of Tsar Ivan during the weeks before the coronation, for he maintained a discreet silence. A tall, handsome courtier, possessed of intelligence and ambition, Godunov had managed to influence Ivan while standing apart from the terrors of his reign. Sometime before 1580 the Godunov family had been elevated above others at court

by the marriage of Irina, sister of Boris, to the then Tsarevich Fedor. Irina was a woman of character who dominated her husband and could sway her brother. Indeed, Fedor, who had no desire to rule and had accepted the throne as a duty, was pleased to surrender to his wife's will and to delegate his powers to his brother-in-law.

At Fedor's coronation Boris took a prominent part, carrying the golden scepter and orb before the tsar in the procession. The English envoy Jerome Horsey reported that almost outshining the tsar himself, "The Lord Boris Fedorovich was sumptuously and richly attired, with his garments decked with great orient pearles, beset with al sortes of precious stones. In like rich maner were appareled al the family of the Godunovs. . . ." The tsar's coronation was always the occasion of bestowing rewards, and far exceeding the grants to others, Boris Godunov was made *Konyushy*, or Master of Horse, and *Blizhny Veliky Boyarin*, or Privy Grand Boyar, and received vast estates. He was soon able to mobilize one hundred thousand fully armed men from his personal estates.

During the fourteen years of Fedor's reign Boris had ample opportunity to usurp the throne, but he devoted himself to the service of the tsar and the nation. He recognized the need to adopt the more advanced techniques of the West, and he encouraged mercantile contacts with other countries. Many new ambassadors came to Moscow, and the number

of Western artisans and specialists increased. He corresponded with Elizabeth of England—the English referred to him as the Lord Protector of Muscovy. He established peace with Lithuania-Poland and with Sweden, and suppressing Tatar outbreaks against the tsar's authority, he encouraged exploration in the recently annexed territory of Siberia.

The supremacy of Boris aroused resentment among the older boyar families, particularly the Shuisky and Mstislavsky. They regarded the Godunovs as upstarts and were constantly seeking ways to overthrow them. Boris dealt first with the Mstislavsky and those close to them, exiling some and imprisoning others. The Shuisky were more astute. They enlisted the support of Metropolitan Dionysius in a conspiracy to force the tsar to divorce his childless wife Irina. In 1587 Boris struck against them and had the leaders executed. He made Dionysius step down from office and had Archbishop Job made metropolitan in his place.

From this time the Church and Boris were allies; ecclesiastic support was greatly strengthened when early in 1588 Boris induced the visiting patriarch of Constantinople to consecrate Job as patriarch, the Eastern equivalent of bishop. The sees of Alexandria, Antioch, Jerusalem, and Constantinople were all under the rule of the sultan of Turkey. The Church of Moscow, the Third Rome, was independent. Muscovites had long felt that their Orthodox Church should have

Political unrest and bickering marked the reign of Fedor, who is shown at far left in royal robes and with the arms of Moscow. The people fared no better under this weakling than they had under his despotic father, Ivan the Terrible. In the uncertain times that followed, suppression and cruel punishments were the only assured way of keeping the populace under control. In the scene at left, boyar soldiers and a churchman stand by as a poor victim, his hands and feet tied, is about to be flogged with the dreaded knout.

its own patriarch who would reside in Moscow. The prestige of Boris Godunov was enhanced by bringing this about.

Boris also tried to deal with the intractable problem of the peasantry. Although legally free to move from the land after the autumn harvest had been gathered, the peasants were usually tied in economic bondage to their landowners. Their only escape was in flight, and in the second half of the sixteenth century the flight developed into a great exodus from the central regions of Muscovy southward and eastward, where the land was plentiful and fertile. Giles Fletcher described the desperate conditions in *Of the Russe Common Wealth*: "Besides the taxes, customes, seazures, and other publique exactions done upon them by the emperour, they are so racked and pulled by the nobles, officers, and messengers sent abroad by the emperour in his publique affaires . . . that you shall have many villages and townes of halfe a mile and a mile long, stande all unhabited: the people being fled all into other places. . . . So that in the way towards Mosko . . . (litle more then an hundredth mile English) there are in sigt fiftie *darieunes* or villages at the least . . . that stand vacant and desolate without any inhabitants. The like is in all other places of the realme. . . ." The manpower shortage became critical. The great landowners had begun enticing, bribing, and even abducting peasants from the estates of small landowners, who were usually the *pomeshchiki*, or serving

gentry, on whom the government depended.

Starting in 1592, Boris attempted to protect both the small landowners and the peasantry; through a series of decrees he prohibited owners of large estates from taking away the peasants of small ones. A system of registers of peasants on service lands was introduced as a means of enabling *pomeshchiki* to recover runaway peasants and those who had been poached by the great landowners. A later *ukaz*, issued in 1597, permitted claimants a five-year period in which to recover peasants—thereby making escape considerably more difficult and enslavement a greater reality.

Early in 1598 Fedor died and the Rurikide dynasty came to an end. It marked the start of a fifteen-year period of struggle against internal and external factions, the Time of Troubles (*Smutnoe Vremya*). Ivan's other heir, the exiled Tsarevich Dmitry, had perished eight years earlier under strange circumstances. The nine-year-old boy had been found with his throat cut in the courtyard of his residence in far-off Uglich. His mother screamed that agents of Boris had murdered him, and the people of Uglich, summoned by the bell of the village church, ran wild, killing all officials and servants in Dmitry's entourage. A commission, headed by Prince Vasily Shuisky, came promptly from Moscow to investigate the death of the tsarevich; it reported that he had killed himself in an epileptic fit while playing with a knife, and the matter

119

Boris Godunov (opposite), boyar favorite of Ivan IV and regent to Fedor, ruled as one born to the office. Although the False Dmitry (above, left) was welcomed as his legitimate successor, the people's support was brief. Soon after Dmitry and his Polish bride Maryna (above, right) wed, he was murdered. The "tsarevna" next became wife to the second False Dmitry and mother of a third claimant.

was officially closed. (It was said by Boris' enemies that he had procured the child's murder in order to remove the one person standing between him and the throne.) As a result, a new tsar had to be found among the princes. On behalf of the Church, the Patriarch Job offered the crown to Boris, who refused to accept it, insisting that the *zemsky sobor* be convened in the matter. The assembly, although widely representative, was probably strongly influenced by the patriarch and by the agents of Boris, and nominal efforts to put other princes in contention were quickly suppressed. Boris was again offered the throne; a man of considerable political acumen, he refused it twice, and only in response to the pleas of the patriarch and other churchmen did he finally accept.

As tsar, Boris began methodically to dispose of his enemies. The Romanov family and their close supporters were condemned on the ground that they had applied witchcraft in their attempt to gain the throne. Fedor Romanov, who had obtained some support as candidate for the throne, was forced to become a monk. His son, Mikhail, destined to be the first tsar of the Romanov dynasty, and other members of the family were banished to distant parts of the country.

From the outset of his reign Boris was beset by calamities. The weakness of his position was dynastic. As regent under Fedor, he had been popular; but the Muscovites could never really accept him as tsar appointed by God. He could

not wield the authority that Ivan or even the feeble Fedor had held. The boyars plotted against him, and discontent erupted among other classes. Boris began to deal more harshly with rebels, and his agents were everywhere, spying and seeking out evidence of treason. Then, in three successive years beginning in 1601 the harvest failed in most parts of the country. Famine, followed by plague, killed off the people in thousands. Boris organized relief. Grain was distributed liberally to Moscow's hungry. Starving peasants, turned out by masters who were unable to provide for them, crowded into the city, where supplies of grain were soon exhausted and the plague was rampant. The suffering became worse and all blamed Boris. He tried earnestly to help his people, but could achieve little under such dire conditions.

The question of Boris' role in the earlier disappearance of Dmitry was opened again, and just when discontent was at its worst, rumors began to circulate that Tsarevich Dmitry was still alive and grown to manhood and that another child had been buried in his grave in Uglich. Many Muscovites, eager to believe that the old dynasty had not died out, readily accepted the story. Then, in 1603, it was reported that, after wandering incognito in Muscovy and Poland, Dmitry had revealed his true identity and had taken up residence in the castle of Sambor on the banks of the Dniester, four hundred miles from the Polish-held city of Kiev. The patriarch

Continuing the centuries-long tug of war over the territories along their common border, Polish troops once again attacked Russian cities in 1609. Typical of their cavalrymen is the Polish rider above, painted by Rembrandt. One objective was Smolensk on the Dnieper, a city the Russians had held for a hundred years. In the German engraving at center, the enemy has breached the outer batteries and with cannon and men approaches the moated inner city.

denounced the pretender as an unfrocked monk who had once been a serf of the Romanovs. The real identity of the pretender will never be known, but he was almost certainly a Russian who had mastered Polish and learned some Latin, and was, moreover, an accomplished horseman and courtier. He was accepted by the Polish nobility and recognized, even if only for political reasons, by Stefan Batory's successor, Sigismund III, who allowed him to organize his forces on Polish territory. In Muscovy belief that he was truly the tsarevich gathered strength.

In October, 1604, the False Dmitry set out from Kiev at the head of a motley army of some four thousand Cossacks, Poles, runaway serfs, and others. His plan was to take Moscow, but the tsar's forces drove him back. He again set out in the spring of 1605, and this time his advance was heralded by proclamations that he was the son of Tsar Ivan coming to claim the throne. His army grew as Russians of every class rushed to join him. In April, 1605, Tsar Boris suddenly died, and his son, Fedor Godunov, succeeded him. He had reigned for only six weeks when the boyars cruelly murdered him and his mother. Ksenia, the beautiful daughter of Boris, was spared, and she was to become the pretender's mistress. On June 20 the False Dmitry entered Moscow and was acclaimed tsar by the populace. His reign proved to be short. His earlier conversion to Roman Catholicism, and his Polish

manners and court, violently antagonized the Russians. Belief in his authenticity vanished, and rivalries among his followers promptly erupted. On May 17, 1606, he was murdered in the Kremlin by the boyars. His body was burned, and his ashes fired from a cannon in the direction of Poland.

Two days later, claiming descent from the house of Rurik, Prince Vasily Shuisky was appointed tsar by the aristocracy without benefit of the *zemsky sobor*. The troubles took a new turn with outbreaks of violence in the provinces, and the nation stumbled toward chaos. The boyar families struggled to establish themselves as the ruling caste; the serving gentry fought to maintain their position and refused to be under the domination of the boyars. The peasants, brutalized by their landlords and the harsh conditions of their lives, once again rose up—burning, murdering, destroying all that stood in their way. A Cossack named Ivan Bolotnikov, who had himself been a runaway serf, led a mass movement of fugitive peasants and slaves in a march on Moscow. Meanwhile, Vasily, anxious to discourage rivals to the throne, declared officially that the real Dmitry was dead. However, a conflicting report that Dmitry was still alive quickly gained wide acceptance among the people. Bolotnikov marched on Moscow, declaring that he would restore Dmitry to the throne. But the threat of peasant mobs occupying the capital rallied the quarreling boyars and gentry in support of

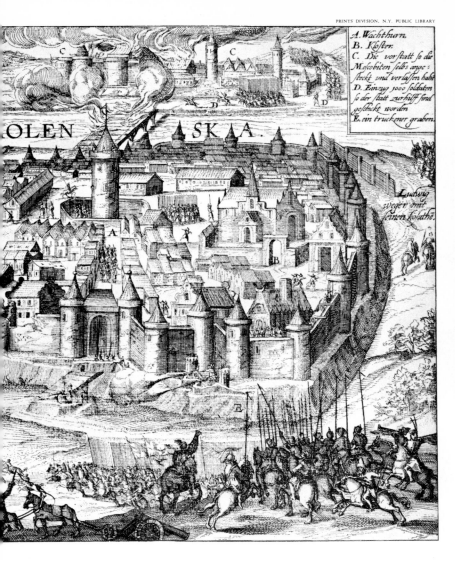

Prince Mikhail Skopin-Shuisky (above) halted Poland's meddling in Muscovite affairs by routing their puppet tsar-pretender, the Thief of Tushino.

Shuisky, and their combined forces then scattered the rebels.

In 1607 a second False Dmitry, known to his enemies as the Thief of Tushino, appeared. He had the support of a well-armed and -led Polish-Lithuanian force. He advanced on Moscow in the spring of 1608, established a rival "court" at nearby Tushino, and managed for a time to partially blockade the city. Prince Mikhail Skopin-Shuisky, a relative of Tsar Vasily and a respected military leader, rallied supporters in Novgorod, and with reinforcements of mercenaries put Dmitry to flight. Sometime later this second agent of the Polish crown was murdered.

Muscovy was now to face still worse disaster. In September, 1609, the Poles intervened directly, and soon Smolensk, Moscow, and other important towns were in their hands. Novgorod accepted the suzerainty of Sweden. Patriarch Hermogen, who had bravely tried to rally the Russians, was imprisoned. The *dvoryane*, a faction composed of disaffected gentry, had brought about the assassination of the embattled Tsar Vasily Shuisky; the duma had disbanded; and the *opolchenie*, or national militia, summoned to defend the country against the Poles, had scattered in disarray. Muscovy was without leadership and defenseless.

Only an upsurge of religious and national feeling, largely inspired by the Orthodox Church, saved Russia. From the Troitsa Monastery, the most renowned monastery in Russia, Archimandrite Dionysius sent out messages calling on the people to rally in defense of the nation. The response was strongest northeast of the Volga region. In Nizhny-Novgorod (a trade center to the east of Moscow) the mayor, a butcher named Kuzma Minin, aroused provincial nobility and townspeople to serve and to contribute men and money to the cause. He also found a minor prince, Dmitry Pozharsky, to lead what became the second *opolchenie*.

In Moscow Cossacks held the Polish occupation forces under siege in the Kremlin. Reports came from the Troitsa that a Polish army was advancing; Minin and Pozharsky were urged to hasten to the capital before the Polish relief arrived. Once there, however, the militia refused to fight alongside the Cossacks. The people who comprised Minin's forces had suffered at the hands of Cossack marauders and saw them as no better than the Poles.

When it became apparent that without cooperation neither would be able to defeat the Poles, the Church gave leadership and succeeded in bringing the militia and the Cossacks together. The combined forces then defeated the approaching Polish army. The remainder of the Poles in the Kremlin were reduced to starvation and, by some accounts, to cannibalism; and in October, 1612, they surrendered. By the onset of winter the capital had been cleansed of foreign invaders. The uppermost need now was to find a new tsar.

Early Moscow had been built entirely of wood; but as the city's wealth increased, stone became the preferred material for public architecture. In the engraving at left, the gleaming white stone and brick that went into the construction of the two-hundred-and-seventy-foot Tower of Ivan the Great is hoisted to the second tier by numerous winches and a block and tackle. Completed in the reign of Boris Godunov, the belfry served not only as the Kremlin's lookout but also as a symbol of the new grandeur of the Muscovite state. The pen drawing of Moscow (opposite) was secretly executed by a local boyar in 1610. The Flemish cartographer who smuggled it out of Russia explained that it was only after solemnly promising not to reveal the artist's name that this rarity was obtained—to record the city's layout was an act of treason, and anyone so bold as to undertake the task was certain to be killed.

Representatives to the *zemsky sobor* began arriving in Moscow from all parts of the country, called by Moscow's temporary leadership, which included Minin and Pozharsky. The time was January, 1613, and they traveled under conditions of great hardship and danger to elect the tsar. This assembly was to prove the most representative that had yet met, for it included the peasantry and urban dwellers, two classes previously excluded. For three days they fasted and prayed for divine aid in their momentous task. However, the early sessions that followed were taken up with rowdy disputes between factions supporting the various candidates. Then, abruptly, they compromised on Mikhail Fedorovich Romanov as tsar.

Mikhail was sixteen years of age and in poor health. His claim to the throne was through his grandfather, Nikita Romanov. The elder Romanov was the brother of Anastasia, the first wife of Ivan the Terrible, and thus the uncle of Tsar Fedor I, the last of the Rurik line. The Romanovs had been highly respected at court and among the people. The sons of Nikita Romanov, whom Boris Godunov had banished to distant parts of the tsardom, were regarded as martyrs. Fedor Romanov, the eldest and most able of the sons, had been compelled to take holy orders, assuming the name of Filaret, and was at this time a prisoner in Polish hands. The element of dynastic continuity appealed so strongly to all Russians that they were at one in demanding that Mikhail be tsar.

Mikhail and his mother were in Ipatyev Convent near Kostroma, some two hundred miles northeast of Moscow. A mission from the assembly, headed by an archbishop, set out at once from Moscow, and on March 11, 1613, arrived at the monastery in procession, bearing icons and chanting prayers. On hearing that they had come to invite him to be tsar of Russia, Mikhail rebuffed them "with great wrath and tears." They pleaded, and then, in the face of his obstinate refusals, Mikhail was warned that God would hold him responsible for the final destruction of the nation if he did not ascend to the throne. Reluctantly the boy agreed to be tsar.

The journey to Moscow distressed Mikhail. Thirty miles from the city, at the Troitsa Monastery, he halted and threatened to go no farther. The country through which he had passed was, like most of Muscovy, devastated. Famine was widespread in the towns. Foreign troops had been expelled, but bands of brigands and Cossack marauders roamed—pillaging, murdering, and preventing cultivation of the land. Russia was near to complete collapse, and he was afraid of the burdensome responsibilities of the throne. Finally he was persuaded to continue. He was forced by his own penury to beseech the wealthy Stroganov family "for the sake of Christian peace and quiet" to lend him money and supplies so that he could complete the trip.

MOSCVA

In July, 1613, Mikhail was crowned in the Uspensky Cathedral in Moscow. The people were jubilant. Adam Olearius, the German secretary to the duchy of Holstein's embassy, observed, "No people in the world have a greater veneration for their Prince. . . . No Muscovite, what quality soever he be of, but makes it his brag to be the Great Duke's *kholop*, or slave."

The troubles continued in the first years of Mikhail's reign. However, Russia was beginning to recover and was soon demonstrating a tremendous will to survive. The immediate task of his government was to restore order within the country. Levies of money, food, and men were made, and constant internal campaigns were waged against Cossacks and other marauding bands. Gradually stability returned, and agriculture and trade revived. But the other pressing need was to come to terms with Russia's enemies, who were eager for further conquest while Russia was weak and vulnerable.

In 1615 the Swedish king, Gustavus Adolphus, not satisfied with the acquisition of Novgorod and the complete possession of the shores of the Gulf of Finland, laid siege to Pskov. The garrison repelled his attacks, and Gustavus Adolphus, who was preparing for the war in Germany—which was to last for thirty years—offered terms to the Russians. By the Treaty of Stolbovo, signed on March 10, 1617, he returned Novgorod, but exacted the permanent surrender of

the towns on the southern shores of the gulf and one hundred thousand rubles.

Lithuania-Poland remained Russia's most hated enemy. In 1618 Ladislas, the son of King Sigismund III, marched on Moscow, supported by Cossacks from the Ukraine; but the Muscovites stoutly defended their capital, and the Poles were forced to retreat. Finally at Deulino, near the Troitsa Monastery, a fourteen-and-a-half year truce was signed. Filaret, the tsar's father, was thus released from Polish captivity. On his return to Moscow he was enthroned as patriarch with the special title of *Veliky Gosudar*, or "Great Autocrat," to rule jointly with his son until his death fourteen years later.

Mikhail had relied mainly on the guidance of the duma and, in major matters, on the *zemsky sobor*. Thenceforth it was Filaret who wielded the supreme power to unite the nation and to strengthen the throne and the dynasty so that they would be beyond challenge by the boyars.

Filaret was determined to recover the territorial losses, confirmed by the treaties of Stolbovo and Deulino, and to renew Russia's westward drive. He was active in strengthening Russia's forces in readiness for war. He sought to form a coalition with Sweden and other countries against Lithuania-Poland. Sigismund III died in 1632, and the Russian armies marched some months later; but they were unable to take Smolensk and were defeated by the Polish forces, led by the

The announcement in Moscow's Red Square on February 7, 1613, that Mikhail Romanov had been elected tsar by a unanimous vote of the zemsky sobor is depicted in the miniature (right) from the contemporary Book of the Election of Mikhail Fedorovich. *From a raised, circular platform a priest gives the word to the joyous throng gathered outside the crenelated walls of the Kremlin. Six years later Mikhail's father, Fedor Romanov, pictured in the seventeenth-century portrait (left), was released from a Polish prison, where he had been held captive. His subsequent consecration as patriarch of Moscow (he changed his name to Filaret) is shown in the illustration at far left, also from the book of Mikhail's election. By nature more of a temporal than religious leader, Filaret took the title of "Great Autocrat" and in effect exchanged roles with his monkish, retiring son to become the real power behind the throne until his death in 1633.*

new king, Ladislas IV, who reimposed a temporary peace.

In spite of these failures, however, Mikhail's reign, lasting thirty-two years, was of great importance. It provided a period of stability during which the national revival could gather momentum. Through his son Alexei he also ensured the continuity of the Romanov dynasty.

Alexei succeeded to the throne on Mikhail's death in July, 1645. He was then only sixteen years of age and, like his father, extremely pious; but he was to prove a remarkable autocrat. He was a strong and robust personality, given to explosions of temper when he would chastise the offending subject, no matter how highly placed. Alexei would not tolerate arrogance or gross incompetence. When his own brother-in-law, Boyar Ivan Miloslavsky, a man of indifferent ability, boasted of his military prowess, Alexei in a fury boxed his ears and literally threw him out of the audience chamber. When in church the priest made mistakes in the liturgy, Alexei stopped the service, cursed him for his inefficiency, and made him repeat the liturgy until he performed it correctly. But Alexei was also quick and generous in pardoning offenders. In a real sense he merited the title of the "Gentlest Tsar" (*Tishayshy Tsar*), by which he is known in history. For many Russians in later generations Alexei was the great exemplar of old Muscovy—with its traditions of just and kindly paternalism and piety, order, and magnificence. In fact, he reflected two currents of Russian life that began to flow strongly at this time: one seeking to keep Muscovy inviolate as the stronghold of Orthodox Christianity; the other driving the nation toward equality and kinship with western Europe. Alexei was devoted to the old ideals and, like Ivan the Terrible, held the conviction that he was appointed by God to rule as absolute monarch and defender of the faith. Yet he also saw the need for Russia to accept innovations from the West.

Russia had recovered superficially from the worst disorders of the Time of Troubles. The basic social problems had been exacerbated by the hasty expedients applied in the previous reign. (Government efforts to strengthen the army, to impose order internally, and to repel the enemies on the frontiers had increased the burdens of taxes and services, which lay most heavily upon the peasantry.) Popular discontent continued to erupt in violent rebellions. Outbreaks took place on the lower Don and in Siberia, where townsmen and peasants refused to pay the new taxes. But the first major revolt in Alexei's reign happened in 1648 in Moscow. The people's hostility was directed primarily against Boris Morozov, a powerful boyar who had been Alexei's tutor and was now his chief minister, and against a number of Morozov's appointees. Most of the officials were killed by the angry mobs. Morozov was spared only because the young tsar tearfully pleaded for his life.

The many foreigners who came to Moscow during the reign of Alexei (shown with Natalya in the medal at left) were rigidly segregated from the native population. The envoys, seen bowling below, conducted their affairs in the Ambassadors' Courtyard beyond the Kremlin walls and lived farther away in the Foreign Quarter. When the tsar chose to receive them, as in the scene opposite, he surrounded himself with boyars and, after each introduction, performed ritual ablutions.

Alexei was deeply shaken by the fury of the people. He summoned the *zemsky sobor* and, on its recommendation, convened a second assembly to draft new laws. The *ulozhenie*, or code, enacted the principle of the primacy of the state and the complete subordination of the people to its military and financial needs. (It would remain in effect until 1833.) The population was divided into five classes to facilitate tax collection and ensure that the army raised its quota of recruits. Serving gentry, urban workers, and peasants were liable; clergy and slaves were not. The duty of the gentry to render military service was confirmed. Serfdom was extended by the abolition of the time limit within which landowners could recover runaway serfs. The peasant became tied not only to the estate but also directly to the landowner.

In regimenting the people in the service of the state, the code was an essential step in the political growth of the country. Russia's immensity, and the need to maintain internal order and to secure defenses against the enemies on its borders, demanded a strong central power, adequate revenues, and an effective army. The tragedy was that, when in the eighteenth century Russia became a powerful nation, the code was not revised to allow a more liberal system in which individual citizens and society as a whole could develop freely and strongly.

Since no attempt had yet been made to alleviate the hard-ships endured by the people, unrest and violence continued. In 1650 rebellions broke out in Pskov and Novgorod. The plague of 1654 only added to the intolerable suffering. Alexei was already involved in another engagement with Lithuania-Poland, and he continued to draw heavily on his subjects for money and men. Indeed, he resorted in 1656 to debasing the currency by minting copper coins with the same value as the silver coins, which were withdrawn from circulation. The people quickly lost confidence in the new coinage, and counterfeiters aggravated their mistrust. (For a time even the government refused to accept copper coins in payment, though it continued to pay its own bills in the new currency.) Food prices rose sharply and the poorer classes went hungry. In July, 1662, the Muscovites rebelled, and seven thousand people lost their lives before order was restored in the city.

The harsh conditions and the burdens of the peasants were, however, the root cause of the continuing unrest. They reacted to the *ulozhenie* with rebellion, arson, murder, and destruction of property. But flight to the free brotherhood of the Cossacks of the Don, the Yaik (a river emptying into the Caspian), and the Kuban (the Azov region) was their only real escape. The revolt found a strong leader in Stenka Razin, a Don Cossack; and his rebellion, which started on the lower Volga, developed into a war for peasant liberation. He asserted his authority over a vast area and in 1670 advanced up

the Volga, intending to capture Moscow. He was defeated by the tsar's army and executed in Red Square. But Stenka Razin and his rebellion made an indelible impression on the Russian people. Meanwhile, Alexei continued his program of defensive modernization, working not toward improving social conditions, but rather toward making the nation economically and administratively stronger. Xenophobic and ultraconservative as the Russians were, most had now accepted that new Western techniques would not defile their Orthodoxy. But soon Western influence was felt in a broader sense, particularly through the *nemetskaya sloboda*, meaning "German settlement," as the Foreign Quarter was called.

The foreign merchants, artisans, and mercenaries who had come to Russia had been few in number at first. They had settled in a quarter set aside for them on the banks of the Yauza River outside Moscow, for Orthodox churchmen had taken offense at the presence of heretics in their holy city. At the beginning of Alexei's reign the quarter had a population of some 1,000, but it grew rapidly until soon it was about a fifth of the size of Moscow, a city of some 200,000 people. The foreigners, who lived amicably together, had built a pleasant town with tree-lined avenues and attractive houses with gardens. By contrast, Moscow was unplanned and untended, the timbered houses standing until they burned or fell to the ground. To the Russians, who were not

allowed to travel abroad except with the tsar's special authority, the order and style of the Foreign Quarter, offering sharp contrasts to their own way of life, was a revelation.

Among the boyars and advisers close to Tsar Alexei were a number who had not only adopted Western standards of personal elegance and comfort, but who were also eager to embrace the culture of the West and to introduce education into Russia on a broad scale. Alexei became more and more enthusiastic in making such innovations in conservative Muscovite life. He turned directly to the West for military and industrial skills; but in the field of education and learning he turned to the Ukraine, Russia's indirect contact with the vast social and intellectual changes sweeping Counter-Reformation Europe.

Russians of the Ukraine, then under the rule of the Roman Catholic Poles, had held stubbornly to their Orthodox faith, despite pressures and persecutions by the Jesuits. Their contacts with Latin culture had, however, aroused them from the intellectual stagnation that engulfed the Muscovites. In 1633 Peter Mogila, the metropolitan of Kiev, had established an academy "for the teaching of free sciences in the Greek, Slavonic, and Latin languages," which had become the center of advanced Orthodox learning. From this Kiev Academy scholarly monks had gone to Moscow in 1649 and 1650 to make a Slavic translation of the Bible. They and other monks

were soon translating not only religious but also secular works—principally geographies and encyclopedias—which were eagerly read by the educated upper classes. In 1665 Semyon Polotsky, a scholar from the Kiev Academy, opened a small school in Moscow. He also became tutor to the tsar's oldest sons and his daughter, Sofia, and he taught them Latin, Polish, and how to write verse.

Fedor Mikhailovich Rtishchev, who encouraged and guided Alexei in these cultural innovations, was one of the most influential men at court. Chief gentleman of the bedchamber and later majordomo, he was also interested in education. In 1649 he engaged thirty learned monks from Kiev and settled them in the Andreevsky Monastery, which he had built at his own expense outside Moscow. Apart from translating books, the Andreevsky brothers were available to teach anyone who wished to learn Latin, Greek, Slavonic languages, rhetoric, and classical philosophy. Rtishchev set an example by going nightly to the monastery to study. Tsar Alexei regarded him as a friend and called often on his services; but while taking on responsibilities, he would not accept the rank of boyar or rewards of any kind. A landowner of moderate wealth, he freed many of his serfs at his death, providing them with property. Rtishchev's personal example lent force to the intellectual awakening in Muscovy.

The new enlightenment, spreading at court and among the Church hierarchy, led to ecclesiastical reforms, which in turn provoked the Great Schism (*Raskol*), that sundered the Church and the nation. The immediate cause of the Schism was the correction of the liturgy and sacred books, which had become corrupted over centuries of copying translations from Greek to Slavonic. Greek monks who visited Muscovy, usually seeking alms for maintenance of their own churches, had long urged that the books be corrected. But the Russians paid little heed to the Greeks, who had failed in their holy duty of defending Constantinople and protecting Orthodoxy against the infidel Moslems. Rather, the impetus for change came from within the Russian Church, largely a result of the rise of the Kiev Academy. Efforts to purge the Church of error would probably have been made gradually over many decades, but for a monk named Nikon, who was a man of dominating personality, implacable will, and bigotry. It was he who provoked the Schism.

Nikon, born the son of a peasant in 1605, had experienced in childhood the horrors of the Time of Troubles and had nearly lost his life. Somehow he had learned to read and write. He became a monk and then changed to the white clergy, serving as a parish priest. He had married, as was required of a parish priest, but his three children died in infancy. His wife then entered the Church and he became a monk again. Tsar Alexei heard of Nikon, and always eager to

RAZIN the Rebell

his Brother

Stenka Razin, the Cossack folk hero, is pictured in the right-hand corner of a contemporary engraving (right), which shows him being driven in a troika to his execution in 1671, after the failure of his peasant rebellion. Another seventeenth-century engraving (opposite) depicts one of Razin's most notorious pillaging expeditions on the lower Volga, when he had with him a Persian Princess. "Being now in the heighth of his Cups, and full of Frolicks. . . . he took her into his Arms and threw her into the Wolga."

meet outstanding churchmen, he summoned the priest to Moscow. From this time the tsar began to come under the domination of Nikon, who advanced rapidly until in 1652 he was consecrated patriarch.

Nikon enforced his reforms at once. Though spiritual changes were his ultimate goal, it was the external, ritualistic changes that would concern the people most: among these revisions were the retranslation and correction of Orthodox texts; the destruction of icons that departed from Byzantine canon; and making the sign of the cross with three fingers, symbolizing the Trinity, rather than the two fingers, representing the human and divine dualism of Christ. The people were deeply distressed, for their icons and the details of the liturgy were an intimate part of their daily lives and a solace they needed. The punishments and excommunication that their patriarch inflicted upon them hardened opposition. The Old Believers, or *Raskolniki*, were banished in thousands, but they stubbornly continued to worship according to the old forms. The monks of the Solovetsky Monastery on an island in the White Sea denounced the change as sacrilege, and in 1668, when government soldiers arrived from Moscow to enforce obedience, they shut the gates of their monastery, manned its defenses, and for eight years defied the tsar and the patriarch. During this time many Old Believers who were settled in the northern forests perished in mass suicides. On

the approach of troops or couriers from Moscow, the schismatics crowded into their wooden churches and set them afire. Singing the old liturgy and crossing themselves with two fingers in the old style, men, women, and children perished in the flames. Between 1667 and 1700 no less than one hundred seventeen of these mass immolations were recorded, and more than twenty thousand were martyred. Those Old Believers living in the settled parts of Russia would for centuries be excluded from the political life of the nation.

Rumors circulated that, since Patriarch Nikon, the Church hierarchy, and the government were united in enforcing these blasphemous innovations, the reign of the Antichrist must have begun. It was even said that Tsar Alexei himself was the Antichrist. The revolt against the Church broadened into a revolt against the state. Runaway serfs, outcasts, and malcontents joined with the Old Believers in a broadening movement of the oppressed. Another effect of the Schism, as of the influx of Western influence and the intellectual awakening, was that the court and the landowning nobility became separated more widely from the masses, and the gulf between them was soon to become unbridgeable.

The widespread opposition to the revision of the sacred books and the liturgy did not hold the Church council, which met in 1666, from confirming the reforms. It anathematized schismatics who continued to observe their practices.

The council also deposed the patriarch. Nikon had been a dynamic force, shattering the complacency that had spread throughout the Church; but he had also shown himself to be arrogant and greedy for power. He had even sought to assert his primacy as patriarch over Alexei the tsar. (The Russians had always accepted the Byzantine precedents by which the tsar and patriarch worked in partnership, but with the tsar, appointed by God, to occupy the throne and to defend the faith.) With his driving energy and leadership, Nikon might have revitalized Orthodoxy, but he forgot the interests of the Church and left it divided and weak.

Tsar Alexei meanwhile pursued the foreign policies of his predecessors. The objectives were still to recover the west Russian lands, held by Lithuania-Poland, and to re-establish direct access to the Baltic Sea. He prepared for war, but early in his reign rebellion against Polish rule in the Ukraine broadened his ambitions.

The Ukraine was a vast fertile steppeland, then lying at the center of a triangle formed by the powerful Turkish empire in the south, by Poland in the northwest, and by Russia in the north. Lithuania had conquered these grasslands in the thirteenth century, and after 1569, when Poland and Lithuania had formed the Union of Lublin—by which Poland was acknowledged as the dominant partner—the Ukraine had come under direct Polish rule. The Orthodox

people of the Ukraine had stubbornly resisted the pressures and persecution of the Roman Catholic Poles, led by the Jesuits, and the vast majority had rejected the Uniat Church. They joined forces with the Cossacks, united by religious fervor and by hatred of the Polish landowning nobility.

The Cossacks had by this time evolved semimilitary communities on the basis of autonomy and equality. The celebrated Zaporozhsky Cossacks, whose headquarters was situated on an island in the lower Dnieper, were renowned for their spirit of independence and their brotherhood. The Poles tried to enlist a frontier force of "registered" Cossacks and to disperse the rest, but without success. Uprisings of Zaporozhsky Cossacks and of Ukrainians were frequent in the first half of the seventeenth century, but they lacked a real leader until the Ukrainian Cossack Bodgan Khmelnitsky appeared.

In 1648 Khmelnitsky, aided by Crimean Tatars, defeated the main Polish army in the Ukraine. He then wrote to Alexei, proposing that the tsar take the Ukraine under his protection. Alexei was eager to recover the steppelands and especially Kiev, regarded by Russians as the mother of Russian cities. He acted cautiously, however, for acceptance of Khmelnitsky's proposal meant war with Poland, and Russia had not yet fully recovered from the war of 1632–34. Khmelnitsky began threatening that, if the tsar would not support

Patriarch Nikon, who instructs his clergy in the contemporary portrait at right, led a movement to purify Russian Orthodoxy by restoring it to the original practices inherited from Byzantium. His reforms, such as the making of the sign of the cross in the Greek manner—with three rather than two fingers—created a long-lasting Schism, or Raskol, *in the Russian Church between his followers and the Old Believers, or* Raskolniki, *who refused to abandon native Church customs. As a result of Nikon's measures, hundreds of Old Believers fled to the north, where many committed mass suicide in wooden churches similar to the Church of Assumption (far left), overlooking Lake Onega, near the White Sea. In the distant north monks continued to carve in the traditional modes of the old faith: typical is the wooden spoon at left, topped by a two-fingered sign of the cross and depicting the divine office.*

him, he would turn to the Turkish sultan, Murad IV, bringing the Turks to Russia's southern frontier.

In 1651 Alexei convened the *zemsky sobor* to consider the question. Deliberation continued in 1653, after which the assembly strongly recommended that the tsar declare his sovereignty over the Ukraine. In January, 1654, Alexei declared war on Poland. A Swedish offensive against the Poles complicated events. But in 1656, by the Treaty of Vilna, the Ukraine and Belorussia were ceded to Russia. Alexei then declared war on Sweden; but his efforts to recover access to the Baltic failed, and the Treaty of Kardis, signed in 1661, merely confirmed the earlier Treaty of Stolbovo, by which Russia had ceded the southern coast of the Baltic.

Meanwhile, Khmelnitsky had been secretly negotiating with Charles X of Sweden, with the Crimean khan, and with others in the hope of securing the independence of the Zaporozhsky Cossacks. After his death, however, dissension arose among his followers in the Ukraine: those living on the west bank of the Dnieper declared allegiance to Poland; and those to the east of the Dnieper swore loyalty to the tsar. By this time Poland and Russia were both exhausted and afraid that the Turks might now advance into the Ukraine. They came to terms and in 1667 signed the Treaty of Andrusovo, by which Russia acquired the whole of eastern Ukraine as well as a small enclave, including Kiev, on the west bank of the

Dnieper River. From this time Poland declined in strength, whereas Russia grew.

The architect of the treaty was Afanasy Ordin-Nashchokin. He was, like Fedor Rtishchev, a man who would have been outstanding in any age. Dr. Samuel Collins, the tsar's English physician, described him as one "who will not be corrupted—a very sober, abstemious man, indefatigable in business, a great politician and a wise minister of state, not inferior to anyone in Europe." Born a son of the minor nobility in the Pskov region, where frequent contact with west Europeans had dispelled the xenophobia and conservatism that gripped Moscow, Ordin-Nashchokin had received a broad education. He possessed a brilliant and original mind. In his policies he was always concerned with the welfare of the individual citizen, for whose benefit, he believed, the state existed. In this humanitarian approach he was far ahead of seventeenth-century Muscovy and western Europe.

Tsar Alexei, quick to recognize his abilities, made him foreign minister and chief adviser. Ordin-Nashchokin reviewed the whole machinery of government. Proposals for reform and development poured forth in a torrent. He offered suggestions for the complete overhaul of the administration, for a more equitable levy of taxes, for the reorganization of the armed forces, for the institution of postal services, for establishing a permanent navy on the Baltic and

ARMORY OF THE KREMLIN, MOSCOW; NOVOSTI

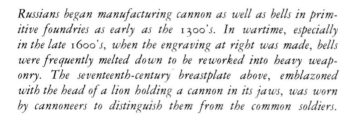

Russians began manufacturing cannon as well as bells in primitive foundries as early as the 1300's. In wartime, especially in the late 1600's, when the engraving at right was made, bells were frequently melted down to be reworked into heavy weaponry. The seventeenth-century breastplate above, emblazoned with the head of a lion holding a cannon in its jaws, was worn by cannoneers to distinguish them from the common soldiers.

Black seas, and for the provision of gardens and other amenities in Russian cities. The development of trade and industry was one of his special interests. While governor of his native Pskov, he organized the merchants into a corporate system designed to protect the weakest from the pressures of excess competition and strengthen the hand of the most proficient in their trade with the West.

Had all his projects been implemented, they would have transformed the nation. Hated by the boyars and others at court for his blunt condemnation of corruption, nepotism, and inefficiency, and for his radical plans, Ordin-Nashchokin remained in office only because of Tsar Alexei's unwavering support. Indeed, Alexei demonstrated the kindliness, loyalty, and understanding, which were among his most attractive qualities, in his relations with Rtishchev and even more with Ordin-Nashchokin.

Ordin-Nashchokin had entrusted the education of his son to tutors, Polish prisoners of war, who influenced the young man so deeply that in 1660 he fled to the West. This was a criminal act in seventeenth- as in twentieth-century Russia. The enemies of the father took full advantage of the incident to condemn both father and son as traitors and apostates. The elder Ordin-Nashchokin was devastated by his son's defection and, expecting punishment for the youth's crime, petitioned to be relieved of office and allowed to re-

tire into a monastery. Alexei rejected the petition. He overruled the criminal law and broke with convention in continuing to support his minister; he even defended the son, writing to Ordin-Nashchokin: "You ask me to allow you to resign; but why do you make such a request? It must be because of your great sadness. But what is so remarkable about your son's foolish behavior? He has acted stupidly. He is a young man and he wishes to see God's world and all its wonders. Like a bird which flies here and there and, when weary, flies back to its own nest, so your son will remember his home and his holy bonds with it and he will return to you."

The tsar's respect and affection for Ordin-Nashchokin were again revealed in the citation, elevating him to the rank of boyar in 1658. Alexei described him as one who "feeds the hungry, gives drink to the thirsty, clothes the naked, is considerate to humble people, and gives no quarter to the wrongdoer." Ordin-Nashchokin was indeed a remarkable man, but his high principles finally brought him into conflict with the tsar. The Treaty of Andrusovo, which he had negotiated, stipulated that Kiev be returned to Poland after two years. When the time came, however, Alexei could not bring himself to surrender this ancient Russian city. Ordin-Nashchokin protested without avail and eventually petitioned again for release from office. Alexei granted his request. He entered a monastery and died as a monk in 1680.

During the thirty-one troubled years of his reign Alexei was faced with crises both internally and in relations with Russia's neighbors. It was fortunate that these crises did not coincide and that the nation was able to gather its strength in time to meet each new challenge. But one anxiety remained constant: the question of the succession to the throne.

Marya Miloslavskaya, Alexei's first wife, had borne him six healthy and energetic daughters and five frail sons—indeed, three had died in infancy. In 1669 Marya died, and all Russians, mindful of the Time of Troubles following the extinction of the previous dynasty, prayed that their tsar would take another wife to bear him sons. Their prayers were granted.

Alexei met his second wife through Artemon Matveev, who had succeeded Ordin-Nashchokin as chief minister. Matveev had married a Scotswoman and lived as a west European, so far as was possible in Moscow. Although it was almost without precedent that the tsar should visit the house of a subject, Alexei, who was strongly attracted by the Western way of life, went occasionally to Matveev's house. There he met Natalya Naryshkina, the seventeen-year-old daughter of an impoverished landowner of Tatar origin and Matveev's ward. In January, 1671, Alexei married her, and in the following year, on May 30, she gave birth to a son, Peter, who was a healthy child with exceptional vitality. Five years later, in January, 1676, Alexei caught a chill and not long after-

ward, at the age of forty-seven, the embattled tsar died.

The succession of Fedor, the eldest surviving son of Alexei, brought into the open the bitter rivalry for power, which had been suppressed during the last years of Alexei's reign. The Miloslavsky, the tsaritsa's family who had enjoyed pre-eminence at court for some twenty years, hated the Naryshkiny, who had displaced them when Alexei had taken Natalya as his second wife. The daughters of Marya Miloslavskaya, in particular, the ambitious Tsarevna Sofia, had bitterly resented their displacement.

The influx of Western ideas, ameliorating some of the harsher customs of Muscovite life, had raised Sofia's hopes that she might escape the usual fate of the tsar's daughters, which was to pass their lives in the seclusion of the *terem*. Able and ruthless, Sofia had grasped at the new opportunities. She had been tutored with her brothers by Semyon Polotsky and had been close to her father. But her young stepmother, Natalya Naryshkina, had merely relegated her to the women's quarters. Now Sofia, who had strong influence over the new tsar, saw an opportunity for revenge against her stepmother and the Naryshkin family. Her first step was to persuade her brother to banish Artemon Matveev, upon whose counsel the Naryshkiny depended. While the fifteen-year-old Tsar Fedor condoned this treatment of his father's chief minister, he was soon to demonstrate that he was no mere tool

in the hands of his family and that he had a will of his own. In particular, he evidently refused to victimize his stepmother and his half brother, Peter.

Although ailing and destined to reign for only six years, Fedor contributed in some degree to the movement of change and reform he had inherited from his father. In this he was aided mainly by a brilliant young boyar, Prince Vasily Golitsyn, who was soon to become the most powerful man in all of Russia.

Vasily Golitsyn was highly educated, and like Ordin-Nashchokin and Matveev, he was a keen Westernizer. He lived in magnificent style, collected works of art, and built up a fine library of manuscripts and printed books in Greek, Latin, Russian, and Polish, the languages he knew fluently. Such breadth of interests was almost unknown among the Russian nobility, and, indeed, Western works of art were generally regarded as sacrilegious. Golitsyn was also advanced in his ideas and policies, even to the extent of planning reforms—never executed—to free the peasants from serfdom and to ensure their independence with grants of open land. And he was probably responsible for Fedor's attempts to moderate the savagery of Russian life. For example, the *ukazy* of 1679–80, abolishing the common punishment for theft (cutting off two or more fingers, or a hand, or a foot) may well have been a result of their joint effort. The

attempts to protect women from the cruelty of their husbands, although limited in success in this severely patriarchal society, also revealed the more humane outlook of Tsar Fedor and Vasily Golitsyn.

Another important achievement was the abolition of the *mestnichestvo*, the pernicious system whereby family seniority dictated appointments to high office. This reform, introduced by Fedor with the support of the patriarch in January, 1682, not only removed an obstacle to the modernization of the army but also weakened the position of the old nobility; thenceforth, they were on equal terms with the serving gentry.

The strength of the army could never be far from the thoughts of Fedor and his counselors. Frequent rebellions in the newly colonized regions to the east and south demanded attention. More important were the disputes over the Ukraine and the Polish claims for the return of Kiev, and then in the summer of 1677, war with the Turks—which the Russians had long feared. But the Turkish invasion of the Ukraine and attempts to take the fortress town of Chigirin were beaten back, and the sultan's armies retreated to the Bug River. In the following year Fedor made proposals of peace, and the sultan, more concerned with his campaign against Austria, agreed. The Treaty of Bakhchisarai, ratified in May, 1681, granted a twenty-year armistice and recognized Russia's possession of the eastern Ukraine and also of Kiev. The treaty

Boyar Afanasy Ordin-Nashchokin, pictured in the seventeenth-century portrait at far left, was foreign minister and chief adviser to Alexei. A great admirer of European civilization, he was one of the first Russians to urge the adoption of Western technology and culture, thereby establishing a trend that became national policy under Peter I. The allegorical print at left, dating from the early 1700's, depicts Alexei's sons, tsars Fedor III, Ivan V, and their baby half brother, the future Peter the Great, in an earthly paradise—presumably Muscovy. Looking on are Patriarch Adrian and a metropolitan. The portrait at right shows Alexei's daughter, regent Sofia, who was overthrown in 1689.

was a major diplomatic achievement for the Russians, giving them a new sense of security.

Concern over the succession was, once again, uppermost in the minds of most Russians. Fedor had married in 1679, and in the following year his wife and newborn son died. He married again in February, 1682, and within a few weeks he himself was dead.

Fedor had not appointed a successor and the two surviving sons of Tsar Alexei held equal title to the throne. Tsarevich Ivan was the elder, but he was ailing and mentally retarded. His half brother, the ten-year-old Tsarevich Peter, was robust and intelligent. The patriarch summoned the *zemsky sobor*, and as most of the representatives were already in Moscow for Fedor's funeral, it met promptly. Its decision was that Peter should be chosen, and the patriarch then proclaimed him tsar. The question of the succession had apparently been resolved peaceably, but all had reckoned without Tsarevna Sofia.

Peter was a minor, and by Muscovite convention his mother, Natalya Naryshkina, would be regent until he came of age. To the twenty-five-year-old Sofia and the Miloslavsky faction, this was a dread prospect. She acted boldly, playing a prominent role at the funeral of her brother, Fedor, and was able to make a moving appeal to the people of Moscow. She lamented aloud that enemies, meaning the Naryshkiny, had poisoned her brother. "Have mercy upon us, orphans," she cried, "or let us depart into the care of a Christian king of a foreign land!"

Sofia's greatest strength lay in the support she had among the conservative Streltsy. Established by Ivan the Terrible as a force of regular infantry, the Streltsy had become a privileged military caste, permitted to engage in trade, exempt from taxes, and enjoying other special rights. Many Streltsy were Old Believers. Moreover, they were normally the only armed force in the capital. They had become increasingly unruly and, by the time of Fedor's death, were near to open mutiny. Natalya Naryshkina, incapable of wielding the authority of regent, had at once recalled Matveev from exile to be her chief minister. In the meantime, frightened by complaints and threats of the mutinous Streltsy against their colonels, she ordered that the offending officers be beaten with rods. Discipline in the regiments declined further, and the Streltsy were on the verge of open rebellion. Sofia, who was inciting them against the Naryshkiny by planting rumors through her agents, waited until Matveev returned before urging the dissidents into action.

On May 15, 1682, after Matveev's arrival in Moscow, two horsemen, sent by Sofia, galloped into the Streltsy quarters, shouting: "The Naryshkiny have strangled Tsarevich Ivan!" The Streltsy grasped their weapons and rushed to the Kremlin. They refused to accept assurances that Ivan was unharmed until Natalya appeared at the grand entrance to the Granovitaya Palace, the tsar's ceremonial hall, holding Ivan and Peter by the hand. The Streltsy began to disperse when suddenly Prince Mikhail Dolgoruky, an old man who was their commander jointly with his son, stepped before them. He harangued them for their undiscipline and threatened them all with the knout. Infuriated, the Streltsy rushed up the Red Staircase, seized Dolgoruky, and hurled him onto the pikes of their comrades below, initiating a general massacre that lasted four days. At all times Sofia was apparently able to control the mutinous troops, and she did not disperse them until a number of her enemies in the Naryshkin clan had been killed. Then, with Streltsy support, her brother Ivan was proclaimed co-tsar—but senior in rank to Peter—and she took over the regency.

The Streltsy terror made a devastating impact on the ten-year-old Tsarevich Peter. He witnessed the savage murder of his uncles, of Matveev, and others, and he greatly feared for his own life. In later years he was to punish the Streltsy without mercy and to disband the regiments. From this time began his aversion for Moscow, which would deepen until he turned his back completely on the ancient capital of the tsars and created a new capital in the west.

Sofia ruled as regent for seven years, sharing power with her lover, Prince Vasily Golitsyn, Fedor's former adviser. The partnership of these two able people was, however, disappointing in its results. They concerned themselves primarily with foreign affairs, ignoring the mounting problems at home. One of her first acts as regent was to send embassies abroad to confirm Muscovy's existing treaties. The Swedes welcomed the reaffirmation of the 1661 Treaty of Kardis, securing Swedish possession of the Baltic shores. The Poles had continued, however, to reject Russian approaches until Kiev had been surrendered in accordance with the Treaty of Andrusovo. But now the Polish king, Jan Sobieski, was at war with Turkey. His army had suffered a calamitous defeat, and he feared the Turks would overrun him. Austria and Venice were anxious to form an aggressive alliance against Turkey and the Crimea, whence they feared massive Tatar invasion. After long negotiations he agreed in 1686 to cede Kiev permanently to Russia on the conditions that Russia declare war on Turkey and mount a campaign against the Crimean Tatars. All Russians were jubilant about the final recovery of Kiev, but they were to find the conditions onerous.

A Russian army of nearly 100,000 men moved southward against the Crimean Tatars in the summer of 1687. Expectations were high, but the campaign was abortive. Prince Vasily Golitsyn, for all his intellectual distinction, was inadequate as commander in chief. Deterred by steppe fires, he ordered his army to retreat without sighting the enemy, and having lost more than 45,000 men through hardships and failures of supplies, he returned to Moscow. Sofia accorded him a triumphal entry into the capital. But under pressure of demands by Russia's Polish and Austrian allies, she and Golitsyn immediately began urgent preparations for a new campaign against the Tatars and their Turkish allies.

At this time the Russians who had settled earlier in the century in the region of the Amur River basin in distant northern Manchuria were sending urgent appeals for help to Moscow. The Chinese were intent on uprooting these foreign settlements, and for some forty years the Russians had been struggling desperately to keep their foothold in the region. But Sofia would not spare troops to help them. Instead, she sent an embassy to negotiate peace with China. At Nerchinsk in Transbaikalia in 1689 a treaty, the first to be signed by the Chinese with a foreign power, was concluded, and under it Moscow agreed to the complete withdrawal of the Russians from the Amur. Two centuries were to pass before Russia was able to renew this advance.

Golitsyn's second campaign against the Crimea, launched in 1689, was also a dismal failure. Again on his return to Moscow Sofia greeted him as a conquering hero. She drew up a proclamation announcing decorations and rewards for all who had taken part. She was astonished when at first the seventeen-year-old Peter refused to sign it and furious when he refused to receive Golitsyn. She recognized that the dreaded time when her regency would be challenged was at hand. In 1686, four years after the regency began, she had assumed the title of *gosudarynya*, or "sovereign," in an attempt to claim the supreme power. She had even tried to rally her old allies, the Streltsy, in support of her coronation as autocrat, but they had shown no enthusiasm for this unprecedented action.

Tension was mounting between Tsar Peter's supporters and the Miloslavsky, led by Sofia and Golitsyn. General Patrick Gordon, the Scot who had long been in the service of the tsars, noted in his diary on July 31, 1689, that "the heat and bitterness are ever greater and greater and it appears that it must soon break out"; and a few days later he wrote of "rumors unsafe to be uttered."

On the night of August 7, 1689, the tension erupted. Warned at the village of Preobrazhenskoe outside Moscow that Sofia was planning to have him murdered, Peter rode to the sanctuary of the Troitsa Monastery. Soon the patriarch and senior churchmen, army leaders and others, were making their way to the monastery to confirm their allegiance to Peter. Sofia fought with courage to retain power, but she failed. Even Vasily Golitsyn took the road to the Troitsa, but Peter refused to receive him. Finally Peter sent word to Ivan, his half brother and co-tsar, that it was time that Sofia's interference in affairs of state ceased, and Ivan agreed. Then, on Peter's orders, Sofia was escorted to the cells specially prepared in the Novodevichy Nunnery outside Moscow, where she would spend the rest of her life.

Cossacks, or "free warriors," like this swashbuckler, were the heroes of Russia's first eastward expansion. These frontiersmen, some of them organized in bands of social outlaws, others formally in service to the tsar, opened the way to an empire beyond the Ural Mountains.

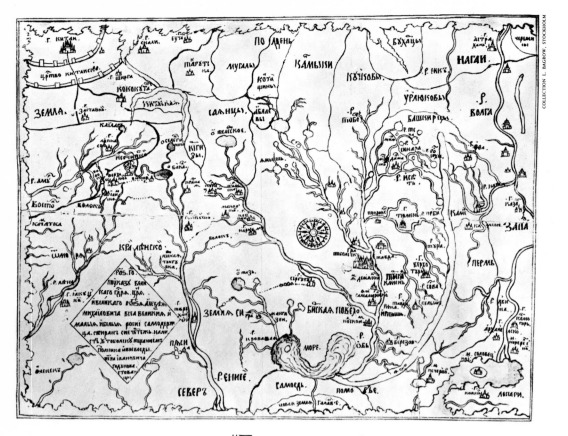

"Eastward Ho!" expressed the spirit, if not the actual cry, of adventurers, who in the 1580's began penetrating the five-million-square-mile expanse of northern Asia called Siberia. It was the Stroganov family, bent on extending its commercial empire, rather than the state, that provided the initial impetus for colonization. Very little was known about these realms of eternal winter and endless forest. Few maps were available until the next century, when Russia's first cartographer, Semyon Remezov, produced the crude chart above. Wishing to enlarge their trade in furs, ores, and salt, the Stroganovs financed a trans-Ural expedition in 1581, delegating the task to the Cossacks, whose days of living on the fringes of Muscovy had hardened them for such a venture. That year, 840 mercenaries, led by a freebooter named Ermak Timofeev, seized the khanate of western Siberia and claimed that area for their employers and the tsar. In sixty years the Russians advanced steadily, unimpeded by natural barriers and aided by a network of rivers, until Russia's frontier reached to the Pacific coast. At junctions, portages, and other strategic places these pioneers built outposts—the most important from west to east being Tobolsk, Yeniseisk, Irkutsk, Yakutsk, and Okhotsk. Contrary to the idealized depiction of Siberian-Russian relations opposite (a detail from a map charted by a member of Vitus Bering's 1729 eastern expedition), the Russians met with fierce resistance from the many Finnish, Turkic, and Mongol tribes they encountered; they committed equally appalling atrocities. Gradually, the hunters and traders were superseded by more permanent settlers. Claiming its share of Siberia's untapped wealth, the government sent out civil servants to collect tribute, and colonists to run the new industries in precious stones, asbestos, iron, coal, and timber. In communities far from the restraining influences of the capital, and where Russian women were still rarely seen, breakdowns of morality occurred: in 1662 the patriarch of Moscow reprimanded the archbishop of Tobolsk for allegedly allowing his parishioners to neglect their religion and to engage in scandalous conduct with native women. By 1730 most tribes had been subjugated, with such exceptions as the remote Kamchadales, who made a last unsuccessful effort to cast off the Russian yoke. A few years later the explorer Stepan Kracheninnikov reported that "all things are entirely quiet. . . . The Cossacks . . . principal happiness consists in the conversion of several . . . [natives] to Christianity . . . and they begin now to be so much improved that they even laugh at their former barbarity."

53
54
55
56
57
58
59
60
61
62
63
64
65
66
N.° 3.
Tungus frau
Tungus mann
Tungus mann
Suchotsky
Korack

SIBERIA'S NATIVE TRIBES *fascinated European explorers, who described them in written accounts accompanied with illustrations like these romanticized engravings. Above and top row opposite, the Tungus, from the icy region of central and eastern Siberia, traveled reindeerback, carrying their children in baskets, tattooed their faces, and left their dead to decay on planks lashed to trees. Center, the Kamchadales of Siberia's easternmost peninsula hunted, fished, and*

herded cows and sheep. Bottom, the Buryats, nomadic herdsmen from the area around Lake Baikal in southern Siberia, wore sheepskin garments, provoking a Westerner's condescending comment: "I should like them much better if they were a little more cleanly." Their priests were "believed by the ignorant vulgar, to be inspired," and during devotions, similar to Mongol rites, worked themselves "up to such a degree of fury that [they] foamed at the mouth."

SIBERIA'S NATURAL WEALTH

by John Bell

Bell, a Scottish physician at the court of Peter I, traveled to China with Russian diplomats in the years 1719–22. The Siberian land and people were particularly surprising to him.

This vast extent of eastern continent is . . . not easy to ascertain. Foreigners commonly are terrified at the very name of Siberia . . . [but] it is by no means so bad as is generally imagined. On the contrary, the country is really excellent, and abounds with all things necessary for the use of man and beast. There is no want of anything, but people to cultivate a fruitful soil, well watered by many of the noblest rivers in the world; and these stored with variety of such fine fish, as are seldom found in other countries. As to fine woods, furnished with all sorts of game and wild fowl, no country can exceed it. . . .

Considering the extent of this country, and the many advantages it possesses, I cannot help being of opinion, that it is sufficient to contain all the nations in Europe; where they might enjoy a more comfortable life than many of them do at present. For my part, I think, that, had a person his liberty and a few friends, there are few places where he could spend life more agreeably than in some parts of Siberia.

Towards the north, indeed, the winter is long, and extremely cold. There are also many dreary wastes, and deep woods, terminated only by great rivers, or the ocean; but these I would leave to the present inhabitants . . . where, free from ambition and avarice, they spend their lives in peace and tranquillity. I am even persuaded, that these poor people would not change their situation, and manner of life, for the finest climate, and all the riches of the east; for I have often heard them say, that God, who had placed them in this country, knew what was best for them and they were satisfied with their lot.

A PETITION TO TSAR ALEXEI

from Senka Dezhnev

After years of unrewarded exploration in Siberia, Dezhnev wrote to the tsar. Customarily, he entreated the tsar by "knocking his head against the ground in humble request."

I, your humble servant . . . established a wintering place and a fort, captured some hostages, and collected, on that new river, as tribute for your Majesty and as tithe 234 sables, 280 sable backs [?] and 4 sable umbilical cords [?] and about 573 pounds of walrus tusk fish bone. I too, your humble servant, with my comrades on the Anandyr River humbly gave your Majesty 2 walrus tusks weighing 32 pounds. And tribute from that new Anandyr River is continuing to come to your Majesty to this day. And I, your humble servant, set out on . . . my own money and my own traveling expenses, and received no salary whatsoever from you, great Sovereign, either in cash or grain or salt from 1642 to 1661. And last year, in 1661, . . . [I received] salt payment for the period of 1642 to 1661 from your Majesty's treasury, but I, Senka, did not receive your Majesty's cash and bread salary. . . . I have risked my life, suffered great wounds and shed my blood, suffered cold and great hunger, and starved. And being in that service, I was impoverished by piracy and incurred heavy debts beyond my ability to repay, and am now perishing in these debts.

Merciful Majesty, Tsar and Grand Duke Aleksei Mikhailovich . . . grant me, your humble servant, for my service to your Majesty and for my fervor and for my hostages, and for my wounds and for the blood and the piracy, and for all I had to suffer the full amount of the salary due me in grain and money for the past years from 1642 to 1661, lest I, your humble servant, be tortured to death in shackling debts and be unable to continue serving your Majesty, and finally perish. . . .

IN SEARCH OF THE "GOLDEN FLEECE"

by Paul of Aleppo

In the eighteenth century a coat of sable was not only prestigious, but it was believed to have a magical effect on its fortunate owner. Gathering perfect pelts required great skill.

The description of the sable, or Scythian weasel, is said to resemble that of the cat. Its offspring is numerous, and it inhabits the hollows of lofty trees. The most healthy situations are required for the well-being of this animal; for if any of them dwell in places unsuitable to their nature . . . their fur is short and white. . . . The hunters repair to the remotest parts of the wilds, mountains, and forests, where they know that these creatures dwell, attended by dogs trained to this chase. On the path which it takes to go to the water they all station themselves in ambuscade: on its return to its abode, they meet it, and the dogs run after it, and catch it, as they are caught, by the neck, that its skin may not be injured. If it escapes from the dogs and ascends its tree, the hunters are there to encounter it, and shoot it with bows and arrows, the head or point of which latter is of bone; striking it below the neck, to avoid injuring the fur. It falls; and, cutting its throat, they skin it with most admirable dexterity. They eat the flesh, and repay themselves for their labor by the sale of the fur. . . . All the princes through out the world send to the Emperor of Muscovy their treasures, riches, and superfluous commodities, and receive from his country furs only. What then shall we say of the blessed creature which supplies the whole world with this valuable article, not found nor produced in any part of the universe except Siberia? Some of its [the sable's] natural properties are, to strengthen the back, benefit the sight, and fortify the heart; and for these causes it is highly esteemed, and bears so high a price. Kings regard it as a rich possession; and wear it even in the summer . . . for it is cool then, though warm in winter. . . .

LE BRUYN, *Voyages par la Moscovie*, AMSTERDAM, 1737

Eighteenth-century Europeans, under the spell of the Enlightenment, were fascinated by Siberian peoples. In the engraving above, executed after 1708, the Dutch painter Cornelius le Bruyn portrays himself on a visit to the Samoyeds.

SALT MINES, *which supplied refineries like the one shown opposite, connote Siberia to the uniniti-*
ated. However, as Siberia's resources began to be exploited, and a profitable trade coursed its rivers, the
accoutrements of civilization were also transplanted there. Situated at the meeting of the Tobol and
Irtysh rivers, the port of Tobolsk served as the Western gateway to Siberia from 1596 until the early
1800's. As described by the Scotchman John Bell in 1719, and depicted in an engraving (below) of that
period, the town's center was a Moscow in miniature, "fortified with a strong brick wall, having
square towers and bastions," and containing a governor's palace, courts of justice, and churches with
gilded crosses and cupolas. Its population included Russian merchants and some 6,000 troops, Tatars
dwelling in "suburbs" along the river, and Swedish prisoners of war, who, according to Bell, enjoyed
"all the liberty that persons in their circumstances can expect. . . . [They] contributed not a little to the
civilizing the inhabitants. . . . I was present at several of their concerts, and was not a little surprised to
find such harmony, and variety of musical instruments, in this part of the world."

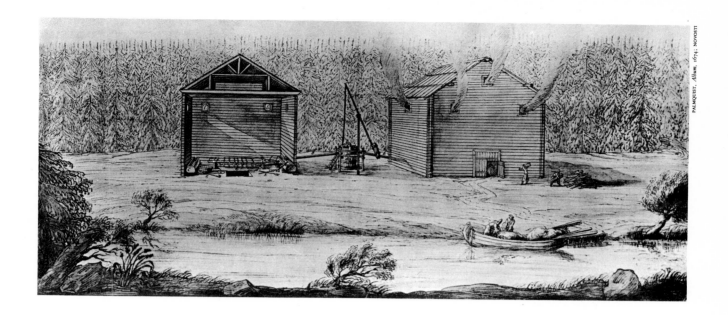

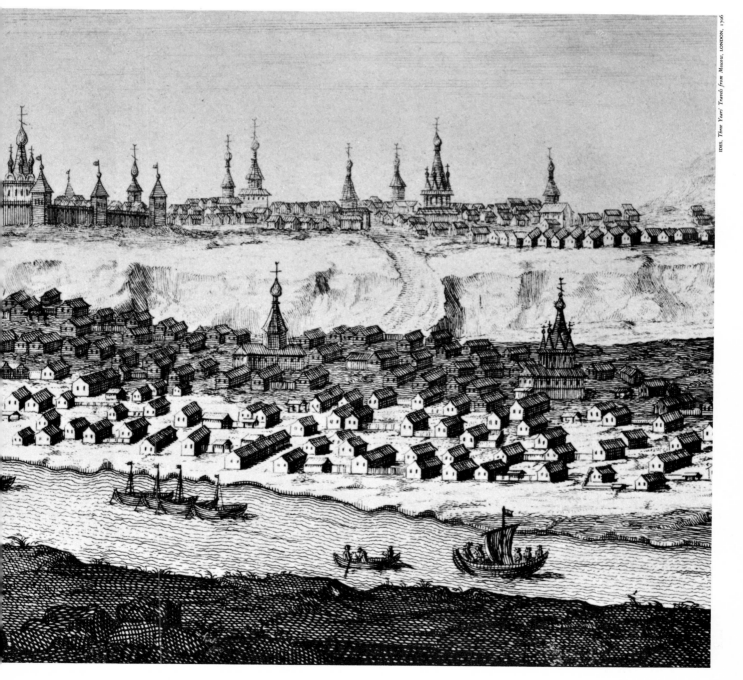

5

Break With the Past

Peter I of Russia was one of the most creative rulers in history. Powerfully built and nearly seven feet in height, he was possessed of dynamic energy, and he worked on a grand scale. To this man was given as a birthright the unlimited power of tsar.

Historians have justly criticized Peter for the brutality of his methods and the heavy human cost involved in his policies. But he was not a cruel man; his were the methods of the age. Moreover, revolutions demand sacrifices, and he devoted himself to making a revolution. His goal was to transform Russia into a great world power, accepted in the comity of European nations, an equal not only in military might but also in trade and industry, government and civilization. He went so far in achieving this vast purpose as to become, in the words of the historian Klyuchevsky, "the central point in our history, combining within himself the results of the past and the trends of the future." He was, indeed, the founder of modern Russia.

Peter was only three and a half years old when his father, Tsar Alexei, died. During Sofia's regency Peter's mother was

Peter the Great, who launched Russia's modernization, is honored in this portrait by Louis Caravaque, his court painter. Behind the sea-obsessed tsar, vessels with English, Dutch, Danish, and Russian flags prepare for combined maneuvers under his command.

uneasy, living in her apartments in the Kremlin. She and Peter spent more and more time at Preobrazhenskoe and other country residences. This suited the boy, who was already rebelling against the ceremonials and restraints of Kremlin life. The tsarevich's passion was military games. In 1687, when only fifteen, he set up his "military headquarters" in Preobrazhenskoe and began enlisting sons of his father's retainers; he soon had two regiments at full strength. Sofia and her chief minister, Vasily Golitsyn, were so deeply involved in their Crimean campaigns that they did not interfere.

Young Peter revealed an insatiable curiosity and an eagerness to learn, which were always to be characteristic of him. His formal education ceased early, and his practical education began. He quickly mastered the skills of smith, carpenter, stonemason, and printer. When the Russian ambassador returned from Paris, bringing an astrolabe, Peter could not rest until he had found someone to instruct him in its use. He could find no one among his own people, but in the Foreign Quarter a Dutch merchant named Franz Timmermann explained it to him, and thereupon became his tutor in mathematics and military science.

Shortly after his sixteenth birthday an incident occurred that was to prove momentous for Peter and for Russia. Visiting a village near Moscow, he came upon a boat of a kind he had never seen before. Timmermann explained it was an

Precocious Peter began his education at two with a book similar to the speller whose Z page is pictured above. In the scene at right, he studies favorite subjects: fortification and naval science.

English boat and that with a new mast and sails it could move not only with the wind, but against the wind as well. Peter worked hard until the boat had been repaired and he had learned to sail it. Soon afterward he engaged two Dutch boatbuilders to teach him their craft, and together they built three yachts and two small frigates on the shores of Lake Pereslavl to the northeast of Moscow.

In January, 1689, Peter returned to Moscow on the insistence of his mother. She had found him a bride, Evdokia Lopukhina, amongst the Russian aristocracy and was anxious that the marriage take place without delay. In this way she was giving notice to Sofia that her regency was no longer legal. Dutifully the tsar married Evdokia on January 27, 1689. Later in the year Peter returned to the lake for maneuvers with his new vessels. During his absence Sofia's power was gradually weakened. With her forced retirement to Novodevichy Nunnery in August, Peter returned to Moscow.

Peter found the city a stifling environment. Moscow and its patriarch, Joachim, were bitterly hostile to all foreigners. Sofia and Golitsyn were believed to have encouraged foreigners to come to Moscow, where they defiled the city, gathered all wealth into their own hands, and kept the Russian people poor. A violent outburst of xenophobia followed Sofia's fall. A frenzied mob even seized a foreign emissary and burned him alive. In March, 1690, Joachim suddenly died. In his testament the patriarch demanded that the tsar, under sacred obligation, avoid contact with Lutherans, Calvinists, Roman Catholics, Tatars, and other heretics; he condemned the wearing of foreign clothes and the employment of foreigners in the service of the state.

Joachim had hardly been buried when Peter ordered a suit of German clothes, and a few days later Peter dined at the house of General Patrick Gordon. To the Muscovites it was unprecedented and disgraceful that the tsar should eat in the house of a foreigner. Peter's Western tutelage now began in earnest. He spent days in the Foreign Quarter learning about the countries of western Europe and making friends—among them General Gordon and François Lefort. Gordon was a Scot from Aberdeen who had enlisted in the Russian service as a major in 1661, when Alexei was tsar. He was a brave, learned, and conscientious man who gained the respect of the Russians, and by distinguished service, especially against the Crimean Tatars, attained the rank of general.

Francois Lefort was the son of a prosperous Swiss merchant who had rebelled against the joyless Calvinistic life of Geneva and had sought his fortune in Russia. He was pleasure-loving and idle, but his warm companionship appealed to Peter, who found in him the perfect drinking partner. Indeed, it was in the company of Lefort that the tsar acquired the habit of hard drinking.

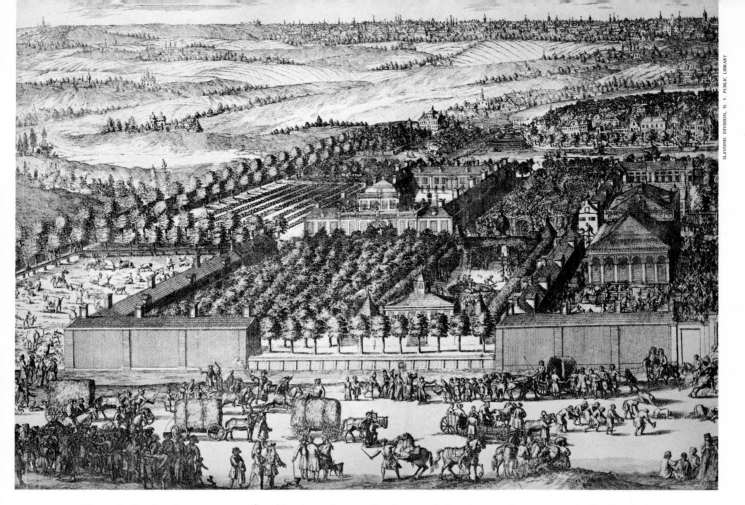

Moscow's Foreign Quarter, a comfortable ghetto for non-Russian professionals, was the young tsar's "university."
One of his most congenial companions there was General Lefort, whose spacious mansion, shown at center in
the engraving above, was the scene of many evenings of lively conversation and high-spirited entertainments.

Besides these men, his inner circle also included Andrew Vinius, a Dutch merchant, and Jacob Bruce, a Scottish adventurer. The remainder of his "company" was composed of a motley society of eighty to two hundred members at a time, mainly from the Foreign Quarter. Muscovites were horrified to see their anointed tsar surrounded by this drunken crowd instead of the dignity and magnificence of the traditional court of his fathers.

In the midst of the orgies, however, Peter was planning military maneuvers for the spring of 1690 and a visit to Archangel, then Russia's principal port for trade with the West. At the first thaw each year ships from England, Holland, and Germany nosed their way through the ice floes of the White Sea. Archangel stirred in readiness for the furious activity of the brief summer, when goods, piled high in the markets and on wharves, had to be cleared before nine months of winter once again locked the White Sea in ice.

He had a new wharf built at Archangel, and he himself laid the keel of a ship to be constructed during the winter months. He also sent instructions to the burgomaster of Amsterdam—who on occasion acted as agent for the tsar—to purchase a forty-four gun frigate to be delivered the following summer. Peter was busy during the winter, turning blocks for the rigging and casting guns for the ship under construction. On January 25, 1694, however, his mother died. Learning of the death of the tsaritsa, Patrick Gordon hastened to Preobrazhenskoe, where he found Peter to be "exceeding melancholy and troubled." But five days after her death he was at work again.

A subsequent visit to Archangel delighted him. On May 20, 1694, he launched the *St. Paul*, built at Archangel, and on July 21, the frigate he had ordered from Holland arrived. It was a sturdy vessel, richly equipped—as was fitting for the Russian tsar. With the *St. Paul* and the yacht *St. Peter* as escorts, he sailed as far as Svyatoy Nos at the entrance of the White Sea; there he turned back, well satisfied. Now he was restlessly planning ahead. He needed warm-water harbors from which he could trade more readily with the West.

On his return to Moscow Peter plunged into preparations for large-scale manuevers. His two regiments staged mock battles outside the city, in what was really a test of their readiness for serious warfare against the Ottoman Porte, as the Turkish court was then known.

Russia was still at war with the Turks and the Crimean Tatars, since no armistice had been signed after Golitsyn's second Crimean campaign. The Poles, supported by the Austrians, had been complaining about Russian inaction. Furthermore, Ivan Mazepa, hetman of the Ukraine, was reporting acute unrest among the Zaporozhsky Cossacks and urging Peter to send an army into the Ukraine to reassert the

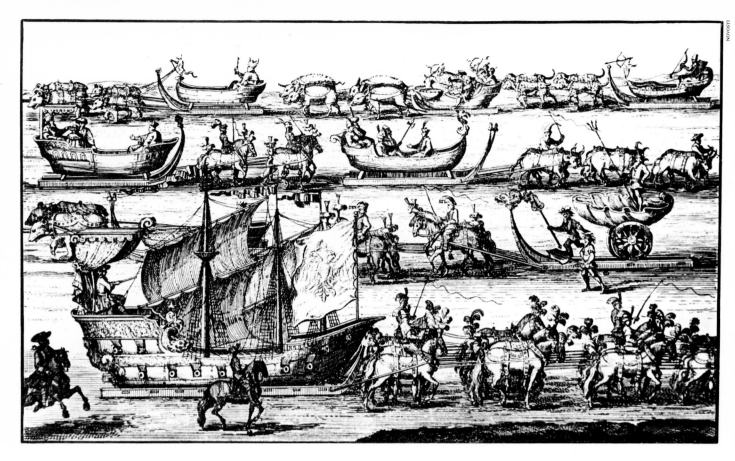

Buffoonery was as engaging to Peter as were war games. He staged mock weddings with grotesque rites and held masquerades, at which, as shown above, he might regale the guests in sleigh-boats drawn by a variety of quadrupeds. His appetites may have inspired the cartoon opposite, "Glorious Glutton and Merry Drinker"; it proclaims: "Anyone who manages to fill my stomach has enough to feed five dozen barge haulers."

tsar's authority. All were sound reasons for launching a campaign against the Turks and the Crimean Tatars. Peter was thinking of his navy. He could realize his ambition in the Baltic, which was closed to him by Sweden, or in the Black Sea, dominated by the Turks (against whom he was already committed). He decided to make his objective the capture of the fortress of Azov—commanding access from the north to the Sea of Azov, which would offer numerous harbor sites.

Preparations for the Azov expedition, begun in January, 1695, only a few months before the campaign was to be launched, were hasty and inadequate. Peter was overconfident, believing that his troops would readily vanquish the Turks. Patrick Gordon, one of the generals, acted with great courage and distinction. He boldly remonstrated against Peter's decision to storm the fortress. As Gordon had warned, the assault failed and losses were heavy. But, far from resenting this opposition, Peter acknowledged his error and made no excuses. Defeat and the first experience of real warfare matured him, and at once he prepared for a new attack.

An important reason for the failure of the first Azov campaign was the lack of a fleet to blockade Turkish supplies. Peter decided to create a galley fleet during the winter months of 1695–96. It was a formidable undertaking, for the Russians, familiar only with the primitive barges that plied the Volga and Don, had no experience in building seagoing

ships. But Peter did not recognize obstacles of this kind. He chose the town of Voronezh, which had direct access to the Don, as the site of the shipyards, and using as the model a galley brought from Holland, he supervised and encouraged the workmen, who had been hurriedly assembled. The fleet he planned was to comprise twenty-five armed galleys, thirty smaller warships, thirteen hundred river barges, fire ships, and other vessels. More than thirty thousand carpenters and workmen labored day and night.

By mid-June twenty-two Russian galleys were anchored off the mouth of the Don, where they effectively blockaded Azov. Meanwhile, the Russian army had taken up siege positions. At the same time fifteen thousand shovel-wielding troops were building up a massive earth rampart, which they moved forward until they were close enough to fire over the walls into the fortress. Soon the mountain of earth was rolling over the walls. The Turks tried to clamber up the rampart to counterattack, but were promptly repelled. On July 19, 1696, the Turks surrendered.

Peter's entry into Moscow with his victorious army was marked by celebrations that bewildered the Muscovites. Instead of the traditional holy icons, the procession of Church dignitaries, and the magnificent thanksgiving services in all the cathedrals, Peter had ordered the construction of a triumphal arch supported by massive figures of Hercules and

Mars, through which secular processions passed. Again the tsar was emphasizing the break with the Muscovite past.

He now inaugurated a plan to send young Russians abroad to learn seamanship, shipbuilding, and navigation—not just by observation but by application. Since Peter could not lag behind his own people, he, too, would study in western Europe. Russians were horrified when the first sixty-one young noblemen received their orders to go to England, Holland, and Italy. They believed the countries to the west were sinister and the tsar was condemning their sons to be corrupted and seducing them from the Orthodox way of life. Worse yet was Peter's decision to go abroad himself; a tsar had never ventured beyond his own frontiers except on rare occasions in wartime. They feared that he would disappear in the West or undergo some evil transformation.

Peter's tremendous energies were in full spate. By the end of 1696 six thousand troops, with their families, were colonizing Azov; a labor force of twenty thousand men was being recruited in the Ukraine to build a town and a harbor at Taganrog, thirty-five miles to the west on the Sea of Azov; and a program was underway for creating the Russian fleet. Responsibility was firmly laid upon the landowners, who, singly or in groups, had to build and maintain one warship for every ten thousand serf households possessed by them.

By March, 1697, Peter was ready to leave Moscow. He was anxious to travel informally in order to avoid the time-consuming ceremonial of state visits. He therefore appointed an embassy to the courts of western Europe, whose ostensible purpose was to negotiate a grand alliance against the Ottoman Porte. The entourage of more than two hundred fifty persons included twenty nobles and thirty-five other "volunteers"—among whom Peter was enrolled under the pseudonym of Peter Mikhailov.

Traveling through Prussia, Peter was impatient of every delay that kept him from reaching Holland. On the advice of Dutchmen in the Russian service, he made straight for Zaandam, where he was plagued by crowds of people curious to set eyes on the Russian tsar. (He was so distinctive in appearance that his incognito was readily penetrated.) The crowds, and the fact that Zaandam offered only limited facilities to study shipbuilding, caused him to move to Amsterdam. Driven by insatiable curiosity, he inspected the buildings, scientific collections, and institutions of that city. But he was excited most of all by the proposal of the East India Company to build a new frigate according to his specifications. Soon Peter was settled in the house of a ropemaker in the Company's yards and hard at work on the new ship, which was launched on November 16. But he had already become restless; Dutch methods disappointed him, for the shipwrights worked by rule of thumb and had no systema-

tized basic principles they could transmit.

Peter suffered another disappointment in Holland. The Russians had hoped to form a grand military alliance against the Turks, but they found that the rest of Europe sought peace with Turkey, since war over the Spanish succession was already threatening. Nor was the Russian embassy able to obtain financial aid or equipment from the Dutch States-General.

The embassy had failed completely in its political purpose. Peter, however, concentrated on his studies in shipbuilding. He was delighted with the unexpected gift from William III of a magnificent yacht, the *Royal Transport*, and on January 8, 1698, he sailed for London.

By the close of the seventeenth century London was the largest and wealthiest city in Europe. The Great Fire of 1666 had destroyed the area between the Temple and the Tower, but new mansions of brick and stone had quickly risen from the ashes. The genius of Sir Christopher Wren had had full scope in designing and rebuilding fifty-one churches; and his masterpiece, St. Paul's Cathedral, towered over all. But the evidence of London's vitality and wealth that impressed Peter most of all was the forest of masts of the ships loading and unloading along the docks of the Thames.

Peter was lodged in a small house on Norfolk Street off the Strand. Here William III called on him informally, and

Peter visited Kensington Palace to return the call. But he had come to England to study shipbuilding, and in February he moved to Deptford, then the center of important docks and building yards. The host government had rented for him the house of John Evelyn, the diarist. Sayes Court was a fine house with magnificent gardens, but Evelyn's bailiff was soon reporting that the house was "full of people and right nasty." Indeed, the damage done by Peter and his suite was so extensive that Sir Christopher Wren was called in to make a report, and Evelyn subsequently received a large sum in compensation.

Peter spent many hours in the shipyards. A journeyman-shipwright commented that "the tsar of Muscovy worked with his own hands as hard as any man in the yard." This was the crucial stage in his apprenticeship, for he was mastering the principles that underlay what he had learned in practice in Russia and Holland. Yet he found time to discuss theology with a group of Anglican churchmen, and to negotiate an agreement for the export of Virginian tobacco to Russia. Earlier, traffic in the "ungodly herb" had been sternly forbidden, and since 1634 its use had been punishable by death, though in practice flogging with the knout, slitting of the nostrils, and chopping off noses were the usual penalties. Tobacco had, nevertheless, been smuggled into the country, and smoking was becoming popular. Peter took the oppor-

154

Archangel, whose northerly location is pinpointed in the map above, was Russia's only seaport and emporium for Western commerce in the 1600's. Its dockside as well as a typical merchant and his wife are shown in the engraving at far left. During his initial visit in 1683, Peter was impressed by the crowded harbor, pictured in the 1700 engraving at left. From there he made his first ocean voyage.

tunity to legalize it, both to stress the break with the past and also to create a new source of taxation. The deal provided him with ready funds to pay for equipment he was buying.

William III was a generous host. Besides the gift of the *Royal Transport*, he allowed Peter full access to naval, military, and other establishments. Peter spent hours at Greenwich Observatory, Woolwich Arsenal, and the Tower of London, which then housed the zoo, the city museum, the Royal Society, and the mint. He made a close study of the English currency and methods of coining, then the most advanced in Europe. (Two years after his return to Russia, he would completely reform Russia's monetary system on the English model, issuing coins of several denominations, all at weights close to the real value of the metal.) A highlight of the visit was the fleet maneuvers in the Solent, which the king ordered for Peter's benefit toward the end of March. The tsar was very impressed.

On April 25 Peter sailed for Amsterdam, where more than seven hundred officers, seamen, engineers, and craftsmen—engaged in Holland and England to serve in Russia—were assembled. Vast quantities of arms and equipment lay piled high on the docks. Ten ships had to be chartered to transport men and materials to Archangel.

Peter himself was in no hurry to return to Russia. He planned leisurely stopovers in several other European capi-

tals. His visit to Vienna proved disappointing. He became enmeshed in imperial etiquette and, moreover, was thwarted in his efforts to dissuade the imperial government from continuing its unilateral peace negotiations with Turkey.

On July 15, however, as he was about to set out from Vienna for Venice, dispatches came from Moscow telling of another Streltsy rebellion. He had disregarded the earlier reports of mutiny that had reached him in Amsterdam; but the latest dispatch, which had taken a month in coming, told of four regiments marching on Moscow. He hurried preparations for the return journey to Russia. Soon after departing Vienna, a courier brought the news that his general, Boyar Shein, had put down the revolt, executing 130 Streltsy and holding 1,860 in custody; but Peter was resolved to deal personally with the Streltsy, and he did not turn back to visit the much-admired naval power of Venice.

En route Peter had a meeting with Frederick Augustus, elector of Saxony and Poland's king. Both monarchs agreed that Sweden was their chief enemy. Frederick Augustus was anxious to win popular Polish acclaim by recovering the province of Livonia, which the Poles had surrendered to Sweden under the Treaty of Olivia; Peter was eager to regain Russia's access to the Baltic. He now adopted the policy of a northern league against Sweden, which Ordin-Nashchokin had promoted during his father's reign.

The western tour had broadened Peter's knowledge and understanding, and had hardened his will to transform his country. Everything in the West—the technical superiority, the intellectual vitality, and the culture and dignity of the way of life—contrasted with the spirit and conditions in Russia. As he traveled toward Moscow, Peter was translating his ideas into practical plans. On the evening of August 25, 1698, Peter slipped quietly into the capital, an entry notable for its rejection of tsarist ceremonies. He remained there briefly and then rode off to Preobrazhenskoe, where he spent the night among his trusted regiments. The news of his return spread swiftly, however, and by dawn next morning crowds of people had gathered to pay homage. When they prostrated themselves before the tsar, he lifted them up; he wanted obedience, but not the old servility. Then he surprised everyone by producing scissors and cutting off the long beards of those present. Only the patriarch and two very old boyars were spared. Orthodox Russians cherished their beards as part of their faith, believing that salvation was impossible without them. The patriarch had thundered from the pulpit, "God did not create men beardless, only cats and dogs. The shaving of beards is not only foolishness and a dishonor, it is a mortal sin." The beard was, indeed, a powerful symbol of old Muscovy, and with this assault on beards and then on the cumbersome national costume, Peter

launched a new campaign for the modernization of Russia.

Three days after his return, Peter ordered his much-neglected wife, Evdokia, to retire into a nunnery by way of divorce. Staunchly Orthodox and conservative, she was wholly out of sympathy with his plans and activities. Evdokia was carried off to the Suzdal-Pokrovsky Nunnery, where in the following year she became a nun under the name Helen. Their seven-and-a-half-year-old son, Tsarevich Alexei, was given into the care of Peter's sister, Tsarevna Natalya.

Next Peter dealt with the Streltsy. He was angry to find that the generals, whom he had left in command of the army, had been perfunctory in investigating the reasons for the rebellion and that they had executed the ringleaders, thereby destroying important testimony. He intended to prove that Sofia, locked away in Novodevichy Nunnery, and the Miloslavsky had somehow instigated the uprisings, and he recalled with cold, savage anger the Streltsy terror that had been visited upon the royal family when he was a child. Fourteen torture chambers were prepared in Preobrazhenskoe, and interrogations—accompanied by the usual flogging and flaying, breaking of arms and legs, and application of fire—continued for several weeks. More than nine hundred of the Streltsy lost their lives by beheading, hanging, or breaking on the wheel. For nearly five months Moscow resembled a charnel house. Evidence of the complicity of Sofia and her

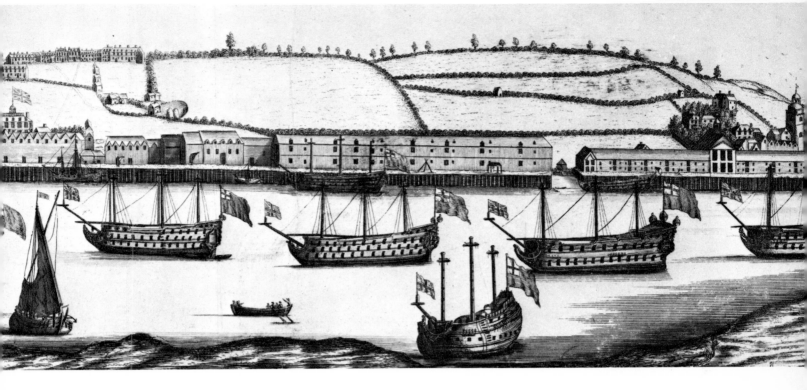

During his Grand Embassy to the West, Peter apprenticed in Holland as a shipwright, his guise in the portrait at left. In England, where a bishop remarked that "he seems designed by nature rather to be a ship-carpenter than a great prince," he mastered new skills at Deptford and the Chatham dockyards, shown above.

faction was inconclusive, and interrogations were carried into the following year. Finally in June, 1699, Peter disbanded Moscow's remaining regiments, dispersing the men and their families to distant parts of the country.

While the Streltsy purge was under way, but after the main executions, Peter went south to the shipyards at Voronezh on the river Don. The building of the fleet was progressing, but the extensive new shipyards were beset with problems. Shortage of labor was acute, and not even harsh punishments deterred the peasant-laborers from flight. Corruption and bureaucratic inefficiency also hindered the work. For once Peter came near to despondency, writing: "A cloud of doubt covers my mind, whether I shall ever taste these fruits or whether they will be like dates which those who plant them never gather." But putting these worries behind him, he laid the keel for a sixty-gun ship, the *Predestination*, and the work continued.

In the spring of 1699 Peter was under pressure from Frederick Augustus to attack Sweden. The monarchs of Denmark and Poland found the time was ripe for war. Young Charles XII, who had succeeded to the Swedish throne on the death of his father in 1697, was reportedly wild and unstable. His nation had long been the dominant power in the Baltic, and its enemies now prepared to seize the territories that they claimed as their own.

Peter had, however, consistently refused to engage in war in the north before he had secured peace with the Turks in the south. Since the sultan could not be hurried, it was not until August, 1700, that Peter received news that a thirty-year armistice with Turkey had been signed.

On the day after word of the armistice had been received, Peter declared war on Sweden, opening the Northern War. He was impatient to recover Ingria and Karelia, but he decided that his first step should be to take Narva, an important trading town on the Narva River, some ten miles from its entry into the Gulf of Finland. He ordered an army of 64,000 into siege positions before Narva, but delays held the Russian strength to less than 40,000 men. Hopes of early capture of the town were diminished by the sturdy resistance of the Swedish garrison even after two weeks of bombardment.

Meanwhile, Peter was disturbed to learn that Charles had forced the Danes to come to terms and that Frederick Augustus had raised the siege of Riga and retreated. Then he received reports that Charles had landed at the Baltic port of Pärnu and was en route to relieve the Narva garrison. Peter hurriedly entrusted the supreme command of the Russian forces to a Frenchman in his service, the duke of Croy, and he withdrew to meet with Frederick Augustus. Eight hours after his departure, Charles took advantage of a sudden snowstorm to hurl his army, some eight thousand strong,

The drummer, enlistment officer, captain, and musketeer pictured from left to right represent members of the Streltsy, the unruly militia that Peter crushed in 1698. The contemporary engraving at center shows the Streltsy being brought in by the cartload to be tortured and hanged from the gallows along Moscow's ramparts. The corpses were left as reminders to potential troublemakers.

against the Russian positions, gaining a swift and complete victory in late November.

Peter's hasty departure had the appearance of flight in the face of the enemy. Many in western Europe believed him guilty of cowardice. Charles was contemptuous. Driven by pride, and hungry for military glory and the excitement of war, he observed criteria that were remote from Peter's standards. Peter was a realist. He had declared war on Sweden to gain certain objectives, but he was not prepared to risk himself in battle with Charles when his army was still untrained and untested. He had, moreover, half expected defeat at the hands of the veteran Swedish troops, and he saw it not as a dishonor but as a stage in the development of his army.

The magnitude of the disaster at Narva nevertheless astonished him. He had lost all his artillery and had been compelled to recognize that his army was little more than a horde of untrained peasants, incapable of standing against Western troops. But he made no recriminations, and in a fury of activity he set about creating a new military machine.

Charles did not follow up his victory by marching on Moscow, as expected. In his contempt for the tsar and the Russians he felt confident that he could deal with Russia when he was ready. He posted small detachments to defend the Baltic states of Livonia and Ingria, and he spent the next six years occupying Poland.

Charles thus gave Peter the respite he needed to train his army in battle. During the years 1702 and 1703 Peter conquered Ingria, and in the following two years he captured Dorpat and Narva. His troops thus proved themselves the equal of the Swedes, but the aura of invincibility still surrounded Charles and his army, and Peter's great duel with him was yet to come.

Among the civilian prisoners taken in 1702, after the capture of the ancient fortress-town of Marienburg, was a seventeen-year-old Livonian girl called Catherine Skavronskaya. She belonged to the family of the peasant Samuel Skavronsky, but was possibly illegitimate. Her mother died when she was three, and, apparently destitute, the child was taken into the home of the Lutheran pastor of Marienburg, Ernst Gluck. Sometime before the arrival of the Russian army she had married a Swedish dragoon; but he was at once recalled to his troop, and she was never to see him again.

The Russian commander, Field Marshal Boris Sheremetev, sent Gluck with his family to Moscow as a translator in service to the tsar, but kept the comely and full-figured Catherine for himself. She next caught the eye of Alexander Menshikov, the son of a humble pie vendor, whose meteoric career had taken him to the innermost circle of the court, and much to Sheremetev's annoyance, he took her into his house. There Peter made her acquaintance, and it was the beginning of an

intimate relationship that endured until his death.

In every way Catherine proved to be the ideal mate. She was a woman of opulent charms, generous, and good-natured, who provided the stability and affection to which Peter could return for renewal. She possessed the amazing physical stamina needed to keep up with him, common sense, and a simple honesty, which held her from being carried away by her exalted position, first as mistress, then as his tsaritsa and empress.

About the time of their first meeting Peter chose the site of a new fortress and port, called St. Petersburg after his patron saint, laying the foundation on May 16, 1703. His choice was extraordinary. The estuary of the Neva River, at the eastern end of the Gulf of Finland, was desolate, marshy, and unhealthy. The winters were long, dark, and bitterly cold; the summers were short and hot. Although his decision appeared hasty and impetuous, Peter was confident that he would ultimately defeat Sweden and secure Russia's access to the Baltic. He was equally sure, in spite of the opposition of his people, that the Neva estuary was the true site for his city.

History has endorsed his decision. Peter was, in effect, transplanting Novgorod, which had been, with Kiev, an early center of Russian trade and kinship with the West. St. Petersburg was to become the capital of a reformed and reorientated Russia. Its rivalry with Moscow symbolized the conflicting currents of Russian life: Moscow stood for the old traditions and the sanctity of Orthodoxy; St. Petersburg represented the new, Westernized Russia.

Peter became obsessed with St. Petersburg. The obstacles to building a new city were enormous. Labor and materials had to be brought hundreds of miles overland to the marshy estuary. Carpenters, peasants, and even troops were drafted in the hundreds of thousands, but the hostile climate killed them off at an alarming rate. Shovels, picks, and other tools needed to build the canals and raise the level of the land were lacking, and men often had to scrape earth with their hands and carry it great distances.

The fortress of Saints Peter and Paul, designed with six bastions, was the first major building that Peter started and supervised. Then, his ambitions growing, he looked west to Kotlin Island, some eight miles from the city and dominating the approach to the estuary. He decided to make this island a channel redoubt. A fortress, renamed Kronstadt and armed with a battery of fourteen canon, was quickly erected. He posted a garrison there and wrote out their orders, which began with the uncompromising instructions: "Hold the citadel, with God's help, and if necessary to the last man."

Peter continued to rebuild his army, recognizing that the trial of arms with Charles could not be held off indefinitely. He was under constant strain, and he suffered bouts of ill-

РАСКОЛЬНИКЪ ГОВОРИТЪ
СЛУШАÏ ЦЫРЮЛЬНИКЪ
Я БОРОДЫ СТРИЧЬ НЕ
ХОЧÜ ВОТЪ ГЛЕДИ Я НА
ТЕБЯ СКОРО КАРАУЛЪ ЗАКРИ

ЦЫРЮЛЬНИКЪ Х
ЁТЪ РАСКОЛЬНИКÜ
БОРОДÜ СТРИЧЬ •

In this contemporary cartoon an Old Believer protests futilely as the barber, probably Peter himself, prepares to modernize his chin. Foreigners reported that many objectors saved their shorn beards and were buried with them.

Conservatives were allowed to keep their beards by paying a tax and wearing the seal (left) stamped with a beard and mustache; many anathematized Peter as the Antichrist or, at least, a Roman Catholic, as in the cartoon above, where he carries a Latin cross.

ness; but nothing diminished his working tempo or his tremendous energy. The new army bore small resemblance to the hastily trained and ill-equipped forces with which he had tried to besiege Narva. The infantry, forty thousand strong, and the cavalry, twenty thousand strong, were now comprised of experienced troops, well equipped with small arms and artillery manufactured in the foundries that he had established in the Urals and the armament works that he had greatly expanded at Tula. New methods of recruiting and training also ensured adequate reserves.

Peter had been playing for time and avoiding head-on conflicts with the Swedes. He was constantly on guard against one of Charles' famed lightning attacks. Indeed, Charles almost caught up with the Russian army at their winter quarters at Grodno in March, 1706, and only the breaking of the ice on the Neman River—delaying the Swedes and allowing the Russian army to withdraw—prevented a decisive battle being fought then.

At this critical stage Peter was distracted by rebellions among his own people, which forced him to detach troops from his main army. In July, 1705, uprisings against the tsar's officials broke out in Astrakhan at the mouth of the Volga. Many Old Believers, men from disbanded Streltsy regiments, and other malcontents had settled there, and they had been incensed by the extortions of the tsar's governor.

Peter did not underestimate the seriousness of this outbreak. Astrakhan was more than a thousand miles from the Polish front, but rebellion could spread swiftly to Azov, to the Cossacks of the Terek and the Don, and sweeping northward, it might threaten Moscow. At once he set aside his plans to drive the Swedes from Courland and sent troops to quell the rebellion in the south.

Peter was now waiting with his army in Kiev in readiness for Charles' invasion. He was astonished to learn that the Swedes had turned westward against Saxony. Menshikov was sent with troops to harry the Swedes in Poland, and on October 18, 1706, near Kalicz, the Russians severely defeated a large Swedish force. Peter was en route to Narva when he was informed that Frederick Augustus, whom he had supported for so long, had just signed a secret agreement with Charles, renouncing his alliance with Russia. Peter now stood alone against Charles.

Discontent and rebellion among his people again threatened in the rear. Peter's projects, so numerous and on such a vast scale, had imposed intolerable burdens on the nation. The army had taken more than three hundred thousand men in the first nine years of the Northern War. The fortification of Azov and the naval base at Taganrog required thirty thousand laborers a year in the period from 1704 to 1706. The building of the Volga-Don canal—Peter's attempt to

Reckless and reputedly invincible, Charles XII of Sweden, portrayed at left, was Peter's adversary in the series of battles that made Russia a Baltic power. Peter's taking of the Swedish-held fortress of Narva in 1704, commemorated in the medal (above, left), was followed by his victory at Poltava in 1709 (above, right). Then in 1714, off Cape Hango on the Baltic, with the help of some twenty warships and about two hundred galleys, he scored his first major naval success, recreated in the engraving at right. With these stunning routs of the Swedes, Europe began to reckon with Russian naval power.

link St. Petersburg with the Caspian Sea—needed thirty thousand men, and the English engineer in charge complained that he could obtain only ten thousand men for the work.

Taxes multiplied, and peasants escaped conscription and taxation by fleeing to the open lands beyond the Urals and to the south. Rumors spread that Peter was a changeling or the Antichrist, not the true tsar. The mass of the people of Great Russia continued to labor and to obey, but threats of uprisings in the frontier settlements were ever present.

Peter had issued strict orders that Cossack leaders must surrender all runaway peasants and deserters who had joined them after 1695. His orders were ignored, and Cossack settlements expanded greatly in size. Finally, he sent Prince Yury Dolgoruky with troops to the Don, where the threat seemed greatest, to enforce obedience. The Cossacks regarded this as a denial of their traditional liberties.

On the night of October 9, 1707, Kondraty Bulavin, the hetman from the Ukraine, led a rebel Cossack force against Dolgoruky's camp, killing him and his men. The victorious Bulavin declared that he would capture Azov and Taganrog, freeing the labor force, and that he would then march on Voronezh and Moscow. But loyal Don Cossacks attacked and scattered Bulavin's army. Bulavin took refuge among the Zaporozhsky Cossacks, whose territory served as the southern

buffer between Russia and the Crimean khanate. The Zaporozhsky Cossacks were not prepared to declare war against the tsar, but they allowed Bulavin to recruit volunteers among them. Leading his new army, he defeated a detachment of the tsar's troops from Azov and also the loyal Don Cossacks who had forced him to flee earlier.

The rebellion mounted dangerously. Voronezh and the vast region of the upper Don were threatened. Peter sent a strong force under the command of Vasily Dolgoruky, brother of the prince killed by the rebels in the previous year, and ordered him "to extinguish this fire once and for all"—and, briefly, the tsar even considered rushing to the Don to conduct operations personally. In April, 1708, Bulavin captured Cherkassk; but by this time many Cossacks had grown dissatisfied with his leadership and were plotting against him. Moreover, he made the mistake of dividing his army into three parts, dispersing them in different directions. Vasily Dolgoruky crushed one of the rebel forces in the north, and a second, advancing to attack Azov, was put to flight. Bulavin lost heart and shot himself. The revolt was at an end, and the Cossacks hurried to reaffirm their loyalty.

Charles, unpredictable alike to his own generals and to his enemies, had been expected to invade Russia in the spring of 1707. His army, rested and brought to full strength, comprised 19,200 infantry, 16,000 dragoons, and 8,450 cavalry.

In August, 1707, however, when Charles at last marched, he moved slowly, reaching the Vistula River at Christmas, and then turned northeast.

In January, 1708, Charles suddenly rushed to the Neman River with a small detachment of troops. He nearly overtook Peter at Grodno, but had to give up his pursuit because the country through which he was passing had been scourged by the retreating Russians. Charles now established his headquarters near Minsk. All assumed that his bold plan would be to advance by way of Smolensk and, hurling his army into the heart of Russia, dictate his terms in the tsar's capital.

From Minsk, however, Charles advanced to the Berezina River, and thence to the Dnieper. At Golovchina he found the Russian army drawn up in strong positions. He attacked at once, and after bitter fighting, the Russians withdrew. Again he had won a victory, but it had been costly in men and equipment, and indecisive, for the Russians had fallen back in good order. In August Charles crossed the Dnieper and marched eastward, harried by Russian light-horsemen.

Charles had expected that the tsar would not dare lay waste his own subjects' lands as he had done in Poland, but the Swedish army found the same vista of smouldering grass and burning villages beyond the frontier. Peter's scorched-earth policy was yielding results. Charles summoned a war council. His generals were united in urging him to fall back

to the Dnieper, but the king rejected such tactics as tantamount to retreat. He moved farther south. He sent orders to General Adam Lewenhaupt to join him with reinforcements and enough supplies for three months for the whole army. Lewenhaupt was appalled. He knew that a large force of the Russian army stood between them. Loyally he set out to obey orders. He crossed the Dnieper, and then, on September 28, at the village of Lesnaya, he met Peter. In the ensuing battle Lewenhaupt suffered complete defeat and lost the whole of the supply train.

Charles' advance was predicated on the support of Mazepa, who had negotiated secretly to betray the tsar. Peter was worried that the old hetman would persuade the Cossacks—whose rebellions had just been quelled—to follow him, and that the Crimean Tatars would join with them. But Swedish expectations were not realized. When at the end of October, 1708, Mazepa entered the Swedish camp, he was followed not by his normal complement of twenty to thirty thousand men, but only by some two thousand Cossacks. Loyalty to the tsar and fear of reprisals had held most Zaporozhsky and Don Cossacks from going over to the enemy.

The climax of the Northern War was yet to come. The winter of 1708 was exceptionally severe. The rivers of Europe were frozen, and in the Ukrainian steppes the cold was even more intense. In spite of the savage conditions Charles

marched his army farther to the south. The bravery and endurance of the Swedes was heroic. Then, in mid-February, freak thunderstorms and heavy rains melted snow and ice, turning the ground into a quagmire. Charles decided to take Poltava, a small but important trading town on the Vorskla River. He began the siege early in May, 1709. The Russian army gathered on the opposite bank of the river, and Menshikov sent word to Peter that battle was imminent.

Peter rejoined his army early in June and assumed supreme command. Some two weeks later he crossed the army over the river and took up positions within a quarter of a mile of the Swedes. On the morning of June 27 the two armies clashed in general battle. The Swedes fought with great spirit, but they were now opposed by a sturdier enemy. Throughout the battle Peter showed great courage, his tall figure conspicuous among the Russian troops as he drove them to greater efforts. Charles, who had suffered a severe wound in the foot, had himself carried on a litter wherever the fighting was most fierce and encouraged his men. But the Swedes were near the end of their strength and yielding ground. Charles, weak from fatigue and loss of blood, was hoisted onto a horse to order the retreat. Three thousand Swedes lay dead on the battlefields, and twenty-eight hundred were taken prisoners. The remnants of the Swedish army retreated southward toward the Dnieper, but, overtaken by

the Russian cavalry, they surrendered. Charles, Mazepa, and a small band of survivors made their escape in boats across the river and found refuge in Turkish territory.

Peter was jubilant. He attended a thanksgiving service on the field of battle, and then he celebrated. The Swedish generals and officers were brought to his tent, where he showed them great courtesy and praised their bravery. He stood up and gave a tribute to his mentors in the art of war. "Who are your teachers?" a Swedish general asked. "You are, Gentlemen," the tsar replied. "Then well have the pupils returned thanks to their teachers," the Swede commented.

Peter wrote at once to all who were close to him, giving them the news. He asked Catherine to come to him in Poltava. In his letter to General-Admiral Fedor Apraksin he expressed most concisely what was for him the chief outcome of this battle. "Now," he wrote, "with the help of God, the final stone in the foundation of St. Petersburg has been laid."

Eager also to raise Russia's prestige, Peter sent a stream of battle reports to Russian ministers abroad. In the chancelleries of Europe the significance of this decisive victory was readily understood. A new power had arisen, displacing Sweden and changing the balance of Europe. Fear and suspicion of the new colossus began to condition the policies of western European countries toward Russia.

However, Peter realized that Charles would not capitulate

Soon after sentencing the heir apparent, Alexei, to death for treason, Peter posed with his second wife, Catherine I, for the enameled portrait opposite. They are flanked by their children, Anna, Elizabeth, Natalya, and Peter, the last of four sons and soon to die, too. Catherine and Peter are also the subjects of the lubok *at right—a type of broadside popular in Russia after the 1600's. Entitled "The Witch Baby going off to Fight the Crocodile," it lampoons Catherine's humble origins by dressing the "Witch Baby" in Livonian costume and putting her astride a pig. Peter is portrayed as a crocodile—a touch of Old Believer satire.*

or come to any terms but his own; he might succeed in persuading the Turks to declare war on Russia and in invading the Ukraine with Turkish and Tatar support. Charles, supported by France and by the Crimean Tatars, was, in fact, bringing every pressure to bear in Constantinople. Through Peter Tolstoy, his ambassador to the Ottoman Porte, Peter demanded that Turkey expel Charles, still in refuge there. The demand was rejected, and on November 20, 1710, the Turks formally declared war on Russia. Tolstoy was then imprisoned in Constantinople's Tower of the Seven Bastions. The following February the Russians declared war against the enemies of the Cross. A few days later Peter, accompanied by Catherine, went south to join his army at the river Pruth.

This campaign against the Turks was another chastening experience for Peter. He embarked on it hastily and in a mood of overconfidence. He planned to strike deep into Turkish territory, and with the support of the Orthodox Christian peoples of Wallachia, Moldavia, and the Balkans, take command of the Black Sea. However, when the campaign opened, the Christians did not rise against the Turks.

Early in July, beyond the Pruth, the Turks attacked the Russian army, but were repelled with heavy losses. The Russians then began to withdraw, only to be engaged in further desperate fighting. Peter's army of 38,000 men was now surrounded by the Turkish army of 120,000 troops, supported by 70,000 Tatars. The Russians were exhausted by the heavy fighting in sultry heat. Fortunately the vizier commanding the Turkish army did not appreciate the strength of his position. He, too, was eager to come to terms, especially since the Janizaries, the palace guards, who had suffered most in the fighting, refused to attack the Russian positions again. Finally, to Peter's great relief, peace conditions were agreed to on July 12. The vizier had demanded far less than the tsar had been prepared to concede. Though Peter gave up all that he had won in his campaign of 1696—including the strongholds of Azov and Taganrog on the Sea of Azov—he was spared the humiliation of Turkish captivity for Catherine and himself. Peter returned to his capital, determined to force Sweden to an early peace that would ensure Russia's position in the Baltic. He needed such a treaty to compensate for the losses in the south and to erase the bungled Pruth campaign.

However, peace with Charles was to evade Peter for a further ten years. He might have succeeded earlier if he had concentrated all his forces against Sweden. But he was more cautious after the Pruth campaign. Peter nevertheless achieved some positive results. In 1713 he dispatched a fleet of ninety-three galleys, sixty brigantines, and fifty large boats—carrying in all sixteen thousand troops—to capture Finland. The expedition succeeded brilliantly. Naval supremacy was achieved in a major victory the following year. To-

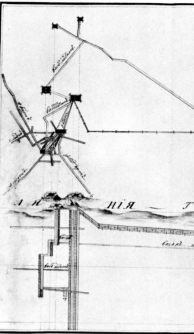

ward the end of June, 1714, the Russian fleet anchored some six miles to the east of Cape Hango, where a small Swedish fleet of sixteen warships, five frigates, and other smaller vessels barred the approaches to the Aland Islands and the Swedish mainland. On July 26 the Russian fleet outmaneuvered the Swedes off Cape Hango and then pursued them into Rilaks Fjord. Peter called on the Swedish admiral to surrender his outnumbered forces on honorable terms. The offer was rejected and the Russians attacked. Fierce fighting raged for hours, but the Swedes were beaten; Russians now held the Aland Islands, a mere twenty-four miles from Sweden.

To Peter this naval victory was equal in importance to his land victory at Poltava. But this further proof of the emergence of Russia disturbed the rest of Europe. England and Holland, in particular, were alarmed that Russia would challenge and even take over their Baltic trade. Rivalries were further complicated by the fact that France had become the ally of England and Holland at the end of the Spanish Succession War. When in 1714 the elector of Hanover became King George I of England, he set out to drive the Swedes from northern Germany. Peter assumed that he would welcome alliance with Russia, but George refused.

Peter's policy of dynastic marriages with the ruling families in the German duchies of Courland, Mecklenburg, and Holstein also led to disappointments, as did his efforts to

strengthen ties with France. In 1717 he visited France to negotiate personally a second marriage of his son, Tsarevich Alexei, with the daughter of the duke of Orleans or, failing that, between his daughter, Tsarevna Elizabeth, and the boy-king Louis XV. Both proposals came to nothing, though Peter made a strong and favorable impression on the French court. The duke of Villeroi wrote to Madame de Maintenon that "this prince, said to be barbarous, is not so at all; he displayed sentiments of grandeur, generosity, and politeness which we by no means expected." Peter spent six weeks in Paris and devoted much of his time to visiting royal buildings, bridges, and industries. The Gobelin tapestry workshops fascinated him, and he engaged skilled workmen to establish similar workshops in Russia. He made repeated visits to Versailles, Fontainebleau, and St. Cloud to study the architecture and decorations of the palaces and of the gardens. He made notes and enlisted artisans of every kind to take back to St. Petersburg.

Peter finally recognized that his ventures into diplomacy had merely aroused suspicion and antagonism, and had probably delayed the peace with Sweden. He subscribed to a plan, proposed by the Holstein minister Baron George Henry von Goertz, to open direct negotiations with Sweden. Charles accepted the idea, although he probably did not fully grasp its implications, which involved the political cession to

Peter promoted heavy industry by exploiting Russia's vast mineral wealth, especially in the Urals. Toward the end of the eighteenth century Russia would supply England with half its pig iron. The wash drawings above depict, from left to right, a furnace and machine hammer, a copper mine, and a forging shop. They are taken from a 1735 manual on the construction and operation of mines and metalworks, written in Russian by Georg de Hennin, one of the many foreign experts brought in to stimulate native technology.

Russia of most of the territories that Peter had conquered. In December of 1718, while Russian and Swedish ministers were debating peace on one of the Aland Islands, Charles was killed in an action against Norway. His sister, Ulrica Eleonora, ascended the throne, and England, Denmark, Prussia, and Saxony hastened to make alliances with the new Swedish government in attempts to halt the expansion of Russian power in the north. George I even sent an English squadron into the Baltic to support the Swedish fleet and to force Peter to accept English mediation. Peter replied by breaking off diplomatic relations with England and launching new attacks on Sweden. Destructive raids on the Swedish mainland were carried out in 1719, 1720, and 1721. The Swedish government was powerless to halt the Russian attacks, and none of Sweden's allies was prepared to risk war with Russia. At last, in April, 1721, through the intercession of the French ambassador in St. Petersburg, Russians and Swedes reopened negotiations at Nystadt.

Disappointed so many times in his efforts to conclude a treaty with the Swedes, Peter was prepared for the negotiations to break down yet again. He was traveling north to inspect the frontier near Vyborg in September, 1721, when couriers overtook him. They brought him the news that on August 30 his envoys had signed a treaty of peace with Sweden on his terms. The Swedes had ceded in perpetuity

the Baltic states of Livonia, Estonia, Ingria, a part of Karelia, and the Vyborg district. For his part, Peter was committed to returning Finland to Sweden, to paying compensation for Livonia, and to making certain minor trading concessions.

The tsar wrote in excitement to Prince Vasily Dolgoruky of his triumphs: "All students of science normally finish their course in seven years: our schooling has lasted three times as long, but, praise God, it had all ended so well that it could not be better." He hurried toward St. Petersburg and sailed into the Neva—with drums beating, trumpets sounding, and cannon firing. The people of the city crowded to greet their tsar, and then all attended thanksgiving services in the Church of the Holy Trinity and other churches. He next set in motion a three-part celebration throughout the country.

As the date of the second celebration approached, government and religious leaders held a joint meeting at which they agreed unanimously to petition the tsar to take the title of Emperor Peter the Great. With some reluctance, for this curiously modest man was more concerned with the glorification of Russia than of himself, he finally agreed.

At the victory service in St. Petersburg on October 22, the thanksgiving was followed by the reading of the treaty and ratification. Lastly, a chancellor, Count Gabriel Golovkin, recounted the tsar's heroic endeavors: "Through which alone and by your tireless labors and leadership, we, your loyal

167

subjects have stepped from the darkness of ignorance onto the theatre of fame of the whole world and, so to speak, have moved from non-existence to existence, and have joined in the society of political peoples—for that and for winning a peace so renowned and so rewarding, how can we render our proper gratitude? And so that we may not be with shame before the whole world, we take it upon ourselves in the name of the All-Russian nation and of all ranks of the subjects of Your Majesty, humbly to pray you to be gracious to us and to agree, as a small mark of our acknowledgment of the blessings that you have brought to us and to the whole nation, to take the title—Father of the Fatherland, Peter the Great, Emperor of All Russia."

Though the West came to know—and admire—Peter as a military and political figure, his internal assault on old Muscovy was equally impressive. The great achievements against Russia's enemies had not distracted Peter from his reforms at home. In his energy he was like an elemental force, bewildering to his people, and he left no aspect of their lives untouched.

The change in the calendar, effective from January 1, 1700, marked the beginning of the new age. Russians had always calculated their calendar from the date, accepted in the Orthodox Church, of the creation of the world, and their new year began on September 1. Peter adopted the Protes-

tants' Julian calendar (ten days later in its calculations than the Gregorian reform calendar—which Roman Catholics had long since accepted).

For some years Peter's efforts at national reform were dictated mainly by the Northern War. The creation of the army and the navy had priority, and with the prosecution of the war the demands on Russia's financial resources became heavier. He adopted numerous expedients to increase revenues. He created a new class of officials, the *pribylshchiki*, whose function was to discover new means of raising revenues. (A servant, Alexei Kurbatov, became director of a municipal department as a reward for proposing a new stamp duty on legal documents.) Taxes and the trading monopolies of the state multiplied. Watermelons, beehives, cucumbers, boots, hats, and leather were a few of the objects that became subject to tax. In 1710 Peter began a review of the established system of direct taxation, whereby the main tax was levied on peasant households. In due course he ordered a new census and then introduced a personal tax, which fell chiefly on peasants and yielded even better fiscal results.

Peter recognized, however, that he could increase revenues substantially only by strengthening and expanding the economy. He promoted prospecting and the utilization of Russia's rich mineral resources, mostly iron and coal, and he encouraged the establishment of heavy industry. Some twenty

Even after his death Peter continued to be lampooned, especially in the various versions of this widely circulated lubok *called "How the Mice Buried the Cat." The trussed-up fat cat is a sarcastic allusion to the tsar, while the gleeful mice in the funeral cortege represent the Russian people reveling in their release from oppression. Some tote instruments—drums, balalaikas, bagpipes—that diverted Peter on even the most solemn occasions; others mimic his undisciplined appetites by carrying food, beer, vodka, and other delights. The crutch-bearing rodent refers to the Russians wounded in his frequent wars, and the "foreign-born mouse" (49) driving a bun-filled sleigh satirizes his second wife, the ample-bosomed Catherine.*

small foundries existed at the time of his accession; he developed seventy-five new iron and brass foundries, far larger in scale and several of them in the industrial region of the Urals. He was also active in establishing light industries, including textile mills, leather works, gunpowder mills, glass and china works. Though his plans suffered delays and setbacks, mainly because of the lack of experienced workmen, some two hundred twenty new industries were in production, and many articles, previously imported, were being manufactured in Russia by the end of his reign.

The visits to Archangel and then to Amsterdam and London had made him realize the importance of foreign commerce. He was tireless in encouraging and compelling merchants to greater activity. During his reign the volume of Russia's foreign trade quadrupled, with St. Petersburg gradually taking precedence over Archangel as the leading center of trade with western Europe.

Government administration was cumbersome, corrupt, and incompetent, and over the years Peter labored to make it more efficient. He was only partially successful; but the system he introduced was to endure in all its main aspects until 1917.

One of his first administrative reforms, introduced in 1707, divided the country into eight provinces. The immediate purpose was to improve financial management and

to lessen the crippling overcentralization. But it soon had to be modified, since it all but left the country without a central government. On the eve of his departure for the disastrous Pruth campaign, he established a senate of nine favorites; they were to hold legislative powers, especially in his absence. The new institution functioned ineffectively, so Peter created the office of inspector-general of *ukazy*, and even posted officers of the guard to ensure that the Senators behaved with dignity and carried out their duties. In 1722 he appointed a procurator-general, responsible to him alone, to supervise the work of the Senate, which gradually began to function more effectively.

The old *prikazy*, or central administrative offices, were another weakness. They were not capable of dealing with the greatly increased volume and complexity of government business. The collegiate system, found in many countries of northern Europe and in England—by which the functions of a minister were carried out by a board—impressed Peter. The advantage of the collegiate board over the ministerial system was that rule by committee restricted possibilities of corruption and the arbitrary power of a single minister. In 1717, after some five years of study and preparation, Peter established nine colleges to run the empire's foreign, judicial, economic, military, commercial, and industrial affairs. As with the Senate, the colleges were beset with problems in their

first years, but eventually they settled down with some improvement in the administration.

In all his reforms Peter was hampered not only by the conservatism of his people but also by their inexperience and ignorance. He introduced numerous schemes for training and educating young people, and strove to inculcate upon them a sense of service. He himself felt strongly that he served the nation, and he exacted the same duty from his people. He abolished the privileged position the nobility had always enjoyed, substituting the Table of Ranks, which created, in effect, a bureaucratic hierarchy open not only to the landowning class but to talented and ambitious persons of humble birth. The Table classified all officers and officials in fourteen parallel grades. Without exception, all had to start in the lowest grade and work their way up by service. On reaching a specific grade in the hierarchy, all persons acquired the titles and rights of the old nobility, and only through service could such status be acquired.

Education was, however, the basic need, if the people were to serve efficiently and if the quality of Russian life was to be raised. Peter persevered with his early policy of sending chosen young men to study abroad. But he also engaged hundreds of foreign officers and experts to serve in Russia, directing them to "teach the Russian people without reserve and diligently." In 1701 he established the first secular school in Russia, the School of Mathematics and Navigation, under Henry Farquharson, a young mathematician from Aberdeen University. In 1714 he made it compulsory for the sons of the nobility to attend the naval, the engineering, the artillery, or the medical academies in St. Petersburg. But the mass of the people remained illiterate.

The range of Peter's innovations and reforms was astonishing. He had the old Church Slavonic alphabet and orthography replaced with a simpler "civil Russian" system, and Arabic numbers substituted for the less workable Slavic ones. He encouraged the printing of books of all kinds, commissioning new works as well as the translation of foreign-language books. His reign marked the beginning of Russia's secular literature. (Peter's personal library was to provide the nucleus of the library of the Academy of Sciences, which he planned in detail and which was inaugurated shortly after his death.) Hospitals, institutions for the care of unwanted children and of the aged, town planning and the laying out of gardens, and the organization of fire-fighting services were among the projects that he promoted actively. He also drafted rules of good citizenship and even insisted on the social emancipation of women of the upper classes.

The Orthodox clergy, the bulwark of conservatism, stood in opposition to many of the reforms, and Peter acted cautiously in dealing with them. On the death of Joachim, the

Vodka was offered as enticement to visitors at St. Petersburg's Kunstkamer, or Cabinet of Curios (pictured above), where such treasures as the "skin of a Frenchman tanned and stuffed" shared exhibit space with fossils, minerals, and such samples of taxidermy as a zebra. Moscow's Printing House (far left) and simple presses, like the one at left, also played a part in Peter's efforts to enlighten his people.

old patriarch, in March, 1690, Peter had appointed as his successor Adrian, a mild, saintly old man; but after Adrian's death in 1700, the patriarchate was allowed to remain vacant. Peter was always on guard against the patriarch using the great authority of his office to rally popular opinion against the reforms. Finally, in 1721, at Peter's instigation, the Spiritual Regulation was proclaimed and, applying the collegiate system, it established the Holy Governing Synod in place of the patriarchate, with special responsibility for cleansing the Church of abuses and encouraging it to play a more positive role in improving the lives of the people and in serving the welfare of the nation.

At the personal and the national level the great tragedy in Peter's life arose from his conflict with his son. Tsarevich Alexei, born in 1690 to Peter's first wife, had grown into a weak and cowardly individual, with the outlook of a conservative Muscovite. His childhood had been difficult. He had spent the first eight years of his life in his mother's care, surrounded by her family and supporters, who were strongly critical of his father's way of life and policies. Entrusted to Peter's sister Natalya after his mother's banishment, Alexei began to be trained for the responsibilities of the throne. Peter ordered that his heir should be present at the storming of fortresses and gave him tasks—such as supervising the mobilization of recruits and the organization of supplies—that

exceeded his abilities. He expected the tsarevich to render the same dedicated service that he himself gave, and instead of encouragement and understanding, he treated the youth with Spartan firmness. Alexei, overawed by his father, was increasingly obsessed with feelings of inadequacy.

In the summer of 1709 the nineteen-year-old prince was sent to Dresden to study, and then to Karlsbad to take the waters, for drink was already undermining his health. In Karlsbad he was introduced to Princess Charlotte of Wolfenbuttel, the charming and dutiful girl who had been chosen to become his wife. Alexei was appalled by the idea of marriage with a foreigner, worse still a Protestant. He did not dare, however, to oppose his father's will, and they were married on October 14, 1711. She bore him a daughter, Natalya, and then on October 12, 1715, a son named Peter Alexeevich. She was just twenty-one years old when, seven days after giving birth, she died.

Disgusted by his son's lax way of life and callous treatment of his wife, of whom Peter was fond, he sent Alexei an ultimatum shortly after the funeral. In this letter he threatened to cut him off from the succession "like a gangrenous growth, and do not imagine," he continued, "that because you are my only son I write this merely to frighten; in truth by the will of God I will do it, for as I have not spared and do not spare myself for my country and my people, how

171

should I spare you who are useless? Better a worthy stranger than an unworthy son!"

Peter's anger struck terror in his son. He hastened to reply in a letter of abject humility and asked to be allowed to renounce the succession. Peter considered the request mere subterfuge. He knew that after his death the tsarevich would be called on to rule and that his renunciation would be set aside. Peter sent a further warning, after which Alexei requested permission to become a monk. Calling on him unexpectedly, Peter spoke kindly and asked him to reconsider his decision to take holy orders. "That's not easy for a young man," Peter said. "Think again without haste, then write to me what you want to do . . . I'll wait another six months."

Peter was abroad during these months, and Alexei spent the time in idleness. A reminder was sent from Copenhagen that the day of decision was approaching. The prospect of facing his father was more than he could endure. On September 26, 1716, he set out from St. Petersburg, accompanied by his mistress, a peasant girl named Yefrosinia, and four servants. On the way he adopted disguise and made secretly for Vienna, where he begged the emperor to hide him, saying that his father was bent on his murder. His presence was an acute embarrassment to the imperial government; but the emperor felt that he could not deny asylum, especially as he believed the tsarevich's story. Attempts to hide him in the Tyrol and then in Naples were, however, of no avail. Peter's trusted officers tracked him down, and the exile, upon promises of the tsar's pardon, finally agreed to return to Russia.

Alexei arrived in Moscow toward the end of January, 1718. He was summoned to the Kremlin a few days later, and there, in the presence of his father, the Senate, the Church hierarchy, and the nobility, he solemnly renounced the succession and swore to acknowledge as heir to the throne his half brother, the new tsarevich, Peter Petrovich, born to Catherine on October 29, 1715. He was then allowed to live in freedom in St. Petersburg and there await the return of Yefrosinia, who was en route from Naples at a more leisurely pace because she was pregnant. On her arrival she gave birth to her baby. Four weeks later she was interrogated.

Alexei's formal renunciation of the succession had not eliminated Peter's suspicions that he would claim the throne and then work to destroy all that had been achieved. Peter himself questioned Yefrosinia, and she spoke readily of Alexei's frequently expressed hatred of his father's policies. She confirmed that he intended to claim the throne, to abandon St. Petersburg and live in Moscow, to leave the navy to rot, and to eliminate from the national life all innovations based on foreign ideas. Alexei was confronted by his mistress; breaking down, he confessed that her evidence was the truth. He was then questioned further, this time under severe torture.

Determined not to try his son himself, Peter convened a court, comprising one hundred twenty-seven of the most eminent men in the land, and he ordered them to try the tsarevich impartially and without fear—even to the extent of treating Alexei leniently if they considered it justified.

However, the evidence of his treason was conclusive, and the court was unanimous in passing the death sentence. But Alexei had been so savagely flayed during the interrogations that he died before the sentence could be carried out.

This personal tragedy did not, however, deflect Peter from his goals. In 1719 he sent an embassy to the Chinese emperor, with the purpose of establishing commercial relations with China. His initiative came to nothing, however, because the Chinese had no interest in trade with Russia. Peter was disappointed, but he was active in promoting exploration of the Pacific coast; he annexed Kamchatka Peninsula and the Kurile Islands. He also sent an expedition by land to chart the shores of the Sea of Okhotsk and to ascertain whether Asia and America were joined. The expedition failed to resolve this problem, and in 1725 he sent Captain Vitus Bering on his first voyage east—a search that was to lead to the discovery of the Bering Straits.

The first attempts to open up trade with Persia and India were also unsuccessful. In 1722, impressed by reports that Persia was near to collapse and afraid that Turkey might occupy the Persian provinces adjoining the Caspian Sea, Peter took command of his army in Astrakhan and embarked on the Persian campaign. He was uneasy, as though fearing a repetition of the Pruth campaign, especially when in the spring of the following year war with Turkey threatened. But in June, 1723, to his great relief, his envoy signed the Treaty of Partition in Constantinople, peace returned, and Russia gained land along the west coast of the Caspian Sea.

Peter was now over fifty. He still worked with the same dynamic energy. John Bell, a Scot who was a member of his staff during the Persian campaign, observed that "he could dispatch more affairs in a morning than a house full of Senators can do in a month." But his health was deteriorating. He suffered from chronic strangury and stone, which were soon to cause his death. In these years he drew comfort from the companionship of Catherine, whom he had married privately in 1707. She had earned his deep gratitude, especially for her staunch support during the Pruth and Persian campaigns. On February 19, 1712, he publicly celebrated their marriage, and on May 7, 1724, in a magnificent ceremonial with full regalia, he crowned her empress.

The problem of the succession was unresolved. Peter Petrovich, his son by Catherine, had died. Peter the Great feared that the elevation of his grandson, Alexei's son, would lead to a resurgence of Muscovite conservatism. On February 5, 1722, he issued an *ukaz* in which, following the precedent of Ivan III, he decreed that the sovereign should appoint whomsoever he chose to succeed to the throne. But, on January 26, 1725, still unable to make a choice, he died.

Far from the bells, boyars, and bulbous domes of Moscow, St. Petersburg was Russia's longed-for "window on Europe." The archway of the former General Staff Building opens onto the plaza before the Winter Palace, the imperial family's residence until 1917.

"Emerging from a rather glum wood, all of a sudden the river curves round and . . . there we were in front of the Imperial Town. On either bank rose splendid edifices grouped together; towers, with gilded spires shaped like pyramids, rose up here and there, and there were vessels with streaming pennons." Such was the brilliant spectacle that met Count Francesco Algarotti's gaze as he approached St. Petersburg by sea in 1740, only twenty-eight years after it had become Russia's new capital. Built on a group of wind-swept islands at the mouth of the Neva (a Finnish word for "swamp"), it was Russia's point of entry into the eighteenth century. From the day in May, 1703, when Peter the Great declared, "Here shall be a town," and began supervising the construction of the Fortress of St. Peter and St. Paul (illustrated above), work progressed unremittingly. His fiat brought tens of thousands of peasants, soldiers, and prisoners to work the insalubrious, swampy site that would become a burial ground for most of them. The tsar also imported the citizenry, specifying the type of house to be built by each social class. By the middle of the century, thanks to the efforts of French, Italian, Dutch, and German architects, St. Petersburg was already "one of the wonders of the world." Sankt Piterburkh, the Dutch name by which the city was first known, was heterogeneous and secular from the start, and in marked contrast to monastery-ringed Moscow, a circle of magnificent palaces, such as Peterhof (whose Great Cascade is pictured opposite), soon adorned its environs. Upper-class women, newly released from the *terem*, wore the damasks and brocades favored by their European counterparts, and danced, played games, and conversed at assemblies, a type of entertainment that Peter quaintly defined as "a number of persons who gather together either to amuse themselves or to discuss their affairs." (Some ladies, who found a touch of Old Muscovy irresistable, wore fur-lined coats under their silk finery.) And whereas the brilliance of St. Petersburg society was often superficial—the finest houses were permeated with mildew and foul canal odors—Peter could remark with satisfaction: "We have lifted the curtain drawn in front of our country's curiosity, which deprived it of communication with the whole world." His successors continued to glorify his legacy: Elizabeth turned the city into a baroque extravaganza; Catherine the Great and her heirs gave it the neoclassical aspect that still predominates in Leningrad (as the city was renamed in 1924 in honor of Vladimir Lenin).

THE TWELVE COLLEGES, *shown in this eighteenth-century lithograph, are a sample of the early St. Petersburg architecture, built when few of the unlit, muddy streets were even cobbled, and prowling wolves occasionally devoured helpless citizens in broad daylight. The extant colleges, begun in 1722 by the tsar's architect general, Domenico*

Trezzini, exemplify the Petrine baroque style, a Russianized adaptation of the baroque architecture then favored in northern Europe. A row of twelve three-story pavilions, they originally housed the various departments of government; in the early nineteenth century they were slightly modified and assigned to the newly founded university.

A DESCRIPTION OF ST. PETERSBURG

from A New Royal and Authentic System of Universal Geography *by Rev. Thomas Bankes*

Building a city under the most primitive conditions, and on land that was thought to be uninhabitable by man, was a herculean task. An eighteenth-century description follows.

The city of Petersburg . . . is situated between Ingria and Finland, in a fenny island, surrounded by the river Nieva, in 60 deg. north lat. and 31 deg. 34 min. east long.

A late traveller, who calls this city a creation of the present century, says further of it, "I am struck with a pleasing astonishment while I wander among havens, streets, and public buildings, which have risen, as by enchantment, within the memory of men still alive; and have converted the marshy islands of the Nieva into one of the most magnificent cities on the earth. The imagination, aided by so many visible objects, rises to the wondrous founder, and beholds, in idea, the titulary genius of Peter yet hovering over the child of his own production, and viewing, with a parent's fondness, its rising palaces and temples . . . . The Muscovites, (Russians,) wrapt in the most profound barbarism, secluded by their illiberal prejudices from an intercourse with European nations, and equally the slaves of superstition and long prescription, were forcibly torn from this night of ignorance, and compelled to accept of refinement and civilization.

The island on which this fine city has been so wonderfully raised, was nothing but a heap of mud in the short summer of these climates, and a frozen pool in winter, not to be approached by land but by passing over wild forests and deep morasses, and had been till then the habitation of bears and wolves, till it was, in 1703, inhabited by above 300,000 Russian, Tartar, Cossack, &c. peasants, whom the Czar called together from all corners of his vast empire, some near 1200 miles; and these made a beginning of this work. He was obliged to break through forests, open ways, dry up moors, and raise banks, before he could lay the foundation. The whole was a force upon nature. At first the workmen had neither sufficient provisions, or even pickaxes, spades, wheelbarrows, planks, or huts to shelter in; yet the work went on so expeditiously, that, in five months, the fortress was raised; though earth thereabouts was so scarce, that the greatest part of the laborers carried it in the skirts of their cloaths, or in bags made of old rags and mats, barrows being then unknown to them. It is computed full 100,000 perished at the place; for the country had been desolated by war, and supplies by Ladoga lake were often retarded by contrary winds. The Czar himself drew the main plan. While the fortress was going on, the city began gradually to be built. He obliged many of the nobility, merchants, and tradesmen, to go and live there, and trade in such commodities as they were ordered. Provisions being scarce, and conveniencies wanting, the place, at first, was not at all agreeable to persons of distinction, who had in Moscow large buildings, and seats in the country, with fish-ponds, gardens, and other rural elegancies. However, he little regarded the complaints of those who only considered their own ease. The boyars (nobility) brought great retinues with them; and merchants and shopkeepers soon found their account settling here. Many Swedes, Finlanders, and Livonians, from towns nearly depopulated by the wars, continued here. Artificers, mechanics, and seamen, were invited hither, to encourage shipping; who, having worked out the time agreed on for the Czar, were hired by the boyars; and also built for themselves, and settled; each man being allowed to pitch on the spot he liked. In one year 30,000 houses were erected, and, in two or three more, double the number, which doubtless are very much increased since. Some, indeed, but chiefly in the . . . suberbs, are mean, and may be taken to pieces in two or three hours, and set up elsewhere. . . .

Petersburg is amazingly increased in size within these fifty years. At the death of Peter the Great, it did not contain 80,000 inhabitants; and now the Russians assert that there are 500,000; but this is deemed an exaggeration. It covers a very great extent of land and water. The streets are some of them very broad, long, and with canals in the middle of them; and others are planted in the Dutch fashion. . . .

Among the public buildings there are many extremely worthy the attention of a traveller, particularly the dock-yards, the naval magazines, the arsenal, foundry, admiralty, &c. without insisting on the imperial palace, the cathedral, or many churches. . . .

The grand market-place is on the southernmost part of the city, with many warehouses, to deposit all kinds of commodities and merchandize, both domestic and foreign, for sale. It is a large square, with four entries, and a range of shops on each side, both within and without, with covered galleries, to secure those who frequent it from the rain.

Woolen and linen manufactories were set up here, of which the latter is brought to great perfection, as we may observe by the linen of late imported from thence. Here is particularly a workhouse, where an old Dutch woman had 80 young nymphs under her care, who are taught, with a whip, how to handle the spinning-wheel; and several regulations are made for improving the plantations of hemp and flax. Paper-mills, and powder-mills, have also been erected, with laboratories for gunnery and fire-works; and other places for preparing salt-petre and brimstone. . . . A printing house is established, and news-papers are now as regularly printed as in other countries of Europe. Several useful books have been translated out of the High-Dutch, and printed; the government encouraging their subjects to enquire into the state of the world abroad, instead of keeping them in ignorance, according to their ancient maxims.

A placid Leningrad canal, the abiding symbol of Peter's dream to make his "paradise" a second Amsterdam

BALLET AND OPERA *at the Bolshoi, or Grand, Theater, pictured in this 1806 print, equaled or surpassed most European performances of the period and contributed to St. Petersburg's growing reputation as a cultural mecca. The old Bolshoi, which was replaced in 1860 by the Mariinsky (now Kirov) Theater, was designed in the French neo-*

classical manner. Its patrons were seated Russian-style, by rank: the first four rows were for high aristocracy and top officials; then came bankers, foreigners, artists, and other notables. Merchants sat no nearer than the sixth row. Outside, patient coachmen kept warm and dry by huddling around fires burning in open kiosks.

ICE SLIDING ON NEVSKY PROSPEKT, *the city's three-mile-long grand boulevard, was one of the highlights of the* *St. Petersburg carnival. The sliding enthusiast would climb to the top of an ice-coated wooden "snow mountain"* *and, perched on a flat sled, whisk to the bottom (in summer pleasure-seekers rode down in carts). This sport was*

also the rage at court, where everyone was forced to try it. One flabbergasted eighteenth-century English lady wrote home: "I was terrified out of my wits for fear of being obliged to go down this shocking place, for I had not only the dread of breaking my neck, but of being exposed to indecency too frightful to think of without horror."

METROPOLITAN MUSEUM OF ART, WHITTELSEY FUND, 1958

the city: "*A hundred years have passed, and the young city . . . / Rises in proud magnificence . . . / Along these busy banks are ranged / Massive and graceful palaces and towers, / And ships from every corner of the earth / Hasten to these richly laden quays. . . . / How fair thou art, O city of Peter, / Standing unshakeable, like Russia herself!*"

6

Age of Splendor

The Russian throne changed hands seven times in the thirty-seven years after Peter's death; and on each occasion the guards—since Peter's time a privileged caste with powers extending far beyond their military duties—were instrumental in choosing the tsar. Peter Alexeevich, the son of Tsarevich Alexei and the only remaining male representative of the Romanov line, was supported by the old nobility and all who had disliked Peter's Westernizing policies. But the men of ability who had served Peter and whom he had ennobled despite their humble origins knew that they would suffer if the old Muscovite party gained power. Menshikov and Tolstoy, two of Peter's foremost lieutenants, feared that Peter Alexeevich's accession would lead to their disgrace and banishment, for they had taken a prominent part in the prosecution of Tsar Alexei. Their candidate was Catherine, Peter's widow, and since she was popular with the guards and the army generally, she was proclaimed empress.

Catherine reigned briefly. Childbearing and a strenuous life with Peter had worn down her sturdy peasant constitution. Moreover, she needed a master like Peter to direct her,

The future Catherine the Great, the feeble-minded Grand Duke Peter, and their weakling son Paul are depicted in this flattering portrait by R. M. Lisiewska. At the time of the 1756 family grouping, the German princess was priming for the role of empress of Russia.

and she began drinking heavily and leading a debauched life. The governing of the nation rested in the hands of Menshikov. At the pinnacle of his career, Menshikov was hated and feared by most Russians for his arrogant and ruthless exercise of power. The Saxon ambassador reported: "Never did anyone so shake with fear even before the deceased autocratic Emperor Peter I as they are forced to tremble now before Menshikov."

Menshikov was sensitive, however, to the unrest that was mounting throughout the country and to the rumors of plots to elevate Tsarevich Peter. To ensure his position, he proposed the creation of a Supreme Privy Council. It had six members of whom three—Prince Alexander Menshikov, Prince Dmitry Golitsyn, and Count Andrei Ostermann—held the real power. The Council's stated purpose was "to relieve Her Majesty of the heavy burden of ruling"; and it became at once the supreme governing body.

The Council's policy, endorsed by Catherine, was to carry on the work of Peter the Great. But the momentum was gone, and the nation was looking for relief from the pressures of his reign. The poll tax, levied on all male "souls" save those exempted by privilege, burdened the peasantry; in 1725 more than one million rubles in taxes were uncollected and many peasants were falling further into arrears. Finally, the Privy Council reduced the tax and moderated other

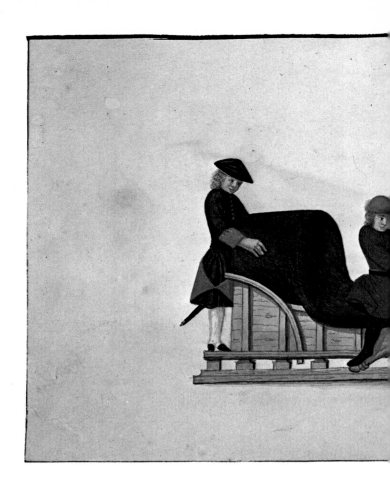

*The pastimes enjoyed by villagers remained the same for centuries.
In these eighteenth-century water colors by an English traveler, men*

demands that were making the lives of the peasants intolerable—minor palliatives at best.

On May 7, 1727, the day after Catherine's death, the imperial family, the Supreme Privy Council, the Senate, the Holy Synod, and the *generalitet* (those in the four highest grades of the Table of Ranks) assembled at the palace to hear the reading of her testament on the succession. Peter Alexeevich was to become Tsar Peter II; but during his minority the Supreme Privy Council—enlarged to include his older sisters, Tsarevni Anna and Elizabeth—was to wield all power. If Peter had no heirs, then Anna and her heirs or, failing that, Elizabeth and her heirs would succeed.

During the first weeks of Peter's reign Menshikov continued to be the most powerful man in the land. Peter, although only eleven years of age, proved to be headstrong and conscious of his privileges, and he hated Menshikov. In this he was encouraged by the Dolgoruky, who, notwithstanding Menshikov's blandishments, were determined to dispose of him. On September 8, 1727, officers of the guard arrested Menshikov; he was subsequently stripped of all honors, property, and authority, and deported to Siberia, where he died in disgrace two years later.

In January, 1728, Peter moved with his court from St. Petersburg to Moscow, where he was greeted with the magnificent ceremonial that had been extended to the old Mus-

covite tsars. To many Russians the change portended the restoration of Moscow; the tsar was said to be abandoning the new Westward-looking capital city and rejecting his grandfather's policies. The boy-tsar probably had slight understanding of the significance attached to the move. His interests were riding and hunting, and little else. When his sister, Natalya, died in 1728, he fell more completely under the influence of the Dolgoruky, whose manipulations were even more harmful than those of Menshikov. He became betrothed to Catherine, the seventeen-year-old daughter of Prince Alexei Dolgoruky, and the marriage was to take place on January 19, 1730. A few days earlier, however, Peter succumbed to smallpox, and he died on the day appointed for the ceremony. Members of the nobility and gentry had thronged to Moscow to be present at the tsar's wedding only to find that they were attending his funeral.

The Supreme Privy Council met hurriedly to consider the succession, which was again contested, despite Catherine's earlier testament. Prince Dmitry Golitsyn was now emerging as the most influential member of the Council. A man of outstanding intelligence and a student of Western political theory, he was eager that Russia be modernized—but without abandoning the traditional values and, above all, without diminishing the powers and privileges of the old nobility. Golitsyn rejected the undeniably strong claims of Elizabeth,

in traditional long shirts, leggings, and bast shoes, and women in homespun sarafans, take part in rustic sports, including a sledge ride.

Peter the Great's daughter, and of her nephew, the young duke of Holstein. He maintained that the peasant girl who had become Empress Catherine I while his first wife still lived could not have been legally married to Peter the Great. The children of Catherine were therefore illegitimate and could not succeed to the throne. He proposed, instead, that since the male line from Peter the Great had died out, they must turn to the branch of the Romanov family represented by the descendants of Peter's half brother and co-tsar, Ivan V. Of Ivan's three surviving daughters, Anna, the widowed duchess of Courland, was his choice. Anna had been married to the duke of Courland when she was seventeen, but within a year of the wedding the nobleman died. She had languished during the following nineteen years in Courland. Prevented by political reasons from remarrying, she had taken as her lover first Peter Bestuzhev-Ryumin, the Russian representative, and then Ernst Johann Biron, the grandson of a local stableman. Biron was soon wielding strong influence over her. Dependent mainly on money from Russia, she was constantly writing to Catherine, Menshikov, the Golitsyn and the Dolgoruky, and others, asking for help.

The Senate, the Holy Synod, and the *generalitet* were called into session at the Kremlin palace to ratify the proposal that Anna succeed to the throne. No mention was made, however, of the secret discussions in the Privy Council concerning the "Conditions," drafted by Dmitry Golitsyn, which limited her powers as autocrat. Prince Vasily Dolgoruky was dispatched posthaste to her estate at Mitau (Yelgava) in Courland to inform Anna of her election and to procure her endorsement of the Council's terms.

Dolgoruky's news came as a miraculous release from the penury and humiliation of her life in Courland. She readily agreed to the "Conditions," which concluded: "And if I do not fulfill this promise then I will be deprived of the Russian throne." In signing, she also promised not to marry or nominate a successor to the throne without the permission of the Supreme Privy Council. In particular, she would not declare war, make peace, impose taxes or expend state revenues, grant military or civil appointments above colonel or its equivalent in the Table of Ranks; she would not deprive members of the gentry of property or honors without trial; she would not confer titles or estates on Russians or foreigners without the authority of the Privy Council. Finally, she had to relinquish to the Privy Council control of the guards and all other armed forces.

Anna accepted Dolgoruky's assurances that the compact represented the will of the Russian people. With the formalities completed, she set forth for Moscow on January 29, 1730. No sooner had she arrived, however, than she discovered that the agreement was the work of only a small

minority, the members of the Privy Council itself. On February 25 some eight hundred of the leading men met in the great audience chamber and petitioned her to appoint an assembly to draft a new and more effective system of government. However, Anna sent for the "Conditions" she had signed in Mitau and publicly tore them up. Had these drastic restrictions on autocratic power prevailed, they would no doubt have amounted to a Russian Magna Charta. They contained the beginning of a movement that might have produced a constitutional monarchy—such as had developed in England. But the old nobility was no more interested in supporting Golitsyn's plan than Catherine was. Other classes feared that oligarchic rule—such as Poland and Sweden had suffered—would be more unbearable than the rule of the most arbitrary autocrat. Common to all but a few was the fundamental belief that the throne was the sole source of power and the true center of the nation.

Anna was now thirty-seven years old. She was coarse and masculine in appearance and in her pleasures. Of her entry into the capital an eyewitness wrote: "It was terrible to see: she has a repulsive face; she is so tall that, when she walks among her officers, she is a head taller, and she is exceedingly fat." Her chief interests were shooting and riding. Loaded guns were kept at the windows of the palace so that she could bring down passing birds. She maintained a large

troupe of dwarfs and freaks at court and took a sadistic pleasure in the deformed and grotesque. A favorite entertainment was to humiliate members of the old nobility. Prince Mikhail Golitsyn, who committed the error of converting to Roman Catholicism, was once required to sit on a basket of eggs and cackle like a hen until they were hatched. When his wife died, Anna chose one of her freaks as his new bride and forced the unfortunate pair to spend a chilly wedding night in a palace built for them entirely of ice.

Anna moved the court back to St. Petersburg in 1732. She now openly declared her mistrust of the Russian gentry and her preference for foreigners in her service. Soon Germans were holding all the most powerful offices in government and the army. She made some attempts to appease the Russian upper classes: she strengthened the Senate and abolished the Supreme Privy Council, which had effectively excluded all but a handful of their number from power. But then she set up a new central administrative body known as the Cabinet of Her Imperial Majesty. At its head she placed Count Ostermann, a Westphalian of remarkable ability whom Peter the Great had promoted. Another powerful figure was Count Burkhard von Münnich of Bavaria, whom she made president of the War College and commander in chief of the army. Anna's favorite, Ernst Biron, was named lord chamberlain. Though this title conferred no real powers of its own,

Empress Anna created the Russian court in imitation of the pomp and spectacle of Versailles, sponsoring fetes and masquerades (like the one opposite), at which elegant courtiers danced the quadrille, gambled, and sipped French wines. Less refined merriment was provided by Anna's resident troupe of buffoons; dwarfs, idiots, and cripples, as well as persons who had incurred royal wrath, were retained to perform on command. At elaborate fireworks displays, like that shown at right, all St. Petersburg shared in the royal fun.

Biron was, in fact, given charge of the government's operations. Arrogant, vain, and cruel, he was hated by all Russians. He controlled, indirectly, the Chancellery for Secret Investigations, and through this office he was responsible for the interrogation, torture, and execution of no less than twenty thousand Russians suspected, usually on false evidence, of criticizing the empress. His reign of terror—the Bironovshchina—gave its name to the last years of Anna's rule.

Shortly before her death, in October, 1740, Anna designated Ivan, the two-month-old son of her niece Anna, duchess of Mecklenberg, as her successor. Biron was to act as the infant's regent. The patience of the Russians was near exhaustion. They had suffered constant humiliation at the hands of Anna's German adventurers without rebelling, for she, at least, held legitimate title; but this new arrangement was completely unacceptable. It took little more than a year for Tsarevna Elizabeth, the daughter of Peter the Great, to become the new champion of the Russian people.

On the night of November 24, 1741, Elizabeth traveled swiftly by sledge—accompanied by a small band of friends—to the barracks at Preobrazhenskoe. At once the guards rallied to her, swearing oaths of loyalty. They then rode with her to the Winter Palace, where they arrested the infant tsar, Ivan VI, together with his parents. Special detachments of guards took Ostermann, Münnich, and other Germans into custody. On the day after this bloodless revolution Elizabeth made a ceremonial entry into St. Petersburg, and the Senate, the Holy Synod, the *generalitet*, and the army then took the oath of allegiance to her as empress and autocrat.

Elizabeth was the youngest daughter of Peter the Great, born in December, 1709, soon after his great victory at Poltava. Her schooling was left to churchmen, who taught her in the spirit of old Muscovy. Although her formal education was slight and she would read only sacred books, she acquired a working knowledge of English, German, and French; and in state affairs she was often clever.

In character Elizabeth recalled her grandfather, Tsar Alexei. She could be quick-tempered, forthright, and, when Russian interests or her own dignity were harmed, severe. She was remarkable, however, for her generosity, and, as one contemporary wrote, for her "tender, indeed bewitching, kindness." She was free of malice and sadism, which Empress Anna had exhibited. She refused to allow Ostermann and Münnich, and others among the arrested German favorites, to be tortured and executed, and early in her reign she abolished the death penalty.

Her court was the scene of constant entertainments. As she reigned in a time of relative peace, there was time and talent available to support more autonomous activities in the arts than in Peter the Great's era. The first play to be per-

Visiting Russia from 1758 to 1763, the French artist Jean-Baptiste le Prince put on canvas his romantic impressions of Slavic exoticisms. Left, amid sumptuous oriental surroundings, musicians produce the melancholy strains of a folk melody. Opposite, at a time when rich robes and pompous ceremony took precedence over piety in the Orthodox Church, a wealthy family smugly watches its infant being baptized by total immersion in a silver font. Upon observing this sacrament, an Englishman wrote: "Parents are . . . very eager, even at the hazard of their children's lives, to embrace the blessed occasion."

formed in Russia had been staged by members of Moscow's Foreign Quarter for her grandfather, Tsar Alexei. Peter had experimented briefly with didactic drama, glorifying Russian history as a means of public instruction; but his efforts had attracted little attention among his subjects. Elizabeth's enthusiasm was unlimited. Though her own taste ran to Italian comic opera and ballet, she encouraged native developments. Alexander Sumarokov, an actor-manager-playwright, wrote and produced the first Russian tragedy in 1747. Mikhail Lomonosov, the great Russian poet, wrote plays. Fedor Volkov, a gifted actor-manager, formed his own troupe of players. Under Elizabeth's patronage it became Russia's first public theater in August, 1756, with permanent headquarters in St. Petersburg.

In architecture Elizabeth was fortunate to inherit the services of Bartolomeo Rastrelli, who had been responsible for much of the important building in Russia during the previous twenty years. Elizabeth gave him the opportunity to express his genius in the design of such magnificent structures as the new Summer Palace, the Anichkov, Vorontsov, and Stroganov palaces, as well as in the reconstruction and refurbishing of the Great Palace in Tsarskoe Selo and of the Winter Palace in St. Petersburg.

In her choice of friends and advisers Elizabeth was also fortunate. Alexei Razumovsky, the Ukrainian peasant whose

fine singing voice had brought him to the attention of the court, became her lover. It was said he had married her secretly, and remained loyal to her until her death. Ivan Shuvalov, the chief favorite in the later years of Elizabeth's reign, was also a man of wide culture, who corresponded with Voltaire and the Encyclopedists, and worked to promote art and education in Russia.

Like the Razumovsky, Ivan Shuvalov was genial and without interest in the struggles for power at court. By contrast, his cousins, both colonels in the imperial guard, were very much involved in the affairs of state. Alexander Shuvalov was feared as the head of the Chancellery for Secret Investigations, but he served Elizabeth honestly. Peter Shuvalov was the most ambitious and able member of the family. He made important contributions to the stability of the nation in several fields. The national finances were chaotic. The amounts of uncollected head tax increased annually, and the nation suffered from chronic budget deficits. His chief reform was to reduce the poll tax and to increase indirect taxation, especially on salt and alcohol, which were state monopolies. He abolished many of the internal tariffs that handicapped the growth of trade, and by a series of army reforms prepared the nation for the heavy burdens that were to come from Elizabeth's wars.

During most of Elizabeth's reign Alexei Bestuzhev-

Ryumin was her vice-chancellor in charge of foreign policy. Bestuzhev, whose father's rise in government service had been aided by an early liaison with Anna, was a man of great talent, but secretive, surly, and feared at court. Elizabeth was said to dislike him, though she respected his ability. Bestuzhev's foreign policy was based on alliance with Austria against Prussia and France. He also sought alliances with the maritime powers—England and Holland—against Prussia and with Austria and Poland-Saxony against the Ottoman Porte. His policies were to involve Russia in two wars during Elizabeth's reign: the first against Sweden; the second over the Austrian succession.

Frederick II, who had come to the Prussian throne in 1740, was the main cause of strife. He had promptly provoked a war with Austria by seizing Silesia. He was eager to strike again, this time to take Bohemia; but he hesitated, unsure how Russia would react. In order to distract Russia, Prussia and France persuaded Sweden to attack its eastern neighbor in the hope of recovering at least part of the Baltic lands annexed by Peter the Great. The Russian army quickly conquered southern Finland. The Swedes, admitting defeat, sued for peace in the fall of 1742; and by the Treaty of Abo, signed in the following year, Russia gained further territories on the Finnish mainland.

Russia did not take part in the War of the Austrian Succession (1740–48) until the last stages of the conflict. In 1746 Elizabeth renewed a twenty-year-old treaty of alliance with Austria. A Russian army marched to the Rhine in 1748 as a show of force. Meanwhile, the fury of diplomatic intrigues in St. Petersburg had intensified. The Prussian minister, Axel Mardefeld, and the French ambassador, the Marquis de la Chétardie, had not given up hope of discrediting Bestuzhev and drawing Russia into alliance with their countries. In addition, the prospective marriage of Elizabeth's heir apparent lent great hope to Prussian interests.

Elizabeth had chosen her nephew, Grand Duke Peter Fedorovich, as her successor. He was the son of her elder sister, Anna, who had married the duke of Holstein and had died in 1728. Soon after her coronation, Elizabeth had sent for him, intending to train and equip him for the throne. The fourteen-year-old Peter Fedorovich proved to be an unhealthy youth, mentally backward, and a German Lutheran at heart. Disappointed and concerned that he might be carried off by smallpox or some other illness, she decided to have him married early in hope that he would father a son. It was important that the bride be of noble blood and also that she not have family connections that would directly involve Russia in political commitments. Sofia, an insignificant princess from Anhalt-Zerbst, was chosen.

Frederick was delighted. He had special hopes that he

Empress Elizabeth, portrayed at left by Louis Caravaque, earned renown as a beautiful and seductive sovereign. Soon after her 1742 coronation at Moscow's Uspensky Cathedral, shown opposite, it became apparent that this eternal debutante was more adept at love affairs than affairs of state. Having narrowly escaped the fate of a nunnery under Empress Anna, the unmarried monarch was described as having "not one bit of nun's flesh about her," and as "a ravenous bacchanante whose skin sweats lasciviousness." In her pursuit of the gay life Elizabeth staged "metamorphoses," at which diplomats in petticoats danced with women in breeches. The future Catherine II admitted that Elizabeth "had the prettiest legs I have seen on any man." She displayed them costumed in such guises as a French musketeer, a Cossack, and a Dutch sailor—the last commemorating Peter the Great's stay in Holland.

would be able to influence the new empress toward an alliance with Prussia, which would secure his eastern flank and free him to attack Austria. When in January, 1744, Sofia and her mother, Princess Johanna, arrived in Berlin on their way to St. Petersburg, he briefed them on his expectations.

Sofia was accepted into the Orthodox Church and rebaptized with the name Catherine; then she was betrothed to Grand Duke Peter in the Uspensky Cathedral in the Moscow Kremlin. Already Elizabeth was aware of Princess Johanna's mischievous activities as the agent of the king of Prussia. The princess had regular meetings with Mardefeld, De la Chétardie, and others who were working to displace Vice-Chancellor Bestuzhev. Frustrated by their failure to make any progress, they blamed Elizabeth, reporting to their capitals that she was lightheaded, obstinate, and incapable of ruling. De la Chétardie was most outspoken in his dispatches, and he wrote warmly of Princess Johanna as the capable agent of the Prussian king. He suspected that Bestuzhev was intercepting his dispatches and having them copied, but he was so confident that no one could break the code in which they were written that he took no further precautions. However, Bestuzhev was managing to decipher every word, and he assembled a dossier of pertinent extracts that he submitted to Elizabeth. She exploded in anger. She reprimanded Princess Johanna and sent her back to Germany. De la Chétardie and

several of his associates were expelled. Grand Duke Peter and Catherine were watched even more closely than before.

Though Elizabeth had satisfied herself that Catherine was not directly involved in court intrigues, she continued to be angry about what she considered to be the young princess' failure in her marital duties: that she did not become pregnant. Elizabeth did not allow any affection she may have felt for Catherine to obscure the fact that the princess had been brought to Russia to marry the grand duke and bear sons to carry on the Romanov dynasty. Peter had nearly died of smallpox soon after Catherine's arrival in Russia. Elizabeth had nursed him herself, without thought of the risks. As soon as he had recovered sufficiently, the marriage was celebrated. Elizabeth's impatience was so great that she ordered her ladies in waiting to undress the sixteen-year-old Catherine and put her to bed early on their wedding night. Later, in her memoirs, Catherine recalled that at the time she had been innocent even of the difference between men and women and that she had sat up in bed not knowing what was expected of her. Her husband, then aged seventeen, was equally unprepared. During the following months Peter, who spent his time in childish games and who was already drinking heavily, began to avoid his young wife.

In 1752, after seven years of marriage, Catherine found herself strongly attracted to a young chamberlain, Sergei

Saltykov. He had married one of the empress' ladies in waiting only two years earlier, but this did not prevent his paying ardent court to Catherine. The grand duke knew about the affair, but showed no concern, as he was forming a close friendship with Elizabeth Vorontsova. There is evidence that the lady in waiting especially appointed by the empress to watch over Catherine's behavior connived at her affair with Saltykov, possibly under instructions. The circumstances will never be known; then, in September, 1754, after two miscarriages, Catherine gave birth to a son, who was christened Paul. Grand Duke Peter may have been the father, but it would seem highly unlikely.

At this time Vice-Chancellor Bestuzhev was hard at work to develop an alliance with England—an essential part of his long-range plans of thwarting Prussian expansion; but he had great difficulty in prevailing upon Elizabeth to endorse his efforts. In June, 1755, however, the new English ambassador, Sir Charles Hanbury-Williams, arrived in St. Petersburg. An elegant and persuasive diplomat, he made a favorable impression on her, and in September she signed an agreement, the main provision of which was that England would pay Russia an annual subsidy in return for a Russian undertaking to field an army of fifty-five thousand men to defend Hanover against attack by Prussia.

Elizabeth hesitated again when it came to ratifying the treaty, and in February the astonishing news reached St. Petersburg that Frederick of Prussia and George II of England had secretly joined in alliance. This formed part of a complete realignment of European powers at this time. England had become involved in a colonial war against France, and George was anxious to secure Hanover against a French attack. France had entered into alliance with Austria, its old enemy. In St. Petersburg pressures were increasing on Russia to join the new Austro-French alliance. Finally, in January, 1757, in spite of Bestuzhev's efforts to prevent it, Russia signed the Treaty of Versailles, thereby joining with Austria, France, Sweden, and Saxony against Prussia.

The gentry of St. Petersburg was now sharply divided between two factions. Elizabeth and official government policy were anti-Prussian, while the pro-Prussian party centered on the grand ducal court. The tsarina had been seriously ill that year, and it was in everyone's mind that on her death the grand duke, mentally unstable and an ardent supporter of Frederick, would immediately reverse her policy. His wife Catherine was assumed to share his outlook.

In the summer of 1756 Frederick invaded Saxony and launched the Seven Years War upon Europe. The Russian army was mobilized and in August of the following year inflicted a major defeat on the Prussians at Gross-Jägersdorf. But Stepan Apraksin, the Russian commander in chief, re-

195

treated across the Neman River instead of pursuing the defeated enemy. Elizabeth suspected him of deliberately
thwarting her policies. Apraksin was, indeed, in an awkward
position, for the empress was ailing and the Grand Duke
Peter was bitterly opposed to war. Apraksin knew that he
could expect instant dismissal and probably banishment to
Siberia as soon as Peter ascended the throne. His fears
quickened when in September, 1757, Elizabeth suffered a
severe stroke and for a time seemed on the point of death;
but she recovered quickly.

The destruction of Prussian power now became Elizabeth's obsession. She dismissed Bestuzhev and Apraksin in
the belief that they were sabotaging her war policy. William
Fermor, the new army commander, occupied the whole of
East Prussia and on August 25, 1758, engaged the Prussian
army at Zorndorf. In nine hours of fighting, the two armies
lost more than twenty thousand men, but the battle was indecisive. Elizabeth was bitterly disappointed, yet she would
not come to terms. She appointed Count Peter Saltykov as
commander, and at Kunersdorf he routed the Prussian army.
In 1760 the Russians took Berlin. Frederick had been
brought to his knees and was ready to capitulate.

The death of Elizabeth came on Christmas Day, 1761.
Peter was at once proclaimed Emperor Peter III. Frederick of
Prussia was anxiously awaiting to learn of the terms of sur-

render that the empress would impose on him. To his delight
he received, instead, the news of her death and the invitation
of the new emperor to draft his own terms. Under the peace
treaty Prussia recovered at a stroke all that it had lost. The
war against Prussia had never been popular; the Western
balance of power was outside the Russians' immediate national interests. But they had been proud of their army and
its victories, won at great human cost. The emperor offended
the army by blandly ignoring both sacrifices and victories,
and by introducing Prussian uniforms, decorations, drill, and
discipline in place of Peter the Great's uniforms and regulations. He formed a regiment of German guards to which he
showed special favor. Finally, he ordered preparations for
war against Denmark to aid the duchy of Holstein in regain-
ing Schleswig. He went out of his way to demonstrate to all
Russians that Holstein meant more to him than the whole
Russian empire. In the same spirit of arrogant stupidity he
demonstrated his contempt for the Russian Church. He had
been brought up as a Lutheran until summoned to Russia,
and he showed neither understanding nor sympathy for the
Orthodox Church. He mocked priests during services. He
tried, unsuccessfully, to ban the vestments worn by Orthodox churchmen, and directed that they should dress in the
manner of German pastors. Finally, he ordered the confisca-
tion of Church property and the closing of private chapels.

Certain of Peter's *ukazy* held promise of liberal policies: he abolished the Chancellery for Secret Investigations in February, 1762, and made the arrest and interrogation of any citizen illegal unless sanctioned by the Senate after preliminary investigation of the charges. As a blow to the established Church, he granted freedom of worship to Old Believers. He reduced the price of salt, a government monopoly, and prohibited factories from the odious practice of purchasing serf villages. Perhaps his most significant change was to relieve the gentry of the duty of service to the state; in the future, service was to be voluntary, and any member of the gentry could resign from the armed forces, except in time of war. This new independence of the gentry, the first class in Russia to be emancipated from compulsory service to the state, was to have far-reaching results. For the first time a sector of the population had both the leisure and the means to support secular education and culture. But Peter's reforms failed to win him support, even among those who gained most; his contempt for tradition had infuriated all classes.

Catherine behaved quite differently. She had taken care from the moment of her arrival to show reverence toward everything Russian. She had studied the language and was punctilious in worshiping according to the Orthodox rites. She had made it clear to all at court that she did not share her husband's pro-Prussian sympathies, but was a patriotic Rus-

sian. At the funeral of Empress Elizabeth, when the people filed past the open coffin, Peter shocked everyone by laughing and joking. Catherine, however, knelt for hours in prayer and her respect was noted with approval.

Estranged from her husband, Catherine was in an unenviable position at court; but, as the French ambassador recorded, she "more and more captures the hearts of the Russians." Attractive rather than beautiful, she possessed what a contemporary called "sheer magic of personality." Her appeal to crowds was irresistible. She was faring equally well with members of her court. When in December, 1757, Catherine had given birth to her second child, a daughter, it was generally accepted that the father was Count Stanislas Poniatowsky, a handsome young Pole, a member of the powerful pro-Russian Czartorysky family, who had come to St. Petersburg to gain experience as a secretary in the embassy of the English ambassador, Hanbury-Williams.

A few months after the Pole's recall in August, 1758, a young officer of the guards, Grigory Orlov, succumbed to her charm. Of the five Orlov brothers, all of whom were renowned for their bravery and handsome bearing, Grigory and Alexei were most remarkable. They had strong following in the guards' regiments and were devoted to Catherine. Grigory became her lover, and in April, 1762, she bore him a son, Alexei, an event that, thanks to the expansive crinolines

then in fashion, happened without her husband ever knowing about it. Her other allies included Count Nikita Panin, formerly Russian ambassador in Stockholm and tutor to Grand Duke Paul, and Princess Catherine Dashkova, a highly intelligent and tempestuous young woman who was the sister of Peter's mistress.

Conspiracies had been forming since Peter's accession, and increasingly they centered on Catherine. Mutinous feelings, encouraged by the Orlovs, mounted among the troops as the time approached for their departure on the Danish campaign. The coup came earlier than expected. On the night of June 28, 1762, Alexei Orlov galloped to the imperial estate at Peterhof. He awakened Catherine, who dressed hurriedly, and together they rode the thirty miles to St. Petersburg. Grigory Orlov met them on the way, and they proceeded to the quarters of the Izmailovsky regiment. The whole regiment pledged allegiance to Catherine and escorted her to the barracks of the Semyonovsky and Preobrazhensky regiments, where she was acclaimed with similar enthusiasm. Her entrance into St. Petersburg, escorted by the three regiments of guards, was triumphal. She attended a special service in the Kazan Cathedral, at which the priests blessed her as "Autocrat Catherine the Second."

Peter III was inspecting troops in Oranienbaum on the Gulf of Finland when news of the coup reached him. He made halfhearted attempts to call on the support of the troops at Kronstadt, but found that the garrison had already taken the oath of loyalty to Catherine. Then, as Frederick II marveled, he "allowed himself to be overthrown as a child is sent to bed." Signing the declaration of abdication, he went to his estate at Ropsha, and there a few days later was killed in a drunken brawl with officers of his guard. Alexei Orlov was present, and as the officer in command of the guards, he was directly responsible. There is no evidence implicating Catherine; but she took no action against her aide and the other guards, and promptly issued a manifesto proclaiming the death of the late emperor from natural causes.

In mounting the throne of the Muscovite tsars, Catherine had achieved an extraordinary triumph. The Russians nursed bitter memories of the rule of the German favorites in the reigns of Anna and Ivan VI, and their antagonism toward Peter III had arisen mainly from his being a German and a Lutheran convert to Orthodoxy. But now, paradoxically, the people were acclaiming another German convert, whose only title to the Russian throne would have been as regent during the minority of her son, Paul. It was a tribute to the genius of her public personality.

At once Catherine set about securing her grip on the throne. The popular mood could change, and she recognized that she must cultivate the guards, the gentry, and the peo-

As the lubok (*opposite*) *of a Cossack fighting two Germans suggests, the Russian people had little affection for the Prussians in the 1700's. They particularly distrusted the wily Frederick II, shown at right, whose diplomatic and marital machinations helped place several Germanophiles on the Russian throne. None was as unpopular as Peter III, who humiliated his subjects by stating: "The will of Frederick is the will of God"—and by kissing a bust of the king.*

ple as a whole if she was to remain empress. Her immediate concern was the preparation for her coronation. The crowning of an autocrat had a special significance for the people and could deeply influence their attitudes. The imposing ceremony took place in the Uspensky Cathedral within the Kremlin. This traditional venue allowed her to appeal astutely to Russian sentiment, and she was careful to show particular respect for Moscow. Twenty bishops, thirty-five archimandrites, and other churchmen, all chanting prayers, processed before her to the cathedral; and the guards regiments, in their brilliant full-dress uniforms, escorted her. From the Uspensky, again according to ancient custom, she proceeded to the Arkhangelsky and Blagoveshchensky cathedrals in the Kremlin to pray before the holy icons. Returning to the palace, she dispensed six hundred thousand rubles to the people, granted amnesties to prisoners, and bestowed honors and rewards on her close supporters. She succeeded in making it a grand and happy occasion. To the Russian ambassador in Warsaw she wrote: "It is impossible to describe to you the joy which the masses of the people show here on seeing me. I have only to make an appearance or to show myself at a window and the cheers are renewed."

Catherine was, however, insatiable in her ambition. She was not content to be empress, acclaimed within Russia; she hungered for the praises of the whole civilized world. Dur-

ing the early years of her marriage to Peter III, and especially after the birth of her first son, she read widely. Montesquieu's *L'Esprit des Lois*, the *Annales* of Tacitus, and Voltaire's *Essai sur les Moeurs et l'Esprit des Nations* made a deep impression upon her. Attracted by these sometimes revolutionary ideas, at least superficially, she launched herself in the role of enlightened autocrat. It was a bold step for an empress of Russia.

With the *Nakaz* (*Instruction*), which Catherine drafted for the guidance of a commission summoned to recast the laws of Russia, she won European renown. She began working on the *Nakaz* in January, 1765, and, devoting three hours daily to it, she completed the task two years later. It was not an original work. She admitted her borrowings in a letter to Frederick of Prussia: "You will see that, like the crow in the fable, I have decked myself in peacock's feathers; in this work merely the arrangement of the material and here and there a line or word belong to me." Nevertheless, she was in no sense modest about its goals. The *Nakaz* closed with the stirring rhetoric: "God forbid that . . . any other nation shall enjoy greater justice and, therefore, greater well-being. . . . The object of the legislation would not have been achieved."

The Grand Legislative Commission, comprising deputies from every part of the vast empire, assembled in Moscow. The first session opened with magnificent ceremonial in the

Though Russia's eighteenth-century rulers differed in their tastes, all wished to create external symbols of imperial grandeur. To bedeck such splendid works as the Grand Imperial Crown (left), Catherine the Great vastly enlarged the royal jewel collection, acquiring precious gems from India and Brazil, as well as from sources in the Urals and Siberia. Diamond-encrusted and topped with a 399-carat ruby, the diadem was designed for her coronation by the Swiss émigré Jeremie Posier. Empress Elizabeth's legacy to St. Petersburg's elegance included the Russian baroque Winter Palace (opposite) by the Italian Bartolomeo Rastrelli. Originally painted a bright turquoise, its 450-foot-wide façade is enlivened by white moldings and classical statues and urns along the roof.

Granovitaya Palace on July 30, 1767. The *Nakaz* was read aloud, and deputies interrupted several times with standing ovations. But, when they began their meetings, they did not understand what was required of them, and the system of committees into which they were divided deepened their confusion. Meetings continued for over a year without result. Toward the end of 1768 the commission was prorogued and never reconvened. In Russia the *Nakaz* was forgotten; but in western Europe it circulated in several versions. Voltaire hailed it as "the most beautiful monument of the century."

The young grand duchess was probably sincere in her dreams of continuing Peter the Great's work—but in the spirit of the new enlightenment. As empress, however, she found herself beset by responsibilities and problems that directly involved her own security on the throne. In particular, she could do nothing that would antagonize the nobility and gentry on whose support she depended. This meant that she considered herself barred from attempting to alleviate conditions of the peasants. The *Nakaz* had revealed her appreciation of the intolerable lives of the peasantry, burdened by taxes and debt, and oppressed by their landowners, but she yielded to the demands of the landowning class for wider and more oppressive powers over their serfs whenever her position as empress was threatened. Also, she recognized that serfdom was the most efficient means of sup-

plying manpower to Russia's vast lands and new industries. In 1765, while working on her *Nakaz*, she had granted to landowners the right to sentence their serfs to forced labor in Siberia. Again, in 1767, when the Grand Legislative Commission was still in session, Catherine endorsed an *ukaz*, proposed by the Senate, that made any serf who petitioned or complained against his landowner liable to the knout and lifelong banishment with hard labor. Peter the Great had protected the right of the serf to make formal complaint against oppression and had insisted that such petitions be promptly investigated and justice done. By this *ukaz* Catherine condemned serfs to suffer in silence without appeal.

Serfs and their families had come to be treated like chattel. In the eighteenth century public auctions normally included the sale of serfs with that of horses, dogs, and cattle. The system itself degraded both landowner and peasant, for the custom of trading serfs as casually as livestock destroyed all sense of human dignity and debased standards of conduct. Industrial serfs, bought to labor in mines and factories, were, in fact, worked to death. Catherine attempted, in 1762, to give some protection to these unfortunates by decreeing that they were to be enlisted voluntarily, but the *ukaz* started rumors of liberation, and serfs in the Kazan and Perm regions stopped work. Troops had to be dispatched to deal with them. The decree was never enforced.

Driven to desperation and thwarted in their attempts to flee, peasants gave way to violence, which often developed into spontaneous bloody rebellions. In 1773 a revolt known as the Pugachovshchina, after its leader Yemelyan Pugachov, erupted on a far greater scale than any preceding. Pugachov had served with distinction in the Russian army, but then had deserted and vanished. He came into prominence again in September, 1773, declaring that he was Peter III and that he had escaped from Ropsha before Catherine's assassins could succeed in murdering him.

Pugachov drew his early support mainly from among the Yaik Cossacks and the industrial serfs in the Ural region. He quickly extended his authority in the Urals and along the Volga, laying siege to the city of Orenburg. He now set up his own court in a bizarre imitation of the imperial court. He named his favorites "Orlov," "Panin," and "Vorontsov"—after Catherine's ministers; and he appointed six concubines as his ladies in waiting. He issued stirring *ukazy*, setting forth his policy to kill all nobles and gentry, to distribute the land among the peasantry to whom it rightfully belonged, and to incarcerate Catherine in a nunnery. Peasants throughout eastern Russia rallied to his banner, leaving destruction in their wake as they went to join the rebels. Soon Pugachov had an army of fifteen thousand men. Landowners who managed to escape took refuge in Moscow, and panic spread among them when Pugachov prepared to march on the city.

Catherine recognized the magnitude of the threat posed, but not until late in the summer of 1774, when she could divert troops from campaigns against the Turks, was she able to send a strong force to put down the rebellion. Pugachov was brought in an iron cage to Moscow, where in January, 1775, he was publicly executed.

The empress knew that unless conditions changed, there would be more "Pugachovs." To her minister of justice she wrote: "If we do not consent to diminish cruelty and moderate a situation which is intolerable to the human race, then sooner or later they will take this step themselves." But the splendor with which she bedecked her capital and the acclaim accorded by Europe engaged her attention.

Catherine was a prodigious worker. Normally she arose at 5 A.M. Mornings were usually devoted to study in solitude; state business, court functions, and entertainments took up the rest of her day. From this busy routine she could spare little time for Grigory Orlov, her lover. Increasingly dissatisfied with his position as male courtesan, Orlov pressed her to marry him, for through marriage he saw the way to power. Catherine, however, was determined that she would never share her throne, for her love of power and the position of autocrat transcended all else in her life. But she treated Orlov with great patience during his frequent bouts of surliness.

201

She entrusted him with special tasks. In the spring of 1772 she decided to make the break; she sent him as her representative to negotiate with the Turks. While he was away, a handsome young officer of the guards, Alexander Vasilchikov, was installed in the palace. He was the first of a procession of young favorites.

Following Vasilchikov was Grigory Potemkin. Potemkin had shown exceptional brilliance as a student. At the University of Moscow, which Elizabeth had established in 1755, he had been presented with a gold medal for outstanding scholarship. Suddenly he lost interest in study and in 1760 was expelled for laziness. He then joined the Semyonovsky guards as a private and soon earned his commission, thereby gaining admission to society. An intelligent and entertaining companion, he could enliven any gathering, and he became a member of Catherine's inner circle. She was strongly attracted to this dynamic young officer—all the more so because he was clearly in love with her. Then he lost an eye, probably through infection (it was rumored to have been the result of a duel with one of the Orlovs). He withdrew from court to live on his small estate, reading and meditating in solitude. For a year and a half he resisted all blandishments to return to the capital; but, finally, Catherine managed to draw him out of his retreat. During the next ten years (1763–73) she assigned him tasks both in diplomatic and military fields as though training him for highest office. By this time, moreover, she was becoming bored with Vasilchikov, and in spring of 1774 she pensioned him off, and Potemkin took his place.

The thirty-five-year-old Potemkin was no longer slim and elegant. The British minister wrote that "his figure is gigantic and disproportioned, and his countenance is very far from engaging." He was sometimes known as the One-eyed Cyclops. Catherine, however, surrendered herself to him almost completely, and it was said that they were secretly married. It was a partnership of opposites. She remained always a German princess, disciplined and industrious. He was Russian in his furious excesses: his moods of exuberance and joy followed by deep depressions; his tremendous bouts of work alternating with spells of lethargy. Often they quarreled; but close intellectual and emotional bonds held them together until his death.

The time of splendor in Catherine's reign commenced after Potemkin had become virtually co-regent. The scale and richness of Catherine's court amazed foreigners. The British ambassador reported that the banquet celebrating the birth of a son to Grand Duke Paul "surpassed everything that can be conceived . . . the dessert at supper was set out with jewels to the amount of upwards of two million sterling." Catherine set the social standard, which the nobility

After discovering the delights of sex, Catherine confessed: "It is my misfortune that my heart cannot rest content, even for an hour, without love." To fulfill her lusty appetites, the empress (depicted in her fading years at far left) took at least twenty-one lovers, including, from left, Sergei Saltykov, Stanislas Poniatowsky, Grigory Orlov, Grigory Potemkin, and Platon Zubov. Potential paramours were subjected to a doctor's examination, "tested" by an éprouveuse, and only then installed in an apartment next to the royal bedchamber, where in return for passion and flattery their worldly successes were assured.

sought to emulate in their patterns of behavior.

Sequestered in the Hermitage, the private wing she had added to the Winter Palace, Catherine carried on an extensive correspondence, principally in French, with her ambassadors and agents abroad, and with the notables of the day—Voltaire, Diderot, and the *philosophes*. She kept abreast of all that was new in the cultural life of Europe. Literature was her greatest interest, and she longed to win literary fame. In 1769 she became the publisher of and principal contributor to her own literary magazine, called *Vsyakaya Vsyachina* (*All Sorts and Sundries*) and modeled directly on the *Spectator* of Addison and Steele. Like Elizabeth, Catherine loved the pageantry of the theater. She wrote several comedies and two historical dramas modeled on the plays of Shakespeare. Her own theater at the Hermitage set the standard for later rival theaters that were established in Moscow, St. Petersburg, and elsewhere. Though the Russian effort was still in bondage to Western, and especially French, models, a number of gifted Russian dramatists—including Denis Fonvizin, Yakov Kniazhnin, and Mikhail Kheraskov—were writing for the stage.

French manners and culture were dominant at the Russian court as well. The fashion had been introduced in Elizabeth's reign, and it had produced a French veneer, beneath which the barbarity of Russian life remained. Catherine's early enthusiasm for the Enlightenment had brought many French-

men to her court, and it became the practice of wealthy Russian families to engage French tutors for their children. Moreover, Russian nobles were now traveling freely in Europe, returning with new modes of dress, books, and ideas.

Nikolai Novikov—an able satirist whose journal *Truten* (*The Drone*) soon proved too trenchant for Catherine's taste and was closed down—published a notice mocking the new snobbism. It read: "Young Russian porker, who has traveled in foreign lands for the enlightenment of his mind and having profitably completed his tour, has returned home a perfect swine; anyone wishing to inspect same may see him free of charge in many streets of this city." The cultural gulf was opening up between the aristocracy and the Russian people as a whole. Gradually losing touch with the land and the people, the gentry was becoming a displaced class.

It was in architecture, rather than in literature and the theater, that Catherine left her most splendid legacy. She inherited from Elizabeth several outstanding architects. A Frenchman, Vallin de la Mothe, built the Hermitage, in which she delighted. A German, Yury Velten, who had studied under Rastrelli, added a gallery to the Hermitage for her rich collection of paintings and other works of art, which her agents had purchased for her in all parts of Europe. Vasily Bazhenov, a Russian, built the impressive new Arsenal in St. Petersburg and the Kamenny Ostrov Palace for Grand

Duke Paul. But the Russian architect who won her full approval was Ivan Starov. He created the Alexander Nevsky Monastery in a simple classic style that appealed so strongly to her that she commissioned him to build the Tauride Palace. Designed for Potemkin, whom she had made prince of Tauris in recognition of his role in the conquest of the Crimea, it was Starov's masterpiece. Among the foreign architects whom she engaged, the Scot, Charles Cameron, who built for her the Agate Pavilion and the Cameron Gallery at Tsarskoe Selo, won her favor. In the last years of her reign she also commissioned an Italian, Giacomo Quarenghi, to erect a Palladian mansion, known as the English Palace, at Peterhof, as well as other buildings. Throughout her reign she set fashions in architecture that wealthy nobles followed in their town and country houses. It was the golden age of architecture in Russia.

Catherine's patronage also extended to scholarship. Peter the Great's Academy of Sciences had stagnated. The first two directors whom Catherine appointed were ineffective. In 1783, however, she called on Princess Dashkova to be director of the Academy, and she proved outstanding in the post. She planned the first dictionary of the Russian language, embarked on an ambitious program of learned publications, and raised the prestige of the Academy abroad. Most interesting among the foreign connections that she cultivated was the American Philosophical Society of Philadelphia, and at her suggestion its president, Benjamin Franklin, was elected an associate member of the Academy of Sciences. Dashkova was responsible also for the establishment of the separate Russian academy devoted to the study of the Russian language.

Catherine expressed special interest in education. She founded several new schools, such as the celebrated institute at Smolny, the first to be opened in Russia for the training of young ladies of gentle birth. She was eager to set up a system of education for a broader segment of the upper classes. In 1764 she sent a commission to Britain to report on universities and schools there, and to propose plans for a similar system in Russia. Again in 1785 a commission visited Austria to study its normal schools; but nothing came of these plans and illiteracy remained widespread.

Catherine's reign was a time of Russia's triumphs over traditional enemies. From the outset she paid close attention to foreign policy, for it was a field offering opportunities for her to appeal to the national pride of her subjects and to make an impression upon the rest of Europe. The army, though neglected, had shown its mettle in the war against Prussia, which had served as valuable training ground for the new generation of officers. Russia was a powerful nation, and its chief enemies were in decline: Sweden had never recovered from the Northern War; Poland was divided and

weak. The Ottoman Porte, although decadent, stood alone as an enemy to be respected.

Catherine's opposition to the policies of her husband, Peter III, was tactical; it allowed her to appeal to the anti-Prussian feelings of the Russian people. Her first thought was to secure peace so that the country could recover from the Seven Years War. The policy she adopted, known as the Northern System, aimed to unite under Russia's leadership the northern countries, including Poland, against Austria, France, and Spain. It proved an impractical scheme, and it had the serious disadvantage of canceling the alliance with Austria against Turkey.

The first international issue Catherine had to contend with concerned the succession to the Polish throne, left vacant by the death of Augustus III in September, 1763. Austria and France promoted the elector of Saxony as their candidate; but Catherine wanted her former lover, Stanislas Poniatowsky, on the Polish throne. She was confident that he would give no trouble and would not disturb the "fortunate anarchy" that kept Poland weak. She made a general defensive alliance with Frederick of Prussia in March, 1764; by a secret compact they had agreed to work together to keep Poland in a state of decline. French and Austrian intrigues to secure the election of their candidate intensified. Catherine sent a strong detachment of troops into Poland in the following May to

ensure that her wishes prevailed, and under the shadow of Russian guns Poniatowsky was unanimously elected king of Poland in August.

Catherine had thus reasserted Russia's domination over Poland. In doing so, however, she had further antagonized Austria and France, and by her alliance with Frederick she had aroused their fears that Russia would support Prussia in any attack on the Austrian empire and, further, that Russia and Prussia intended to divide Poland between them. To ensure that Russia would be fully engaged, Austria and France persuaded the Turkish sultan to declare war on Russia.

Catherine was far from ready for the declaration of war issued in October, 1768. Russia stood alone against Turkey. While its army and navy were hurriedly mobilizing that winter, the Tatars of the Crimea, subjects of the sultan, ravaged southern Russia. By the spring of 1769, however, Russian forces had taken up positions at strategic points along the frontier from the Danube to the Kuban rivers.

Catherine had ordered the refitting of all ships and the building of new squadrons in the Baltic shipyards in readiness for an expedition into the Mediterranean, a part of her campaign against Turkey. Under her English admirals, John Elphinstone and Samuel Greig, two squadrons set sail from the Baltic in September, 1769, revictualed in English ports, and headed for the Mediterranean. Russian warships had

never before sailed around the European coast, and many in the West saw in it a portentous event.

The squadrons were directed to challenge the Turks in the Aegean Sea by supporting a rebellion among the Greek Christians, and then to capture Constantinople and join up with the Russian armies on the northern shores of the Black Sea. It was an ambitious plan, and it nearly succeeded. Indeed, it might have been completely successful but for the inexperience and inadequacy of the Russian commander in chief, Alexei Orlov. The Turkish fleet appeared off Lemnos, and since it had overwhelming superiority in ships and guns, the Russian squadrons withdrew. Soon afterward, however, off Chios, the Russians attacked and defeated the Turkish fleet, which took refuge in a bay along the Turkish coast. Admirals Elphinstone and Greig then barred the entrance to the bay and sent in fireships that destroyed the enemy fleet. The obvious tactics now were for the Russian ships to sail with all speed to the Dardanelles, where the Turks were in a state of panic. Orlov hesitated and missed the opportunity.

News of further victories over the Turks now reached St. Petersburg. Prince Peter Rumyantsev, commanding the Russian land forces, had advanced into Moldavia and taken Jassy, the capital. He had then gained a major victory over the Turks at Bucharest, and at the end of July, although heavily outnumbered, he had defeated the Turks decisively at the Bessarabian fortress town of Kagul on the Pruth River.

Austria and France, alarmed by these proofs of Russian power, feared that Catherine was planning the conquest of the Balkans. Austria nervously mobilized its armies. Frederick of Prussia saw the tension erupting in a major war, into which the rest of Europe, including his own country, would be drawn. He acted to avert this danger. In September, 1770, at Neustadt, he met Joseph II of Austria, who urged him to intercede with Catherine and, in particular, to dissuade her from seeking to penetrate south of the Danube or into the Balkans. Frederick sent his brother, Prince Henry, to St. Petersburg to suggest that she halt her campaign against Turkey and seek compensation in annexing part of Poland.

Catherine was attracted by this proposal. In the campaign of 1771 Prince Dolgoruky captured the Crimea, whence in past centuries the Tatars had terrorized Russia. It was a triumph that all Russians would normally have celebrated jubilantly; but now they were in no mood to celebrate, for central Russia was in the grip of the plague. (In July and August there were as many as a thousand deaths per day.) Political considerations also made Catherine look favorably on the Prussian proposal. Her armies had been weakened by the fighting, disease, and hardship. The task of maintaining Russian authority in Poland was also proving to be a severe strain on Russian resources. The Polish nationalists, sup-

At the outbreak of the Turkish war, Voltaire wrote Catherine: "I think that if ever the Turks are expelled from Europe, it will be by the Russians." His words seemed to support the empress' own grandiose dreams of a Russian "Constantinople," and her ensuing campaign was so impressive that Voltaire compared it to Hannibal's march on Rome. Russian gains were acknowledged in a 1774 treaty and commemorated in broadsides like this one, showing the arrival of the Ottoman ambassador at the St. Petersburg court. Both governments regarded the peace as temporary, and Catherine herself allowed: "Now the sleeping cat is roused, and it will not rest until it has eaten the mouse."

ported by Austria and France, were resisting boldly. Russia needed a respite from war and from the burdens of Poland. In January, 1772, Catherine accepted Frederick's plan for the partition of Poland—in which Austria was invited to participate. In July the treaties were signed, and Catherine annexed most of Belorussia, which Russians had claimed as their territory since the fifteenth century. Meanwhile, two peace congresses, one at Focşani and the other in Bucharest, broke down because the Turks would not accede to Catherine's demands. War was renewed, but in the campaign of 1773 fortune did not favor Rumyantsev. At this time, too, Catherine was worried by Pugachov's rebellion and by the threat of war with Sweden.

In a desperate attempt to recover their losses on the western shores of the Black Sea, the Turks mobilized a massive army for the campaign of 1774. The sultan and the grand vizier expected that with Russia torn by rebellion they would readily triumph; but morale was once again high, and Catherine's generals were at the peak of their power. In a series of Russian victories in the spring of 1774 three thousand men routed elements of the demoralized Turkish army. Finally, at Shumla, Rumyantsev compelled the sultan's army to surrender. The Turks now sued for peace. On July 21 the grand vizier signed the Treaty of Kuchuk Kainarji, renouncing their claim to the Crimea and the northern shore of the Sea

of Azov. But it was no more than an armistice, for both nations recognized that a renewal of the war was inevitable.

The next twenty years were a time of remarkable triumph, largely through the efforts of Potemkin, who was elevated to foreign minister in 1775. Catherine had found Frederick of Prussia to be a treacherous ally, and while careful not to reject him openly, she had turned again to Austria as her ally against the Ottoman Porte. When conflict broke out between Austria and Prussia over the succession to the elector of Bavaria, both Joseph II of Austria and Frederick appealed to her to mediate. The Peace of Teschen, which resulted in 1779, was acclaimed throughout Europe. Again she raised the prestige of Russia and of herself by the part she played in bringing together the European powers in an attempt to oppose English domination of the seas during the American War of Independence.

Gratifying as these triumphs were, Catherine was obsessed with plans for the expansion of Russian power in the south. The vast lands, wrested from Turkey and now known as New Russia, were under the direct rule of Potemkin as viceroy. His dynamic energies and his capacity for planning on a grand scale were producing amazing results. He created the new naval station of Kherson on the lower Dnieper and pressed on with schemes to colonize the region. He scattered the remnants of the Zaporozhsky Cossacks, who had been

AN IMPERIAL STRIDE!

Russia.

Constantinople.

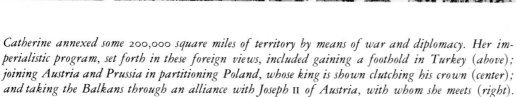

Catherine annexed some 200,000 square miles of territory by means of war and diplomacy. Her imperialistic program, set forth in these foreign views, included gaining a foothold in Turkey (above); joining Austria and Prussia in partitioning Poland, whose king is shown clutching his crown (center); and taking the Balkans through an alliance with Joseph II of Austria, with whom she meets (right).

disbanded in 1775 after the Pugachov rebellion. He knew, however, that this new domain would never be secure while the neighboring Crimea remained independent, as had been provided in the Treaty of Kuchuk Kainarji. Finally, in 1783, he persuaded the Crimean khan to abdicate in favor of the empress, and Catherine proclaimed at once that the Crimea formed part of the Russian empire. Demoralized and unwilling to challenge Russia's might again, Turkey accepted Catherine's terms for peace. By the Treaty of Constantinople Russia's sovereignty over the Crimea, the Taman Peninsula, and the Kuban was recognized—and also the right of Russian ships to free passage through the Black Sea and the Dardanelles. Since the fifteenth century the tsars had been striving to reach the natural frontier of the Black Sea and to trade freely with the lands beyond. And now this historic objective had been achieved.

In 1784 Potemkin devoted his energies to building the naval depot and harbor of Sevastopol and to creating the Russian Black Sea fleet. He was also building Yekaterinoslav (meaning "Catherine's glory") as the capital of the New Russia. At the same time he was working on a grand project that fired Catherine's ambition: this was the dismemberment of the Turkish empire, the revival of Byzantium, and the creation of the new kingdom of Dacia (roughly equivalent to modern Romania). It was generally accepted that Potem-

kin himself would become king of Dacia, and Catherine intended that her second grandson, named Constantine, should be the first of the new line of Byzantine emperors. She planned to take him with her on a journey through the southern lands to the frontier of his future empire. When the time came for their departure, however, he had smallpox and had to remain in the palace.

Catherine's triumphal procession to the Crimea in 1787 came as the splendid climax of her reign. Potemkin was responsible for all the arrangements, and he ensured that she would be surrounded with magnificence, which would impress Turkey and Europe. In his anxiety to show her how rapidly New Russia was developing, he even erected false façades of villages that did not exist, the legendary "Potemkin villages." Nevertheless, Potemkin had achieved real and amazing results within a brief period. This was revealed most dramatically when from the heights near Inkerman he pointed out to her the new town and harbor of Sevastopol. As Catherine first set eyes on the scene, forty newly built warships, alerted by a complex series of signals, fired salvos in her honor. Comte de Ségur, who traveled with the foreign ambassadors on the journey, wrote that "it seemed incredible to us that, at a distance of eight hundred leagues from the capital and in a country so recently conquered, Prince Potemkin had found it possible in two years to raise such an establish-

ment, to build a town, construct a fleet, to erect forts, and to assemble such a large number of inhabitants: this was truly prodigal activity." Its military import was not lost on anyone.

Alarmed by Russian might and by the openly discussed plans to dismember the Turkish empire, the Turks saw the imperial journey to the Crimea as the final provocation. On August 18, 1787, soon after Catherine's return to St. Petersburg, the sultan declared war. Potemkin had been impatiently awaiting this event. He had an army of one hundred thousand men ready; like many Russians before him, he saw the war both as a crusade against Mohammedanism and an opportunity for glorious conquests. During the following four years the Russian armies gained a series of brilliant victories, finally compelling the Turks to sue for peace.

The war and the development of New Russia had kept Potemkin away from the capital. In the spring of 1791, however, he visited St. Petersburg, where he held a banquet in honor of Catherine. "Potemkin's Feast" was colossal in scale and splendor, and it was to be his final act of homage to her. Three thousand guests—all masked and in full court dress —attended, and a sumptuous meal was served in an adjoining square. Potemkin received in a suit of red silk, a cloak of black lace, and a broad hat decked with precious stones. Several orchestras played; two ballet companies and two companies of actors provided entertainment. As Catherine

prepared to leave, an orchestra and choir rendered a cantata, especially composed in her honor.

A few months later Potemkin set out for the south to supervise new projects and to conduct negotiations with the Turks. He fell ill on the journey and on October 5, 1791, at the age of fifty-two, he died. Catherine was inconsolable at the loss of her trusted partner and friend. The Prince de Ligne, a longtime friend of the court, wrote: "He is the emblem of the immense Russian empire; he also is composed of deserts, of gold mines, and of diamonds—he is the most extraordinary man that has ever lived."

By the treaty, finally concluded at Jassy on December 29, 1791, the sultan confirmed all Russian gains under the earlier Treaty of Kuchuk Kainarji, surrendered all claims to the Crimea, and also conceded the Black Sea lands between the Bug and the Dniester rivers, where Odessa was to become the great port. Although the treaty did not establish the kingdom of Dacia or allow the revival of Byzantium, as Catherine and Potemkin had dreamed, it triumphantly concluded a long chapter in Russia's history. Peter the Great had defeated Sweden and had established Russia's power on the Baltic; now Catherine had crushed Turkey and asserted Russia's possession of the northern shores of the Black Sea and its direct access to the sea. This was possibly the greatest achievement of her long and glittering rule.

BOTH: PORTER, *Travelling Sketches*, 1809

From the time of Catherine on, Russia was periodically invaded by tourists bored with other European vacation spots, by youths with their tutors making the grand tour, and by curious observers, like the English artist Robert Ker Porter. The record of his visit, comprised of painted and written vignettes, reveals mixed fascination and revulsion. Of the figure at left, Porter stated: "You would hardly believe . . . this is a man, that it were not rather a Russian bear." He noted that in the rural posthouse (right) the oven also served as a veritable hotbed. A loft built above always accommodated several persons huddled together in a manner "not more decent than disgusting."

The Russian economy appeared to be flourishing under Catherine. The national revenue was 14.5 million rubles at the beginning of her reign; at the end it had swelled to 55.4 million rubles. Contributing to this rapid growth were the acquisition of new territories, increases in poll tax and customs and other duties, and the expansion of trade and industry. Russian exports rose from 11 million rubles in 1763 to 19 million rubles in 1778, but imports also increased in this period from 8 million to 13 million rubles. The ships arriving in St. Petersburg alone rose in number from 150 in 1750 to nearly 1,000 in 1790. The main exports to the West were flax, hemp, linen, timber, iron, and other raw materials.

The figures suggested a healthy economy, but they were misleading. Russia was in the grip of chronic inflation. Revenues were rising, but expenditures rose more steeply. The army and navy, and the wars against Turkey, were costly, and the corruption of officials and officers at every level added to the debt; Catherine's own extravagance contributed notably to the recurrent deficits. The Reverend William Coxe, a traveler from England, observed: "It is difficult to conceive how she is able to maintain the magnificence of her court, the number of public institutions, the numerous buildings which are constantly erected at her expense, the liberality with which she encourages the arts and sciences, the purchases which she is constantly making in every country

of Europe, and the immense donations which she confers upon the most favored of her subjects."

Catherine was able to spend on an extravagant scale because she treated the national revenues as her own. Her expenditure on her court alone was, according to a conservative estimate, some four million rubles annually from the early 1770's until her death. She was prodigal in her generosity to her favorites. In her patronage of the arts, her commissions to architects, and her acquisitions she never counted the cost. She made occasional efforts toward economy, but she was not really interested in cutting back her private budget. The remedies she adopted were to increase revenues, and increasingly she resorted to various dangerous expedients.

The peasantry suffered most from the financial crises and the inflation. The nobles, living up to the style of the imperial court, had to exact additional income from their estates. They increased the *barshchina*, the amount of compulsory labor required of their serfs. In many districts serfs worked five or even six days for their masters and had no time for their own holdings on which their livelihood depended. Other serfs, who worked a portion of an estate for their own gain or plied a craft or trade, paid a proportion of their earnings, known as *obrok*. Many landlords took so much of these earnings that the serfs were reduced to penury and hunger. On top of the landowners' demands came in-

creases in the poll tax, assessed solely upon the peasantry.

In her search for revenue Catherine required the state monopolies to produce more. The sale of alcohol was the chief monopoly, contributing as much as a third of internal revenues. By opening new taverns, and ensuring that they were set up promptly in the new territories as well, she increased the yield from the alcohol monopoly by six times during the years from 1764 to 1795. When these and other methods failed to keep pace with rising expenditure, she resorted to raising loans and issuing paper money. As early in her reign as 1768 she set up a Bank of Assignation, with a capital of one million rubles, and issued bank notes to that amount convertible into silver or copper money. In 1774 the bank notes in circulation were increased to the value of 20 million rubles, and this was later raised to 100 million and then 150 million rubles to meet the expense of the second Turkish war and the inexorable rise in expenditure. Inevitably, inflation followed (the value of the ruble had fallen by half at the end of her reign). Moreover, she began borrowing abroad. Loans totaling 52.7 million rubles had been raised by the 1790's, and the cost of servicing the loans was six million rubles a year. Peter the Great had waged major wars and carried through a tremendous program of development, but he had not imposed such financial burdens on his people, nor had he incurred debts on this scale. The Russian

economy, although poor, had been solvent at the time of her accession; by the end of her reign it was in deep trouble.

The revolutionary ideas that Catherine embraced had meanwhile been fermenting, and with the fall of the Bastille on July 14, 1789, they erupted. In France the old regime collapsed, and in the midst of spreading anarchy men believed that they were living at the dawn of a new age of freedom. They saw the revolution as the logical outcome of the ideas of the Enlightenment. But the rule of the moderates was short-lived. The Jacobin extremists seized power, and the terror, culminating in the death of Louis XVI and then of Marie Antoinette in 1793, alarmed the rulers of the other countries—and none more than the empress of Russia.

At first Catherine expected Louis XVI to act firmly to restore order, but then she realized that the French monarchy had crumbled. She feared that the French Revolution would spread like a contagion through the rest of Europe; the conditions that had given rise to the upheaval in France were, she knew, present in Russia in more extreme forms. Pugachov's rebellion had shown how easily popular discontent could develop into a massive threat to the throne and the whole structure of society.

The Russian people were, however, not ready for full-scale revolution, largely because the Russian Orthodox Church had a strong restraining influence. Over the years the Church had inculcated a Christian humility, patience, and a sense of community of suffering that were alien to the Western outlook. The Church had also discouraged demands for material and social rights that men had claimed and won in the West. Catherine recognized that the Orthodox Church was a sturdy champion of the autocracy, and she was assiduous in cultivating close relations with the Church hierarchy.

The immediate task was, however, to eradicate the enlightened ideas that she had herself once encouraged. Her flirtation with the Enlightenment had come to an end early in her reign. The *Nakaz* had been withdrawn from circulation soon after the dismissal of the Grand Legislative Commission. In the last years of her reign she became more and more reactionary and prompt to suppress the least suggestion of liberal thinking. The works of Voltaire, her old friend and correspondent, were banned. She instructed the censors to examine all foreign works with care and to scrutinize everything French minutely. Her new conservatism was demonstrated in May, 1790, in her treatment of Alexander Radishchev, a gentle idealist and a customs official who had the temerity to write and print on his private press a book called *A Journey from St. Petersburg to Moscow*. Patterned closely on Laurence Sterne's *A Sentimental Journey through France and Italy*, then widely read in Europe, it appeared to be a series of simple travel sketches. Though the book passed the censor, Catherine was quick to discover that it was a severe indictment of serfdom and absolutism. She at once ordered the arrest of this "rebel worse than Pugachov," and had the book banned. Copies, often written out by hand, circulated secretly, and an hour's private perusal cost the borrower as much as twenty-five rubles.

On July 24, 1790, Radishchev was sentenced to death; but with a display of clemency Catherine commuted the sentence to banishment to central Siberia. Weighed down with heavy chains and closely guarded, Radishchev, already a sick man, was borne off in an open cart on his long journey. As a Frenchman at the imperial court wrote: "His courage has not been useless to his country; in spite of house-to-house searches by this despotic regime, his work subsists in the hands of several of his countrymen, and his memory is dear to all men of honor and sensibility." Indeed, the persecution of Radishchev caused several of the most prominent people at court, including Princess Dashkova, to withdraw.

The last years of Catherine's reign were marked by severe reactionary policies internally and by repression abroad, especially in Poland. A national revival had taken place among the Poles after the first partition. In 1789 they had abrogated the hated constitution that Catherine had imposed upon them, and on May 5, 1791, with a unanimity almost unprecedented in Polish history, they approved a new constitution designed to end the anarchy and the divisions among them. Catherine condemned these demonstrations of independence as revolutionary. At this time, however, Russia was engaged in the last phase of its war with Turkey, and the empress waited until an armistice had been concluded before she took action. A group of reactionary Polish nobles had agreed at

Targovitse to secede from the regime established by the new constitution. The Russian army marched into Poland to support this cadre, and the empress' will was reimposed. Declaring that Poland had become a hotbed of Jacobinism, Catherine then negotiated with Frederick William of Prussia for a further partition. Their agreement was signed on January 23, 1793, and under pressure the Polish king accepted it. Russia's gains included half of Lithuania, the remaining parts of Belorussia, and the Ukraine west of the Dnieper—all territory that, it was claimed, had originally been Russian.

Among the Poles a desperate movement to expel the Russians gathered force. Its leader was Thaddeus Kosciusko, a Polish patriot who had studied military engineering in France and had taken part in the American War of Independence. Returning to Poland in 1785 he had made Krakow, the old capital in independent Poland, his headquarters. The remnants of the Polish army and crowds of peasants rallied to him there, and on March 24, 1794, he declared war on Russia. It was a bold challenge. His forces fought gallantly, with no possibility of victory against the Prussian and Russian armies that converged upon them. On October 10, 1794, Kosciusko suffered complete defeat and was taken prisoner. A few weeks later Warsaw was captured and the Polish insurrection extinguished. Catherine now agreed with her fellow monarchs in Austria and Prussia on the division of the spoils in a third partition that removed Poland from the map.

No claim could be made that Russia had any ancient right to the territories gained under the third partition. This partition was a blatant act of aggrandizement, which intensified Polish enmity toward Russia at a time when wise statesmanship might have won Poland as an ally. But Catherine was concerned with immediate gains and her own prestige.

Although in her sixties, Catherine continued to live her exceedingly busy and orderly life, and to pursue her varied interests, and she took even more care in selecting the young men who served as her favorites (there had been sixteen since Potemkin). She still cherished her ambition of realizing the Greek Project and of reviving the Byzantine empire. However, events in France clouded these last years of her reign. The gaiety and splendor of her era had already proved transient by the time of her death on November 6, 1796. But her life had been an amazing adventure. An insignificant German princess, she had usurped the Russian throne, and by intelligence, courage, a certain brilliance of personality, and good fortune, she had reigned for thirty-four years with magnificence. She had compelled the admiration and at times had aroused the anxieties of the whole civilized world. But she had also increased the burdens and sufferings of her people, and at her death Russia was seething with unrest.

The serfs' anguish, expressed in this wooden carving, was largely ignored by the state until 1861, when Alexander II abolished the "hundred headed monster of serfdom." Until then the majority of Russian peasants were considered the "baptized property" of their owners.

The Soul of Russia

"For the largest part the peasants of Russia are slaves; I do not need dilate on the degradation and misfortune of such a position." So wrote Alexander I in the early 1800's as the Russian aristocracy was tightening its grasp on the mass of once-free peasants, or muzhiks. The typical peasant lived under the control of a village commune (*mir* or *obshchina*) like the one shown opposite, a type of community that persisted in one form or other from Kievan times until 1906. The communer possessed a hut, farm implements, livestock, and the right to work a small tract of land, but shared common acreage, taxes, and military obligations with his fellow villagers. However, as early as the eleventh century, when it became the practice for princes to donate communes to boyars and the Church, many peasants were deprived of their economic autonomy, becoming the renters, contract workers, indentured laborers, or domestics of their landlord. During the chaos of the Mongol era the landlord was given the right to govern and judge the peasantry. By the 1500's the peasant's overburdening obligations to lord and state were established. Aside from a constantly increasing poll tax, which he remitted to the state, he either paid his landlord an annual quitrent (*obrok*) in cash or kind, or performed labor duties (*barshchina*) for him. However, the enserfment process was not fully completed until the promulgation of the law code of 1649, which would remain in force until 1833. It abolished freedom of movement for the peasant and his family, and denied him the right to own property (his master held title to all his belongings), while allowing the landlord an unlimited period of time in which to recover fugitive peasants. By Catherine the Great's reign—the golden age for the Russian aristocracy—serfs were the pawns and base of credit of the gentry, the only class that could legally own land and serfs. A slightly more fortunate group was the state-owned peasants. Although they escaped the whims of an individual owner, they were often forced to spend part or all of the year working in Russia's fledgling industries, both government and private, such as mines, factories, and ironworks. Still another category of peasants were those belonging to the tsar or his imperial family; they were little better off than the serfs, but if the property to which they were attached was given as reward to a member of the gentry—a frequent occurrence—they immediately became serfs. Despite the system, a significant number of serfs bought their way to freedom through demonstrated talents as factory owners, merchants, entertainers, or artists. The rest remained an ever-present threat to internal peace—awaiting the inspiration of a leader. One of the most effective organizers was Yemelyan Pugachov (above), pictured after his capture in 1774. But even the emancipation statute of 1861 would do little to better the muzhik's lot.

THE INTERIOR OF A PEASANT HUT, *the one-room* izba, *is shown in this eighteenth-century engraving. The family (which often included two or more married brothers and their children and parents), as well as poultry, livestock, and an unsavory assortment of vermin, all lived in the cramped quarters. The allocation of space followed a traditional pattern. Domestic activities were assigned to the cooking corner, which contained the oven, or* pech; *and this also was a sleep area in winter. At other times the paterfamilias and the younger men slept on benches, and the rest of the family in the loft (right). Babies lolled in bast cradles suspended from a crossbeam. Socializing took place in the icon corner (left), which was always diagonally across from the* pech. *(When a stranger entered, he was expected to remove his hat and cross himself in front of the icons before greeting his hosts or sharing their meal.)*

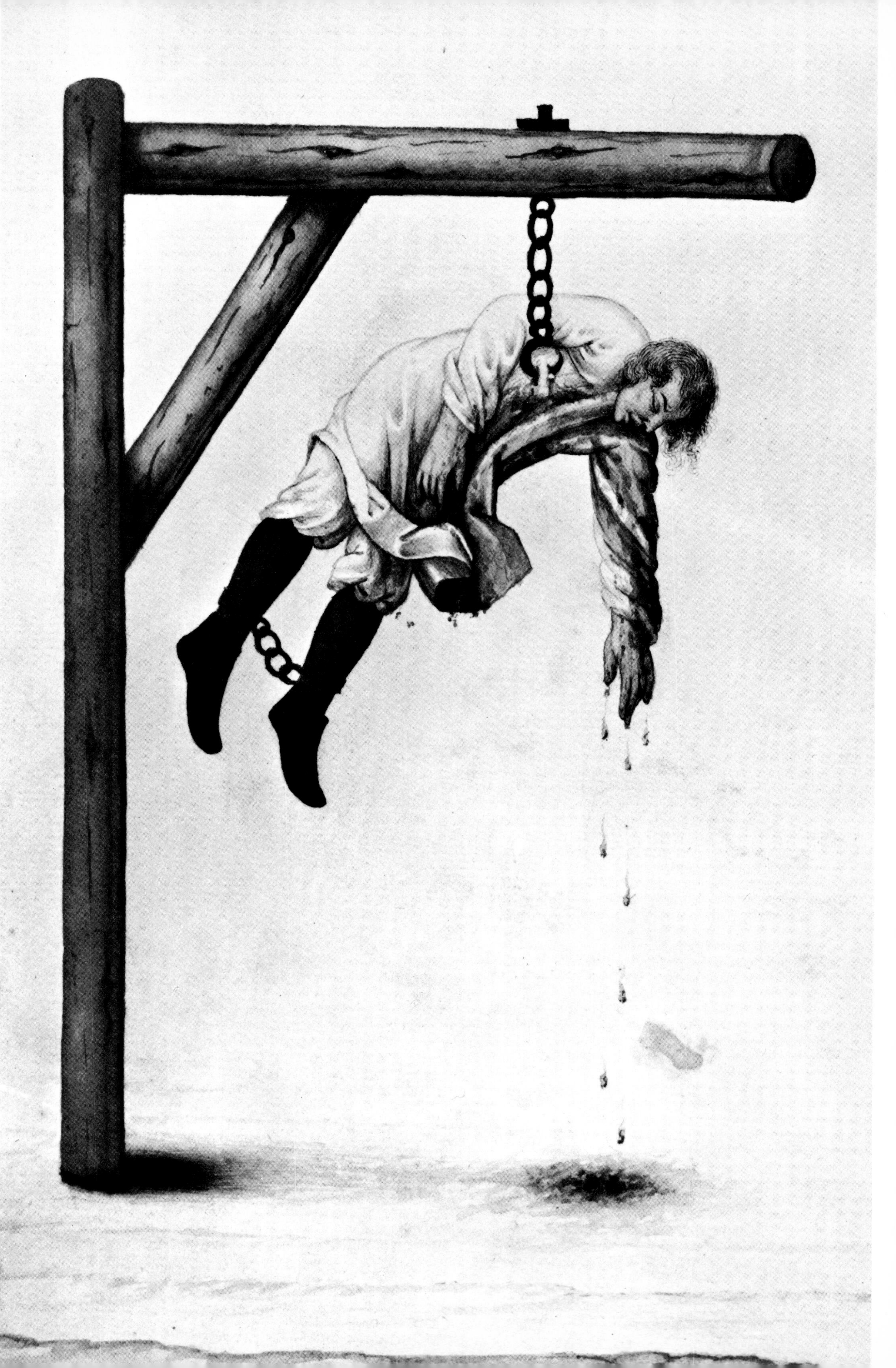

THE AGONY OF OPPRESSION
by Alexander Radishchev

Radishchev's criticism of the social order in A Journey from St. Petersburg, 1790, *stirred intellectuals. He was considered a threat to Catherine and was exiled to Siberia.*

O inhabitants of Petersburg, who feed on the superabundance of the fertile districts of your country, whether at magnificent banquets, or at a friendly feast, or alone, as your hand raises the first piece of bread meant to nourish you, stop and think. . . . Have not the fields on which it grew been enriched by sweat, tears, and groans? . . . Upon [that bread] are grief and despair, upon it is made manifest the curse of the Almighty, who in His anger said: "Cursed be the earth in its fruits." Beware lest ye be poisoned by the food ye covet. The bitter tears of the poor lie heavy on it. Put it away from your lips, and fast, for that may be a sincere and wholesome fast. . . .

A certain man who . . . did not make his mark in the government service . . . left the capital, acquired a small village of one or two hundred souls, and determined to make his living by agriculture. . . . This nobleman forced all his peasants and their wives and children to work every day of the year for him. Lest they should starve, he doled out to them a definite quantity of bread . . . [and] thin cabbage soup on meat days, and on fast days bread and kvas, to fill their stomachs. If there was any real meat, it was only in Easter Week. . . .

With such an arrangement it is not surprising that agriculture in Mr. So-and-So's village was in a flourishing condition. . . . He increased his holdings year after year, thus multiplying the number of those groaning in his fields. Now he counts them by the thousand and is praised as a famous agriculturist.

Barbarian! You do not deserve to bear the name of citizen. What good does it do the country that every year a few thousand more bushels of grain are grown, if those who produce it are valued on a par with the ox whose job it is to break the heavy furrow? . . . The wealth of this bloodsucker does not belong to him. It has been acquired by robbery and deserves severe punishment according to law. . . . Destroy the tools of his agriculture, burn his barns, silos, and granaries, and scatter their ashes over the fields where he practiced his tortures; stigmatize him as a robber of the people, so that everyone who sees him may not only despise him but shun his approach to avoid infection from his example.

The day and the hour of the auction have come. Prospective buyers are gathering. In the hall where it is to take place, those who are condemned to be sold stand immovable. An old man, seventy-five years of age . . . is anxious to find out into whose hands fate will deliver him, and who will close his eyes. He had been with his master's father in the Crimean Campaign. . . . In the Battle of Frankfurt he had carried his wounded master on his shoulders from the field. . . . The old woman, his wife, is eighty years of age. She had been the wet-nurse of the young master's mother; later she became his nurse and had the supervision of the house up to the very hour when she was brought out to his auction. . . . The forty-year-old woman is a widow, the young master's wet-nurse. To this day she feels a certain tenderness for him. Her blood flows in his veins. . . . The eighteen-year-old girl is her daughter and the old man's granddaughter. Beast, monster, outcast among men! Look at her, look at her crimson cheeks, at the tears flowing from her beautiful eyes. When you [the master] could neither ensnare her innocence with enticements and promises nor shake her steadfastness with threats and punishments, did you not finally use deception. . . . She is holding a little one, the lamentable fruit of deception or violence, but the living image of his lascivious father. . . . The lad of twenty-five, her wedded husband, the companion and intimate of his master. Savagery and vengeance are in his eyes. He repents the service he did his master. . . . It is not difficult to guess his thoughts. . . . You will become the property of another. The master's hand, constantly raised over his slave's head, will bend your neck to his every pleasure. Hunger, cold, heat, punishment, everything will be against you. Noble thoughts are foreign to your mind. You do not know how to die. You will bow down and be a slave in spirit as in estate. And if you should try to offer resistance, you would die a languishing death in fetters. . . .

For the first time I looked closely at all the household gear of a peasant hut. For the first time I turned my heart to things over which it had only glided heretofore. The upper half of the four walls, and the whole ceiling, were covered with soot; the floor was full of cracks and covered with dirt at least two inches thick; the oven without a smoke-stack, but their best protection against the cold; and smoke filling the hut every morning, winter and summer; window holes over which were stretched bladders which admitted a dim light at noon time; two or three pots (happy the hut if one of them each day contains some watery cabbage soup!). A wooden bowl and round trenchers called plates; a table, hewn with an axe, which they scrape clean on holidays. A trough to feed the pigs and calves, if there are any. They sleep together with them, swallowing the air in which a burning candle appears as though shrouded in mist or hidden behind a curtain. If they are lucky, a barrel of kvas that tastes like vinegar, and in the yard a bath house in which the cattle sleep if people are not steaming in it. A homespun shirt, the footwear given them by nature, and leggings and bast shoes when they go out. Here one justly looks for the source of the country's wealth, power, and might. . . . Here may be seen the greed of the gentry, our rapaciousness and tyranny; and the helplessness of the poor. Ravening beasts, insatiable leeches, what do we leave for the peasants? . . . The law forbids us to take their life—that is, to take it suddenly. But there are so many ways to take it from them by degrees!

After punishment had been administered, the bloodied peasant might be gibbeted for public instruction.

Flailing the grain, a vital activity in a country where the peasants' main food was bread, was more strenuous than this ideal-

ized nineteenth-century painting suggests. It took place in the threshing barn or outdoors, and the whole family participated.

FOLK ARTISTRY *found one of its most spontaneous expressions in the wooden sculpture of peasant carvers who fashioned everyday objects. The long-nosed country-woman (left) and her pipe-smoking husband (far left), made by a nineteenth-century artisan, are actually birdhouses for starlings, who would enter through the face and nest in the head. Because of the abundance of wood in many areas of Russia, woodcarving became a favorite medium of folk art, and nearly every peasant was a carpenter of sorts, turning out ladles, buckets, beehives, and utensils vital to his personal needs. His repertory also included religious figures and other decorative objects done in stylized natural forms and geometric patterns, as well as realistic likenesses of his fellow muzhiks.*

FROZEN FOOD MARKETS, *like the one shown in this late eighteenth-century engraving, were picturesque centers of commerce and gossip, where peasants sold their own or their landlord's produce. Foreign visitors were amazed to discover that the Russian winter acted as a natural refrigerator, freezing food that was subsequently thawed without much loss of flavor. "Your astonished sight," reported one Englishman, "is there arrested by a vast open square, containing the bodies of many thousand animals piled in pyramidical heaps on all sides. Cows, sheep, hogs, fowls, butter, eggs, fish are all stiffened into granite." The open-air winter market was a truly Russian spectacle, for the bearded merchants and peasants who gathered there wore traditional Muscovite costume—long, heavy caftans and fur caps.*

224

THE PARISH CHURCH, *the hub of peasant life, was situated in the* selo, *or village, and it served a cluster of communal settlements. Most muzhiks accepted Orthodoxy, laden with pagan deities and rites. They worshiped in stark, wooden churches, such as the nineteenth-century structure pictured opposite, in which an ornately carved iconostasis was usually the main decorative element—in contrast to the Byzantine opulence of most urban churches. The village priest, or* pop (*who, unlike the monastic clergy, could marry*), *eked out a meager livelihood by working the land and collecting fees for ecclesiastical services. Although the majority of the priests were pillars of sanctity, instances of moral laxness were not unknown. The holy procession, depicted in the 1860 drawing above, has the overtones of a drunken brawl and confirms a report issued to Grand Duke Constantine, brother of Alexander* II, *which asks: "Can the people respect the clergy when they hear how one priest stole money from below the pillow of a dying man at confession, how another was publicly dragged out of a house of ill fame, how a third christened a dog, how a fourth . . . was dragged by the hair from the altar by the deacon?"*

227

7

The Iron Rule

The French Revolution had given new impetus to the demand for liberal reforms in Russia, but, more importantly, it rallied the strong reactionary elements around the empress. Talk of reform became treasonable and all hope of change vanished. Conditions in Russia continued to deteriorate alarmingly. Inflation, food shortages, the extravagances of the court, mounting military expenditures, and the underlying gangrene of serfdom combined to present the nation with a massive crisis. Russia needed an activist emperor, but the forty-two-year-old Paul, who had succeeded Catherine, was unstable and impetuous.

Paul hated his mother. He blamed her for his father's murder, and he bitterly resented the fact that she had usurped his throne for so many years. He rejected as far as possible all that his mother had done. He shared Peter III's hero worship of Frederick the Great and revered all things Prussian. He was obsessed with military parades and the paraphernalia of war. During the years when he was grand duke and heir to the throne he had not been allowed to take part in state affairs. Virtually confined to his estate at Gatchina, he had

Rather than surrender Moscow to Napoleon, on September 14, 1812, the evacuating citizens reportedly set fire to their ancient capital. In this lithograph detail, after a painting by Johann Rugendas, crudely armed Russians deliver parting blows at the invaders.

spent his time drilling and parading his private army of some two thousand men. Now as emperor he had the armies of the nation at his command. St. Petersburg was transformed into a military camp. Army discipline became more savage. Men who were guilty of real or imagined mistakes were cruelly flogged. He further antagonized the army, and especially the regiments of guards, by introducing Prussian uniforms in place of the ones Peter the Great and Potemkin had designed.

The army and the parade ground defined Paul's attitude toward the state. In his view the emperor held the absolute power of a general over subjects, who were to be ordered about as though they were troops on parade. He regarded obedience and discipline as the basic needs of a healthy society. Apart from the regimentation he sought to impose, Russia began to suffer even more from the excessive centralization of all the government's functions in St. Petersburg.

Under Paul's erratic rule, certain *ukazy* were issued to ease the burdens of the peasantry. A decree promulgated in April, 1797, for example, laid down that landowners, some of whom exacted five or six days of labor a week from their serfs, should, in the future, require them to work only three days; the remaining three days belonged to the serfs for the cultivation of their own lands, and Sunday was for rest. However, it is doubtful whether this important and progressive enactment was ever enforced. As the serfs had no means

of recourse against landowners who ignored it and as Paul was eager to limit the power of the upper classes, he restored, in part, the right of the peasants to petition the throne with their grievances. But it was difficult to exercise this right, and landowners could still uproot their peasants and send them to Siberia. As if to negate these limited benefits, Paul insisted that unrest among the peasantry must be dealt with firmly, and he issued a manifesto calling on all serfs to obey their masters without question.

At the same time Paul antagonized the gentry by assailing privileges that Catherine had bestowed. In 1785 she had granted a charter guaranteeing them immunity from corporal punishments, payment of taxes, and deprivation of rank and estates except by judgment of their peers. He did not impose taxes on the gentry, but would "invite" them to contribute to the treasury for special purposes. He also required them to serve in the army. Refusal resulted in disgrace, banishment from court, and more serious punishments—often so savage that they caused severe injury or death. It was not uncommon for Paul in one of his bouts of temper to take away an offender's noble rank; this loss of privilege was of great importance.

Foreign policy was also subject to Paul's whims. He had criticized Catherine's extensive military commitments and had vowed that on ascending the throne he would cancel them. But he was so strongly opposed to the revolutionary movement that he involved Russia in several European squabbles. He joined a coalition against France in 1799. He sent an army under the command of the brilliant Russian General Alexander Suvorov to join with the Austrian forces in northern Italy. But when the Austrians failed to support their allies sufficiently, relations between the two states quickly became strained. The combined armies nevertheless gained several victories in Italy and were preparing to invade France when Suvorov received orders to march on Switzerland without delay. In a feat of remarkable military derring he led his army over the Alps by way of the St. Gotthard Pass. In Switzerland, however, relations between Russians and Austrians deteriorated further, and in 1800 Paul, angered by Austrian complaints about the disrespectful behavior of the Russian troops, suddenly canceled the accord and recalled Suvorov and his army. He next severed relations with Great Britain, mainly because the British failed to make good their promise to cede the island of Malta. By banning British ships from Russian ports he inadvertently damaged Russia's trade. He then joined the new Armed Neutrality with Sweden, Denmark, and Prussia to oppose British sea power, thus bringing Russian trade with its principal customer to an official standstill.

Meanwhile, Paul had reversed his earlier policy with

Paul I, who inherited his mother's throne at forty-two, strikes a pose of unwarranted dignity in the painting opposite. Reviled both at home and abroad, he was more often portrayed in the spirit of the British cartoon above, which characterizes "Crazy Paul"—"Fickle as the passing air, / Led about by Bonaparte, / Growling like a dancing bear." His son, the thoughtful Alexander I (right), seemed to represent a new breed of ruler.

France and decided that Napoleon was a necessary ally. He became enthusiastic about alliance with France, Austria, and Prussia for the purpose of partitioning Turkey and destroying British power. Russia and Britain now came close to war. In January, 1801, the tsar formally annexed Georgia, which had been under divided Turkish and Persian suzerainty, and then he ordered a force of twenty-three thousand Cossacks to proceed toward British India, which he dreamed of conquering.

Paul had antagonized the regular army and the gentry, the two main pillars of his throne, to the point where a palace revolution had become almost inevitable. The military governor of St. Petersburg, Count Peter Pahlen, was the leader of the final conspiracy. On March 11, 1801, he and several officers of the guard dined together and then set out for the Mikhailovsky Fortress, which Paul had had rebuilt for greater security. The sentries did not hesitate to admit the military governor and the officers with him. They made for the emperor's bedchamber, but it appeared to be empty. Paul had heard them approaching and had hidden in the chimney of the fireplace, but one of the party noticed his dangling feet. They dragged him out, screaming for mercy. Someone struck him with a gold snuffbox and then strangled him with a scarf.

A proclamation had been prepared in advance, giving the cause of his death as apoplexy, and it was generally accepted

without close question. St. Petersburg and the nation as a whole were eager to welcome Paul's son, Alexander, as emperor, for great things were expected of him, and the matter of the succession was free of all uncertainties. When Paul had finally attained the throne, he had issued an *ukaz* rescinding Peter's 1722 decree and establishing that the throne must pass in future according to the laws of primogeniture.

Alexander ascended the throne with reluctance, despite his strong idealism and sense of mission, which César de La Harpe, his Swiss Jacobin tutor, had instilled in him. Soon after his accession Alexander declared his policy of peace, based on agreements with Great Britain, France, Austria, and Prussia. "If I ever raise arms," he stated, "it will be exclusively in defense against aggression, for the protection of my peoples or of the victims of ambitions that endanger the peace of Europe. . . ." His immediate task was to avert such disasters as Paul had inflicted upon the nation. He recalled the Cossacks from their advance toward India. He revived friendly relations with Britain and in June, 1801, signed a new Anglo-Russian convention in St. Petersburg. He also agreed to a treaty with France in October, 1801, and in June of the following year reached close understanding with Frederick William III, king of Prussia. Having laid the foundations for peace, he felt free to devote himself to reforms.

The first *ukazy* of his reign gave promise of a broad and

231

enlightened program. The security police were abolished, and he declared that "all crimes must be provided for, tried, and punished by the general laws." He replaced the Privy Council that Catherine had established by a permanent council of twelve prominent advisers. He appointed a special commission to examine the problem of reducing the accumulated decrees of previous reigns and setting them out clearly in a law code. He made the Senate the highest judicial and administrative organ in the land, subordinate only to the autocrat. He completed the changeover from Peter the Great's Twelve Colleges, which had proved cumbersome, to ministerial departments. He calmed the anxious gentry by reinstituting their charter of privileges, which Paul had limited; and he revived Catherine's system of local government, which Paul had set aside.

In planning his liberal reforms Alexander relied on four trusted friends, Count Viktor Kochubey, Prince Adam Czartorysky, and Nikolai Novosiltsev, all keen students of the British parliamentary system, and Count Pavel Stroganov, who had studied in France. The four friends formed the Private Committee, which met frequently from mid-1801 until the end of 1805. The Private Committee had as its first task the drafting of Alexander's statement of principles, his so-called Charter of the Russian People, to be proclaimed with full ceremony at his coronation on September 15, 1801.

Their draft charter was an enlightened document; it guaranteed freedom of the individual, freedom of the press and of speech, religious tolerance, and other fundamental rights. When the time came, however, Alexander feared the hostile reception that it would receive from the conservative gentry, and the charter was not proclaimed. Similarly, the work of the Private Committee in preparing a legal constitution for Russia was stillborn.

Alexander had also considered reforms to relieve the peasantry of their heavy burdens; but little of substance was achieved. In May, 1801, he decreed that landowners should not advertise serfs for sale as though they were livestock, rather they should simply announce serfs "for hire," which in practice meant for sale. His *ukaz*, proclaimed in February, 1803, allowing serfs to achieve their freedom through voluntary release by their owners under certain conditions, caused general excitement, but only 47,153 male serfs, representing about one per cent of the serf population, were able to take advantage of this law during the twenty-four years of Alexander's reign. The redemption price that serfs had to pay was far beyond the means of the great majority. Of more lasting significance were his pioneering efforts to promote education. He established forty-two secondary schools and many primary schools, as well as several universities for able and deserving children of all classes, though, in effect, the lower

Described by Pushkin as a "crowned drill sergeant," Alexander indulged his love of the military by inspecting troops on the St. Petersburg parade grounds, as in the engraving at left. Battlefield engagements were entrusted to Mikhail Kutuzov, subject of the painting above, who led the fight against Napoleon.

classes rarely dared to exercise the newly won privilege.

The war of the Third Coalition was soon to engage Alexander's full attention. Napoleon had signed treaties with Russia in October, 1801, and with Great Britain in March, 1802, primarily to provide time to rebuild his armies; but he maintained his blockade of Britain and continued to mass troops along the North Sea and Channel coasts until an army of two hundred ten thousand men stood ready to cross the Channel. However, Admiral Horatio Nelson's fleet kept the French squadrons under close observation, and to protect his invasion force for the crossing of the Channel, Napoleon suddenly turned eastward against Austria.

Meanwhile, Napoleon had become increasingly critical of Russia and especially of the friendly relations the emperor maintained with Britain. Alexander, who had worsened matters by sending a note to Napoleon, ostensibly protesting the callous murder of the duke of Enghien, son of the duke of Bourbon, was chastened by the sharp reply, which referred to his complicity in the murder of his own father. From this time Alexander saw that war with Napoleon was inevitable, and he became the architect of a grand alliance with Britain —supported by Sweden, Austria, and the Kingdom of Naples—with the purpose of creating a new Europe free of French domination. Alexander's scheme also provided for Russia to acquire by force vast areas of Poland, which were

under Prussian and Austrian rule, as well as Moldavia, Corfu, Constantinople, the Dardanelles, Malta, and other territories. Alexander, even in his most idealistic moods, seldom missed an opportunity for Russia's aggrandizement.

Britain's Prime Minister, William Pitt, whose sole concern was to defeat Napoleon, readily accepted those parts of Alexander's scheme that would further this purpose. An Anglo-Russian treaty was signed on April 11, 1805, by which England promised total subsidies of five million to those monarchs who would put troops in the field against France. With Russia's help, pressure was brought to bear on Sweden, Prussia, and Austria. Only Prussia remained neutral.

Turning eastward in August, 1805, Napoleon made one of his famed advances. The Austrians were taken completely by surprise, and at Ulm, on October 9, their army capitulated. As a result of this easy victory, Napoleon was faced with a difficult decision. He was far from his home base and winter was approaching. News of Admiral Nelson's destruction of the French fleet at Trafalgar, establishing British mastery of the seas, had just reached him. He also recognized that the Russian army was a formidable force. At this stage, however, Alexander made a fatal mistake. His commander in chief had advised that the Russian army fall back, drawing the French farther and farther from their bases and exposing them to the rigors of winter. But, under pressure from Emperor Francis

of Austria, Alexander ordered the Russian army to go to Vienna's defense, and at Austerlitz they suffered an overwhelming defeat. It was Napoleon's most brilliant victory, and a disaster for Alexander. Austria and then Prussia signed ignominious treaties at Napoleon's dictation.

Matters worsened when in December, 1806, largely as a result of French pressure in Constantinople, Turkey declared war on Russia. Alexander nevertheless sent Russian troops to the West and in the savage but inconclusive battle of Eylau engaged the French. They met again at Friedland in East Prussia in June, 1807, and his troops were put to flight. Alexander was pressured by his closest advisers to sue for peace.

The confrontation of Alexander and Napoleon, on the magnificently decorated raft in the middle of the Neman River opposite Tilsit, is one of the dramatic meetings in history. The two men talked alone for some three hours. Napoleon persuaded Alexander to reverse the policies Russia had followed for decades. Alexander became convinced that alliance with France should be the cornerstone of Russian policy and that Britain was the real enemy.

The discussions at Tilsit resulted in the Franco-Russian treaty, which Alexander then proceeded to implement. In November, 1807, he broke off diplomatic relations with Britain. In the following February, at Napoleon's instigation, he invaded Sweden, annexed Finland, and joined the con-

tinental blockade against Britain. When in February, 1808, Napoleon proposed joint Russo-French actions in Scandinavia and Turkey, and also a campaign in Asia, the ultimate object of which was the conquest of India, Alexander reacted with enthusiasm. He seemed incapable of refusing Napoleon anything, except when it came to annexing Prussia.

Quixotically, Alexander refused to betray Frederick William, although he was forced to stand by while the Prussian king ceded to France all Prussian territory west of the Elbe as well as its Polish provinces, which were thenceforth to be formed into the grand duchy of Warsaw. The creation of this duchy amounted to a reversal of the policies of Catherine the Great, and it represented a threat to Russia itself. Alexander and Napoleon met again in Erfurt from September 27 until October 14, 1808. This meeting was surrounded with even greater panoply than the famed meeting at Tilsit. Kings and princes from all parts of Europe were present to pay homage to Napoleon and to the Russian emperor. Despite Alexander's suspicion when he could obtain no satisfaction concerning the partition of Turkey, the Franco-Russian alliance was reaffirmed. The tsar had to be content with Napoleon's guarantee of the annexation of Moldavia, Wallachia, and Finland, in return for which he bound himself to declare war on Austria, if it were to attack France.

The Austrians were, in fact, preparing desperately to renew

In the engraving opposite, a defeated Alexander I meets Napoleon (the shorter monarch) on a lavishly equipped barge moored midstream in the Neman River near Tilsit. At this peace conference held on June 25, 1807, the emperors apparently spent most of three hours exchanging flatteries, for Napoleon later wrote that if the tsar "were a woman, I think I would make him my mistress." He made a pact with Alexander and granted Russia liberal terms, agreeing to divide Europe between their nations. Armistice negotiations ended in displays of camaraderie like the fete at right, at which grenadiers introduce Russians to French cuisine.

the war against France, and in May, 1809, they came near to defeating Napoleon's army at Aspern and Essling. In July, however, the Austrian army was routed at Wagram, and the Treaty of Schönbrunn, reducing Austria to a second-class nation, was imposed. Alexander had given Napoleon no assistance during the war, although his troops had been massed at the Galician frontier, and he now felt strong misgivings over the destruction of Austrian power.

Russian opinion had already become anti-French. The fear was growing that Napoleon, having conquered the rest of Europe, would finally turn on Russia. A further factor intensifying hatred of the French was the dislocation of the Russian economy, resulting from the continental blockade. The export of flax, linen, tallow, grain, hemp, timber, and metals, especially iron ore, had dropped critically, and the import of such British goods as manufactured wares, wines, spirits, wool, and various other luxuries had stopped. Galloping inflation was felt in every part of the country, but it was the cessation of trade with Britain that made the burdens insupportable. In 1810 Alexander relaxed the embargo on trade with Britain. Napoleon began talking of the inevitability of war with Russia.

Moreover, Napoleon's persistence in concluding a political marriage had offended Alexander. Having divorced Josephine, Napoleon sought the hand of Alexander's fifteen-year-old sister, Grand Duchess Anna, offering in return the assurance that Poland would never be resurrected. Alexander did not welcome the marriage, especially as his sister was so young, and delayed his reply. Losing all patience, Napoleon suddenly informed the Russian court of his change of mind in two notes: one withdrawing his original marriage proposal; the other announcing his intention to marry Archduchess Marie Louise of Austria. The latter crossed with a courteous note from Alexander asking Napoleon to wait two years for his sister to reach maturity. Napoleon's inept handling of this delicate matter caused great offense in St. Petersburg, which was at the same time alarmed by this evidence of a change in French policy from alliance with Russia to alliance with Austria. Relations between Russia and France now declined rapidly. Alexander began concentrating troops on the western frontier, while in Prussia and in the duchy of Warsaw French troops were massing.

In the months after the Tilsit meeting, Alexander had turned his attention to internal reforms and had come under the influence of Mikhail Speransky, an outstanding liberal. Speransky, modest and retiring in personality, was the son of a village priest; he had reached the St. Petersburg Theological Academy and then by good fortune had become secretary to the then minister of internal affairs, Count Viktor Kochubey. Alexander had taken him on the visit to Erfurt as a mem-

Raging from dawn to dusk on September 7, 1812, the bloody battle of Borodino, depicted at right in the heroic painting by Louis-François Lejeune, was Russia's major defensive effort to stop the French advance toward Moscow. The fighting signaled the age of artillery warfare, as canon bombardments, blinding gunsmoke, and deafening explosions threw traditional formations of infantry and cavalry into confusion and made organized assault by either side impossible. Although the Grand Army technically triumphed, opening the road to Moscow, French troops (seen in the foreground) were demoralized, for few prisoners were taken and the Russians remained steadfast. As Napoleon reflected: "The French showed themselves worthy of victory, and the Russians of being invincible."

ber of his suite and had then appointed him assistant to the minister of justice, and two years later, secretary of state.

The first major task that Alexander entrusted to Speransky was to prepare a plan of constitutional reform. In October, 1809, Speransky submitted "An Introduction to the Code of State Laws," which was both a critical review of the existing system and an impressive proposal for major reforms. In his review Speransky was remarkably outspoken. He wrote in one typical passage: "People complain of the confused finances. But how can finances be organized in a state which lacks public confidence, where there are no national laws or order which would protect them? Of what use is education? Only to enable the public to observe more clearly its miserable condition . . . I do not mention here subjects of a more important character, namely, the relation of the peasants to their owners, that is, the relation between millions of people, composing the most useful part of the population and a handful of parasites who acquired, God knows why and how, all rights and privileges." Despite his devastating condemnation of the existing system, and particularly of serfdom, Speransky did not envisage immediate emancipation of the peasants. But his proposals included strict separation of legislative, administrative, and judicial powers. The government was to be organized like a pyramid with the autocrat at the apex and beneath him a state council, which would serve as an advisory body on legislation and coordinate the other executive and judicial organs of government.

Alexander was a secretive man. None, not even those closest to him, ever succeeded in probing his mind. It is not known what he thought of Speransky's proposals. The draft plan was kept in his private archives and never published. Speransky managed, nevertheless, to obtain approval for the state council and for certain basic reforms in the financial organization and structure of the central administration. His views were, however, so critical of the regime that the gentry, with few exceptions, were soon ranged solidly against him. Their hostility mounted when his plans to reform the administrative system became known. An *ukaz* of April 6, 1809, aroused bitter antagonism, especially as it laid down that promotion beyond certain grades depended on passing examinations or holding a university degree. His proposals to check inflation were equally unpopular. Alexander eventually yielded to demands, and Speransky was exiled in 1812.

Three months later, in June, 1812, Napoleon made the momentous decision to invade Russia. Alexander was taking part in an imperial ball in Vilna when the news of the French invasion was brought to him. He received it calmly, made excuses to his hostess, and at once joined his army. Despite preparations, the Russians were not ready to meet the French onslaught. A treaty of peace with Turkey, concluded on May

28, 1812, had relieved Alexander of the problems of engagement on two fronts, but he could oppose only 220,000 troops against the French army of some 500,000 men. The Russian commander, Mikhail Barclay de Tolly, retreated before the French forces. Napoleon advanced swiftly to Vilna. All Russians expected him to be halted at Smolensk, but Barclay de Tolly surrendered the city and retreated toward Moscow. His conduct aroused a storm of criticism. Alexander, whose presence with his army was hampering battlefield operations, was urged to return to the capital.

Reluctantly, Alexander then appointed Prince Mikhail Kutuzov as commander in chief of the imperial army. Kutuzov was already a legendary figure. At this time he was sixty-seven, had only one eye, and was so fat that he could hardly walk (his father had served under Peter the Great, and the younger Kutuzov had been one of the leading generals under Catherine the Great). Above all, his leadership inspired the troops. The tactics of retreat that had brought about Barclay de Tolly's downfall were continued when Kutuzov assumed command. As a concession to Russian feeling, he attempted against his better judgment to engage the French army at Borodino, a village seventy miles southwest of Moscow. The battle, which resulted in seventy thousand casualties, was inconclusive, with each side claiming victory. Napoleon considered it the most savage battle he had ever fought, and the loss of forty-seven of his generals was to affect the future course of the campaign. Withdrawing his army in good order, Kutuzov made a surprising decision: he directed the army guarding Moscow to evacuate and march southeastward in the direction of Ryazan. The order to evacuate the city, the symbolic heart of the nation, was a deep shock, but Kutuzov recognized that he had to choose between saving Moscow and saving his army.

On September 14 Napoleon entered Moscow. The city was almost deserted, and fires, breaking out on the same evening, raged for four days—reducing most of Moscow to ashes. Though it was widely rumored that the French had perpetrated this fearful act of desecration, the fires may have been started by the Russians in the final evacuation. Napoleon, who had taken it for granted that Alexander and the Russian nation would surrender on the fall of Moscow, now spent thirty-three days in the ruins of the city while his attempts to negotiate peace were ignored.

Alexander and his subjects shared an unshakable faith that no invader could survive in their vast land. The Austrian ambassador reported to Vienna: "The emperor has little confidence in the talents of his generals. . . . He puts his trust in the courage of his troops, their discipline, and their passive obedience, but even more so in the obstacles, which in his dominions are offered by the terrain—wooded, swampy,

237

The Napoleonic Wars were accompanied by savage propaganda campaigns. Above and center, Russian artists take aim at France's recruitment of its "enthusiastic and voluntary" army and at Bonaparte's excessive appetite for additional territory. At right, a British caricature depicts the unequal contest between the Russian colossus and "Bony."

primitive, and sparsely populated. His Majesty greatly relies on the difficulty of supplies and the rigor of the climate." The governor of Moscow, Count Fedor Rostopchin, expressed this more succinctly when he wrote to the emperor: "I am not afraid of reverses; your empire has two powerful defenders in its peasants and its climate. The emperor will always be formidable in Moscow, terrible in Kazan, and invincible in Tobolsk."

On October 19 the troops of Napoleon's Grand Army, laden with booty and encumbered by sick and wounded, began their retreat from Moscow. The winter cold and the partisan bands that harried them incessantly made their progress painfully slow. On November 8 they arrived at Smolensk; some twenty days later they reached the Berezina River. Kutuzov had been following at a distance with the main Russian army; he now made an unsuccessful attempt to halt Napoleon's forces. The French army continued its weary retreat, finally crossing the Neman River on December 14. The Grand Army, which with reinforcements had numbered 600,000 at the time of the invasion five months earlier, was reduced to 30,000 ragged survivors.

Napoleon's invasion had made a profound impression on Alexander. He had never been overtly religious, but from this time his belief in his messianic world role deepened. He came under the influence of mystics. Alexander now be-

lieved that he was engaged in a terrible struggle against the "reign of Satan" and that he was the "depository of a sacred, holy mission." In Vilna Alexander joined his army. He ignored Kutuzov's urgent pleas that the troops be allowed to rest, for he was determined to pursue Napoleon until French power had been crushed and peace signed.

The Russian army crossed the Neman River on January 13, 1813. Soon afterward, in Silesia, Kutuzov died, worn out by his last campaign. Alexander felt that he could now press forward more rapidly. The Russians joined with Austrian and Prussian troops, and at Leipzig the allied forces decisively defeated the French, who fled over the Rhine. The Austrian and Prussian commanders urgently sought to make peace, but Alexander insisted that the threat to Europe could only be removed by the expulsion of Napoleon.

On March 31, 1814, Alexander entered Paris at the head of the allied army. He was welcomed with enthusiasm by the French people, who were weary of war. And in the liberal terms of the Treaty of Fontainebleau, by which Napoleon was forced to abdicate, and of the first Treaty of Paris, he gave evidence of his generosity toward former enemies.

That September emperors, kings, ruling princes, and their envoys convened the Congress of Vienna to consider terms by which "a real and permanent balance of power" could be revived. Its ostensible purpose was to distribute the

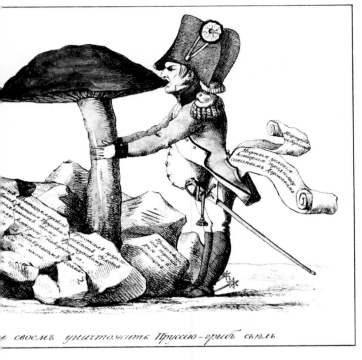

extensive territories reconquered from France, but its long-range goal was to restore the European state system as it had existed before the French Revolution and ensure peace for the future. Alexander, who was conspicuous among the monarchs present as the only man free to form his own foreign policy without interference from his home government, was determined, above all else, to secure agreement to his annexation of the grand duchy of Warsaw. However, the assembled powers forced a compromise: the grand duchy of Warsaw became a constitutional kingdom with the Russian emperor as its sovereign; Prussia regained some Polish territories it had previously held; Austria recovered Galicia; and Krakow became a free city.

Alexander's conduct at the Congress of Vienna had aroused strong suspicion of his loudly professed ideals. Napoleon's return to Europe from Elba in March, 1815, which was generally attributed to Alexander's excessively benevolent terms, had further diminished the tsar's influence. Alexander's request that he should be commander in chief of the allied army was curtly rejected by Wellington. Indeed, after the battle of Waterloo (June 18, 1815), the duke of Wellington dominated the allied camp, and Alexander, who reached Paris nearly a month later, was able to contribute little to the second, more severe Treaty of Paris.

In an attempt to regain his self-appointed role of the Christian emperor, providing the whole world with moral leadership, he proclaimed on September 26, 1815, his Holy Alliance. This manifesto, couched in lofty language, pledged the signatories to observe the teachings of Christianity in their conduct toward each other and toward their subjects. Alexander saw it as a declaration of faith and the beginning of a "universal union." All the European sovereigns but the pope and the Turkish sultan were asked to subscribe. All but Britain agreed. Viscount Castlereagh, the British foreign secretary, who considered it a piece of "mysticism and sublime nonsense," brought the allies together on a more practical basis in the Quadruple Alliance of November, 1815, which was intended to exclude the House of Bonaparte from power and to maintain the international peace and security of Europe. Alexander assumed that this principle extended to the maintenance of legitimate governments against attack from revolutionary forces within (in each of the five revolutions that erupted in 1820–21 he proposed allied intervention). Unlike Alexander, Castlereagh and his successor, George Canning, were opposed to involving the signatories in the internal affairs of foreign states.

During these years Alexander had continued to cherish vague plans of internal reform. Then in October, 1820, a mutiny among the Semyonovsky guards—the regiment that had figured in bringing him to the throne in 1801—pro-

OVERLEAF: *Pursued by Russians, remnants of the Grand Army retreat across the Berezina River, abandoning baggage, jamming make-shift bridges, and swimming the waters in their panic.*

vided proof that dangerous revolutionaries were gaining a hold on the country. He disbanded the Semyonovsky guards and now became openly reactionary. His fears of the spread of revolutionary ideas were indeed justified. Many young officers who had seen action in western Europe and had served in the army of occupation in France for as long as three years looked with new eyes upon the miserable conditions of their own people. Justice was nonexistent and corruption widespread. They saw that Russia was fearfully backward compared with the countries of the West. The young liberals and army officers had to take great care in their criticism of reactionary policies and their discussions of reforms. Although Alexander had proclaimed the abolition of the security police at the beginning of his reign, a far larger secret police was now operating under the control of Alexei Arakcheev, a figure who had gained Alexander's confidence and had served him in an advisory capacity. With typical thoroughness Arakcheev had instituted a special security branch within the guard regiments and had spread this secret elite throughout the army. Officers and men suspected of liberal ideas were imprisoned or banished to Siberia. Nevertheless, secret societies, influenced by reformist members of the older Freemasons lodges, began to organize.

One of Alexander's most hated projects, launched in 1801, was the creation of military colonies, at first in the Novgorod district and later in the Ukraine and elsewhere. The purpose of such colonies was to enable Russia to maintain an army equal in size to the armies of Austria and Prussia together, and thus to ensure Russia's dominant position in European affairs. The economic burden would, he believed, be reduced by converting districts into military colonies in which all members would receive military training and live under military discipline, but at the same time work the land. Official permission was required to marry. Children were to be educated in local military schools and recruited into the army at the age of eighteen. Alexei Arakcheev was placed in charge of the colonies, which, despite massive opposition and repeated rebellions, were maintained until 1857.

Alexander had often talked of abdication, but no one knew his true thoughts. He had made up his mind, however, that since he had no legitimate children by his empress, Princess Louise of Baden, his younger brother Nicholas should succeed him. His brother Constantine, who stood next in line, had declared categorically in 1801, at the time of their father's murder, that "after what has happened my brother may reign if he likes, but if the throne ever comes to me I shall certainly not accept it." Constantine had held to this refusal, making it official with his request to marry a Polish Roman Catholic. In July, 1819, Alexander informed Nicholas of his decision. As always, the tsar acted with great

Christian Wilhelm Faber du Faur, a German officer in Napoleon's army, kept a pictorial diary of the 1812 campaign. These sketches reflect the rigorous life experienced by fellow soldiers on their retreat from Moscow. Center, on the road to Plevna (marked by a sign-post), the emperor and troops huddle around a fire, trying to fend off cold and hunger. Hardships have already taken their toll, as evidenced by corpses littering the snowscape. Other scenes show "tattered ghosts" of the Grand Army trudging westward; an officer riding in a sled; and an infantryman carrying off stolen provender.

secrecy. He had signed a manifesto, drafted by the metropolitan of Moscow, appointing Nicholas as his heir, but this and Constantine's letter of renunciation were deposited under seal in the Uspensky Cathedral in Moscow. Three copies of each document were kept in sealed envelopes in the offices of the State Council, the Senate, and the Holy Synod. Nicholas and Constantine both understood their own positions, but had no knowledge of any other dispositions made by the emperor. Six years later, while the imperial couple was on a visit to Taganrog on the Sea of Azov, Alexander fell ill; he died on November 19, 1825.

The death of Alexander, which had come so unexpectedly and in a remote corner of his empire, gave rise to a mystery that has never been resolved. Many refused to believe the official report. It was rumored that Alexander had slipped out of the country on an English yacht bound for the Holy Land. Then, when a holy man known as Father Fedor Kuzmich appeared in Siberia in 1836, many concluded that he was Alexander I in disguise. Evidence accumulated that Kuzmich closely resembled the emperor, who, when laid out in his coffin, was so changed as to be unrecognizable to those close to him. Finally, many recalled that Alexander had frequently said that he wanted only to be free from the burdens of the throne and to retreat from the world. At court, and even in the tsar's family during the reign of the next tsar, there would

be many who persisted in the belief that the holy father was none other than Emperor Alexander I.

When the news of Alexander's death reached St. Petersburg eight days later, Constantine was in Warsaw and Nicholas was in the capital. Nicholas was unsure of what action to take. He wanted to be tsar, and he had Alexander's promise that he would be the successor. However, in the eyes of the people Constantine, the oldest surviving brother, was the legal heir, and Nicholas, little better than a cruel martinet. Governed by a stern sense of duty and anxious to avoid an interregnum, Nicholas at once swore allegiance to his brother and ordered the nation to do the same. Despite Alexander's earlier attempt to settle the matter in Nicholas' favor, the State Council, the archbishop of Moscow, and the Senate recognized Constantine as emperor of Russia.

Constantine, who now resided in Warsaw, had no intention of accepting the throne. Couriers galloped between St. Petersburg and Warsaw, carrying messages of loyalty from one brother to the other. Nicholas urged Constantine to make a public statement and to return at once to the capital. Constantine's reply was blunt: "I am not able to accept your proposal to hasten my departure for St. Petersburg, and I warn you that I shall leave Warsaw only to retire to some greater distance if everything is not arranged according to the will of our deceased emperor."

"His name should be written not in ink, but in blood," wrote a contemporary of Count Alexei Arakcheev, portrayed at left before the stone barracks of one of the military colonies he created. Alexander's minister of war proved to be a martinet in the Prussian mold, and before the experiment was ended, some 800,000 rebellious souls had been forcibly turned into soldier-peasants. Arakcheev's rule extended even to mothers—who were to "give birth, every year, preferably [to] a son."

Inspired with the reformist spirit they had met in western Europe, a secret society of officers staged the abortive Decembrist Rising of 1825, depicted at right. Braving subzero weather, nearly 3,000 guards mutineers and sympathetic civilians milled about for hours on St. Petersburg's Senate Square. Loyal troops finally fired upon the rebels. That night, traces of the bloodbath were camouflaged with clean snow, and bodies of the dead and wounded were reportedly dumped through holes cut into the ice of the Neva River.

Tension in St. Petersburg mounted when dispatches came from Taganrog with news of a conspiracy among members of the army. A confirmatory report was given Nicholas by a young officer whom the group had tried to enlist. Faced with the immediate danger of mutiny among the guards, Nicholas decided to proclaim his own accession on December 14.

The conspirators, who became known in history as Decembrists, were an aristocratic group of young officers. Service abroad during the Napoleonic wars had provided them with firsthand knowledge of Western liberal movements and given them a clearer perspective of the desperate backwardness of their own nation. One of their number recalled: "Events had passed before our eyes which had determined the fate of nations . . . and it was unbearable to look at the empty life in Petersburg and listen to the babbling of the old men who praised the past and reproached every progressive move. We were away from them a hundred years." A secret society, the Union of Salvation, was founded in 1816, and for several years its members were committed to legal, economic, educational, and social reform—all apparently to be accomplished by peaceful, unrevolutionary means. Divisions began to appear, however, and in 1821 the members regrouped as the Northern Society, led by Captain Nikita Muravyov of the guards, and the Southern Society, headed by Colonel Pavel Pestel of the Vyatsky regiment.

Muravyov and his followers were bent on establishing a constitutional monarchy. "It is not permissible to let the basis of government be the despotism of one person; it is impossible to agree that all rights shall be on one side and all duties on the other," he wrote in the preamble to his proposed constitution. To broaden the base of power further, he argued for the division of Russia's vast lands into a federation of autonomous states and provinces, to be drawn along the lines of nationality groups. But his moderate program for the peasants and his protection of the traditional rights of the landowners were rejected by Pestel as a legalized continuation of the evil system the reformers sought to destroy. The radical Pestel called for nothing less than the destruction of the royal family, the elimination of class structure, the integration of national minorities into a single Russian people, and the redistribution of land.

As the day of Nicholas' accession dawned, St. Petersburg, gripped by icy cold, lay under gray winter mists. The insurgents gathered in the Senate Square about 10 A.M. Their plan was to prevent the Holy Synod and the Senate from swearing allegiance to Nicholas. They had come too late, however, for the Senate and the State Council had already sworn the oath, as had the St. Petersburg garrison. The insurgents were joined by some seven hundred soldiers of the Moscow regiment who were calling for "Constantine

and constitution." (It is said that many of the uneducated soldiers were under the impression that constitution, or *konstitutsia*, was the name of Constantine's wife.) Other soldiers joined them, until some three thousand rebels were gathered in the Senate Square. Civilians were urging them to attack the government troops, who were taking up positions in front of the Senate building.

The young Prince Yevgeny Obolensky, who appeared to be in charge, was unsure what action to take. The explosion came when the governor-general of St. Petersburg, Count Miloradovich, dashed onto the square in an open sleigh. This gallant and beloved old soldier approached the rebels, and addressed them simply. "I myself would rather Constantine became our emperor," he said. "I am his friend. This sword was given to me by him, but if he refuses the throne what can we do?" His presence calmed the noisy crowd, and the rebels began to disperse. At this point Obolensky approached him and told him to go. Miloradovich took no notice, and then another of the Decembrists fired his pistol at pointblank range, and the old general fell dead.

The rebels became more defiant, and they were undeterred when Nicholas came across the square, placing himself at the head of the first battalion of the renowned Preobrazhensky guards. Nicholas moved with quiet courage, lining his troops opposite the rebels, with the horse guards on the right flank. Although Nicholas was an easy target, the rebels did not fire on him. They stood firm and refused to disperse in response to admonitions by the metropolitan of St. Petersburg. Growing desperate, Nicholas ordered the horse guards to charge the rebels; but the ground was covered with ice and the horses slid and fell. The rebels jeered and threw snow balls.

The rebellion was spreading, and as the early dusk gathered, Nicholas feared that it would grow into an uprising of the whole city. He had a battery of four guns brought to the square. Shots were fired over the heads of the rebels, who reacted by fixing their bayonets to attack. Then Nicholas ordered the gunners to fire into the hostile crowd. Panic spread among them and they began to flee. The square emptied rapidly except for fifty or sixty bodies sprawled in the snow. This was the end of the Decembrists' revolt. It had been a fiasco, as was the attempted uprising by members of the Southern Society; but it was a momentous failure. The resident British minister, reporting on it to London, blamed "want of management and want of a head to direct it . . . but I think the seeds are sown which one day must produce important consequences."

Nicholas at once set up a committee of inquiry, and about 570 people were interrogated; some 121 of these were tried. Most of them were sentenced to banishment with hard labor,

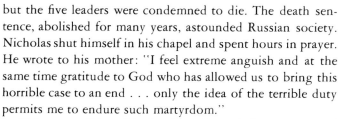

A uniformed Nicholas I, his wife, and the future Alexander II are depicted above enjoying a rare hour of frivolity aboard a river yacht. The public feast in 1825 (at right) was Nicholas' coronation gift to his subjects. Set among temporary pavilions outside Moscow, tables of delectables and fountains of wine are receiving last preparations, as mounted troops hold the guests at bay.

but the five leaders were condemned to die. The death sentence, abolished for many years, astounded Russian society. Nicholas shut himself in his chapel and spent hours in prayer. He wrote to his mother: "I feel extreme anguish and at the same time gratitude to God who has allowed us to bring this horrible case to an end . . . only the idea of the terrible duty permits me to endure such martyrdom."

This sense of "terrible duty" made Nicholas a harsh and inflexible reactionary throughout his life. Alexander Herzen, the brilliant Russian publicist and revolutionary, wrote of him at about this time that "he was handsome, but there was a coldness about his looks; no face could have more mercilessly betrayed the character of the man than his. The retreating forehead and the lower jaw, developed at the expense of the skull, were expressive of an iron will and feeble intelligence, rather of cruelty than of sensuality; but the chief point in the face was the eyes, which were entirely without warmth, without a trace of mercy, wintry eyes." Many years later, when Nicholas visited Britain, Queen Victoria, then aged twenty-five, noted that "the expression of his eyes is terrible. I have never seen anything like them; he is severe and gloomy, imbued with principles nothing on earth could change; I don't think he is very intelligent; his mind is without refinement; his education is very inadequate; politics and the army—those are the only subjects that interest him." The

young Victoria's observations on her guest were astute.

Nicholas' interest in the military was fundamentally different from that of his father, Tsar Paul. Looking far beyond the panoply of military life, Nicholas observed: "Here in the army there is order; there is a strict unconditional legality, no impertinent claims to know all the answers, no contradictions, all things flow logically one from the other; no one commands before he has himself learned to obey; no one steps in front of anyone else without lawful reason; everything is subordinated to one definite goal, everything has its purpose."

The purpose, which was ultimately the glorification of tsar and country, was to be achieved through total commitment to "Orthodoxy, Autocracy, and Nationality." This ideological trinity, which was first elucidated by Nicholas' new minister of education, Sergei Uvarov, became the standard by which all later programs and public behavior was judged. Uvarov tolerated no waivering: "A Russian, devoted to his fatherland, will agree as little to the loss of a single dogma . . . as to the theft of a single pearl from the tsar's crown."

Both the schools and the army provided excellent laboratories for instilling Nicholas' doctrine of "Official Nationality," as it became known. Consequently, education expanded greatly, especially in fields that could produce graduates use-

ful to the state: law, scientific agriculture, technology, architecture. Though a very tight rein was kept on the curricula and on the students (among the many rules imposed upon them was the wearing of uniforms), the ministry was generous in granting increased salaries and financing better facilities for research and teaching.

The military also received a substantial boost in its numerical strength and in the attention given to training the officers, for Nicholas regarded his army as an institution for maintaining both the security of the nation and the legitimacy of thrones throughout Europe. Known as the "gendarme of Europe," he kept the largest standing army on the continent. He had declared: "I consider the entire human life to be one of service, because everybody serves." His "beloved soldiers" did not share his joy in their calling. Among the Russian peasants nothing was dreaded so much as being conscripted into the army. Landowners provided a prescribed number of recruits for every thousand male serfs on their lands. In principle, the village decided by lots who would be chosen; but landowners had considerable discretion as to who should be sent into the army, and often sent unsatisfactory serfs to the recruiting office when there was no call. The masters then received a receipt that could be sold to other landowners who were more willing to part with some of their money than be short-handed in running their estates.

In his *Memoirs of a Revolutionist*, Prince Peter Kropotkin has given a moving description of the distress in a peasant household when one of its members had been named as a recruit. The ill-fated young man was immediately placed under guard so that he would not escape. All his fellow serfs would come to the *izba* to give their blessings. He would bow deeply to them, asking forgiveness if he had offended any of them. His family would lament his departure, using the same words as for the burial service, for he was being taken away from family and village for twenty-five years (later in Nicholas' reign it was reduced to fifteen). His male children were sent away to a military orphanage to be trained for service in the army; his wife, suddenly deprived of husband and children, was virtually a widow (she was allowed to remarry after three years).

Having committed the nation to a huge army, Nicholas then had to build adequate governmental machinery to finance and administer it. These centralized bureaucracies, staffed by a new class of functionaries, were conceived as civilian branches of Nicholas' military establishment. Discipline, rank, and even uniforms underscored this philosophy of government. His personal rule was exercised through His Majesty's Own Chancery of which the Third Section, in charge of the state and security police, was feared and hated. Indeed, through the Third Section he virtually created a

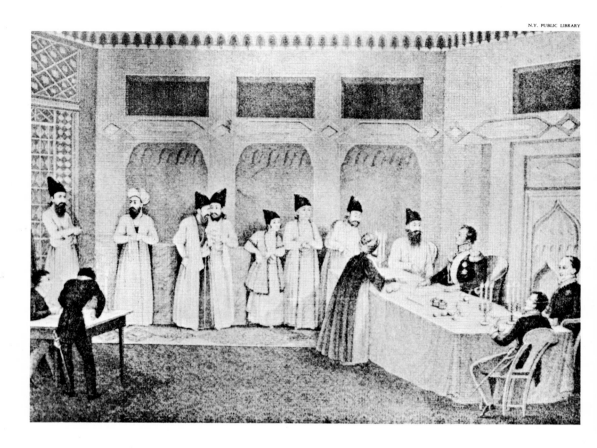

police state, the only means, he believed, of maintaining public security and carrying on the struggle against corruption and inefficiency.

The burning issues of reform to which earlier autocrats had given token approval were now even more acute, as Nicholas was well aware. "There is no doubt that serfdom, in its present form, is a flagrant evil that everyone recognizes," he declared to the State Council in 1842, "yet to attempt to remedy it now would be, of course, an evil even more disastrous." He consistently maintained this negative approach throughout his life. He appointed a number of secret committees to consider possible alleviations of harsh conditions on the land. The proposal was even put forward by Count Pavel Kiselev, a member of the court, that the only solution was emancipation of the serfs with grants of land. Though this proposal was ignored, an *ukaz* in 1842 enabled peasants to obtain their freedom, provided a contract was drawn up guaranteeing a transfer of hereditary land to the worker and the fixed obligation of payment or service to the master. Known as "bound peasants," they were like the serfs emancipated in Alexander I's reign; but again, the number of serfs able to secure their freedom under this *ukaz* was small.

The reign of Nicholas was, oddly enough, a time of great intellectual vitality and a golden age of Russian literature. The emergence of the intelligentsia as a new class in Russian society had been accelerated by the Decembrist rebellion, and it was to play a role of increasing importance. Meeting secretly in small groups, members of the intelligentsia discussed social and political questions. They were concerned with the works of the German philosophers and increasingly with the French utopian socialists. Alexander Herzen, the bastard son of a minor landowner, became one of the most influential men of this new class. His activities as a student in promoting independent socialism and revolutionary action at Moscow University brought him to the attention of the Third Section, and he was banished to a distant province. Soon after his return from exile in Vyatka, he went abroad and in London edited *Kolokol* (*The Bell*), the first Russian emigré journal, which had a wide and flourishing clandestine circulation in Russia.

In the 1840's the intelligentsia rallied around two opposing groups: the Slavophiles and the Westernizers. The Slavophiles believed that a modern Russia could only be built upon its indigenous, Slavic institutions. They sought to explore popular and folk culture—giving the first real impetus to the study of native music, dance, literature, art, ethnography, and history.

The Westernizers sought to pattern Russia's modernization on European institutions. Peter Chaadaev, an officer of the guards and an elder statesmen among the Westernizers,

Victorious Russians and defeated Persians are shown at left concluding the 1828 Treaty of Turkmanchai, which ended their two-year war. Russia's spoils included the part of Armenia bordering on Russian Georgia and exclusive naval rights in the Caspian Sea. Despite the apparent unease of these Persian diplomats, Nicholas left the throne intact, well-satisfied with his gains.

A caricature entitled "Social Attitudes of Bureaucrats" (right) depicts a functionary tyrannizing his underlings. To run his state, Nicholas created an enormous bureaucracy largely staffed by gentry. Unskilled for their new calling, and assisted by incompetent low-level clerks, administrators often fell prey to inertia and corruption.

argued: "Through our entire existence as a society we have done nothing for the common good of man; not one useful thought has been born on our arid soil. . . . Led by a malevolent fate we have borrowed the first seeds of our moral and spiritual enlightenment from decadent, generally despised Byzantium." He even maintained that Russia would have fared better had it embraced Roman Catholicism or Protestantism. Expressing such iconoclastic views in his letters, which were circulated and eagerly read in St. Petersburg and Moscow, it was inevitable that he should fall foul of the notorious Third Section. Nicholas concluded that Chaadaev must be mad, ordering as punishment that he receive a daily visit from a doctor.

Indeed, all those who were searching for answers to the country's numerous problems ran the constant danger that they would be arrested and banished. One such group, calling itself the Brotherhood of Saints Cyril and Methodius, and espousing the dual causes of emancipation of the serfs and autonomy in the Ukraine, was suppressed as impugning "our state principle, on which throne and altar are firmly grounded, our properly *Russian* principle, . . . our sacred treasure"; the members were rounded up and imprisoned. The Petrashevsky group, with which Fedor Dostoevsky was associated, did no more than hold Friday literary meetings at which reformist ideas were discussed. Charged with a "con-

spiracy of ideas," fifteen, including Dostoevsky, were sentenced to be shot; six others were condemned to hard labor in Siberia. The harrowing pre-execution ceremonial was carried out, and only as the drums were rolling and they were awaiting the order to the firing squad did a courier bring the proclamation of the tsar's clemency, commuting their sentence to banishment in Siberia. It was an experience that Dostoevsky in particular was never to forget, as he revealed subsequently in his novels. Among the many other writers who won fame and the close observation of Nicholas' security force were Alexander Pushkin, Mikhail Lermontov, and Nikolai Gogol.

In his foreign policy Nicholas naturally stood for the maintenance of the legitimate regimes and opposed nationalists and revolutionaries. He had inherited this policy from his brother, and it was completely in accord with his own views. But his reign was to close with the Crimean War, which showed not only the bankruptcy of the regime but the failure of the army and the principles to which he had devoted his life.

The Eastern Question, involving the control of the Bosporus and the Dardanelles, the protection of the Christian minorities in Turkey, and the control of Constantinople, raised considerable problems throughout his reign. Europe was becoming increasingly obsessed with the dangers of

The orderly aspect of this British encampment, photographed by the reporter Roger Fenton near the Crimean town of Balaklava, belies the largely uncoordinated efforts of 57,000 soldiers from Britain, France, Turkey, and Austria, who took to the field against Russia in 1854. Nicholas precipitated the Crimean War by invading Turkish territory, purportedly to "restore the independence of Christian states which for years had fallen under the Ottoman yoke." Other European powers saw the tsar's crusade as a pretext for turning the Black Sea into a Russian lake; thus threatened, they rallied to the sultan.

Russian domination of the eastern Mediterranean. Nicholas believed it to be his duty to maintain the existing order in Europe and the Mediterranean, for the tide of revolution, which was flowing in many parts of Europe, was threatening his internal control.

Concurrent with a war against Persia, by which Russia eventually gained part of Armenia and the right to maintain a fleet in the Caspian Sea, Nicholas declared war on Turkey. His pretext was protection of Russia's Christian brothers, the Greeks and Serbs, who were rebelling against the sultan. In the spring of 1826 an Anglo-Russian agreement on the Greek question, and in particular the setting up of an autonomous Greek state under Turkish rule, was negotiated in St. Petersburg with the duke of Wellington.

As other nations were quick to protest, this support for people rebelling against a legitimate master was a departure from the principles reaffirmed at the Congress of Vienna. However, Nicholas was more concerned about Russia's interests. He sent a series of demands based on the Anglo-Russian agreement to the sultan, who yielded and signed the Treaty of Akkerman—by which Moldavia, Serbia, and Wallachia regained a measure of autonomy from their Ottoman suzerains. Turkish and Russian sovereignty over certain disputed areas in the Caucasus was recognized.

Nicholas had acted without reference to Britain, and the

British Prime Minister, George Canning, was incensed. Nevertheless, Britain joined with France and Russia in the Treaty of London, recapitulating their mutual determination to settle the Eastern Question. Three months later, in October, 1827, their combined naval squadrons became involved in a battle with the Turkish fleet in the Aegean. The Ottoman fleet was destroyed. The sultan reacted strongly, breaking off diplomatic relations with the three powers by revoking the Treaty of Akkerman.

Nicholas was now eager for war against Turkey. Britain, however, refused to become involved. Wellington, who had become Prime Minister in January, 1828, was quite prepared to allow Russia and Turkey to fight it out together. In April, 1828, Nicholas again declared war on Turkey, and in the following year the Russian armies won several victories. With Constantinople threatened, and faced with unrest among his own people, the sultan, on September 14, 1829, accepted the Russian terms, which were embodied in the Treaty of Adrianople. Russia gained the mouth of the Danube and further Caucasian territories, and virtually annexed Moldavia and Wallachia—although they continued to be under nominal Turkish suzerainty.

The revolutions of 1830, threatening the established order, prompted Nicholas to propose that Russia, Austria, and Prussia prepare an armed crusade to defend Europe. Re-

bellion in Poland came before he could proceed with this plan. The Poles had become more and more restive under the constitution of 1815, which Alexander I had granted to them. This constitution provided for Polish autonomy, but Nicholas, who disliked the Poles, had nevertheless sworn at the time of his coronation as king of Poland to maintain the constitution. The spirit of revolution that was spreading through Europe stimulated the Poles to rebellion. In 1830 an extraordinary meeting of the Polish diet proclaimed a national insurrection and the removal of Nicholas as king. The Poles were ill-equipped to face the Russian armies dispatched by Nicholas. They fought bravely, but were crushed. Nicholas promptly revoked the 1815 constitution and on February 26, 1832, proclaimed the Organic Statute, making Poland "an integral part of the Russian empire." Poland, thenceforth directly governed from St. Petersburg, was subjected to a policy of extreme repression.

A crisis in Turkey next claimed the attention of Nicholas. The Ottoman sultan, Mahmud II, was threatened by the pasha of Egypt and appealed to the Western powers for support. Nicholas alone was prepared to assist him—to strengthen Russia's hold on Turkey. British and French alarm was increased in July, 1833, by the signing of a treaty that forged an alliance between Russia and Turkey, giving authority for Russia to intervene directly in Turkish affairs. A secret article

concerning the closing of the Dardanelles to foreign ships of war became known in London; it was taken as further evidence of Russian duplicity.

Nicholas was blind to the antagonism he had aroused. He was most anxious to reach some agreement with Britain, for he recognized the British influence in Constantinople continued to be very strong. Further, he saw in rapprochement with Britain an opportunity to revive the Quadruple Alliance of 1814, which would isolate France, a country now showing an unhealthy interest in events in the Middle East. Even on the Eastern Question Nicholas favored an agreement among the powers for the maintenance of Turkey, but the British could never accept this as sincere.

Turkey staggered toward collapse following Mahmud's death and the succession of his sixteen-year-old son. Nicholas, who was compelled to give in to Britain's broader policy, entered into negotiations with Britain, Austria, France, and Prussia; it resulted in successful mediation between Turkey and Egypt and in the 1841 Straits Convention. This treaty guaranteed the integrity of Turkey and, in particular, accepted the principle that the sultan would not allow foreign warships to pass through the Straits. But while the Convention was promptly signed by the British and Russian governments, it gave impetus to their rivalry in the region. Russia began building up naval strength within the Black Sea; Britain and France concentrated their fleets outside.

Responding in 1848 to revolutions in France, Italy, Austria, and Prussia, Nicholas ordered preparation for military intervention in France. His constant fear was that the spirit of insurrection would infect the Russian people. In March, 1858, he issued a proclamation that called on the people to stand fast "for our Holy Russia . . . for faith, tsar and country." Its concluding words were: "God is with us! Understand ye people and submit, for God is with us!"

The uprisings among the Italian and Czech people were quickly suppressed, but the Hungarians proved more determined. Finally, in May, 1849, the Austrian government called on Nicholas for assistance, and in June a strong Russian army invaded Hungary. By August the insurgents had been crushed. The Russian intervention had, however, caused an outcry throughout Europe. The plight of the Hungarians had aroused strong sympathy, and reports of tortures suffered by the insurgents had angered Western public opinion. Many Hungarians had sought refuge in Turkey, and when Nicholas and Franz Joseph, the Austrian emperor, demanded their surrender, the sultan, on British and French advice, refused.

Britain and France continued to suspect that Russia and Austria were interested less in the fate of the Hungarian refugees than in extending their power over Turkey. Nicholas finally yielded, and the demand for the refugees was dropped. Meanwhile, Nicholas was disturbed by the movement among the German states toward unity; he also noted with alarm that his brother-in-law, Frederick William IV of Prussia, had accepted the upsurge of German nationalism and the demand for unification.

The powers had become increasingly suspicious of Russia's intentions in the Near East. The British people in particular were hostile toward the policy they believed Russia was pursuing of challenging British power in India. The two countries had long been drifting toward war, but Nicholas failed to appreciate completely the danger until the Crimean War was upon him. The immediate source of hostilities was found in the rival claims of the Orthodox and Roman Churches for the custody of the holy places in Jerusalem within the Ottoman empire. This "churchwardens' quarrel," as Palmerston called it, was merely a subterfuge. The basic reason was continuing fear of Russia's threatened dominance in the eastern Mediterranean and the maintenance of the balance of power. The French had championed the pope's claim to custody of the holy places while the Russians championed the Orthodox claims.

When in December, 1852, the Turks decided in favor of France, Nicholas began massing his troops on the Pruth River. His special envoy to the sultan demanded not only custody for the Greek Church but also a secret alliance and rights giving Russia direct responsibility for the twelve million Orthodox Christians under Turkish rule. The sultan rejected these demands, and in July, 1853, the Russian army advanced. Britain, France, Austria, and Prussia protested; they agreed among themselves the terms on which a settlement of the Russo-Turkish dispute should be reached. Nich-

olas himself accepted the settlement, known as the Vienna Note. The Turks were now in a belligerent mood, however, and counting on British and French support, they rejected the plan. On October 8 Turkey declared war on Russia. In the following February Britain and France presented an ultimatum in St. Petersburg, demanding the withdrawal of Russian troops, and in March, 1854, Britain and France formed an alliance with Turkey.

Nicholas now found the European powers ranged against him. He sent a special envoy to Vienna seeking assurances that Austria would not exercise its influence against Russia. He felt sure that the emperor would readily support him in view of the help he had given in suppressing the Hungarian uprising. But the Austrians refused; moreover, the Austrian emperor and the king of Prussia joined in the demand for the withdrawal of Russian troops and support for maintenance of the Turkish empire. Meanwhile, the representatives of Britain, France, Prussia, and Austria met in Vienna and agreed on four conditions for peace negotiations: first, European guarantee of the principalities of Serbia, Moldavia, and Wallachia in place of the protection of Russia alone; second, free navigation of the Danube; third, revision of the 1841 Straits Convention, which had provided that the sultan would allow no foreign warships through the Straits; fourth, protection by the five powers of the Christians in Turkey in place of Russia's sole claim.

Nicholas felt that he had been betrayed. An eyewitness wrote that he was "unrecognizable, his face had a greenish pallor, his profile had lengthened and his eyes had a fixed expression; only his step was firm." Involved now in a war he had not anticipated, Nicholas experienced further disappointments. His Danubian campaign failed. The Russians fought bravely in the Crimea, but without success. British and French warships landed some sixty-two thousand troops on the peninsula, with the purpose of capturing the naval port of Sevastopol. The Russians suffered defeat at Balaklava and at Inkerman. Nicholas accepted that he must negotiate on the basis of the four conditions set out in the Vienna Note. He recognized that this amounted to surrender, but he was already broken in spirit. Throughout his life he had bestowed loving care on his army, and he now saw that against the armies of the West it was inferior in organization, in equipment, and in transport, and that victory was not to be his.

Early in 1855 he caught a chill and on March 5 he died. The tragedy of his whole life perhaps was expressed to the priest who gave the last sacraments—"I believe I have never done evil knowingly." He was incapable of understanding that for the Russian people his reign had been another long and barren period of suffering.

Russia's rise to international power and prestige in the 1800's was due in large part to the efforts of the intellectual class—represented here in Leonid Pasternak's painting of the writer Leo Tolstoy, the historian Mikhail Solovyov, and the philosopher Nikolai Fedorov.

The Intelligentsia

Throughout the first half of the nineteenth century the Russian government suffered from a chronic lack of qualified men to match its national ambitions. Waivering attempts to solve the problem reflected a genuine dilemma: to retain its position among European nations, Russia had to raise technology and culture to the level of its neighbors; as the bastion of autocratic rule, it had to preserve its political stability amid the chaos of revolution by censoring the educative institutions that fostered progress. In the early years of Alexander's reign Count Mikhail Speransky had made a daring attempt to upgrade the civil service by requiring university degrees of higher officials, but the ruling had so outraged the anti-intellectual gentry that the tsar had rescinded the order, exiling the unfortunate minister as well. Paradoxically, the aristocratic government was for the first time forced to open wide its ranks to lower-class aspirants with advanced degrees, adding another small but significant challenge to the old order. Beginning in 1833 Nicholas and his minister of education, Sergei Uvarov, also addressed themselves to the problem of creating a competent, educated bureaucracy; but the building of more and better schools, and the raising of academic standards, were coupled with rigorous censorship of curricula, scholarly journals, and the activities of learned societies. (Above, a satirist presents one view of government control.) Every aspect of science, education, and public opinion was to pass through the crucible of "Official Nationality," whereby its conformity to the tenets of orthodoxy and autocracy could be tested. Foreign scholars and books redolent with forbidden ideas were removed from positions of influence. Upper-class Russians were to be given stronger inducements to become educated and to serve; lower classes were to receive "only that part needed" to be useful. But the tide proved irreversible. Control merely acted as a stimulant to ideological opposition; even the gentry was spawning unreliable doctrinaires. Russian intellectual life, which had existed largely in isolation and had begun its emancipation with the works of the French *philosophes* and German romantics, was coming alive to its own possibilities. (The gallery of literary and philosophical giants opposite indicates the greatness of only a part of that outpouring.) Sons of priests, teachers, the new professionals of the law and medicine, statesmen, and bureaucrats came increasingly to discuss literature, aesthetics, and philosophy—and stayed to argue reform, experimentation, and revolution.

Alexander Pushkin, poet

Nikolai Gogol, social satirist

Fedor Dostoevsky, novelist

Anton Chekhov, dramatist

Nikolai Nekrasov, poet-journalist

Mikhail Bakunin, pamphleteer

Bottom row, from left to right: Ivan Goncharov, Ivan Turgenev, Alexander Druzhinin, Alexander Ostrovsky. Top row: Leo Tolstoy, Dmitry Grigorovich.

Alexander Herzen, journalist

Vissarion Belinsky, literary critic

Nikolai Dobrolyubov, polemicist

Nikolai Chernyshevsky, radical publicist

ГУДОКЪ

САТИРИЧЕСКІЙ ЛИСТОКЪ СЪ КАРРИКАТУРАМИ.

ВЫХОДИТЪ ОДИНЪ РАЗЪ ВЪ НЕДѢЛЮ

НАШИ НА НѢМЕЦКОЙ МАСЛЯНИЦѢ

Видимые знаки признательности къ начальству

SATIRICAL JOURNALS *like the two shown above*—Gudok (The Alarm Whistle) *at left and* Iskra (The Spark) *at right—flourished briefly during the* 1860's, *at the height of Alexander* II's *liberal administration. Government*

ИСКРА

ГОДЪ I.
СЕНТЯБРЯ 11.

ПОДПИСКА ПРИНИМАЕТСЯ: въ конторахъ журнала, при книжныхъ магазинахъ: въ С.-Петербургѣ, В. П. Печаткина, въ Москвѣ, Г. Свѣшникова и въ Таганрогѣ, К. Д. Данилова.

№ 35.
1859 ГОДА.

ПОДПИСНАЯ ЦѢНА: Въ С.-Петербургѣ 6 руб. сер., съ доставкою на домъ 7 руб. сер.; съ пересылкою во всѣ города Имперіи 7 руб. 50 коп. серебромъ.

САТИРИЧЕСКІЙ ЖУРНАЛЪ СЪ КАРРИКАТУРАМИ.

БИРЖЕВЫЕ ТИПЫ.

Лица изыскивающіе причины пониженія курса.

officials and their practices, and the evils of society, were ridiculed in biting caricatures and rhymed ditties. Featured on the cover of Gudok are drunken revelers being led off to jail; Iskra takes aim at avaricious stockbrokers.

257

Young intellectuals after the 1860's preferred action to theorizing; they settled among the peasants and workers to preach socialism.

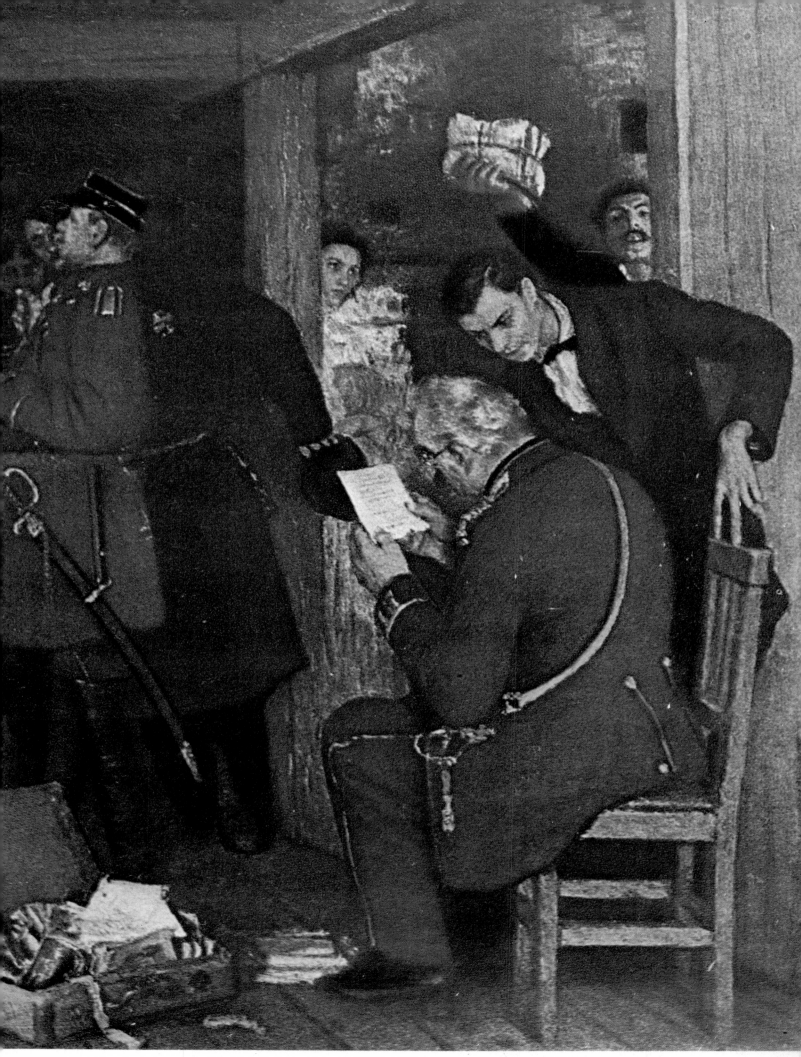

Ilya Repin's painting, Arrest of a Propagandist, *shows one of the ways the government responded to the radical movement.*

ПЕРИОДИЧЕСКАЯ СИСТЕМА ЭЛЕМЕНТОВ

ГРУППЫ ЭЛЕМЕНТОВ

РЯДЫ	I	II	III	IV	V	VI	VII	VIII			O
I	H 1 — 1,008										He 2 — 4,003
II	Li 3 — 6,940	Be 4 — 9,02	5 B — 10,82	6 C — 12,010	7 N — 14,008	8 O — 16,000	9 F — 19,00				Ne 10 — 20,183
III	Na 11 — 22,997	Mg 12 — 24,32	13 Al — 26,97	14 Si — 28,06	15 P — 30,98	16 S — 32,06	17 Cl — 35,457				Ar 18 — 39,944
IV	K 19 — 39,096	Ca 20 — 40,08	Sc 21 — 45,10	Ti 22 — 47,90	V 23 — 50,95	Cr 24 — 52,01	Mn 25 — 54,93	Fe 26 — 55,85	Co 27 — 58,94	Ni 28 — 58,69	
V	29 Cu — 63,57	30 Zn — 65,38	31 Ga — 69,72	32 Ge — 72,60	33 As — 74,91	34 Se — 78,96	35 Br — 79,916				Kr 36 — 83,7
VI	Rb 37 — 85,48	Sr 38 — 87,63	Y 39 — 88,92	Zr 40 — 91,22	Nb 41 — 92,91	Mo 42 — 95,95	Ma 43 — —	Ru 44 — 101,7	Rh 45 — 102,91	Pd 46 — 106,7	
VII	47 Ag — 107,88	48 Cd — 112,41	49 In — 114,76	50 Sn — 118,70	51 Sb — 121,76	52 Te — 127,61	53 J — 126,92				Xe 54 — 131,3
VIII	Cs 55 — 132,91	Ba 56 — 137,36	La 57 ★ — 138,92	Hf 72 — 178,6	Ta 73 — 180,88	W 74 — 183,92	Re 75 — 186,31	Os 76 — 190,2	Ir 77 — 193,1	Pt 78 — 195,23	
IX	79 Au — 197,2	80 Hg — 200,61	81 Tl — 204,39	82 Pb — 207,21	83 Bi — 209,00	84 Po — 210	85 — —				Rn 86 — 222
X	87 — —	Ra 88 — 226,05	Ac 89 — 227	Th 90 — 232,12	Pa 91 — 231	U 92 — 238,07					

★ ЛАНТАНИДЫ 58—71

Ce 58 — 140,13	Pr 59 — 140,92	Nd 60 — 144,27	61 —	Sm 62 — 150,43	Eu 63 — 152,0	Gd 64 — 156,9
Tb 65 — 159,2	Dy 66 — 162,46	Ho 67 — 164,94	Er 68 — 167,2	Tu 69 — 169,4	Yb 70 — 173,04	Cp 71 — 174,99

THEORETICAL SCIENCES *had consistently lagged behind applied sciences in the century after the founding of Peter's Academy of Science because of untrained men, restricted university teaching facilities, and a persistent fear of disputes that these studies might engender. With such notable exceptions as the native physicist-chemist-poet Mikhail Lomonosov and the mathematician Nikolai Lobachevsky, most early researches were undertaken by scholars invited from abroad, and their studies were channeled primarily toward the limited technological needs of the state. However, with the Crimean defeat, the government underwent a fundamental change in attitude. The teaching of all sciences was given priority: between 1853 and 1860 the number of university-graduated scientists rose from 22 to 508. Soon many Russians were gaining recognition for original work as, for example, Dmitry Mendeleev, whose 1869 Periodic Table of Elements (above) provided the basis of the international system for classifying elements by atomic weight. A model public servant, Mendeleev also developed tariff laws, presided over the bureau of weights and measures, and advised the petroleum industry. In the drawing at left he makes a balloon ascension to study the 1887 solar eclipse.*

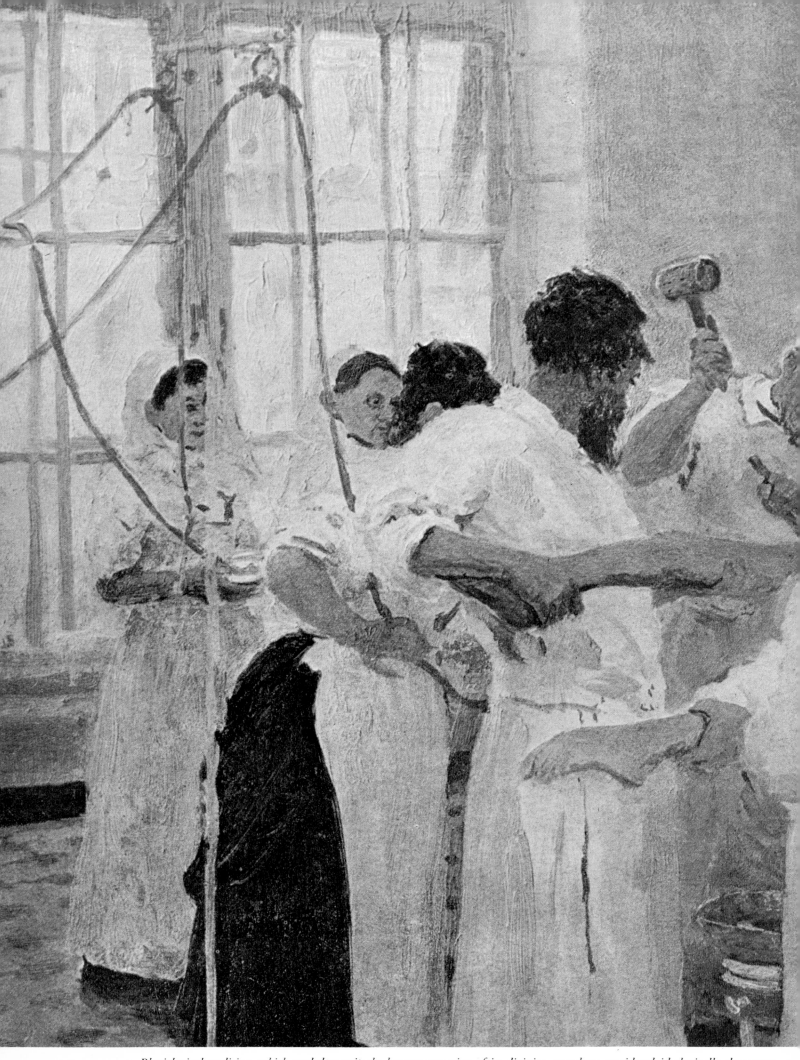

Physiological medicine, which tended to strip the human organism of its divinity, was long considered ideologically dangerous.

Belated government support was particularly aimed toward military needs. Ilya Repin's surgeons are specialists in amputation.

BIRTH OF AN INTELLECTUAL

MY PAST AND THOUGHTS
by Alexander Herzen

In the following excerpt from the memoirs of one of nineteenth-century Russia's leading political theoreticians and journalists, the "marvelous decade" of the 1840's is described.

Thirty years ago the Russia of the future existed exclusively among a few boys, hardly more than children, so insignificant and unnoticed that there was room for them between the soles of the great boots of the autocracy and the ground—and in them was the heritage of the 14th of December, the heritage of a purely national Russia, as well as of the learning of all humanity.

Little by little groups of them are formed. What is more nearly akin to them gathers round their center-points; then the groups repel one another. This dismemberment gives them width and many-sidedness for their development; after developing to the end, that is to the extreme, the branches unite again by whatever names they may be called—Stankevich's circle, the Slavophiles, or our little *coterie* [of Westernizers].

The leading characteristic of them all is a profound feeling of alienation from official Russia, for their environment, and at the same time an impulse to get out of it—and in some a vehement desire to get rid of it.

The objection that these circles, unnoticed both from above and from below, form an exceptional, an extraneous, an unconnected phenomenon, that the education of the majority of these young people was exotic, strange, and that they sooner express a translation into Russian of French and German ideas than anything of their own, seems to us quite groundless. . . .

What halted them was the complete contradiction of the *words* they were taught with the *facts* of life around them. Their teachers, their books, their university spoke one language and that language was intelligible to heart and mind. Their father and mother, their relations, and their whole environment spoke another with which neither mind nor heart was in agreement—but with which the dominant authorities and financial interests were in accord. This contradiction between education and

custom nowhere reached such dimensions as among the nobility and gentry of Russia. . . .

The number of educated people amongst us has always been extremely small; but those who were educated have always received an education, not perhaps very comprehensive, but fairly general and humane: it made men of all with whom it succeeded. But a man was just what was not wanted either for the hierarchical pyramid or for the successful maintenance of the landowning regime. The young man had either to dehumanise himself again—and the greater number did so—or to stop short and ask himself: "But is it absolutely essential to go into the service? Is it really a good thing to be a landowner?" After that there followed for some, the weaker and more impatient, the idle existence of a cornet on the retired list, the sloth of the country, the dressing-gown, eccentricities, cards, wine; for others a time of ordeal and inner travail. They could not live in complete moral disharmony, nor could they be satisfied with a negative attitude of withdrawal; the stimulated mind required an outlet. . . . The government did its best to strengthen us in our revolutionary tendencies. . . .

In 1835 we were exiled. Five years later we came back, tempered by our experience. The dreams of youth had become the irreversible determination of maturity. . . . There was nothing to go on with, there was no one and nothing around him that appealed to a lively man. A youth, when his mind had cleared and he had had time to look about him after school, found himself in the Russia of those days in the position of a traveler waking up in the steppe; one might go where one would—there were traces, there were bones of those who had perished, there were wild beasts and the empty desert on all sides with its dumb threat of danger, in which it is easy to perish and impossible to struggle. The one thing which could be pursued honorably. . . .

What was it touched these men? Whose inspiration re-created them? They had no thought, no care for their social position, for their personal advantage or for security; their whole life, all their efforts were bent on the public good, regard-

less of all personal profit; some forgot their wealth, others their poverty, and went forward, without looking back, to the solution of theoretical questions. The interests of truth, the interests of learning, the interests of art, *humanitas*, swallowed up everything. . . .

It was just the same in the two contiguous circles, the Slavophiles and ours. Where, in what corner of the Western world of to-day, will you find such groups of anchorites of thought, of ascetics of learning, of fanatics of conviction, whose hair is turning grey but whose enthusiasms are for ever young? . . .

But what does all this prove? A great deal . . . whenever she [Russia] has had a chance of stretching her limbs, such fresh, young powers have appeared. This does not in any way guarantee the future, but it does make it extremely *possible*. . . .

Both they [the Slavophiles] and we had been from earliest years possessed by one powerful, unaccountable, physiological, passionate feeling, which they took for memory and we for prophecy—a feeling of boundless love, that embraced the whole of one's existence, for the Russian people, the Russian way of living, the Russian cast of mind. And like Janus, or the two-headed eagle, they and we looked in different directions while one heart throbbed within us.

They transferred all their love, all their tenderness to their oppressed mother. In us, brought up away from home, this tie was weaker. We had been in the hands of a French governess, and learned later on that our mother was not she but an over-driven peasant woman, and this we ourselves divined from the likeness in our features and because her songs were more akin to us than the *vaudevilles*. We loved her dearly, but her life was too narrow. We were stifled in her little room which was all blackened faces looking out from silver settings, all priests and church servitors to frighten the unfortunate woman, knocked silly by soldiers and clerks. Even her everlasting wailing for her lost happiness rent our hearts: we knew she had no bright memories; we knew something else too: that her happiness lay in the future, that the new life was stirring under her heart; this was our younger brother, to whom . . . we should yield our seniority.

Russia's late-developing universities were subordinated to the ministry of education. The typical lecture hall was dominated by a pedagogue of proven orthodoxy, with the result that students were often bored, as drawn below.

Physiology of Petersburg, 1844

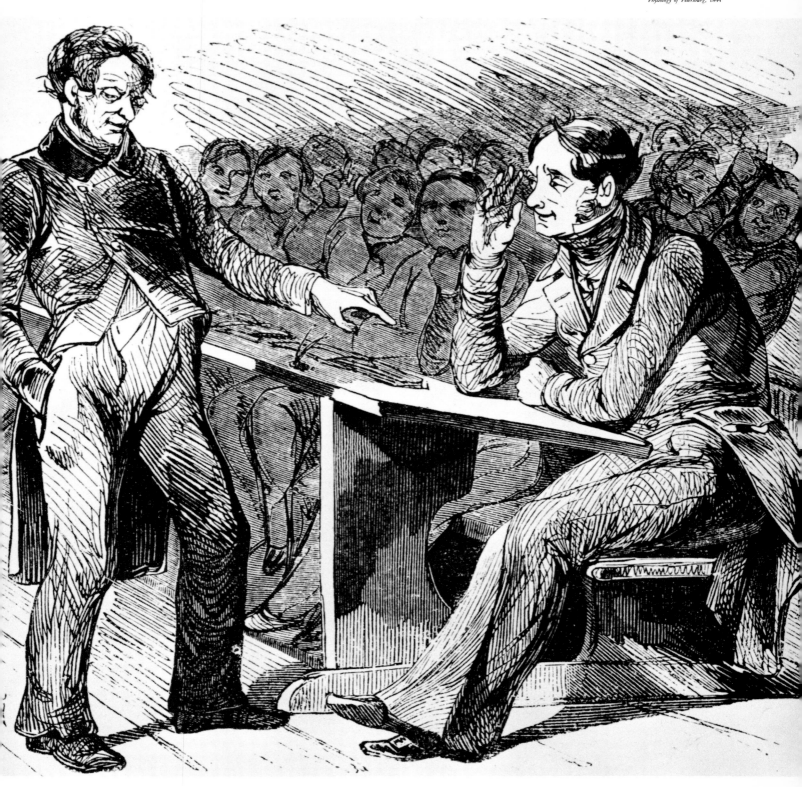

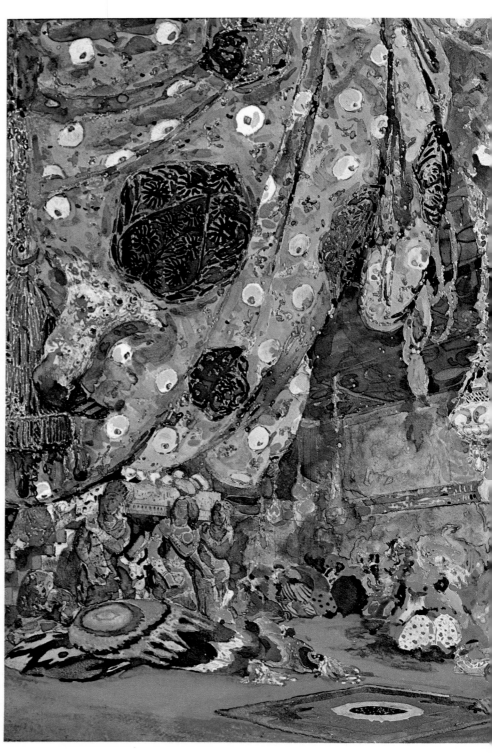

ETHNOLOGY AND HISTORIOGRAPHY *developed along with the growth of national consciousness and broader social concerns. Events from Russia's heroic past as well as stories from the neighboring cultures of central Asia had a profound effect on the arts. Following Mikhail Glinka's example, nationalism and exoticism began to play an especially important role in music, inspiring such leading composers as Alexander Borodin, Modest Mussorgsky, and Nikolai Rimsky-Korsakov to produce scores for ballet and opera. Korsakov's "Scheherazade" is interpreted here in set and costume sketches by Leon Bakst.*

x

266

8

Experiments in Reform

The reign of Alexander II marked the beginning of a new era in Russia's history. The nation was liberated from the militaristic paternalism of his predecessors. In the words of a contemporary: "It seemed as if out of a depressing dark dungeon we were emerging, if not into God's light, at least into an anteroom where we could sense refreshing air."

Alexander's formal education concluded when he was nineteen years of age. He spoke Russian, English, German, Polish, and French, had had a six-months course on the laws of the Russian empire conducted by Count Mikhail Speransky, and special classes in finance, diplomacy, and military matters. He then made a seven-months tour, which intensified his love of "our mother Russia," as he called his country. Moreover, at the urging of his tutor, Vasily Zhukovsky, he visited peasant huts and villages, where he saw how his people lived. He met certain of the Decembrists, who had now been in exile for more than twenty years, and was delighted when his father granted his request that restrictions on them be relaxed.

In Vyatka Alexander met Herzen, who wrote in his memoirs that "the tsarevich's expression had none of that narrow severity, that cold merciless cruelty which was characteristic of his father; his features were more suggestive of good nature and listlessness." Through Alexander's intervention Herzen was allowed to return from his exile in Vyatka to Vladimir, which was less isolated.

In 1839 Alexander went on a foreign tour, lasting sixteen months, during which he visited most of the countries of Europe. In Darmstadt he met Princess Maria of Hesse-Darmstadt, a girl of fifteen. They were married in 1841.

When Alexander ascended to the throne in 1855, Russia was involved in the Crimean War. The populace had no enthusiasm for this war, which Nicholas had regarded as an opportunity to assert Russian power over Turkey. Reports of conditions among the tsar's armies in the south horrified the people of St. Petersburg. The troops had been drilled on the parade grounds, their uniforms and buttons gleaming, but their weapons were out-of-date and unserviceable. Food and other supplies were desperately short because of the inefficiency of the commissariat and the breakdown of communications. Railways linked Moscow and the Baltic, but did not run to the south. Roads were primitive, and in the autumn and winter months, unusable. Corruption was widespread, even in the senior ranks of the army.

Alexander could not bring himself to evacuate Sevastopol,

In September, 1855, after bravely defending Sevastopol for almost a year, the ill-equipped Russians abandoned their Black Sea port, thus ending the Crimean War. This detail from an English print shows them fighting the British on the ramparts of Redan fortress.

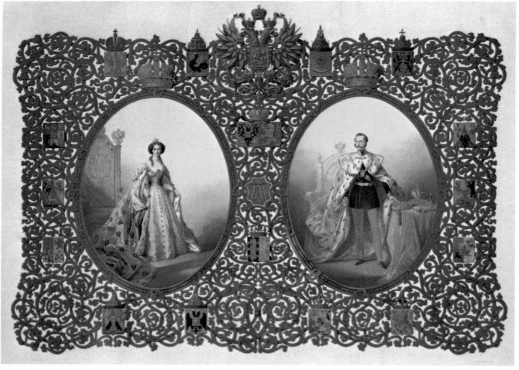

For all Russians Alexander II's 1856 coronation in Moscow seemed a promising prologue to better times. Celebrated by more than three weeks of festivities, the joyous occasion was recorded in a commemorative album, from which two paintings are reproduced here. Formal portraits of the emperor and his German-born wife, Maria, appear at left. The unbridled exuberance of hat-tossing, merrymaking peasants (opposite) suggests that the masses already thought of Alexander as the long-awaited "Tsar-Liberator" who would release them from age-old servitude.

which was under siege by the allies. However, after the fortress was stormed in September, 1855, and after the loss of more than a hundred thousand Russian men, the Council of Ministers unanimously demanded that peace be negotiated —and he bowed to the inevitable. On March 30, 1856, the Treaty of Paris was signed. It amounted to the surrender of all that Nicholas had struggled to attain. Russia had to evacuate Wallachia and Moldavia and give up its rights to maintain a fleet in the Black Sea.

Alexander's manifesto announcing the end of the Crimean War closed with a promise of reform. Even earlier, his first *ukazy* had repealed certain of the harsh restrictions that Nicholas had imposed in the last years of his reign. At his coronation, in the autumn of 1856, Alexander showed a benevolence far beyond what was customary at the coronation of the emperor. All political prisoners were given amnesty; arrears of taxes were canceled for many people, and other tax concessions granted; all recruiting was halted for three years, and the military colonies were abolished. Foreign travel was permitted again; limitations on the number of students admitted to universities were eased; and censorship was greatly relaxed. The Russian people welcomed these measures as a forecast of major reforms to come.

However, the central problem of serfdom continued to undermine the nation. This had been recognized since the

reign of Catherine the Great, but no tsar had had the courage to attempt to deal with it. Alexander's predecessors had been deterred by the fact that the security of the throne rested to a large extent on the support of the landowning gentry, who strongly opposed any diminution of their powers and privileges. Unrest among the peasantry had been increasing. Historians have estimated from official records that in the first half of the nineteenth century there were as many as 1,467 peasant uprisings.

Alexander found the courage to deal with the problem almost immediately. Excited rumors spread through the capital and into the countryside that he would emancipate the serfs and grant them land. Referring to these rumors, Alexander called on the gentry to give thought to the problem. "I consider it necessary to inform you that I have no intention to do this now," he stated. "But, of course, you yourselves understand that the existing order of serfdom cannot remain unchanged. It is better to abolish bondage from above than to wait for the time when it will begin to abolish itself spontaneously from below. I request, gentlemen, that you think over how this can be accomplished."

This request for cooperation was ignored. The landowners refused to even consider action in the interests of the peasantry. Disappointed, Alexander named a secret committee to study the problem. Although the committee agreed that serf-

HERB ORTH, *Life* MAGAZINE, © TIME, INC.

dom was an evil system, it went no further than recommending that any change must be undertaken "gradually and with great caution." The members of the committee were so conservative that even when Grand Duke Constantine—the younger brother of Alexander and an ardent champion of emancipation—became its chairman, the committee continued to concern itself with palliatives.

Then in October, 1857, some landowners of Lithuania submitted a petition for permission to free their serfs, but without transmitting land. Alexander welcomed the "initiative taken by the Lithuanian nobles," but he did not give his approval. Instead, he instructed them to prepare proposals that would give the serfs their freedom, together with an opportunity to buy their homestead lands over a limited period and make further purchases through payments of money or labor. This scheme, devised by S. S. Lanskoy, the minister of internal affairs, was intended to abolish serfdom slowly: it allowed landowners to retain title to their lands, but required them to lease parcels of it to the peasants in return for service or tribute. The imperial instruction to the landowners of Lithuania was then sent to all provincial governors and marshals of the gentry, who were called upon to pursue similar action.

Alexander took care that his resolution to deal with serfdom was understood by the gentry. In St. Petersburg he warned the governor and an assembly of the gentry: "I hope that you will turn your attention to a class of people who deserves that their situation should be justly assured, further delay is impossible. The matter must be dealt with now . . . that is my unshakable resolution."

The problem was vast in scale, involving more than fifty million peasants; and the bureaucratic system cumbersome and obstructive. But by the spring of 1859 local committees of landowners were meeting in every province. They had to report before the end of the year to the central committee, composed of nine senior advisers, in St. Petersburg. The landowners, as a whole, accepted the fact that reform was inevitable, but were united in their resolution to secure their own interests. The gentry of southern Russia, where the soil was exceptionally fertile, were concerned with retaining as much of the land as possible for themselves. By contrast, the landowners of northern and central Russia considered peasant labor as their greatest asset and were more prepared to part with their land in return for exorbitant financial or labor compensation. The drafting commission, created in February, 1859, was entrusted with the task of preparing the emancipation statutes to be submitted to the central committee.

Alexander found himself surrounded by strong pressure groups. He had the support of the intelligentsia and of the small but wealthy merchant class, and, of course, of the peas-

The callous indifference of Russian serf owners is satirized in this 1854 engraving by Gustave Doré. It refers to the practice of certain masters who, hard-pressed for cash but rich in the number of "souls" at their disposal, were occasionally known to bet their chattels as stakes in poker games.

ant masses. He also had the machinery of government now fully committed to change. The majority of landowners, however, remained stubborn opponents. They resisted every stage of the emancipation and fought most bitterly over the ownership of the land. The struggle continued in the editing commission and the central committee, but finally, on February 19, 1861, six years after the date of his accession, Alexander signed the statutes, and the release of the serfs from their age-old bondage was promulgated. Twelve days later the momentous manifesto was read from the pulpits of all churches and proclaimed in all provincial centers. The preamble to the main statute declared: "In considering the various classes and conditions of which the state is composed, we came to the conviction that the legislation of the empire, having wisely provided for the organization of the upper and middle classes and having defined with precision their obligations, their rights, and their privileges, has not attained the same degree of efficiency as regards the peasants attached to the soil, thus designated because whether from ancient law or from custom they have been hereditarily subjected to the authority of the proprietors, on whom it was incumbent at the same time to provide for their welfare. The rights of the proprietors have been hitherto very extended and very imperfectly defined by the law, which has been supplied by tradition, custom, and the good pleasure of the

proprietors. . . ." The tsar's proclamation went on to explain: "As the paternal relations between the proprietors and the peasants became weakened, and, moreover, as the seigneurial authority fell sometimes into hands exclusively occupied with their personal interests, those bonds of mutual good will slackened, and a wide opening was made for an arbitrary sway, which weighed upon the peasants, was unfavorable to their welfare, and made them indifferent to all progress under the conditions of their existence. . . .

"We thus came to the conviction that the work of a serious improvement of the condition of the peasants was a sacred inheritance bequeathed to us by our ancestors, a mission which, in the course of events, Divine Providence called upon us to fulfill. . . ."

The mood of enthusiasm and exaltation that followed was short-lived. The emancipation statutes were immensely complex, understood only by few people. The peasants had interpreted the reform to mean simply that they had been completely liberated and given possession of the land that they had always regarded as their own because they worked it; but now they found that their bondage had been changed only in form and that their burdens were undiminished. Serfs who had worked on the land received allotments; but domestic serfs, who were wholly engaged in personal service to the landowner, received no land as a rule. They had gained

After emancipation, provincial committees of gentry were appointed to arbitrate between serfs and landowners in achieving fair land settlements and redemption terms. Tver's thirteen "peace mediators" proved so sympathetic to peasant interests that they were arrested as mentally insane.

their personal freedom, but if they could not find work, they starved. Moreover, the statutes enabled the peasants to receive only part of the land they had farmed. The peasants also found that they were burdened with redemption payments to the landowners for the land they did acquire, such payments being spread over a period of forty-nine years. An alternative whereby they could take a quarter of their normal allocation of land—known as the pauper's allotment—and avoid the redemption fees was not sufficient to maintain a family.

Landowners were ruthless in retaining as much land as they could in the south or exacting the highest compensation in money or labor in the north. Prior to emancipation a large part of the gentry was heavily mortgaged to the state, and the sale of land to peasants was seen as an opportunity to cancel debts. Consequently, the government often erred in the gentry's favor in determining land values. Official figures showed that seventeen years after their emancipation 13 per cent of the peasants were well endowed with land; some 45 per cent had sufficient land; and the remaining 42 per cent had received land so small in area or poor in quality that they lived in conditions of severe distress.

A further disadvantage was that, except in parts of the Ukraine, much of the land was not given to the individual peasant but to the commune (*mir* or *obshchina*). Communal

organization had appeared as early as the tenth century. Its original purpose was to handle the economic and legal relationships of the peasants within their villages. The commune had developed, however, as the basic organization of peasant life, with certain distinctive features. The family, rather than the individual, was the important unit, and commune membership was hereditary. Internal affairs were decided by the heads of families. They elected the peasant elders, who were the responsible leaders of the commune. They decided on the division of state taxes among the families of the commune, and they convened the meetings at which the periodic redistribution of the land was arranged. The commune became responsible for the payment of taxes, the provision of recruits for military service, and other state liabilities. Under the emancipation statutes not only the land but also the responsibility for redemption payments was vested in the commune. These shared responsibilities, and liabilities, made it a matter of importance to all in a commune that none of its members should leave the district except in special circumstances. Travel was checked by the use of written passports, which had been instituted by Peter the Great and maintained by local authorities. Indeed, the peasant was in many ways as enslaved within the commune as he had been under his landowner.

Alexander now found that the emancipation statutes were

Konstantin Savitsky's 1880 *painting* Off to War *shows peasant recruits being herded aboard a train, unable even to complete their farewells. Despite drastic reforms in the conscription laws—compulsory military service was extended to all men in* 1874 *and length of service reduced from sixteen to a maximum six years—the burden still fell on the lower classes, for university students were hurried through in six months.*

the target of general criticism. Thousands of serfs were un-employed or working under conditions of near starvation. Many began to talk of the real liberation yet to come; some expected that it would happen after the end of the first phase of the emancipation program, which would be completed in two to four years. In a few districts, however, the peasants did not wait; they rebelled. In the province of Penza they attacked the landowners with farming implements; and in the province of Kazan government troops were called in, killing fifty and wounding more than three hundred insurgents before order was restored.

Alexander, shaken though he was by these violent reactions, did not revert to the oppressive policies of his father and grandfather. The reform of the entrenched system demanded further major measures as a preliminary to the modernization of Russia. Carried along by the momentum of the emancipation statutes, Alexander instituted basic reforms in local government, in education, and in the armed forces.

Local government had always been one of the most ineffective areas of the Russian administration. Alexander inherited the system that Catherine the Great had organized. The fifteen vast provinces into which European Russia had once been divided had proved unwieldy, and had been redrawn in 1781 by Catherine to form forty provinces (later further divided into fifty provinces). But even the smaller units, each

under the rule of a governor-general and dominated by elected and appointed representatives of the local gentry, suffered badly from maladministration and especially from central control, which meant in practice that all final decisions had to be made in St. Petersburg. In March, 1859, Alexander appointed Nikolai Milyutin, the assistant to the minister of internal affairs, as chairman of a commission to prepare a plan of reform, but Milyutin was soon dismissed for what were regarded as too-liberal views. His successor, Peter Valuev, produced the commission's report. The new element introduced by these reforms was the zemstvo, an elected council in which all classes participated. The activities of the zemstvos were strictly limited to local government and specifically to such matters as road and bridge maintenance, prisons, hospitals, the promotion of local industry, education, trade, agriculture, and relief for the poor.

This innovation was received with considerably less opposition from the gentry than were peasant reforms. They saw in the zemstvos an opportunity to recoup some of the local authority lost through the emancipation of the serfs. A statute signed by Alexander on January 1, 1864, provided that zemstvos were to be elected by the people of the district, grouped in three electoral colleges. Landowners and townspeople could vote in their appropriate colleges if they had the necessary property qualifications. A third col-

To the state, and its burgeoning bureaucracy, was given the task of reconstructing the complex economic system of land management and ownership. The benevolent scene opposite, the work of Vladimir Makovsky, shows an interview between a peasant and a local administrator, one of the thousands of men who mediated between the government and the citizenry.

Peter Valuev, shown walking a tightrope in the cartoon at right, typified the middle-of-the-road minister chosen to implement Alexander's reforms. In charge of internal affairs from 1861 to 1868, Valuev struck a precarious balance between forces of liberalism and reaction by suppressing anarchist activities while working to eliminate the maltreatment of peasants.

Iskra, 1862, NO. 21

lege, representing the village communes, was elected in two stages: the householders in the commune elected "elders," who in turn elected representatives to the college.

Each zemstvo, which varied in membership from ten to as many as one hundred delegates, was supposedly ordered so that no single social class could dominate, but in fact the gentry played a leading role. Members of the district zemstvos, elected for three-year terms, appointed from among themselves the members of the provincial zemstvos. A major disability of the system was that the chairmen of the district councils had to be approved by the provincial governor, and of the provincial zemstvos by the minister of internal affairs. Moreover, zemstvos had no executive powers and had to rely on the cooperation of the local officials and police. The councils were also restricted in their work by a shortage of funds. Their sources of revenue, provided by the statute, were rates levied locally on agricultural and urban lands, on commerce and on industry. The total revenues of all zemstvos rose from 5.6 million rubles in 1865 to 24.2 million rubles in 1870 and 33.1 million rubles in 1880. But they were required to pay out roughly one half of their funds on matters that were not really of local interest.

Notwithstanding the difficulties that hampered their work, the zemstvos at once introduced new elements of order and enterprise into local government. Their most strik-

ing work was done in establishing schools and promoting education. Russia had always been lamentably backward in education. In 1856 a mere 8,000 elementary schools existed throughout the whole country, and these were for the most part under Church control. The Church's claim was now rejected, and largely through the efforts of the zemstvos, which were given a free hand, education expanded rapidly. In European Russia alone the number of schools increased to 23,000 by 1880, with zemstvo-assisted schools being founded at the rate of 1,000 a year.

The dumas, or elective town and city councils, were set up with similar powers. The dumas acted with energy, providing public services that had for so long been part of Western life but had been lacking in Russia, such as water supplies, paving and lighting of streets, maintenance of essential services, and other amenities; but again, as with the zemstvos, the greatest achievement was in the area of education. In the course of seven years the dumas increased the number of schools in St. Petersburg from 16 to 88.

One of the most striking developments in education in this period was the university statute of June, 1863. The new minister, Alexander Golovnin, sent professors to study universities in western Europe and to make recommendations on the basis of their observations. The statute that resulted revived the universities' autonomy, which had been abol-

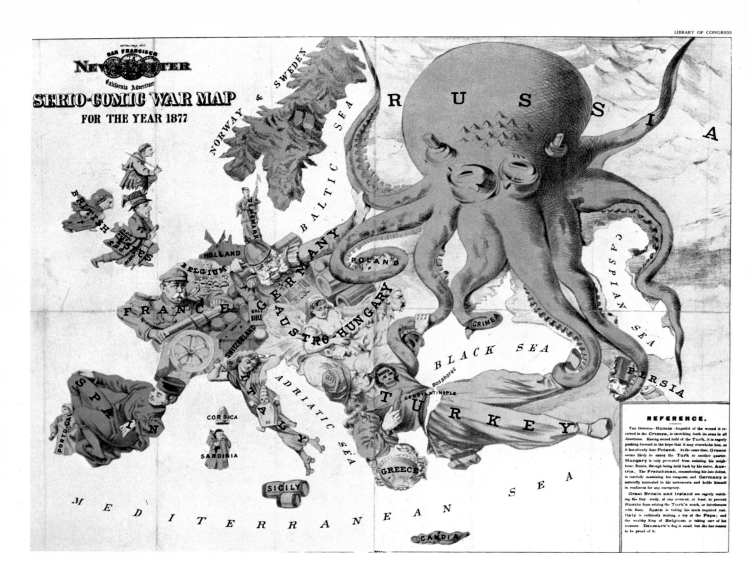

ished by Nicholas I, and granted them administrative independence. Academic freedom was restored, and many measures were introduced to encourage higher education. By 1881 Russia had eight universities, attended by 9,860 students and with a teaching staff of 600. Again, the figures are low in relation to the size of the population, but compared with the past, the development was significant. Golovnin's reforms began a brilliant and active period in the universities, which were to contribute greatly to the movement for the liberalization of Russian life.

The judicial system, too, had long been in need of fundamental reform. The courts were corrupt, arbitrary, dilatory, and savage in their sentences. At the outset of his reign Alexander had declared that one of his purposes was to establish in Russia "expeditious, just, merciful, and impartial courts for all our subjects; to raise the judicial authority by giving it proper independence, and in general to increase in the people that respect for the law which national well-being requires and which must be the constant guide of all and everyone from the highest to the lowest." The need for improvement in this area had indeed been recognized by Nicholas I, but it was not until the end of 1861, when Alexander appointed new members to the commission set up by his father, that the task of reform was advanced. New proposals, enacted on November 20, 1864, and put into effect by Dmitry

Zamyatin, Alexander's minister of justice, involved complete separation of the judiciary from other branches of the administration, public trial by jury, the simplifying of legal procedures, and full publicity for court proceedings, an innovation that in the second half of the century did much to further the liberal cause. Apart from the reorganization of the judicial system, there was a notable emergence of a new impartiality and courtesy in the courts. The idea that the individual deserved respect and consideration was suddenly advanced, almost as a by-product of the liberation of the serfs and the spirit of reform.

The inhuman conditions that applied throughout the army and navy, and the inefficiency and corruption that had contributed to the disastrous defeat in the Crimean War, also demanded change. Grand Duke Constantine had served as minister of marine, during which time he abolished barbaric punishments and emphasized technical training over parade-ground precision, and he recommended the appointment of General Dmitry Milyutin, brother of Nikolai Milyutin, as minister for war. A remarkable man who had served first in the guards and then for fifteen years as a professor in the military academy, General Milyutin was, in Bismarck's words, "the most daring and radical spirit among the reformers and the bitterest enemy of the nobility."

One of Milyutin's first acts as minister was to abolish the

By staking out new colonies Alexander antagonized other empire-building nations. The British in particular watched warily, as seen in the American cartoon opposite, in which a Russian octopus clutches Turkey in its tentacles and is about to ingest the rest of Europe. Britain's Middle Eastern domains also were threatened by its rival's steady annexation of lands in Central Asia. Among the chief prizes forming Russian Turkistan were Bukhara, Tashkent, and fabled Samarkand (below), once Tamerlane's capital.

JOHN FEENEY

savage discipline and punishments that marked army life. Milyutin next introduced up-to-date training methods and improved the conditions of the troops, including provisions for teaching them to read and write. In place of the elite cadet corps, he set up army gymnasiums in which talented young men might be trained to become officers, skilled in the most advanced military methods.

The most drastic change introduced by Milyutin, after nearly ten years of struggle against the conservative opposition, was the adoption of universal conscription. When he finally signed the statute on January 1, 1874, Alexander spoke of the basic principle that it embodied: "Under present legislation the duty of military service falls exclusively on the lower class of town dwellers and on the peasants. A significant section of the Russian people is exempt from a duty which should be sacred to all. Such an order of things . . . no longer agrees with the changed conditions of national life; nor does it satisfy our military needs. Recent events have shown that the strength of armies is based not only on the number of soldiers but on their moral and intellectual qualities. These attain their highest development when the defense of the fatherland has become the common concern of the whole people and where all, without exception and without distinction of calling or estate, combine in this sacred task."

The new statutes provided that all men on attaining the age of twenty would become liable for military service. Conscripts from each military district were to be chosen by ballot each year. They would serve for six years in the regular army, then for nine years in the reserves, and up to the age of forty they might be called for further service. Compassionate exemption could be obtained on the ground that a man was the sole support of his parents or siblings; civilian skills valuable to the state could shorten the term of service.

Alexander had chosen his ministers and advisers wisely. The Milyutin brothers, Golovnin, Zamyatin, and Valuev were matched by Count Mikhail Reutern, the minister of finance who reviewed the whole system of financial administration. The corruption and inefficiency that had hampered the conduct of government finances in the past were now greatly reduced by the controls he instituted. All government departments, for example, were made subject to effective methods of auditing under the supervision of his ministry. These and other measures were of particular importance at a time when the nation was still burdened by the costs of the Crimean War and by the maintenance of a huge army.

Reutern did not limit himself to reform of the existing system. He was also eager to develop the backward economy of the country. Attempts to improve communications and build railways had met with opposition earlier in the century.

279

The Russian empire's trade monopoly in Alaska, established in 1799, came to an end in 1867 with the 7,200,000-dollar sale to America of territory south to 54° 40'. Fort Mikhailovsky, one of a chain of fur-trading centers, is shown in the water color above. By contrast, Russian presence in Mongolia was extended: the village in the sketch opposite, dominated by an Orthodox church, would eventually become part of the empire.

Indeed, Count Yegor Kankrin, one of his predecessors, had held that railways would "encourage frequent purposeless travel, thus facilitating the restless spirit of our age." Lack of communications had, however, been an important factor in the Russians' defeat in the Crimean War, and there were many who recognized that railways were essential to industrial development. Reutern made this a prominent part of his policy, and between 1855 and 1881 the mileage covered by railways in Russia increased from 660 miles to about 14,000. This was, indeed, one of the major factors in the general economic expansion that began in Alexander's reign and continued into the twentieth century. Trade improved and exports increased. A social shift in which the relative power of the landed gentry declined, while that of the industrial and merchant classes increased, was the consequence. The great reforms had put Russia on the road to becoming a capitalist nation.

The Treaty of Paris, which had brought the Crimean War to an end, had not dispelled Western suspicions of Russia. The only ally to whom Alexander could turn was Prussia. William I and Chancellor Bismarck met with the emperor and his foreign minister, Alexander Gorchakov, at Ems in June, 1870. They reached an agreement that Russia would stop Austria from going to the aid of France in the Franco-Prussian War and that William would support Russia's claims to moderate the terms of the fourteen-year-old peace pact.

Gorchakov then notified all signatories of the Treaty of Paris that Russia repudiated the provisions restricting its rights in the Black Sea. This blunt action provoked a new crisis and infuriated the British government. Alexander and Gorchakov had, however, timed the note well. Austria was isolated; France and Prussia were at war; and Britain, alone, was not prepared to declare war on Russia. On the initiative of Bismarck, a conference was held in London in January, 1871; it resulted in a Russian diplomatic victory.

Russia and Prussia were uneasy allies. Bismarck feared particularly that Alexander might realign Russia with Austria and France. Alexander was carried along, however, by Bismarck's plan for the formation of the League of the Three Emperors in 1872. According to this agreement, the emperors of Russia, Germany, and Austria would exchange views on all matters relating to the Eastern Question and act on threats of revolution or aggression against any one of them by another power. Alexander saw the League as a revival of the Holy Alliance, which his uncle, Alexander I, had conceived, and his father, Nicholas I, had supported.

Meanwhile, the Eastern Question was raising urgent problems. The Bulgars and Serbs in Bosnia and Herzegovina were restive, and Serbia and Romania, although autonomous, were demanding independence from Turkish rule. Among

the Russians a movement developed that favored action to free all Slavs from foreign rule. The doctrine of Pan-Slavism made a strong emotional impact on many Russians. It expressed their sense of a historical mission to free the Slavs and was inextricably bound up with chauvinist policies for the expansion of the Russian empire. The doctrine of Pan-Slavism also contained religious elements, stemming from the idea of Moscow as the Third Rome and defender of the pure Orthodox faith. The leading publicist of Pan-Slavism was Rostislav Fadeev, who, in a series of articles entitled "Opinion on the Eastern Question," developed the idea of Russia's spiritual and cultural supremacy and its destiny to overcome in war the Western, and especially the German, powers and to liberate the Slav countries, which would then form a Slav federation under Russia's leadership.

Alexander and Gorchakov saw Pan-Slavism as a source of embarrassment and contrary to Russia's interests. The principle of maintaining legitimate regimes against rebellion and revolution, which Alexander I had supported so strongly, was still a fundamental of Russian policy. But more immediately, Alexander II and Gorchakov were unnerved because their policy was based on an alliance with Germany and Austria, and the Pan-Slavist agitators were stirring up public hatred of the Germans. Also, memories of the Russian defeat in the Crimean War were sharp, and they did not want

to provoke the Western powers into embarking on a new war. In the West the ideas and activities of the Pan-Slavists were interpreted as chauvinist Pan-Russianism in a new guise. Alexander was deeply disturbed by the strong reactions of the Western governments. He could not, however, simply reject Pan-Slavism. The grand duke and heir to the throne, and many of the nationalists prominent at court and in the government, were its enthusiastic supporters. Official policy wavered, as though uncertain how to handle this emotional doctrine.

In 1875 rebellions broke out in Bosnia and Herzegovina, and soon afterward among the Bulgars. The Great Powers had agreed under the Treaty of Paris to act together in the event of a rebellion, but they proved incapable of concerted action in a crisis. Benjamin Disraeli, now the British Prime Minister, was on guard against any expansion of Russian power; Austria and Germany were concerned about avoiding a further European war. Russia alone was ready to act. In 1876, when both Serbia and Montenegro declared war on Turkey, Alexander proposed an armistice to the sultan, who rejected this approach, confident that he could depend on British support. Preparations began in Russia for war against the Turks; Alexander, remembering the way in which the Crimean War had suddenly developed, was cautious. But events took control, and in April, 1877, he de-

clared war. The Russian armies advanced on the Balkan and Transcaucasian fronts, and were soon threatening Constantinople. Disraeli sent a British fleet to guard the Straits, but by the time it arrived, the Turks had come to terms, and on March 3, 1878, they signed the Treaty of San Stefano. Bulgaria became an autonomous state, nominally under the sultan's rule, and the independence of Romania, Montenegro, and Serbia was recognized. Alexander was horrified to find that a European war was now threatening, for the Western countries were disillusioned with the terms of the treaty. Determined to avoid a confrontation at all costs, he agreed to attend a congress of the Great Powers to reconsider the terms of San Stefano. The congress, meeting in Berlin in June and July, 1878, agreed to the Treaty of Berlin, which modified many of the provisions of the Treaty of San Stefano. Russia secured substantial gains; nevertheless, the new treaty was strongly criticized for partitioning Bulgaria and handing over Bosnia and Herzegovina to Austria. Many Russians regarded the treaty as a humiliation, and again, Britain had been primarily responsible. Deeply hurt by the treatment he had received at the hands of the European powers, Alexander readily agreed to revive the League of the Three Emperors.

The continued expansion of Russian interests in Central Asia and the Far East at this time provided some compensation. Not since Catherine's time had the government so

actively supported territorial expansion on the eastern borders. But a new movement now developed, which led to the conquest of this vast region. The first stage in the advance had been to secure the river valleys of the Syr Darya and Amu Darya, which brought the Russians into conflict with the rulers of Khiva, Bukhara, and Kokand. In June, 1865, Russian troops took Tashkent, which became the capital of the province of Turkistan, an important center of agricultural, commercial, industrial, and military activity. Soon Russia had reached the frontiers of Afghanistan and Persia.

Meanwhile, the Russian American Company, the trading monopoly in North America since 1799, had declined, mainly because of corruption and inefficiency. Indeed, Alaska had become an economic liability, and early in the Crimean War the threat of an attack by a Franco-British naval squadron on the port of Petropavlovsk-Kamchatsky made Nicholas I realize that the defense of Alaska was beyond Russia's capability. With this in mind, the Russians had begun in 1854 to discuss with America the sale of Alaska. These negotiations continued, and finally an agreement was reached in 1867 whereby Alaska and all the claims of the Russian American Company were sold to the United States for 7,200,000 dollars.

Russian expansion in the Far East, however, continued undiminished. Britain's defeat of China in 1842 (the Opium War) had emboldened Nicholas I to develop Russian inter-

Russians had tried to establish trade with Japan since the early 1700's. However, it was only under pressures brought to bear by the 1853 arrivals of an American expedition, led by Commodore Matthew Perry, and of a Russian fleet, headed by Admiral Evfimy Putyatin, that the Island Kingdom reopened its doors to the outside world. Subsequent diplomatic maneuvers won for the tsar the sizable island of Sakhalin off the Asian-Russian mainland in exchange for the lesser Kurile Islands. As these Japanese wood-block prints of a soldier (left) and a duet-playing couple (right) show, the Slavs—with their wavy hair, beards, pointed noses, and Western attire— were regarded as curiosities. Cultural differences did not prevent fraternizing in the small village set aside for the Russians on the outskirts of Nagasaki. There, according to the pleased report of the Russian admiral, kimono-clad officers were permitted to take temporary Japanese "'wives' and conscientiously spend their honeymoons."

ests in the Amur Basin and along the Pacific coast. The success of his policy was largely the work of Nikolai Muravyov, who was governor of eastern Siberia from 1847 until 1861. He proved a brilliant and dynamic administrator. The Russian foothold in the vast area north of the Amur River was strengthened in 1850, when he established the frontier trading town of Nikolaevsk, and in 1854, when he advanced up the Amur River and founded Khabarovsk. In 1857–58, while China was engaged in war with France and England over the opening of Chinese ports to trade, Alexander approved the creation of Amur Province, embracing the whole of the north Amur region. China was in no position to contest this seizure of its territory, and de jure recognition of joint Russian-Chinese occupation of the land from the Amur and Ussuri rivers to the Pacific coast was made in a treaty negotiated by Muravyov with the local Chinese commander. In 1858 further negotiations with the Chinese government gained for the Russians the rights to trade in certain Chinese ports and to maintain a legation in Peking—concessions that China had been forced to grant to England, the United States, and France. Suddenly, however, the Chinese government repudiated these trade agreements. War between China and England and France broke out afresh, and toward the end of 1860 China was reduced to signing the Treaty of Peking, by which Russia obtained the vast region between the Amur and

Ussuri rivers and the Pacific and special trading concessions in Mongolia and in Chinese Turkistan. This new region was promptly divided into two provinces: the Amur Province, with its capital at Blagoveshchensk; and the Maritime Province, with Vladivostok as its center.

Russia's advance to the north Pacific coast now brought it face to face with Japan. The two nations clashed first over the island of Sakhalin. An attempt was made to administer the island jointly, but this failed. Finally, in 1875, Japan yielded Sakhalin to Russia in return for the Kurile Islands, to which the Russians had laid claim almost a century earlier.

Despite the remarkable achievements of Alexander's reign, he found himself increasingly the target of bitter hostility and criticism. Not even against his father, Nicholas I, who had represented all that was most negative and reactionary in autocracy, had the voice of the people risen so shrilly. The emancipation statutes had caused the most disappointment. So much had been expected. The reforms themselves had defects that, with patience and application, could have been corrected; but a mood of impatience and criticism overshadowed all honest liberal thinking among the Russians. The ferment was greatest among the intelligentsia. Many of them had advocated revolutionary and socialist programs, and they now became more vocal. Students demonstrated against the authorities in the universities in St.

Sofia Perovskaya

When a decree in 1863 denied women a university education, many went to study abroad. Numbers returned home radicalized, giving a feminine cast to the growing terrorist movement. Sofia Perovskaya was hanged for plotting to assassinate the tsar. Vera Zasulich, admitted assailant of the governor of St. Petersburg, was acquitted by a sympathetic jury. Vera Figner was jailed in 1884 for her belief that "the only way to change the existing order was through violence." Imprisonment often meant a trip to Siberia; the drawing opposite, sketched in 1861 by the American Bayard Taylor, shows convicts en route to punishment.

Vera Zasulich

Vera Figner

Petersburg, Moscow, and Kiev. Alexander Herzen's London-based journal, *Kolokol*, endorsed violent action. In 1861 new regulations, directed toward restoring discipline in the universities, led to large-scale student demonstrations at the University of St. Petersburg. Police and troops were called in, the university was closed, and some three hundred students were arrested and imprisoned.

Alexander intervened personally. Appalled by the brutality of the police, he ordered that the students be released at once. He also dismissed the governor of St. Petersburg and the minister of education. But his sincere efforts to calm students had no lasting effect. Demonstrations were renewed in the following year. Arsonists set serious fires in St. Petersburg, and some two thousand shops and warehouses were burned. Saboteurs were active in other parts of the country, but no one was charged. The tendency was to blame the Poles and the socialists.

Angered by this lawlessness, Alexander applied firmness. Publishers and writers suspected of stimulating unrest were prosecuted. A poet named Mikhail Mikhailov, believed to be one of the chief instigators, had been arrested in September, 1861, and condemned to penal servitude in Siberia, where he died four years later. The eminent writers Nikolai Dobrolyubov and Nikolai Chernyshevsky, leaders of the young Russian radicals, were also influential in the revolu-

tionary movement. Both were able men; they had, in their economic and social paper, *The Contemporary*, created a major vehicle for the discontent of the intelligentsia. In 1862 Chernyshevsky was arrested; he made use of his time in prison to write a novel called *What Is to Be Done?* (*Chto Delat?*), which managed to pass the censors and quickly became the bible of alienated youth.

In the beginning popular Russian opinion had supported the demonstrations of the intelligentsia against the government, and particularly against the emperor, but the violence, the fires, and then, in January, 1863, the Polish rebellion were beginning to turn the general mood against the radicals. Nevertheless, the idea of a national assembly persisted. The reformers who supported the assembly, known as the constitutionalists, won increasing support. In one incident thirteen "peace mediators" from Tver petitioned the emperor to convene a national assembly in which all classes of the people would be represented. The gentry had gone so far in their planning as to have the petition printed and circulated before it was presented to the emperor. Alexander was incensed and ordered their imprisonment in the Fortress of St. Peter and St. Paul. They were later sentenced by a special court to lose all their civil rights and to be incarcerated in a lunatic asylum. Though detained for only four days, they were never to recover their civil rights.

Prisoners for Siberia.   *Moscow*

Among the members of the intelligentsia who became prominent in the 1870's Peter Lavrov and Mikhail Bakunin were outstanding. Bakunin, a nobleman, had for years propagated his belief in revolutionary anarchism. His disciples, including Sergei Nechaev, were wholly dedicated to the revolutionary ideal, and terror was an essential element of their tactics. Lavrov, like Chernyshevsky, was an ardent socialist who believed that the peasant commune was Russia's greatest contribution to solving the problems of the age. It could lead the people to develop a truly socialist society without suffering the evils and injustices of Western capitalism. Lavrov, a professor of mathematics who had studied the works of Karl Marx, accepted the view that socialism must develop from a proletarian revolution within the capitalist system, which existed in western Europe and the beginnings of which could already be observed in Russia. His contribution to this theory, however, was the idea that since most Russian workers remained peasants and the proletariat was still relatively small, the revolution would erupt among the peasantry and develop from the natural socialism of the commune. He therefore urged that the task of the revolutionaries must be to educate the peasantry politically so that they could consciously develop the commune toward the goal of enlightened involvement.

Inspired by the writings of Herzen and his followers,

Populism became the most active socialist movement in the 1870's. Most Populists saw their mission as one of "going to the people" to teach, though some enthusiasts, carried away by Bakunin's doctrines of destruction and anarchy, wanted to instigate rebellion. In 1874 some two thousand young urban men and women, wearing peasant clothes, went into the countryside to be with the peasants. They expected to be welcomed as brothers and comrades. They found, however, that the peasants regarded them with suspicion and hostility, attacking the young Populists and even handing them over to the police. Altogether 4,000 were arrested, and numbers of these were sentenced to imprisonment or sent to Siberia.

This setback left many Populists completely disillusioned in their hopes that the peasantry would lead in the regeneration of Russia. In 1876 remnants of the Populists joined the *Zemlya i Volya* ("Land and Liberty"), the first important Russian revolutionary society—which had been originally established in 1862. Terrorism was their chief weapon against the authorities. But revolution among the peasantry was basic to their policy. They therefore organized a new movement to the people and this time had greater success because they did not invade the countryside in the spirit of missionaries, but settled quietly among the peasants and sought in the course of daily life to gain their confidence and to influence them toward political action, and ultimately revolution.

The Populists enjoyed the active support, or at least the silent sympathy, of all but the most conservative elements among the educated classes and the urban population in Russian society. They represented the opposition to autocracy and bureaucracy and, irrespective of their revolutionary policies, were seen as the champions of reform. This widespread support was especially noteworthy at the trial of Vera Zasulich in February, 1878. She was accused of shooting and wounding General Fedor Trepov, the governor of St. Petersburg. He had visited a prison in the city where a number of young Populists were being held to await trial. In a fit of anger he ordered that one of them be flogged, and as a result of the savage beating, the young man went mad. One morning soon afterward, when the governor was receiving petitioners, Zasulich appeared among them and at close range fired a revolver, wounding him only slightly. Her trial was the talk of St. Petersburg and, indeed, attracted attention in western Europe. The evidence against her was irrefutable, but the jury found her not guilty.

Encouraged by the decision, Populist acts of terror became more frequent. In 1878 General Nikolai Mezentsov, and later Prince Kropotkin, governor-general of Kharkov, were assassinated. Others highly placed were now to suffer the same fate. But the person on whom the terrorists concentrated with greatest determination was the emperor himself.

While Alexander was walking in the Lenty garden in April, 1867, a young revolutionary named Dmitry Karakozov, a student from the universities of Kazan and Moscow, had tried to assassinate him. Karakozov was hanged, and all who had been closely associated with him were banished. On April 2, 1879, another revolutionary fired five shots at Alexander, but all missed. In the following June the revolutionaries held a conference in Lipetsk, at which the Land and Liberty split. One group adopted the name *Narodnaya Volya* ("People's Will") and called for immediate political action. They unanimously endorsed terrorism as their main weapon and made assassination of the emperor their first priority. At least five more attempts were known to have been planned on Alexander's life. In November, 1879, the imperial train was blown up in the approaches to Moscow. In the following February terrorists posing as workmen succeeded in planting a massive charge of dynamite beneath the banquet hall of the Winter Palace, where the emperor and his family were to entertain Prince Alexander of Bulgaria. However, on the evening of the scheduled event the royal party was late, and the dynamite exploded before the emperor entered the hall.

The ingenuity and daring of these fanatic revolutionaries increased the general uneasiness pervading the capital and the rest of the country. The police were unable to cope with

Extremists, disillusioned by Alexander's failure to continue reforms, saw regicide as the way to cure Russia's ills. The tsar's life was in danger even outside his own country: the print opposite shows an advocate of Polish independence in an unsuccessful attempt on Alexander's life during his visit to the Paris Universal Exposition in 1867. The anarchist revolutionary group, the People's Will, finally accomplished the deed in St. Petersburg in March, 1881. The conspirators are depicted at right receiving last rites before being hanged.

them. Alexander began to lose his nerve, becoming bitter and mistrustful. Once, on hearing that someone had spoken critically of him, he made the comment: "Strange, I do not remember ever having done him a favor; why then should he hate me?"

In his private life, too, Alexander was under severe strain. He had become estranged from his wife, Empress Maria. He had had affairs with other women, which she had learned to overlook, and for a time they had been reconciled. About 1864, however, Alexander, then aged forty-seven, fell in love with Princess Catherine Dolgorukaya, a girl of seventeen, and in the following year she became his mistress. Despite clandestine meetings, their relationship quickly became the subject of gossip at court and throughout St. Petersburg.

Alexander's affair became a matter of public concern when, in May, 1872, Catherine gave birth to a son. In May, 1880, the empress died, and forty days later Alexander married Catherine morganatically, granting her the title Princess Yurievskaya. He had long been concerned about the security of his new family (she had by this time given birth to four children), and he derived great comfort from the fact that he had made her his wife and had legitimized the children. At this time, too, feeling more and more hunted by the terrorists, he found solace only in her company.

The mounting terrorism led inevitably to changes among

his ministers. The conservatives were returned to positions of authority, and among those who had held liberal ideas many now became intensely nationalistic. Golovnin, who as minister of education had inaugurated the new liberal era in the nation's schools was now dismissed. Count Dmitry Tolstoy, a stern reactionary, took his place in April, 1866, and at once instituted police methods in an effort to eradicate liberal and revolutionary ideas from the universities.

Alexander himself had been consistent in his policies. He believed in reform and even accepted constitutional government as advantageous. The unrest among the Poles, who in their hatred of Russia could never accept the tutelage that had been imposed by Nicholas I's Organic Statute, aroused his sympathy to some degree, and he sought means of giving the Poles a measure of autonomy. Always inflexible, they would accept nothing less than complete independence and restoration of their boundaries of 1772. They rebelled in January, 1863, expecting support from France, which did not come, and they were suppressed in the following year. At first Alexander dealt leniently with the nationalists and continued to consider ways of extending greater self-rule while keeping Poland part of the Russian empire. But in the face of the intractable mood of the Poles he imposed more severe restrictions on the Roman Catholic and Uniat churches and reinforced the policy of Russification, whereby Russian was the sole language of instruction, even in the universities.

The Finns behaved with greater wisdom in regard to their colonial rulers. Though they continued to press for a diet and for complete autonomy, they did not resort to violence and rebellion. By making their institutions function effectively, they gained the emperor's confidence. In 1863 they were permitted to hold elections for representatives, and Alexander traveled to Helsinki in September to open their diet. It was on this occasion that he declared: "In the hands of a wise nation . . . liberal institutions not only are not dangerous, but are a guarantee of order and well-being." In fact, the concessions that Alexander readily made provided the foundation for the independence of Finland. The Finns themselves recognized that he had been their benefactor, and at a time when liberals and revolutionaries were criticizing and even reviling him, they held him in high regard. Later they were to erect a statue in Senate Square, the heart of Helsinki, commemorating the tsar-liberator.

Alexander's acceptance of constitutional government did not, however, extend to Russia. He believed that conditions in Russia would never permit government by popular representation. Like all his predecessors, he accepted completely that he had been appointed by God and that his special responsibility for the good of his people could not be delegated. When, in 1865 and again in 1866, the St. Petersburg zemstvo proposed that a central zemstvo office be established, virtually to serve as a national assembly, he rejected the proposal outright. The moderate liberals who favored some form of constitutional government continued to press their views. To one of them Alexander replied: "I suppose you consider that I refuse to give up any of my powers from motives of petty ambition. I can give you my imperial word that this very minute, at this very table, I would sign any constitution you like, if I felt that this would be for the good of Russia. But I know that, were I to do so today, tomorrow Russia would fall to pieces."

The growing activity of the terrorists, and in particular their near success in blowing up the banquet hall of the Winter Palace in February, 1880, had led to urgent consultations. Grand Duke Alexander, the thirty-five-year-old heir to the throne, proposed that the fight against terrorism be co-ordinated by one person who had exceptional powers. On February 12, 1880, the popular Count Mikhail Loris-Melikov, who had been governor of Kharkov, was appointed president of the newly created Supreme Executive Commission, with almost unlimited police powers. He made it his main purpose to gain support for the government among the liberals and the people generally, describing his policy as "a dictatorship of the heart." Count Dmitry Tolstoy, who had antagonized so many people as minister of education, was dismissed. A further significant step was the abolition of the Third Section of His Majesty's Own Chancery, which had managed the security police. Loris-Melikov reassured the nation that the major reforms introduced by Alexander would remain in force and announced that an assembly of elected representatives of the zemstvos and city dumas would be convened to advise the government in preparing new legislation. While falling short of the constitutional reforms proposed by several zemstvos and supported by many liberals, this was a significant advance, and it was welcomed. In August, 1880, Loris-Melikov advised the emperor to dissolve the Supreme Executive Commission on the ground that it had fulfilled the function for which it had been set up.

The tension and unrest had relaxed appreciably as a result of his measures. The liberals, in particular, saw hope of further advance. The revolutionaries had suspended their activities while awaiting the recommendations of the commission. Loris-Melikov's proposals fell far short of their expectations. His recommendation was that a commission be set up to examine legislation before it was finally enacted. The commission, on which representatives of the zemstvos and the dumas of the main cities would sit, was to have only advisory powers. The dissolution of the Supreme Executive Commission, and the minor changes proposed, caused general disappointment. The revolutionaries decided at once to revive their policy of terror, in the conviction that they could promote revolution only by the assassination of the emperor.

Alexander signed the statutes containing Loris-Melikov's proposals on the morning of March 1, 1881. He then attended the Sunday Parade. His wife, Princess Yurievskaya, had pleaded with him on the three previous Sundays not to make himself so vulnerable. She begged him now to avoid two streets, and it was later discovered that both had been mined by terrorists. After the parade Alexander returned by a street that, through a mistake by the police, had not been closed to the public. A student named Rysakov hurled a bomb at the imperial sleigh as it passed along the route. It missed the sleigh, but wounded several Cossacks in the emperor's escort. Alexander was unhurt and jumped from his sleigh to help an injured man; it was at this moment that a Polish student cast another bomb at Alexander's feet. It exploded, shattering his legs and lacerating his body and face. His brother, Grand Duke Mikhail, ran to his aid. Alexander could only whisper, "Home to the palace to die there."

The assassination of Alexander II was one of the most tragic, destructive acts in Russia's history. It shocked the whole nation and, at a stroke, destroyed the general sympathy that all liberal Russians had felt for the revolutionaries. It inaugurated a period of reaction at a time when Alexander II's great reforms might have developed further and, with the institution of Loris-Melikov's constitutional proposals, might have introduced the beginnings of the political freedom and social justice that liberal opinion craved. When, some twenty years later, the constitutional reforms were finally introduced, they came too late.

With Russia's belated industrial revolution of the 1880's, urban workers, like this machinist, emerged to staff the nation's factories. The latest innovations were borrowed from the West; consequently, Russian industries were among the most modern in all of Europe.

The Emerging Proletariat

"In proportion as capital accumulates, the lot of the laborer must grow worse. Accumulation of wealth at one pole is at the same time accumulation of misery, agony of toil, slavery, ignorance, brutality, mental degradation, at the opposite pole." So wrote Karl Marx in *Das Kapital*. In the 1880's the Russian government embarked on a deliberate policy of industrialization aimed at transforming the nation into a capitalistic society. As Marx predicted, the deepening misery of the peasants and proletariat would ultimately lead to revolution. (The women barge haulers of the early 1900's, shown above, exemplify the serflike existence of many "emancipated" peasants.) Ignoring the starving populace and the stagnating condition of agriculture, the state encouraged the use of machines, steam power, and Western technology on an ever-increasing scale, and since private initiative played only a secondary role in Russia's industrialization, the greatest progress was made in fields connected with state interests. The government sponsored a vast railroad-construction program that linked vital centers of industry and mining with each other and with shipping ports, and instituted high tariffs—the highest in the world in 1891—to protect native enterprises. Furthermore, it sought to stabilize the economy through such measures as the adoption of the gold standard in 1897; the consequent flow of foreign investments and loans—mainly from France, Britain, Germany, and Belgium—played a major role in the development of Russia's metal, chemical and electrical engineering, and oil industries. By the turn of the century foreign capital underwrote one half of the big industrial companies, seventy per cent of the mines, and forty per cent of the metallurgical works. Only textiles, still the largest branch of Russian industry, remained principally in domestic hands. By World War I Russia was the world's greatest producer of wheat and fourth largest producer of coal, iron ore, pig iron, and cotton textiles. However, industry was mainly concerned with the production of raw materials for export; most machines and finished goods were imported. Industrialization created Russia's first middle class—manufacturers, entrepreneurs, and technicians—as well as a sizable urban proletariat, largely composed of the land-hungry peasantry. Although the peasant-turned-laborer often maintained strong ties with his native village, where he could find occasional relief from the sterility of his factory, as shown in the photograph opposite, it was the urban experience that made him conscious of his potential strength as a member of a proliferating proletariat. The factory emerged as a rallying point for the discontented workers of the vast Russian empire.

The doubling of Russia's population in the fifty years after emancipation provided a sufficient labor force to run the country's new

industries and still work the land in a primitive, unmechanized manner, as this 1909 photograph of hay harvesting indicates.

Market day, traditionally an important part of rural life, was still observed at the turn of the century, although a great many

of the goods once traded locally were now being transported over Russia's vast railway system to less picturesque urban centers.

Russian labor legislation kept pace with industrialization. The boys in this shoe factory, photographed in 1888, were protected

under laws that called for an eight-hour day for youths under fifteen and obliged their employers to let them attend school.

Kvas seller

Keymaker

Sturgeon vender

Blini peddler

Scarf seller

Plasterer

In the last half century of tsarist rule Russian cities resounded with the brouhaha of street venders, bustling porters, troika drivers, and other individual entrepreneurs, most of whom came from peasant backgrounds and were unable or unwilling to settle into regimented urban occupations. They were part of a floating population of casually employed laborers and were known as meshchane, or "without guilds," a motley social category that also included small shopkeepers, white-collar workers, and artisans.

Knife sharpener

Street sweeper

Fruit hawker

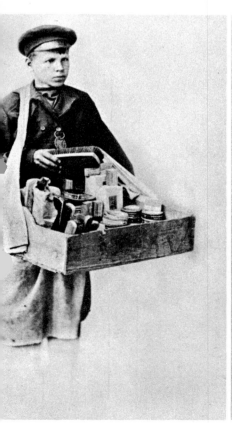

Bootblack

Thread merchant

Dried fruit peddler

Heavy industry expanded rapidly in the late nineteenth century, when this picture of a St. Petersburg foundry was taken. The

capital was a center of the empire's metal-processing and machine-building industries, and a chief producer of its locomotives.

The rich oil deposits of the Caucasus, notably the Baku fields pictured above, supplied Russia's burgeoning industries with fuel.

The vast region was first exploited in the 1880's, and within twenty years it was leading the world in the production of petroleum.

The building of the Trans-Siberian Railway, linking the Urals with the Pacific, was accompanied by equally important, though

less spectacular, construction in more populous areas such as the Ukraine, where this railroad workers' celebration took place.

The Last Romanovs

Alexander III was a large, powerfully built man who possessed a natural authority and dignity that commanded respect. He had not expected to succeed to the throne and had only been proclaimed heir after his elder brother, Nicholas, died from consumption in 1865.

Alexander's concept of autocracy derived from the ideas of his tutor, rather than from those of his father. Konstantin Pobedonostsev, a man of great learning and for a time professor of law at the University of Moscow, was a nationalist and reactionary devoted to autocracy and convinced that parliamentary government was "the great lie of our time." The cruel assassination of Alexander II appeared to both the student and the teacher as conclusive proof of the dangers of relaxed rule. The new tsar was determined he would permit no liberal policies.

One of the first problems that Alexander faced on his accession was what to do about the Loris-Melikov statutes his father had approved. Pobedonostsev, who now held the office of chief procurator of the Holy Synod, attacked the liberal proposals at a meeting of high officials in March. With

Despite growing demands for constitutional limits on the monarchy, Alexander III's Russia continued to be administered at the top by aristocrats responsive to him. One of his ministers is shown in Ilya Repin's study for The Ceremonial Meeting of the State Council.

Alexander's endorsement, the statutes were set aside.

The keynote of the new reign was sounded in the manifesto, drafted by Pobedonostsev, which was proclaimed on April 29, 1881. It read, in part: "In the midst of our great grief God's voice commands us to stand courageously at the helm of the government, relying upon divine Providence, with faith in the power and truth of the autocracy, which for the benefit of the people we are called upon to strengthen and protect from any encroachments."

This reactionary declaration, made in Alexander's name, appalled the ministers of his father's regime. Dmitry Milyutin, Grand Duke Constantine, Mikhail Loris-Melikov, and Alexander Abaza, the minister of finance, resigned their offices. Pobedonostsev was active in recommending their successors. Count Nikolai Ignatiev succeeded Loris-Melikov as minister of internal affairs. Ivan Delyanov became minister of education. Soon Count Dmitry Tolstoy, who had made himself widely hated as minister of education and had been dismissed by Alexander II, was to succeed Ignatiev.

One of the first steps to restoring order was introduced by Ignatiev. On August 14, 1881, he instituted a law providing for two degrees of emergency powers to be invoked in any part of the empire where local officials detected unrest. Pobedonostsev had urged Alexander to tighten censorship again. "I believe that the government should not allow the

control of the press to slip from its hands," he wrote, "that it should not relieve itself of this responsibility. To entrust it to the courts would give the press unbridled license; this would cause great injury to the state and to the people." New regulations were promptly introduced setting up a committee, of which Pobedonostsev as chief procurator of the Holy Synod was a member; it was empowered to ban offending publications and prevent their editors from carrying on editing or writing for any other journals.

Educational policies became more restrictive, too. Education minister Delyanov imposed tuition fees, intended to make it difficult for "children of coachmen, servants, cooks, laundresses, small shopkeepers, and the like" to gain access to higher education. The autonomy of the universities was denied, and student costs were raised, with the purpose of limiting admission.

Alexander and Pobedonostsev were bound to regard the zemstvos and the urban dumas with distrust, especially as they were elective bodies. It was fundamental to their policy that the gentry be strengthened. Three successive *ukazy* in 1889, 1890, and 1892 (mainly the result of the work of Dmitry Tolstoy before his death in 1889) had the effect of restoring the gentry to a dominant position on the land and in the towns; this was achieved through severe restrictions on those franchised to elect delegates to the zemstvos and

the dumas. The electorate in St. Petersburg, for example, was reduced from 21,000 voters to 8,000, and in Moscow from some 20,000 to 7,000. The voting rights of the peasant were sharply curtailed through a system that gave the provisional governors the final selection of candidates from a list of peasants' nominees. Furthermore, in order to ensure that the gentry would be able to oversee the peasantry directly, the new office of the land captain was set up. Chosen from the gentry in each district and subject to confirmation by the minister of internal affairs, the land captains exercised almost unlimited powers over the communal life and even the personal life of the peasants, most of whom were forced to revert to the subservient status they had known before the emancipation of 1861.

Another feature of the policy was the establishment in 1885 of the Nobles' Land Bank. Its function was to provide credit for the gentry on generous terms as a means of preserving for their descendants the estates in their possession. The government had been increasingly disturbed by the vast areas of land that since the emancipation had passed from gentry ownership. It was hoped that this measure would halt the process; the traditional landowners were improvident. (By 1904 the Nobles' Bank would advance more than seven hundred seven million rubles, holding as security a third of the land still in the hands of the gentry.) But this did not prevent

Nearly half the world's Jewish population lived in the empire at the turn of the century, mostly in ram-shackle shtetls, or villages, like the one above. As one of the major unassimilated minorities, the Jews were frequently an object of official persecution (Nicholas II was outspokenly anti-Semitic). The photograph oppo-site was taken after the 1903 pogrom at Kishinev in Bessarabia; hundreds were massacred as police watched.

the further breakup of their estates, which were acquired by merchants and the small but growing percentage—three to five per cent—of wealthy peasants. The landed gentry were, as Anton Chekhov so eloquently described in *The Cherry Orchard*, disintegrating as a class.

In the last two decades of the century rapid industrializa-tion and growth of capitalism had accelerated the rise of two new classes: the middle class and the proletariat. The local government reforms and the expansion of education, and particularly of the universities, had led to increases in the numbers of lawyers, doctors, teachers, veterinarians, and specialists in various fields. Among these people, liberalism and a sense of social responsibility found ready acceptance. During the terrible famine of 1891–92 the national govern-ment attempted to aid the suffering peasantry in the prov-inces affected, but the zemstvos, including a large represen-tation from this new middle class of professionals, had proved far more effective in organizing relief.

Meanwhile, conditions on the land continued to de-teriorate seriously. The peasants held more than half of the arable land; but with the natural increase in population, holdings were subdivided until they became too small to be economically productive. Moreover, farming methods were antiquated, with production per man acreage the lowest in Europe. To aid peasants in raising the capital with which to

buy or rent more land, the Peasants' Land Bank was set up in 1882, with powers to lend money to individuals and to communes. But in European Russia the shortage remained an acute problem.

Many peasants sought work in the expanding industries in the towns, and others moved to Siberia, where land con-tinued to be plentiful. The majority, however, preferred to remain in their own villages. Certain liberal reforms were in-troduced by finance minister Nikolai Bunge, who had estab-lished the Peasants' Land Bank. He abolished the poll tax and also pioneered factory laws in Russia. His law of 1882 made it illegal to employ children under twelve and limited the work week to eight hours per day, with no work on Sun-days and holidays for those between the ages of twelve and fifteen; factory managers were also compelled to release young people to attend schools. A further law in 1885 for-bade night work for women and children in the textile in-dustry. Factory owners generally evaded these regulations; but teams of inspectors were subsequently appointed, and they did much to ensure that the new laws were obeyed.

However, Bunge's principal concern, and that of his suc-cessors, was to promote Russia's belated industrial revolu-tion. The development of Russia's railways was one of the most remarkable feats attributable to the government. The lines, which increased from some 13,719 miles in 1880 to

The amount of land available for farming was considerably greater in Russia than in western Europe, yet Russian agriculture was much less productive. Primitive farming methods and poor management resulted in frequent crop failures and famines. The bread line at left occurred during the devastating famine of 1891–92. The situation was alleviated somewhat by a privately organized relief mission from America, commemorated in the heroic painting opposite, by a grateful if somewhat imprecise Russian (he gave Old Glory eleven stripes instead of thirteen). The artist depicts the arrival of a troika carrying American supplies to a Crimean town.

35,769 miles twenty-four years later, linked the chief industrial regions in the Donets and Dnieper basins and in the Urals with the nearest ports and the growing industries in the cities. The crowning achievement was the construction of the Trans-Siberian Railway between 1891 and 1903, linking the 5,500 mile distance from the Urals to Vladivostok. For this, Sergei Witte, who succeeded Ivan Vyshnegradsky as minister of finance, is chiefly credited. A man of vision and a brilliant administrator, Witte had in the course of his government service become an expert on railways and for a time was employed by the Odessa Railway after it became a private company. In 1889 he established a new railway department within the ministry of finance. Witte was also concerned with ensuring a stable financial structure. He accumulated reserves sufficient to allow him to establish a gold standard in Russia in 1897, a most important measure in that it not only brought Russia prestige but attracted foreign capital. At the same time he protected Russian industry against foreign competition by increasing import duties as much as five hundred and even a thousand per cent.

Alexander's reign was also marked by some very negative policies—chief among them the Russification and persecution of all non-Orthodox peoples. Religious persecution was directed particularly against the Jews, of whom there were some five million, concentrated mainly in western Russia.

The Jews in Russia had been few in number until the partition of Poland in the second half of the eighteenth century. They were numerous in the eastern provinces of Poland, and after their incorporation into Russia, anti-Semitism began to grow. In December, 1791, a decree established the Pale of Settlement in the western and southwestern provinces; Jews were required to live there, and they could move outside the Pale only if they had special permission from the authorities. Attempts were made by Alexander I and Nicholas I to absorb them into Russian life and to persuade them to embrace Orthodox Christianity, but without success. The assassination of Alexander II and terrorism were generally blamed on the Jews, and in mid-April, 1881, and in the following weeks no fewer than two hundred fifteen pogroms erupted, resulting in the destruction of property and the murder of thousands of Jews. Police and military authorities were usually slow to restore order and, indeed, were often suspected of instigating pogroms.

Efforts were made to impose Russification even on Finland, which in 1809 had passed from Swedish rule to semi-autonomy as a grand duchy of Russia. Early in his reign Alexander appointed a new governor-general in Finland, whose instructions were to absorb the Finns into the Russian empire. The Finns responded with passive resistance. They ignored the new law, withheld their taxes, and failed to pro-

vide recruits for the Russian army. The tsar gave the governor-general increasing authority to deal with this resistance, but he found himself faced with stubborn opposition, and in the end he was assassinated. The Finns were readily involved in the revolution that broke out in 1905. In Poland the policy of Russification was applied even more rigorously and the mood of rebellion among them intensified.

In Russia's relations with other sovereign nations, the reign of Alexander III was a period of peace and relative stability. The new League of the Three Emperors, concluded in June, 1881, and renewed for a further three years in 1884, provided that if Germany, Austria, or Russia were involved in war with any other power, the two remaining allies would maintain neutrality. The alliance between Russia and Austria was, however, uneasy, for their interests came into conflict in the Balkans. By 1890 Alexander had become convinced that he should seek allies elsewhere.

Subsequently, Nikolai Giers, the foreign minister, managed to overcome Alexander's antagonism against France as the home of revolution and republicanism; and the two nations concluded an alliance. Giers himself had no love of France, but he recognized that such an alliance had much to offer. There was, indeed, no alternative, for Russia was virtually without allies. A military convention was signed, and an alliance concluded in January, 1894. It marked the birth of the division of Europe into two opposing camps, with the Triple Alliance of Germany, Austro-Hungary, and Italy on one side and of Russia and France, soon to be joined by Britain in the Triple Entente, on the other. The immediate advantage to Russia was, however, the ready flow of French capital into the Russian economy.

Meanwhile, the first revolutionary secret societies had lost much of the support they had once enjoyed among the progressive elements in Russia. The assassination of Alexander II had destroyed confidence in their goals. And when Alexander III had set aside the Loris-Melikov statutes, which had given promise of political freedom and social justice, some revolutionaries left the country. One of the most prominent members of the revolutionary party, Georgy Plekhanov, had emigrated to Switzerland, where he became converted to Marxism. With Pavel Akselrod, Vera Zasulich, and a few others he had founded the first Russian Marxist party, the Group for the Liberation of Labor, in Geneva in 1883.

During the next ten years Plekhanov and his fellow Marxists who were in exile had little contact with their native land, but small circles, calling themselves Social Democrats or Marxists, began to form inside Russia. The first volume of *Das Kapital* had passed the censor and appeared in Russian translation in 1872, and the question whether capitalism could develop in Russia on Western lines was earnestly de-

bated. The Populists argued that since the Russian people were peasants they would create their own socialism through the commune, without passing through the stages of capitalism experienced in the industrialized West. The Marxists countered that capitalism already existed in Russia. In the early 1890's, when industry was expanding rapidly, demonstrations against conditions and long work hours became more frequent. The famine of 1891-92, which had brought thousands of starving peasants into the towns in search of food and work, resulted in many being engaged in the factories at miserable wages, further aggravating discontent.

During these years of unrest Vladimir Ilych Ulyanov was practicing law in Samara on the Volga River and actively studying the works of Marx, Engels, and Akselrod. He was soon to be known to the world as Lenin, one of the greatest political leaders in history. He was born in 1870 in Simbirsk (now Ulyanovsk). His father, who had come from Astrakhan and was probably of mixed Russian and Kalmuk blood, was a stern man of high principles, an inspector of schools dedicated to his work. Lenin's mother, Marya Alexandrovna, was the daughter of a medical doctor. Neither parent took any active interest in politics, yet all six of their children became revolutionaries. The older brother, Alexander, had gained entrance to St. Petersburg University to study science and had there been converted to the doctrine of revolution. In 1887

he was arrested, tried, and condemned to death for having taken part in a terrorist plot to assassinate Alexander III. The sentence would probably have been commuted to imprisonment and exile if he had petitioned for mercy, but he refused. During this period Lenin embraced Marxism as the only ideology that would resolve the problems of Russia and the world.

In 1895 Lenin was granted a passport to travel abroad. He spent four months visiting Germany, France, and Switzerland, but his main purpose was to meet Georgy Plekhanov and the other members of the Liberation of Labor Group in Geneva. At first he was impressed by Plekhanov; but he was unable to accept anyone as his leader, and at this early stage he probably resolved to supplant him. Young Lenin made an impact on the Marxists in exile. Pavel Akselrod, who was to become a bitter enemy in later years, commented on this first meeting: "I felt then that I was dealing with the man who would be the leader of the Russian revolution. He was not only a dedicated Marxist—there were many of them—but he knew what he wanted to do and how it had to be done."

On his return to St. Petersburg in September, 1895, Lenin began organizing the many factions of the Marxist movement into a single party. He founded the St. Petersburg Union of Struggle for the Liberation of the Working Class and began preparing to publish a new revolutionary periodical. On

The Trans-Siberian Railway, the longest of the new railway lines that were laid in Russia in the 1890's—and still the longest railway on earth—linked the western and eastern shores of Russia's vast empire. Labor was provided mostly by convicts and exiles, though soldiers and natives were also recruited. The men at left, brought over from the hard-labor camp on Sakhalin Island, worked on the stretch of track running along the Ussuri River between Vladivostok and Khabarovsk.

December 22, 1895, police raided his rooms and found plentiful evidence of his revolutionary work. Lenin spent the whole of 1896 in the House of Preliminary Detention in St. Petersburg, and then in February, 1897, he learned that his sentence was to be three years exile in Shushenskoe, Siberia.

Shushenskoe offered a pleasant and healthy way of life. Food was plentiful and good, and renting a room in a peasant's house, he had the basic necessities that he required. He was permitted to correspond widely with revolutionaries in western Russia and abroad, and to receive mail regularly. He also completed *The Development of Capitalism in Russia*, which was published in St. Petersburg in 1899 and gained him renown as a Marxist ideologist. While in Shushenskoe he was joined by Nadezhda Krupskaya, a tall, serious schoolmistress who was a convinced Marxist. In July, 1898, they were married, and Krupskaya, self-effacing and dedicated, began her long service to Lenin and to Marxism.

In 1898, while Lenin was still in Siberia, the First Congress of the All-Russian Social Democratic Workers' Party took place in Minsk. The police were extremely active, however, and only nine delegates were able to attend. They were arrested and sent into exile soon afterward, but the congress marked the beginning of the Social Democratic Party, which Lenin was to bring under his sole leadership.

Alexander's death in 1894, from a kidney infection, came as a surprise to everyone. His eldest son, who succeeded as Nicholas II, was twenty-six years old, slight in build, shy, and unsure. Another handicap, which was to prove one of the reasons for his downfall and the collapse of the tsarist regime, was his wife, Princess Alice of Hesse-Darmstadt, a granddaughter of Queen Victoria of England. She was statuesque and intense, but lacked elegance and had none of the poise that the court of St. Petersburg expected. Nicholas had to overcome the opposition of his parents to marry her, for they were both strongly anti-German. He had also had difficulty with the princess, who as a confirmed Protestant was reluctant to embrace Orthodoxy. After a crisis of conscience, however, she was persuaded by the new emperor and Queen Victoria to adopt the Orthodox faith, and Nicholas and Alexandra (the name she took upon conversion) were married on November 14, 1894, one month after the funeral of Alexander III.

Nicholas' reign was early overshadowed by disaster. On May 18, 1896, the day after his coronation in Moscow, the traditional public celebration was arranged on Khodynka Field outside the city. It turned into a stampede in which one thousand three hundred men, women, and children died.

Affecting the whole nation were the crop failures in 1897, 1898, and 1901, which brought peasants swarming into the cities. Economic recession amidst the rapid industrialization

"*In world affairs,*" *wrote an Englishman in* 1902, "*wherever you turn you see Russia; wherever you listen you hear her. She moves in every path, she is mining every claim.*" *The illusion of Russia's strength was shattered two years later by a series of humiliating defeats during its war with Japan. Left, in the aftermath of one battle a priest administers last rites to Russia's dead. The print opposite is a Japanese version of the fall of Port Arthur, Russia's Manchurian base; the fortress cannon (right) are silent as Japanese destroyers send one of the tsar's warships to the bottom.*

gave rise to increasing unrest, and strikes became frequent. However, most of these were short-term stoppages in which workers demonstrated against intolerable conditions. Mass organized strikes were only later to become part of the Russian industrial scene. The revolutionaries, divided now between the Socialist Revolutionary Party, which had been formed in 1900, and Lenin's Social Democratic Party, were preparing for action.

Nicholas II, accepting that his duty was to carry on the same strong autocratic policies that his father had pursued, discovered soon after his accession that many of his subjects looked to him for liberal reform. The zemstvos in particular were centers of such hope. On January 17, 1895, Nicholas took the opportunity in addressing a gathering of zemstvo delegates to declare his policy. He referred to the fact that "lately there have been in certain zemstvo assemblies raised voices of certain persons who have permitted themselves to be carried away by the senseless dreams of participation by zemstvo representatives in internal government. Let all know that, in devoting all my strength on behalf of the welfare of my people, I shall safeguard the principles of autocracy as firmly and unswervingly as my deceased father."

All liberals had hoped that the Loris-Melikov statutes might even be revived, but Nicholas had now dismissed them as "senseless dreams." They recognized that a further

period of repression and reaction lay ahead. But the demand for reform could not be denied indefinitely, and Nicholas, lacking the capacity to rule with the same authority as his father, was soon compelled to yield to popular demands. Demonstrations against the tsar and his government increased in fury during the early years of his reign. Russians in every part of the country began to gather secretly to discuss plans for reform. The police were active. The number of people charged with political crimes mounted from 1,580 in 1900 to 5,590 in 1903, and these figures did not include the numerous cases of secret arrest and exile.

Terror, the weapon of the revolutionaries, developed into a regular campaign. The first political assassination of the reign took place in February, 1901, when a Socialist Revolutionary killed the minister of education. In the following month an attempt was made on the life of Pobedonostsev. In April, 1902, the internal affairs minister was assassinated.

Nicholas reacted as he thought his father would have done: he appointed a harsh reactionary, Vyacheslav Pleve, as the new minister of internal affairs. Pleve's career had been limited to police service, and he had earned promotion through his thorough investigation into the assassination of Alexander II and the arrest of all those implicated. Strongly anti-Semitic and xenophobic, Pleve devoted his energies to strengthening police action. His agents were insinuated into

the army and into political groups not only in Russia but also abroad, and he soon supplanted Pobedonostsev as the most hated man in Russia. In July, 1904, he was killed by a terrorist bomb.

Nicholas, who rarely displayed wisdom in his choice of ministers, had paid great attention to Pleve's advice, and it had been he who had suggested "a small victorious war" to appeal to the patriotism of the Russian people and put an end to the general unrest. Nicholas was strongly attracted by the possibility of expanding Russia's territories and influence in the Far East, and he was soon drawn into war.

Japan had defeated China in the war of 1894–95, and under the Treaty of Shimonoseki had gained Formosa, the Pescadores islands, and the Liaotung Peninsula. China appealed to the European powers, however, and Russia, France, and Germany, acting together, forced Japan to yield the Liaotung Peninsula. In 1896 Sergei Witte negotiated an alliance with China against Japan, thereby gaining rights to continue the Trans-Siberian Railway across northern Manchuria to Vladivostok, and later, in 1898, a southern Manchurian branch line from Harbin to Mukden and Dalny. He secured a twenty-five-year lease of the eastern tip of the Liaotung Peninsula with the right to establish a naval base at Port Arthur and a commercial port at Dalny.

In 1900–1901 the Chinese rose against their foreign over-

lords in the Boxer Rebellion. Russian troops helped to suppress the revolt. They then remained in Manchuria on the pretext of defending the railroad. Nicholas even gave his approval to a scheme to negotiate timber concessions on the Yalu and Tumen rivers as a step toward the expansion of Russian power over Korea. Finance minister Witte was the only realist and statesman in the Russian government; he strongly criticized the new advances, for he recognized the risks they entailed. But Nicholas refused to heed his warnings and eventually dismissed him from office.

In February, 1904, the Japanese suddenly attacked in what was to be a foretaste of their tactics at Pearl Harbor nearly thirty-eight years later. Their assault on Port Arthur and Chemulpo immobilized the Russian naval forces. Japanese armies landed in Korea and in a series of battles inflicted humiliating defeats on the Russians. The Japanese had trained and organized their forces well in advance, and their equipment was far more up to date than that of the Russian army. They counted on gaining a quick victory before massive reserves could be rushed eastward from European Russia. World opinion, which tended to favor Japan, was astonished by the extent of the Japanese successes, the climax of which was the battle of Tsushima. The Russian Baltic fleet had sailed south around Africa to the Far East, and on May 27, in the Tsushima Strait the Japanese navy—under the command

315

of Admiral Heihachiro Togo—annihilated the force.

The Japanese were unable, however, to gain a decisive victory on land. They had exhausted their resources and were now faced with the Russian forces massing in Manchuria. The Japanese secretly approached President Theodore Roosevelt, who brought Russians and Japanese together at a peace conference at Portsmouth, New Hampshire, in August, 1905. Nicholas recalled Witte from retirement to lead the Russian delegation, and by skillful diplomacy he obtained favorable terms. Under the Treaty of Portsmouth (signed September 5, 1905) Russia surrendered the Liaotung Peninsula, including Port Arthur and Dalny, and the southern portion of Sakhalin to Japan, evacuated Manchuria, and acknowledged Korea as being within the Japanese sphere of interest. But Russia retained both the Amur region and the Maritime Province, its main foothold in the Far East.

From the outset the war with Japan was unpopular among the Russians, and the military defeats they suffered gave rise to public anger. Against this background a tragic event irreparably damaged the position and authority of Nicholas as tsar. A massive strike took place in January in the Putilov metallurgical factory in St. Petersburg. The demonstration— protesting conditions and pay—was led by an Orthodox priest named Father Georgy Gapon. He had formed the Assembly of Russian Factory Workers at the end of 1903 with

the purpose of protecting workers' interests, and the authorities had given approval in the expectation that legally constituted bargaining agencies were the best means of curbing the activities of subversives.

Gapon organized the workers to march to the Winter Palace to petition the tsar on January 22, 1905. The procession of workers and their wives and children, some carrying icons and portraits of the tsar, was orderly. As it moved through the city, however, others joined the group, and the police and troops on duty feared that they would attempt to storm the palace. Officials called on the procession to halt, but the number of marchers had become enormous and they moved forward in a mighty wave. Officers commanding troops and police lost their nerve as the procession surged into the square before the palace, and they ordered the troops to fire. Panic ensued with thousands seeking to escape. In the aftermath one hundred thirty dead lay on the ground.

Throughout Russia the news of this massacre aroused a fury of indignation. The general belief was that the tsar had callously ordered his troops to shoot down innocent people. In fact, Nicholas had not been in the Winter Palace and had not known of the procession. But "Bloody Sunday," as this day was called by all Russians, was attributed to him. Father Gapon, who had quickly made his escape from the square, was to tell Lenin later: "We have no tsar any more. Rivers of

On January 22, 1905, thousands of factory workers marched on the Winter Palace to petition the tsar for relief from the untrammeled power of both capitalists and bureaucrats. They had been encouraged by Georgy Gapon, the priest at right, who worked at first with police approval (he is shown with St. Petersburg's chief of police at his elbow). However, the labor movement that he organized proved uncontainable, and when the unarmed demonstrators reached the palace, they were fired on by troops (left). The massacre that followed proved a triumph for the revolutionaries and a prologue to the cataclysm to come.

blood separate the tsar from the people."

News of humiliating defeats in the war against Japan, coming after the massacre of Bloody Sunday, provoked a new wave of violence. In 1904 Nicholas had appointed Prince Dmitry Svyatopolk-Mirsky, a man of relatively liberal outlook, as minister of internal affairs to succeed Pleve. Encouraged, the liberals became more active, and at a conference of zemstvos in St. Petersburg in November, 1904, they approved a petition to the tsar calling for the grant of civil liberties to all classes and races and the formation of a national assembly. Nicholas immediately rejected the petition; but in directing the zemstvos to cease discussing political matters, he promised some reforms. But when the urgently awaited decree proclaiming what was known as Bulygin's Law was found to contain provision for only a consultative body without real powers, the liberals reacted strongly. By October, 1905, strikes had spread from Moscow and St. Petersburg to the provinces, and the whole country became paralyzed.

Nicholas reluctantly turned to Witte for advice. The minister outlined two alternatives: Nicholas must either establish a military dictatorship in which Witte himself would refuse to be involved, as it would lead inevitably to a bloody civil war; or the tsar must grant civil rights and set up a constitutional monarchy. Nicholas was confronted with the task of

introducing policies that ran counter to the principles of autocracy, the maintenance of which he regarded as a sacred trust; but he knew that he had no real choice.

On October 17, 1905, a manifesto was proclaimed in his name, known as the October Manifesto, granting civil rights, announcing the institution of the Duma, to which all classes would elect representatives. Initial enthusiasm gave way to distrust and confusion. It was too late to quell the general mood of disaffection. Trotsky was to write: "The proletariat knows what it does and does not want. . . . It rejects the police whip wrapped in the parchment of the constitution."

Shortly after issuing his October Manifesto, Nicholas noted in his diary: "We have got to know a man of God, Grigory, from the Tobolsk region." The priest Rasputin, who now entered the life of the imperial family, was to be an instrument of the collapse of the Romanov dynasty. Rasputin, which means "the debauched," was a peasant. Forced to flee from Tobolsk, he had wandered for some years as a penitent, or *strannik*, living on charity and searching for salvation. Somehow he had learned to read and write, and had acquired basic religious training. He had twice made the pilgrimage to Jerusalem and late in 1903 had been accepted into the St. Petersburg Theological Academy. The bishop of Saratov and the inspector of the academy, Archimandrite Feofan, both members of the Orthodox hierarchy, had been

impressed by his powers of healing and had given him their blessing and support.

On July 30, 1904, Alexandra gave birth to the Tsarevich Alexei. Both parents were overjoyed, but ten weeks later it was learned that the boy suffered from the incurable disease of hemophilia. Alexandra was overwhelmed by this tragedy. She devoted herself to protecting and nursing the boy, and spent hours in prayer that a miracle might cure him. She lived in fear of every small accident that could bring on a near-fatal hemorrhage, and when Alexandra met Rasputin, she readily believed that he had been sent by God. The fact that he was a crude, debauched peasant with long greasy hair and beard who smelled unpleasant did not affect her faith in his holy powers. True to his name, Rasputin became involved in drunken, sexual orgies, but she refused to heed the scandals and reports even where the evidence was beyond doubt.

Following on the proclamation of the October Manifesto, the Fundamental Laws were hurriedly drafted and promulgated on April 23, 1906. The Laws were the constitution of the new political system. Extensive powers were reserved to the tsar: he had full control of bureaucratic machinery, the armed forces, foreign policy, as well as of succession to the throne. He could dismiss appointed officials and dissolve the Duma at will, although this authority was limited to the extent that he had to declare at once the date of the new elec-

tion and of the meeting of the new Duma. Even the important powers of the Duma in respect of legislation and particularly of finance were restricted. Some forty per cent of the national budget, covering the armed forces, the imperial court, and state loans, was outside the Duma's jurisdiction. Moreover, Article 87 of the Fundamental Laws gave the executive power to legislate in any emergency when the Duma was not in session, although any laws enacted under this article had to be submitted for the Duma's approval within two months of its next meeting. The constitution nevertheless broadened the base of policy formation. The new bodies were empowered to do more than merely advise the tsars as in earlier centuries. The constitution was also revolutionary in that it established a legislature, comprising the Duma, or lower house of deputies, to be chosen by elections, the first in Russia's history, and an upper house, an enlarged State Council. Half of the latter were chosen by the tsar, the rest selected by such conservative elements as property owners, business and commercial interests, and the Church. It also set up a council on the model of the British Cabinet with the Prime Minister or "President" and ministers, appointed on the tsar's recommendation.

Formal political parties began to function actively. The Constitutional Democratic Party, the Cadets, led by Pavel Milyukov, was the chief liberal party. The Monarchist-Con-

By mid-1905 a general strike had taken hold, with the proletariat fighting street wars (opposite) in cities all over Russia. The tsar promised representative government, but the first Duma proved to be too radical and was dissolved. A group of deputies angrily adjourned to Finland, where, eighty miles from St. Petersburg, they met alfresco (above).

stitutionalists supported autocracy and accepted the October Manifesto with reservations. The Octobrists, or Union of October 17, who were in the center politically, were to play an important part in the Duma. There were also several other parties, some of them of the extreme right-wing. The electoral system, as provided by a law enacted in December, 1905, was in a broad sense based on manhood suffrage. But it was complex and had many faults, in particular the application of indirect election by the peasants and the inadequate representation of cities and towns.

Following the elections, the first Duma met in the spring of 1906. Its composition indicated a massive defeat for the government. Of its 497 members, 184 were Cadets and 124 represented left-wing groups. The left-wing representation might well have been far stronger, but the Social Democrats and Socialist Revolutionaries had in the main boycotted the elections. The 112 deputies who had no party affiliation were nearly all peasants who were in general opposed to the government but refused to accept any party label.

As the first Duma was preparing to assemble, Witte resigned from the government (he had acted as Nicholas' first President of the Council of Ministers). Witte, who had served Alexander III wholeheartedly, had not concealed his contempt for Nicholas. The minister was a rough and vindictive man who respected authority, ability, and efficiency, and

despised weakness. He had been primarily responsible for the October Manifesto and the Fundamental Laws, and he was a politician of experience and vision on whom Nicholas should have relied at this juncture. The new president was Ivan Goremykin, an aged bureaucrat and archreactionary whom Alexandra affectionately called "the old man."

The Duma at once agreed on an address to the emperor that outlined demands for further reforms. Goremykin appeared before the Duma and angrily denounced their proposals as wholly inadmissible. Increasingly, the sessions of the Duma were taken up with impassioned attacks on the government. Nicholas felt that the Duma was exceeding its powers and was anxious only to dissolve it. He hesitated to do so, however, as many advised him that such action might upset public opinion in France and Britain, with whom Russia was now in alliance. He considered suggestions that he should call on the liberals to form a government, but approaches made to Milyukov, the leader of the liberal Cadet Party, were unsuccessful. This was an opportunity for the liberals to compromise in order to allow the new system time to work out its problems. But Milyukov was inflexible, making conditions that Nicholas could never accept. In July the Duma was finally abrogated.

Shortly before the dissolution of the first Duma, Nicholas had dismissed Goremykin and named as president in his place

Throughout the turmoil of his reign Nicholas II, who took little pleasure in governing his empire, found refuge with his family. "Heavy trials everywhere," the empress wrote to her husband in 1915, "but at home in our nest bright sunshine." Nicholas and his family are shown in the photograph opposite, taken about 1911: seated to his right is the Empress Alexandra; at her feet, the Tsarevich Alexei; the daughters are, from left, Anastasia, Tatyana, Olga, and Marie. But an éminence grise haunted the family—Rasputin (left), whose presence at court provided an issue that enemies could use to discredit the monarchy.

Peter Stolypin, one of the most able men of the time. Stolypin was a massive, impressive figure of a man who had courage, vision, and integrity. He accepted office with two objectives in mind: to suppress revolutionary terrorism and to accelerate reforms, especially land reforms. The second Duma, which met in February, 1907, was dissolved in June by Stolypin on the ground that it refused to waive the immunity of fifty-five of the Social Democrat deputies whom he wanted tried for treason. Nicholas set the date for the election of the third Duma in accordance with the Fundamental Laws, but he then unconstitutionally amended the electoral law so that the left-wing elements would be virtually excluded. As a result, the moderate conservative Octobrists and right-wing groups became preponderant in the third Duma. Stolypin managed to work effectively with the Octobrist leader, Alexander Guchkov, and the third Duma continued until June, 1912, and was the only one to complete its full term.

Terrorism had mounted dangerously. It had been responsible for some 1,400 deaths in 1906 and 3,000 in the following year. Bombs and other crude methods of the terrorists claimed the lives not only of their victims but also of many innocent citizens. A daring attempt was made in August, 1906, to blow up Stolypin's summer residence; some thirty-two people, including the terrorists, were killed. Stolypin

himself escaped harm, but his daughter was maimed for life. Stolypin applied firm measures. He placed some eighty-two districts under special regulations and introduced summary court martials to try and execute terrorists. In a few months, more than one thousand people had been hanged, and the expression "Stolypin's necktie" became commonplace. But his drastic methods restored order and the incidence of terrorism showed a marked reduction.

Though a conservative, Stolypin was a constitutionalist eager to work with the Duma and "to show the country that it parted company forever with the old police order of things." In fact he introduced many of his reforms under the controversial Article 87. He acted under the emergency article because he believed that the essential reforms were overdue and that further delays were dangerous. In the autumn of 1906 he introduced the first of a series of *ukazy* transforming conditions on the land. He sought to break up the peasant commune and to establish a class of independent yeoman farmers. Every peasant gained the right to claim his share of the communal lands as his personal property that he could bequeath to his heirs. It was a far-sighted measure, which in effect completed the emancipation of 1861. The fact that between 1906 and 1915 more than 2,500,000 peasants withdrew from their communes indicated that it was full independence that they wanted. His agrarian reforms supported this meas-

ure in other ways, and especially in drastically limiting the powers of the land captains. A partial solution to overpopulation and poverty on the land was internal colonization. Largely as the result of new legislation in 1906, 759,000 colonists had resettled in Asiatic Russia by 1908. Time was needed now to allow the reforms and the application of new methods in agriculture to develop, and for the migration to continue relieving the pressure on the land. A prominent landowner and liberal exclaimed: "Give us ten years and we are safe!" A series of good harvests and a new spirit of enterprise brought prosperity such as had not been known before.

Stolypin was also aware of the people's growing political consciousness. He favored a system close to Britain's constitutional monarchy and was anxious that nothing disturb this development. He wrote in July, 1911, to the Russian ambassador in Paris that "every year of peace fortifies Russia not only from the military and naval point of view but also from the economic and financial. Besides, and this is most important, Russia is growing from year to year; self-knowledge and public opinion are developing in our land. One must not scoff at parliamentary institutions. However imperfect, their influence has brought about a radical change in Russia. . . ."

A further ten years with Stolypin in power might indeed have made a world of difference. In September, 1911, how-

ever, he accompanied the tsar on a visit to Kiev for the unveiling of a statue to Alexander II. Toward the end of a gala performance in the Opera House a terrorist named Dmitry Bogrov fired pointblank at Stolypin, who returned toward the imperial box, made a sign of the cross in the direction of the tsar, and fell, mortally wounded.

The assassination of Stolypin caused a public outcry. The police had been guilty of gross negligence in failing to provide protection for him. There was a general demand for an official inquiry into their conduct. Nicholas refused to sanction it, and this gave rise to rumors that he condoned the failure of the police and the murder of his Prime Minister.

Count Vladimir Kokovtsov succeeded Stolypin as Prime Minister. He possessed great ability but did not command the same authority. He was, moreover, plagued by the mounting storm of criticism of Rasputin both in the Duma and in the press. The priest was described as "that cunning conspirator . . . that fornicator of human souls and bodies." Again, unconstitutionally, for censorship had been abolished, Nicholas forbade references to Rasputin in the press. His ban was ignored. Rumors began circulating widely that Rasputin was the empress' lover, and this seriously diminished respect for the imperial couple. Members of the tsar's family were increasingly alarmed by Rasputin's influence. The empress dowager, mother of Nicholas, promised

to speak to him, but added, "my poor daughter-in-law does not perceive that she is ruining both the dynasty and herself." A number of high officials, including Mikhail Rodzyanko, the president of the Duma, had an audience with Nicholas and warned him forthrightly of the harm that Rasputin was causing. Nicholas did nothing.

Meanwhile, Lenin was devoting himself to the task of bringing the Social Democrats under his leadership. He began printing in Stuttgart *Iskra* (*The Spark*), the first issue of which came out in December, 1900, and which was soon circulating through the hands of agents in Russia. Despite a brief period back in Russia earlier that year, he had been detached from events inside Russia and even from the industrial unrest that had intensified in the period leading up to the October Manifesto. He worked on the tactics for promoting revolution and seizing power, setting them down in 1902 in a pamphlet entitled *Chto Delat?*— after Chernyshevsky's celebrated political novel of the same name. His basic idea was that a small, highly centralized party of chosen, disciplined revolutionaries was essential to lead the working class to revolution. This amounted to a departure from the Marxist expectation that the proletariat, the majority of people in a capitalist society, would seize power. In April, 1902, Lenin moved to London, where he met for the first time Lev Bronstein, the son of a Jewish landowner in the Ukraine who was soon to be known widely as Trotsky. Bronstein had been exiled to Siberia and had escaped, making his way to London, where his reputation as a brilliant polemicist and a bold revolutionary had already been established. Meanwhile, the Social Democrats were riven by internecine disputes. In July, 1903, they held a congress in Brussels. The party was still small in strength, and delegates to this meeting numbered only fifty-seven. They argued incessantly among themselves, but it was in this congress that Lenin managed to obtain a majority in the Central Committee, that body which directed party operations between sessions. On this basis he took the name of *Bolsheviki*, meaning the "majorityites," calling his opponents the *Mensheviki*, or "minorityites." The division was fundamental. The Mensheviks, arguing in the Marxist tradition, held that the revolution must await the growth of a proletariat with political understanding. The Bolsheviks were convinced Lenin's strategy was the most effective means to drive the masses on the path to socialism and, ultimately, communism.

The 1905 revolution had taken the revolutionary parties by surprise. They awoke to the fact that the Duma and constitutional government had wide support among the people, and that only the extreme right and left wing parties opposed it. The parliamentary regime might well develop successfully, and this would delay revolution indefinitely. In April

In 1905, with Russia's armies defeated in the Far East and famine and revolt stalking the countryside, Nicholas II was unpopular both at home and abroad. In the cartoon at left, the American magazine Puck *seems to take particular relish in portraying the tsar's predicament. Nicholas, clutching the baby "Autocracy," is shown in a runaway troika, being pursued by the wolves of revolt, while Death lurks in the trees.*

and May, 1906, the Bolsheviks and Mensheviks held a congress in Stockholm and agreed to merge. It was there that a young Georgian Bolshevik named Joseph Dzhugashvili, who used the name of Koba (after a Georgian patriot) and was soon to take the symbolic pseudonym of Stalin (meaning "made of steel"), had his first meeting with Lenin, "the mountain eagle of our party" as Stalin called him.

The urgent problem facing the Bolsheviks and Mensheviks concerned their policy toward popular elections. The Bolsheviks were convinced that the Duma would be reactionary and would come to terms with the autocracy, a belief that was to prove wholly mistaken; but on this ground they boycotted the elections. The Mensheviks were not so strongly opposed to participation in the elections and decided finally to leave the matter to local party groups. The result was that the Social Democrats and the Socialist Revolutionaries were weakly represented in the first Duma. Recognizing their mistake, they participated fully in the elections for the second Duma, in which the Social Democrats gained 64 seats and the Socialist Revolutionaries 20; indeed, left-wing members of this Duma increased from 124 to 216.

As the revolutionaries feared, interest in their cause declined. The elections and the Duma, the new freedom of the press and the policies of Stolypin, had opened up vistas of reform and development. Revolution, which was the policy

of desperation, no longer appealed to the mass of Russians. But the exiles continued to argue and quarrel among themselves, and Lenin, iron-willed and utterly singleminded, pursued his campaign to weld the Bolsheviks into a small disciplined revolutionary vanguard under his leadership. In Stockholm he had supported the union with the Socialist Revolutionaries, and at the Fifth Party Congress, held in London in May, 1907, he had again endorsed the union. Within the party, however, he had maintained his own Bolshevik group, answering only to him.

The London congress condemned violence and "expropriation," the euphemism for robbery of banks and similar institutions in order to obtain funds for the party. Lenin went on record as endorsing this decision, but when in the following month a bold bank robbery, engineered by Stalin, took place in Tiflis, gaining a haul of 341,000 rubles, it emerged that Lenin had approved it. He had even entrusted to one of his closest supporters, Dr. Yakov Zhitomirsky, the task of smuggling the ruble notes out of Russia for the support of the Bolsheviks in exile. The Central Committee considered expelling Lenin for his disregard of the resolutions of the Fifth Party Congress.

Lenin now began preparations to split the party. Realizing that the Mensheviks would never endorse his policy wholeheartedly, he was impatient to discard them. Finally, in

The heroic advances initially made by Russian troops in World War I were soon halted by lack of equipment, poor organization, and chaos at the rear. Within the first year Russia lost nearly four million men—killed, wounded, or captured. Those bivouacked in a Galician field in the 1914 photograph above were among the first to be taken prisoner. In a later photograph (opposite) Russian soldiers flee, dropping their weapons at word of a German attack.

January, 1912, in Prague, the Bolsheviks proclaimed that they were the party, and they condemned as apostates the Mensheviks and all who did not accept the leadership of Lenin. A new Central Committee was elected, and among its members were Yakov Sverdlov, Grigory Zinoviev, a young man named Vyacheslav Scriabin, later known as Molotov. That same year the official organ of the party, *Pravda*, began daily publication.

Meanwhile, conflicts of interests between Austria, Russia, and Germany in the Balkans had erupted, leading to World War I. The German declaration of hostilities, made on August 2, 1914, rallied the Russian people to their tsar. The war against Japan had been resented as an irresponsible adventure, but war against the Central Powers united the whole nation in a mood of patriotic fervor. From all parts of St. Petersburg they gathered in front of the Winter Palace, and their exaltation mounted as Nicholas publicly swore the same oath that Alexander I had sworn at the time of Napoleon's invasion: that he would never make peace while a single enemy soldier remained on Russian soil.

Nicholas himself was deeply moved by the popular demonstrations. He had longed for this union with his people. Kokovtsov and certain others among his advisers warned him that Russia was not financially prepared for such a war. Rasputin even sent him a cable, which read: "Let Papa not

plan for war, for with war will come the end of Russia and of yourselves." Nicholas angrily swept aside warnings and prophecies. To the president of the Duma, which in a special one-day session on August 8, 1914, voted a huge war budget, he said: "I am your friend until death. I will do anything for the Duma, tell me what you want."

Preparations for the war and the mobilization were hurriedly put in hand. Full mobilization required at least three months; but, despite the poor communications and the vast distances of Russia, 4,215,000 men had enrolled by the end of September. The army was well led and disciplined, and its morale was high. In equipment and transport, however, it could not bear comparison with the German army. In response to urgent French demands for a Russian invasion of Germany, Nicholas ordered two armies to march into East Prussia. This was in August, 1914, when the Russian forces were far from ready. The result was the disastrous defeat at Tannenberg. To the south, however, the Russian armies won decisive victories, but Russian casualties in the first ten months of the war amounted to the staggering figure of 3,800,000 dead. Erich Ludendorff, the German chief of staff, wrote with horror of the fighting near Warsaw and referred to the Russians' "supreme contempt for death."

Morale in the Russian armies remained high, but increasingly they suffered from lack of arms, ammunition, and trans-

port. In 1915 as many as twenty-five per cent of Russian soldiers moving to the front were unarmed and had to wait until they could pick up the rifles of comrades killed in action. The death rate among the officers, the professional soldiers who provided the backbone of the whole army, was particularly high in the first months. General Sir Alfred Knox, the British liaison officer with the Russian armies, reported on the courage and chivalry of the officers, who ordered their men to take cover but themselves refused to crawl forward under fire and were mown down, standing, by German machine guns. The failure in supplies was in part due to the War Office under General Vladimir Sukhomlinov (who was later impeached). But it was soon clear that the government ministries could not cope with the crisis. The Duma, convened in August, 1915, for a short session, was outspoken in its criticism of the War Office.

Nicholas was deeply distressed by the casualties and sacrifices of his soldiers, and was consumed with anxiety to take a more direct part. He wanted to be with his army and to demonstrate that he was personally committed to the war. From the best motives he made the fatal decision to assume the supreme command.

Again, Alexandra's dire influence on the tsar was discernible. She had conceived a hatred of her husband's uncle, Grand Duke Nicholas, who was commander of the Russian armies. Like Stolypin, he seemed to overshadow the tsar and he further antagonized the empress by his blunt rejection of Rasputin. When her holy man proposed visiting military headquarters at Mogilev, some four hundred miles to the south, to present a new icon to the grand duke, the commander had responded with a telegram which read: "Come and I'll hang you."

The tsar's new move was heard with dismay. Ten of his twelve ministers sent him a letter in September, begging him to change his decision. Holding tightly a small icon, which Alexandra had given him, Nicholas left St. Petersburg for Mogilev, and the government of the country passed into the hands of the empress and Rasputin.

The shortages of arms and ammunition had been largely made good by the spring of 1916. This was primarily the work of voluntary organizations, which had also performed miracles in providing the medical and other equipment so desperately needed by the forces. Meanwhile, in May, 1916, the Austrians launched an offensive against Italy, and the king of Italy sent urgent appeals to the tsar to attack Austria from the east. Nicholas showed chivalrous concern to help his allies, although it meant advancing the schedule of the Russian offensive, which was planned to take place late in the summer. In June, 1916, General Alexei Brusilov attacked along a three-hundred-mile front, advancing rapidly until an Austrian collapse seemed imminent. The Austrian forces were saved by the hurried arrival of fifteen German divisions. The campaign continued until September, and for the Russians it was highly successful, but at the cost of over two million men.

Notwithstanding the terrible casualties they had suffered, the Russian armies showed no sign of collapse. Plans were already in hand for a new offensive in the spring of 1917. In the rear, however, conditions were deteriorating. It was generally felt that Russia was drifting without leadership. The new ministers appointed by the empress and Rasputin were the objects of popular contempt. The Duma at its new session, which began in November, 1916, criticized the government so violently that Boris Stürmer, Rasputin's choice to succeed Goremykin as Prime Minister, was forced to resign. The Duma failed to dislodge another Rasputin favorite, Alexander Protopopov, the minister of internal affairs. Relations between the Duma and the court had reached explosion point when on December 30 the Duma was prorogued.

Coincident with its dissolution Rasputin was murdered. Vladimir Purishkevich, a conservative who had condemned Rasputin as a Judas and the destroyer of the nation and the dynasty, had planned his death. He was supported by Grand Duke Dmitry Pavlovich, a nephew of the tsar, and by a young nobleman, Prince Feliks Yusupov. Yusupov invited Rasputin to his house, where he plied him with cakes and wine containing cyanide. When Rasputin showed no ill effects, Yusupov, who feared the "holy man's" supernatural powers, summoned up his courage and shot him near the heart. Rasputin fell to the ground, wounded, but then suddenly arose to his feet and like an enraged animal pursued the conspirators. Purishkevich followed Rasputin into the courtyard, firing his revolver until Rasputin fell and ceased moving. The conspirators, by this time in a state of hysteria, hurriedly dragged his body to the river and pushed it through a hole in the ice.

Meanwhile in Petrograd (as St. Petersburg had been renamed at the beginning of the war) and throughout the country, strikes and food riots were increasing. Prince Nikolai Golitsyn, the new Prime Minister, was an old man incapable of dealing with the situation. The State Council, composed of strong conservatives, at this stage joined with the Duma in demanding the appointment of a president and Council of Ministers that would command the confidence of the nation. Hatred of the empress was boldly expressed, and there was even talk of removing or killing her. Mikhail Rodzyanko, the president of the Duma, and even the British ambassador Sir George Buchanan warned Nicholas against her influence. Still he failed to act.

Strikes and unrest became so serious in Petrograd in the first weeks of 1917 that finally Rodzyanko sent an appeal to Nicholas at the headquarters in Mogilev that read: "The situation is serious. There is anarchy in the capital. The government is paralyzed. It is necessary immediately to entrust a person who enjoys the confidence of the country with the formation of a government. Any delay is equivalent to

death." When he received no reply, Rodzyanko sent a further urgent message, to which Nicholas again did not respond. At Mogilev conditions were orderly, but in Petrograd the explosion had come. Mutiny had broken out in the Preobrazhensky guards regiment and other regiments. The troops made their way across the ice of the Neva River to the Vyborg district. There they joined with strikers. This was the turning point; so long as the soldiers had obeyed orders, the regime was secure. But now, when even the guards were making common cause with strikers and revolutionaries, the tsarist regime collapsed.

Still unaware of the gravity of the situation, Nicholas boarded his train to return to Petrograd on February 28. It had to be diverted to Pskov, which was the headquarters of General Nikolai Ruzsky, commanding the northern front. Nicholas now told Ruzsky that he accepted the proposals of Rodzyanko and others and would appoint the Prime Minister, commanding popular confidence and possessing full authority in all matters except foreign policy and the armed forces. Ruzsky spoke with Rodzyanko by telephone and learned that already it was too late. The Soviet of Workers' and Soldiers' Deputies had been formed, and the Provisional Committee of the Duma was striving to avert violent revolution. As a result of communication between Rodzyanko and General Alekseev, the chief of staff in Mogilev, who in turn consulted the commanders on all fronts, the unanimous opinion emerged that Nicholas must abdicate. Alekseev told Ruzsky, who reported to the tsar on March 2.

It had never occurred to Nicholas that he would face the demand from his own generals for his abdication. He did not hesitate, however, and sent a telegram to Alekseev, which read: "In the name of the welfare, tranquillity, and salvation of my dearly beloved Russia I am ready to abdicate from the throne in favor of my son. I request all to serve him truly and faithfully."

Independently of Ruzsky's consultations with the army commanders, the Provisional Committee had appointed two spokesmen to travel by train to Pskov to propose to Nicholas that he abdicate. When they arrived he received them kindly and at this time it seemed that he was almost relieved. He had been burdened by the responsibilities of the throne and of his Romanov heritage all his life. He had tried sincerely to honor his coronation oath, but he recognized now that the task was beyond him. Quietly he signed the abdication deed. He made one change: he knew that his son could not live for long, and concerned to keep the boy in his care, he appointed his brother, Mikhail, as successor. Mikhail declined the office pending a decision by the Constituent Assembly. Thus in March, 1917, after ruling for three centuries, the Romanov dynasty came to an end.

In this water color by E. Barnard Lintott, an American eyewitness, the Petrograd garrison holds a Bolshevik rally by the light of bonfires. The garrison's defection to the insurgents' camp was a key factor in the revolutionaries' seizure of power in November, 1917.

1917: The Onslaught

When the German intellectual Karl Marx (left) and his colleague, Friedrich Engels, published their *Communist Manifesto* in 1848, they believed Europe was on the verge of violent proletarian revolution. Schooled in the rationalism of the Enlightenment, Marx conceived "the history of all hitherto existing society" to be determined by economic conditions, played out in a succession of class struggles between the haves and the havenots. Marx predicted that in one final revolutionary conflagration the oppressed proletariat would rise to crush the bourgeoisie. Since Marx defined political authority as "the organized power of one class for oppressing another," it followed that "as soon as there is no longer any class of society to be held in subjection, there is nothing more to be repressed which would make a State necessary. The State is not abolished, it withers away." Marx's theory failed to account for human nature: it soon became apparent that in the highly industrialized West workers were winning higher wages and improved living and working conditions through the agitation of trade unions and that they were not automatically resorting to revolutionary tactics. In 1917 revolution finally came, not to western Europe, but to underdeveloped Russia. (The photograph opposite shows a 1917 May Day parade in Petrograd's Palace Square, where soldiers hail the overthrow of tsarism with a banner that reads, "Down with the Old!") The fact that socialism was able to take root in Russia is attributable to the superior political acumen of Lenin, who, using Marxism as his platform, constructed a sophisticated strategy to fit his nation's special condition. More in the tradition of Russian populism, he saw that the peasantry could play an important role in creating the new socialist order; and whereas he employed Marxist slogans such as "dictatorship of the proletariat" to enlist the support of rural and urban masses, he actually had little faith in the political effectiveness of unorganized labor. Lenin was an elitist with no trace of Marx's utopian faith in the common man. In his 1902 pamphlet *Chto Delat?* he wrote: ". . . the spontaneous labor movement is pure and simple trade unionism . . . and trade unionism means the ideological subordination of the workers to the bourgeoisie. . . . the task of social democracy is to *combat spontaneity*. . . ." What is needed, he added, is a party made up of "a small, compact core, consisting of reliable, experienced, and hardened workers, with responsible agents in the principal districts and connected by all the rules of strict secrecy with the organization of revolutionists. . . ." In Soviet Russia the Communist Party and the bureaucratic state became virtually indistinguishable, and a succession of totalitarian dictators would promote national interests rather than international revolution.

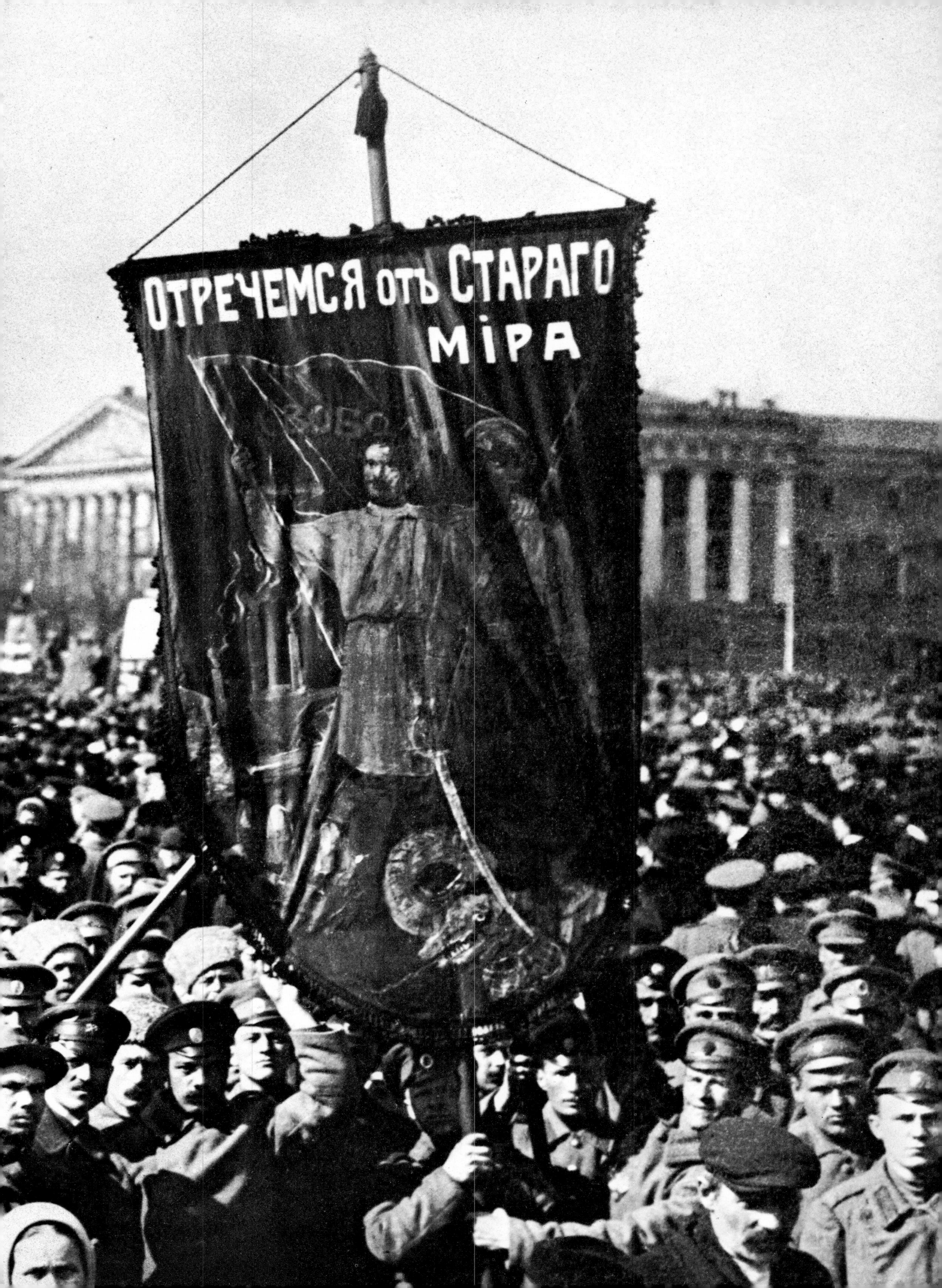
ОТРЕЧЕМСЯ ОТЪ СТАРАГО
МІРА

In this March, 1917, photograph, pro-Bolshevik soldiers, with red flags fixed to their bayonets, patrol the streets of Petrograd from a car they have commandeered from the Provisional Government.

HISTORY'S TURNING POINT
by Alexander Kerensky

In the excerpt below, Russia's Prime Minister at the time of the October Revolution gives a jaundiced analysis of the Bolsheviks' motives for planning their coup in early November.

I can still say, just as I did 48 years ago, that despite three years of war and blockade . . . the democratic government, which devoted itself to the service of the people and was obedient to their will, would never have been overthrown if the struggle against it had been waged by fair means and not by lies and slander. . . .

The decisive moment was rapidly approaching. November 25 was the date fixed for the elections to the Constituent Assembly. But Lenin could not afford to wait for them, because . . . they would not have brought him a majority. . . .

The most important thing was to wrest power from the Provisional Government before the Austro-German-Turko-Bulgarian coalition disintegrated. . . . Here, once again, the interests of Lenin and the German General Staff coincided.

The Germans needed a coup d'etat in Petrograd to stop Austria from signing a separate peace treaty. For Lenin, an immediate peace with Germany after his accession to power was the only way he could establish a dictatorship. . . .

I am firmly convinced that the uprising of [November 6–7] was deliberately timed to coincide with the serious crisis in Austro-German relations. . . . Lenin's plan was to seize power before the government could play this trump card, which would have robbed Lenin of any chance of seizing power. . . .

The night of [November 6–7] was a time of tense expectation. We were waiting for troops to arrive from the front. They had been summoned by me in good time and were due in Petrograd on the morning of [November 7]. But instead of the troops, all we got were telegrams and telephone messages saying that the railways were being sabotaged.

By morning . . . the troops had not yet arrived. The central telephone exchange, post office, and most of the government offices were occupied by detachments of Red Guards. The building that housed the Council of the Republic, which only the day before had been the scene of an endless and stupid discussion, had also been occupied by Red sentries. . . .

After a brief discussion it was decided that I should drive out at once to meet the troops. We were all quite sure that the paralysis of will that had seized democratic Petrograd would pass as soon as it was recognized that Lenin's plot was by no means a "misunderstanding," but a perfidious blow that left Russia entirely at the mercy of the Germans.

FALL OF THE WINTER PALACE
by Leon Trotsky

By November 7 Bolsheviks held nearly all the government offices. In this selection from his History of the Russian Revolution, *their leader dramatizes the final triumph.*

Shortly after six the Winter Palace was at last solidly surrounded by the troops of the Military Revolutionary Committee. . . . Imposing cordons extended from the iron fences of the Winter Palace garden, still in the hands of the besieged, from the arch between Palace Square and Morskaia Street, from the canal by the Hermitage, from the corners of the Admiralty, and the Nevsky nearby the palace. . . . The *Aurora* looked in from the Neva with her six-inch guns. Destroyers steamed back and forth patrolling the river. The insurrection looked at that moment like a military maneuver in the grand style.

. . . It is time to have an end. The order is given. Firing [from the *Aurora*] begins —not frequent and still less effectual. Out of thirty-five shots fired in the course of an hour and a half or two hours, only two hit the mark, and they only injure the plaster. . . .

The palace did not surrender but was taken by storm—this, however, at a moment when the power of resistance of the besieged had already completely evaporated. Hundreds of enemies broke into the corridor . . . through the defended door. . . . A considerable group of junkers got away in the confusion. The rest—at least a number of them— still continued to stand guard. But the barrier of bayonets and rifle fire between the attackers and defenders was finally broken down.

That part of the palace adjoining the Hermitage is already filled with the enemy. The junkers make an attempt to come at them from the rear. In the corridors phantasmagoric meetings and clashes take place. All are armed to the teeth. Lifted hands hold revolvers. Hand-grenades hang from belts. But nobody shoots and nobody throws a grenade. For they and their enemy are so mixed together that they cannot drag themselves apart. Never mind: the fate of the palace is already decided.

Workers, sailors, soldiers are pushing up from outside in chains and groups, flinging the junkers from the barricades, bursting through the court, stumbling into the junkers on the staircase, crowding them back, toppling them over, driving them upstairs. Another wave comes on behind. The square pours into the court. The court pours into the palace, and floods up and down stairways and through corridors. On the befouled parquets, among mattresses and chunks of bread, people, rifles, hand grenades are wallowing. The conquerors find out that Kerensky is not there, and a momentary pang of disappointment interrupts their furious joy. . . . Where is the government? That is the door—there where the junkers stand frozen in the last pose of resistance. The head sentry rushes to the ministers with a question: Are we commanded to resist to the end? No, no, the ministers do not command that. After all, the palace is taken. There is no need of bloodshed. We must yield to force. The ministers desire to surrender with dignity, and sit at the table in imitation of a session of the government. . . .

Below, blood is shed in Petrograd during the summer of 1917, when the Bolsheviks made their first, and abortive, attempt to seize power.

„Пролетарии всех стран, соединяйтесь!"

ЦАРЬ, ПОП И БОГАЧ
НА ПЛЕЧАХ У ТРУДОВОГО НАРОДА.

Три владыки, три господина мира едут на плечах рабочих и крестьян по тощей, разоренной земле, по трупам и костям погибших бедняков.

Эти три владыки—царь, поп и жадный, ненасытный богач-капиталист.

В руках у капиталиста—бич, на боку у него висит меч, покрытый кровью. Бичом он хлещет рабочий народ, заставляет тащить проклятую ношу. Мечом он гонит народ на войну, на бойню. Пускай бедняки завоюют ему в чужих странах новые земли и богатства.

Так было раньше в России. Теперь рабочие и крестьяне сбросили жадных кровопийц. Но во Франции, Англии, Америке короли, попы и богачи еще уцелели. Они гонят теперь свои полки на Россию, хотят помочь царскому отродью, попам, кулакам снова сесть на шею русского народа.

Рабочие и крестьяне! Хотите ли вы опять проливать для грабителей пот и кровь? Хотите ли жить в голоде и холоде и отдавать бездельникам все свои богатства? Хотите ли опять катать на своих плечах царя, попов, помещиков, богачей?

Если не хотите, отбивайте поход иностранных королей и богачей. Помогайте Советской власти, давайте побольше хлеба, работы, солдат в Красную Армию! Подымайтесь все защищать свою власть, землю и волю!

Вторая Государственная Типография. Москва, Трехпрудный пер., 9.

Издательство Всероссийского Центрального Исполнит. Комитета Советов Рабочих, Крестьянск., Красноарм. и Казачьих Депутатов.

1 МАЯ.
РАБОЧИМ НЕЧЕГО ТЕРЯТЬ, КРОМЕ СВОИХ ЦЕПЕЙ, А ПРИОБРЕТУТ ОНИ ЦЕЛЫЙ МИР.

К. Маркс и Ф. Энгельс.

Издательство Всероссийского Центрального Исполнит. Комитета Советов Рабочих, Крестьянск., Красноарм. и Казачьих Депутатов.

10

Aftermath of Revolution

In the chaos of the February-March revolution the abdication of the tsar was hardly noticed. The Provisional Committee of the Duma was striving to establish its authority in Petrograd. It was rivaled, however, by the Soviet of Workers' and Soldiers' Deputies. (An organization of the same name had existed briefly during the revolution of 1905, at which time the Russian word *sovet*, "council," began to be used by left-wing groups to signify popularly elected legislative bodies at all levels of government.) It now quickly revived. The resurgence was led by a number of extremist groups in cooperation with sympathetic members of the Duma. On March 12, 1917, they set up a temporary Executive Committee, the Excom, of the Soviet of Workers' Deputies. Almost three thousand representatives of the workers and soldiers convened in a mass meeting, more like a rally than a session of a deliberative body. That same evening the Soviet of Workers' and Soldiers' Deputies was formally proclaimed.

The deputies were divergent in their views. The Bolshevik minority opposed any suggestion of cooperation with the Provisional Committee of the Duma and argued in favor of

This painting shows Lenin addressing a tumultuous meeting of the Second All-Russian Congress of Soviets after the start of the October Revolution. Cheers rang out as he urged the toilers of the world to unite in liberating the masses "from all slavery and exploitation."

setting up a temporary revolutionary government until the Constituent Assembly could be elected. Certain deputies pressed for coalition with the Provisional Committee of the Duma. However, the majority held strongly that the Petrograd Soviet should not yet grasp power or share responsibility with the Duma, reasoning that since Marx had maintained that the bourgeois revolution must precede the proletariat seizure of power, the bourgeois committee of the Duma should govern for a time. Many deputies also feared that any attempt by them to take over the government at this stage would rally the propertied class in defense of the old regime.

The first priority of any government hoping to stay in power was to establish some order. The armed soldiers and workers who roamed the streets of Petrograd might at any moment become a dangerous mob. But the Provisional Committee of the Duma was seriously hampered in its efforts to exercise authority. De facto power was in the hands of the Soviet of Workers' and Soldiers' Deputies, which was more closely in touch with the revolutionary elements. The Petrograd Soviet had gained strong support with its Order No. 1, which delegated command of the armed forces to committees elected by the soldiers and sailors. The result was that troops —even those fighting the Austro-German forces—were in a position to countermand directives from their officers.

Order No. 1, and the more sweeping Declaration of the

The basic territorial organization of the U.S.S.R. was fixed by the constitution of 1936. Today there are fifteen union republics, all ostensibly self-ruling; within them are smaller administrative entities, most of which have developed around ethnic groups. In practice, the whole Soviet Union is controlled from Moscow.

Rights of Soldiers that followed, seemed to give the troops freedom to do as they wished. They became impatient to leave the fighting and return to their villages to seize their share of the landlords' estates. A massive wave of desertions followed, and the eastward surge of thousands of soldiers added to the general chaos.

Meanwhile, on March 15 and 16, the Duma committee and deputies from the Petrograd Soviet met in the Tauride Palace, once Potemkin's residence, to discuss the future government of the country. Pavel Milyukov, the leader of the Cadet Party, which supported the idea of parliamentary government, dominated the meeting. He was not able to shake the extreme leftists from their ideology; but in the face of the urgent need for some authority, the two blocs reached agreement over a surprisingly wide range of issues. A new government was set up, and on the following day the Excom announced its support in *Izvestia*, the Petrograd Soviet's newly founded daily newspaper. The Provisional Government was committed to the granting of political amnesty, to the elimination of class, religious, and all other forms of discrimination, and to the extension of full civil rights to all citizens. It had the urgent task of convening an assembly that would draft a constitution under which a permanent legislative body would be elected by secret, direct, and equal ballot. The need to restore military discipline was also emphasized.

But one factor that was to prove an important element in the ultimate collapse of the new executive was the leftists' insistence that the Petrograd garrison not be disarmed or dispatched to the front. This meant that it would remain at the disposal of the Bolsheviks.

Milyukov tried strenuously to persuade the Petrograd Soviet to appoint members to serve in the Provisional Government, which would commit them more firmly, but the Excom refused. Only Alexander Kerensky, a brilliant lawyer and orator, and the leader of the revolutionary labor group, agreed to cooperate, accepting the ministry of justice.

The most urgent problem facing the Provisional Government concerned the war in Europe. With the exception of the Bolsheviks, all the parties were politically and morally sworn to continue the fighting. Workers and troops in the city generally believed that if the Germans were victorious they would at once restore the tsarist regime. But the breakdown of order in the capital had spread rapidly to the provinces, and the nation's defenses were all but shattered.

Against this background of anarchy the All-Russian Conference of Soviets convened in Petrograd. Lev Kamenev, speaking on behalf of the Bolsheviks, demanded that the national struggle be transformed into a "prologue to the uprisings of the peoples of all the warring countries against the Moloch of war, the Moloch of Imperialism." Irakly

Alexander Kerensky, shown studying battle plans and wearing the uniform he adopted as minister of war, was the leading member of the Provisional Government. His policy of continuing the nation's participation in World War I—an undertaking that was far beyond Russia's capabilities—facilitated the Bolshevik coup.

Tsereteli, a Georgian Menshevik, declared that the Russian workers must fight alone against foreign enemies until other peoples followed the Russian example and overthrew their governments. In the voting the moderate Tsereteli received 325 in favor of his policy, while Kamenev was able to muster only 57 votes. Among the Bolshevik minority this numerical weakness was, however, soon to be offset by the return from exile of some of their leaders.

Upon Lenin's arrival at the Finland Station in Petrograd on April 16, he received a tumultuous welcome, but from the outset he made it clear that he did not regard the members of the Petrograd Soviet as his colleagues. He was so forceful in proclaiming his radical policies that he came near to turning the most moderate factions of the Soviet against him. As set forth in his *April Theses*, he would not tolerate the Provisional Government as an interim bourgeois democratic government from which the dictatorship of the proletariat would take over at some distant date. Rather, he insisted on the immediate seizure of power by a revolutionary government, by which he meant the Bolshevik Party.

Meanwhile, the Provisional Government, despite frequent crises, remained in power and, indeed, under the threat of increasing violence, was joined in a coalition with the Excom at Kerensky's impassioned urging. (In June at the first meeting of the All-Russian Congress of Soviets, convoked by the April conference, the Bolsheviks again voted their support.) Kerensky, the outstanding member of the new coalition and now minister of war, believed that he could revive in the troops the sense of discipline and duty; he made furious preparations to renew the offensive against Germany. He named General Alexei Brusilov commander in chief and placed commissars in charge of inspiring a new fighting spirit among the troops. His tireless efforts usually evoked enthusiastic if temporary responses. On July 1 Brusilov ordered the start of an offensive on the Galician front and broke through the Austrian lines. But the German troops brought up to support the Austrians halted the headlong advance, and the Russian victory was turned into a rout.

Under the leadership of Lenin and Leon Trotsky, who had returned from exile on May 17, the Bolsheviks gathered increasing support. They could claim, moreover, that they had consistently urged an end to the war. But in the period of mass madness known as the July Days, they, too, were overwhelmed by the eruption of anarchy. In an apparently spontaneous movement beginning on July 16 armed soldiers, sailors, and workers suddenly filled the streets of Petrograd and made for the Tauride Palace. Rifles and machine guns were fired at random. On the next day thirty thousand workers from the Putilov metallurgical factory and twenty thousand sailors from the fortress at Kronstadt renewed the demon-

Trotsky, who served as commissar for war from 1918 until 1925, was the chief organizer and leader of the Red Army during the civil war. The propaganda poster at left was one of the many issued over his signature. It warns Red troops to be on guard against Polish interventionists who, under the leadership of Marshal Pilsudsky (waving a top hat), are trying to "stir up war" in the Ukraine. French imperialists (represented by the aged soldier in Gallic uniform) are supporting the Poles; but, proclaims the poster, "the Red Army will do its work and nothing will stop it." The 1921 photograph opposite shows Trotsky and his staff crossing Moscow's Red Square to inspect Red Army soldiers engaged in military exercises organized for the entertainment of delegates attending a convention of the Communist International.

stration. The situation became more threatening as they surrounded the palace, preparing to lynch or shoot unpopular members of the Petrograd Soviet. The Provisional Government brought in loyal troops and the agitators fled.

On July 18 the Provisional Government, backed by the majority of the members of the Petrograd Soviet, accused the Bolsheviks of attempting a counter-revolution. In a further effort to undermine support for the Bolsheviks, the new minister of justice released documents alleging that Lenin and other party leaders were German agents. At this stage the government might have destroyed the Bolsheviks, but it made little attempt to suppress or disarm the Red Guards—armed units that the Bolsheviks had begun to organize in late June through factory committees—and it arrested only a few leaders, including Trotsky and Kamenev. Lenin, however, went into exile.

He was still in hiding in Finland when the Sixth Bolshevik Party Congress met secretly in Petrograd in mid-August. Stalin was given the task of arguing Lenin's policy. Lenin had dropped the slogan "All Power to the Soviets" in favor of a broader-based concept of a "revolutionary proletariat . . . supported by the poorest peasantry" as the agency to seize power. The congress went on to discuss future tactics. Stalin and others now argued that the revolution could be achieved in Russia alone. But to the optimistic Bolsheviks the whole

of Europe seemed on the verge of revolution.

Kerensky had become head of the Provisional Government on July 21, and with Lenin in hiding and the Bolsheviks discredited, the appearance of stable government was restored. The two basic problems remained: continuing the war and dealing with land reform in such a way as to win the support of the peasants. The feeling was still widespread that to desert the Allies and make a separate peace with the Germans would be dishonorable, and there was also strong opposition from the moderate Mensheviks to the surrender of the land to the peasants. In a bold attempt to rally the various groups behind his government, Kerensky called a state conference to meet in Moscow in August. Two thousand four hundred fourteen delegates, representatives from nearly all classes and sectors of the population except the Bolsheviks, attended, but they at once divided into two hostile camps. The fact that the conference had been convened in Moscow, the bastion of conservatism, made many left-wing delegates fear that the interests of the reactionaries were being promoted.

Kerensky tried without success to bring right and left groups together at the meeting. Right-wing delegates were now looking to General Lavr Kornilov for leadership. Kornilov had been appointed commander in chief in the belief that he would help gain Kerensky the support of the right wing and, equally important, restore order and discipline in

342

the armed forces. But Kornilov soon became disenchanted with the government's caution, and under pressure from reactionary factions, he began organizing a military coup from the army's general headquarters in Mogilev. With three cavalry divisions assisted by two right-wing patriotic groups and some two thousand sympathizers in Petrograd, he planned to seize power.

Despite an order on September 9 to step down, Kornilov commanded his troops to advance. Rumors circulated that the insurgents would not meet with real resistance, for the Provisional Government had no professional forces to protect it. However, the military challenge to the government and the threat of a right-wing dictatorship brought most of Petrograd's citizens behind Kerensky. The Committee for Struggle against Counter-Revolution was formed with the support of all parties, including the discredited Bolsheviks, who were shrewd enough to see their own advantage in the emergent crisis. In the face of the Kornilov threat, the Bolsheviks gained authority to muster and supply an armed workers' militia responsible to their will; this gave them the opportunity to enlarge the Red Guard—soon 25,000 strong. However, none of these preparations proved necessary to Petrograd's defense. Kornilov's troops were undermined by local soviet propagandists and saboteurs, who met them at every step in their advance on the city. By September 12

Kornilov's plans had collapsed without a shot being fired.

Kerensky now found his position greatly weakened; in seeking to mediate between left and right he had lost the confidence of the workers and soldiers. Moreover, the Bolsheviks had managed to take control of both the Moscow and Petrograd soviets, and Trotsky was elected president of the Petrograd Soviet on October 8.

In an attempt to shore up the coalition government, Kerensky convened the Democratic Conference in Petrograd. Right-wing delegates were excluded, and the soviets, trade unions, and smaller bodies were represented by some twelve hundred delegates. But the meetings were disrupted by the Bolsheviks, and Kerensky could not obtain real support. The conference did agree to establish the Council of the Republic; it would serve as a consultative body, guiding the government until the Constituent Assembly could assume power.

Meanwhile, the Bolshevik Party was growing in strength. The July Days and the campaign against Lenin as a German agent were already forgotten. The Bolshevik Party was greatly helped by Kornilov's attempted coup. In May membership had been in the region of 75,000, and in August it was estimated to be 200,000, the increase resulting in part from the Socialist Revolutionaries who had joined up. As yet a very small party, it represented an average 5.4 per cent of the factory workers in the cities.

Even when Lenin was in hiding, first in Helsinki and then in Vyborg, his influence was felt throughout the Bolshevik Party. He was tireless in writing pamphlets and in pressing for the seizure of power in the name of the revolutionary masses. Nevertheless, his ideas were slow to gain wide support. He returned secretly to Petrograd late in October and attended a meeting at which he convinced the Bolshevik Central Committee that "an armed rising is inevitable and the time is perfectly right."

The Military Revolutionary Committee of the Petrograd Soviet was set up under Trotsky's chairmanship. Controlled by Bolsheviks, this committee planned the revolution more or less openly, for the authority of the Provisional Government was dwindling. The celebration of a Day of the Petrograd Soviet on November 4 was the occasion for a peaceful but intimidating demonstration by workers and soldiers, an overt challenge to the government and its forces.

Kerensky took immediate action. He gave orders to close down the Bolshevik newspapers and to arrest the leaders involved in the July Days. On November 6 the naval cruiser *Aurora*, controlled by Bolsheviks and anchored in the Neva River, was ordered to sea as a precautionary measure. Army cadets together with a small Cossack detachment, which formed the government's main military forces, were deployed in the Winter Palace, where they were joined by a

newly formed battalion of women soldiers. The Bolshevik Military Revolutionary Committee now acted. It ordered the *Aurora* to remain at its anchorage, and by placing guards at the printing shops, ensured that the Bolshevik newspapers were published.

The revolution began on November 7 (October 25 by the old calendar). The two main railway stations, the Nikolai and the Baltic, were occupied first. The Bolsheviks then captured the State Bank and the telephone exchanges, disconnecting government communications. Early in the afternoon they surrounded the Mariinsky Palace and dispersed a frantic session of the Council of the Republic. By late afternoon the Bolsheviks had the whole of Petrograd, except for Kerensky's military headquarters at the Winter Palace, under their control. The operation had been carried out efficiently, with little opposition and few casualties.

At 6:30 in the evening an ultimatum was delivered to the headquarters of the Petrograd Military District demanding the surrender of the Winter Palace. When this was not met, the Military Revolutionary Committee ordered armored cars and troops to surround the palace. The *Aurora* fired a blank round at 9 P.M., followed by sporadic rifle and machine-gun fire from the troops. A battalion of women attempting to rescue General Mikhail Alekseev, who was in command at the palace, was at once captured by the Red Guards and

After his abdication Nicholas II and his family were interned for five months at Tsarskoe Selo, a royal summer palace south of Petrograd. Then, anticipating further revolutionary outbursts in the capital, Alexander Kerensky ordered them moved to Tobolsk in Siberia for security reasons. The snapshot opposite shows the emperor and his children (Empress Alexandra was sick) sunning themselves on the roof of a greenhouse attached to the provincial governor's house, their temporary residence. The photograph at right, showing villagers inspecting the bodies of four Bolsheviks who have just been hanged by a lynching party of the White troops, is a grisly reminder that both sides resorted to terrorism during the bitter civil war.

soldiers, who then rounded up the government ministers.

Meanwhile, the Second All-Russian Congress of Soviets was meeting at the Smolny Institute, the former girls' school. The Bolsheviks had 390 deputies out of a total of 650, but they had also the support of some 100 left-wing Socialist Revolutionaries. Signifying its formal approval of the Bolshevik revolution, the congress thus provided legal authority for the creation of the new regime; the Mensheviks and the moderate Socialist Revolutionaries responded by walking out, taunted by Trotsky as "miserable bankrupts. Your role is played out; go where you ought to be into the dustbin of history." They at once withdrew to the City Duma to join with them and other anti-Bolshevik groups, forming the Committee for the Salvation of the Country and the Revolution. The group then proclaimed itself legal heir to the powers of the fallen Provisional Government and became the rallying point for anti-Bolshevik activity.

Kerensky was reported to be marching on the city with a force of 700 Don Cossacks, commanded by General Peter Krasnov. But an anti-Bolshevik rebellion of cadets within the city, supposed to be coordinated with the Cossacks' advance, collapsed. On November 12 Krasnov launched his small Cossack force against the Red Guards on Pulkovo Heights, and they were fiercely repelled. Recognizing the hopelessness of the situation, Kerensky disguised himself in

a sailor's uniform and managed to escape to Murmansk and thence overseas.

Although the Bolsheviks had seized power easily in Petrograd and in other towns where they dominated the local soviet organizations, Moscow was captured only after bitter struggle. On a Bolshevik resolution the Moscow Soviet had appointed its own Military Revolutionary Committee, commanding some 50,000 soldiers and armed workers. Ranged against them were supporters of the Moscow City Duma, some 10,000 cadets, officers, armed students, and volunteers. Violent fighting took place between the two forces, culminating in the taking of the Kremlin by the Bolshevik Red Guard on November 15. By the end of November European Russia was under their control.

Having gained the approval of the Second All-Russian Congress of Soviets to the Bolshevik seizure of power, Lenin appointed the Council of People's Commissars, the new policy-making executive body known as Sovnarkom, which was wholly composed of Bolsheviks. Lenin himself was president of Sovnarkom; Trotsky was commissar for foreign affairs, and Anatoly Lunacharsky, commissar of education. Among the other commissars was Joseph Dzhugashvili (Stalin) as commissar of nationalities; he was at this time virtually unknown and received no ovation.

Lenin and the Sovnarkom were soon issuing a spate of

345

This Bolshevik poster of the civil war period shows the foreign and domestic enemies of the revolution joining forces and driving themselves to their own ruin. General Wrangel and Poland pull a wagon bearing the Entente (sym-

proclamations and decrees. Lenin announced the abolition of private ownership of land—"immediately and without purchase." The accent now was on attaining a "democratic dictatorship of workers and peasants." He achieved his purpose on November 25, when the All-Russian Congress of Peasants' Deputies agreed to merge with the Congress of Workers' and Soldiers' Soviets, thus broadening the base of his government to three classes: workers, peasants, and soldiers. Also proclaimed was the right of Russia's diverse peoples to national self-determination, and the abolition of all titles and class divisions in civil and military life, with special attention given to the "eradication of every inequality in the army." Women's rights were extended by the declaration of full legal equality of men and women and the liberalization of strict marriage and divorce laws. The Russian alphabet was revised for the first time since Peter the Great's modernization some two hundred years earlier. As of February 1, 1918 the Gregorian calendar replaced the Julian calendar, which at that time was thirteen days behind the calculation of the rest of Europe. Another decree effected the separation of Church and state, and gave every citizen the right to profess any religion or choose to be an atheist.

The tsarist legal system was rejected, and a new system of civil, criminal, and political courts established to enact the Sovnarkom's decrees. Political crimes were under the juris-

diction of the police organization known as the Cheka, the Extraordinary Commission to Combat Counter-Revolution and Sabotage. It would become the regime's secret weapon, more ruthless than the tsarist Third Chancellery.

Though the Bolsheviks had proclaimed in one of their most effective slogans "All power to the Constituent Assembly," Lenin would now have preferred that a new coalition government, based on the elected soviets, be given a permanent role. But under pressure of colleagues and of popular demand he agreed to the elections. When the Constituent Assembly convened for the only time on January 18, 1918, the Socialist Revolutionaries won an absolute majority, with the Bolsheviks polling only twenty-five per cent. The Assembly refused by a 237 to 136 vote to approve the earlier decrees passed by the Second Congress of Soviets. Faced with being removed from power, the Bolsheviks acted boldly, dissolving the Constituent Assembly. When the deputies attempted to resume their session at the Tauride Palace on the following day they found Red Guards barring all entrances.

In the international arena Lenin was presented with the need to make peace with the Central Powers: Germany and Austro-Hungary. The German supreme command was eager for peace with Russia. General Erich Ludendorff in particular knew that the Germans' one hope of victory now lay in a massing of all his forces in the West for a final, desperate

bolized by the whip-cracking driver), a well-fed bourgeois, a wizened Social Democrat, a landowner, and the tsar.
White leaders—Admiral Kolchak and Generals Denikin and Yudenich—have fallen to the ground, defeated.

offensive against the Allies, and he needed the troops that were tied down on the Eastern Front. An armistice was agreed on without difficulty early in December.

Trotsky headed his government's delegation. He proved an energetic negotiator, challenging the Germans at every point. He believed that time was on the side of the revolution and that proletarian uprisings were about to destroy both the Hapsburg and Hohenzollern empires. Suspecting that he would drag on the discussions interminably, the Germans presented the Russians with an ultimatum to sign or face renewed hostilities. Trotsky went to Petrograd for consultations. Lenin, always the realist, recognized that an attempt to prolong hostilities or stall the negotiations might well lead to the overthrow of the Soviet government. When Trotsky returned to Brest-Litovsk, he was confident that he could arrive at "an honest democratic peace" or at least achieve a propaganda victory.

The Germans were flabbergasted when after a brilliant diatribe Trotsky declared his refusal to sign a peace treaty on the terms proposed. They announced that they would resume fighting on February 18. Against strong opposition Lenin persuaded a majority of the people's commissars to accept the German terms. A telegram was sent immediately to Berlin. The Russians waited anxiously for the reply. The Germans were advancing on a broad front and were in a position to demand unconditional surrender. Finally on February 23 the new terms—far harsher than those proposed at Brest-Litovsk—were received. The Soviet Central Committee reacted with hysterical fury. Members demanded that they should wage a holy revolutionary war to the bitter end. Only Lenin remained cool. He demanded that the peace treaty be accepted without delay, if they were not to be guilty of signing the death sentence of the revolution, and threatened, "If this is not done, I resign from the government." He presented with remorseless logic his case for the treaty and finally gained their endorsement.

On March 3, 1918, the Treaty of Brest-Litovsk was signed. Russia lost 1,300,000 square miles of territory, embracing thirty-two per cent of the arable lands, thirty-three per cent of the factories, and some seventy-five per cent of the coal and iron resources, as well as a population of sixty-two million. It was a humiliating peace, made worse by a loss of more than two million dead, four million wounded, and two and a half million prisoners of war.

The name of the party was changed in March, 1918, from the Social Democratic Workers' Party to the Communist Party. Another decision was the transfer of the Soviet capital from Petrograd to Moscow. Lenin argued that the government would be less exposed to a renewed German attack if established in the old city, and the Sovnarkom and the Party

347

head offices were shortly transferred to the Kremlin. This return to the ancient capital was especially significant in forecasting the change that was to come in the outlook of the Bolshevik Party. Lenin and most of his comrades had belonged in spirit to Petrograd; they had thought of themselves as Westerners and of Marxism as a philosophy of international revolution. The successors of Lenin were to proclaim socialism in one nation and, like the ancient Muscovites, were to isolate the nation from the West.

The central provinces were now reasonably secure, but in the borderlands independent counter-revolutionary forces were massing. Disillusionment over the opening of the Brest-Litovsk talks had provoked many Russians to join together at first with the idea of renewing the war against the Central Powers, but they soon were challenging the Bolshevik regime. In the early phase of the civil war, which began as peace talks continued in January, 1918, a volunteer army calling itself the White Army was formed in southern Russia, led first by General Alekseev, at one time Kerensky's chief of staff. All over Soviet Russia various White governments were set up in opposition. On the Volga at Samara a counter-revolutionary government, drawn mainly from members of the abortive Constituent Assembly, was established and supported by Cossacks of the Ural and of the Orenburg regions. A directory of five members was set up in Omsk in western

Siberia. In eastern Siberia Grigory Semyonov, who commanded the Cossacks of Transbaikalia, ruled over a vast area with Japanese support. In Estonia General Nikolai Yudenich, a figure backed by the British, recruited an anti-Communist force and planned an assault on Petrograd. Lenin recognized the dangers posed by these White armies, but neither he nor his comrades expected the bizarre turn the civil war would take as a result of the Czechoslovak Legion.

Soon after the outbreak of World War I in 1914, Czechoslovaks had formed a separate unit, fighting alongside the Russian army. (Their numbers consisted of deserters from the Austro-Hungarian army and Czechoslovakian conscripts.) Professor Tomas Masaryk, the Czechoslovak nationalist leader, had obtained permission to transfer the Czech forces to the French front—by way of the Trans-Siberian Railway to Vladivostok, then by ship to western Europe. The Czechoslovak Legion was thirty thousand strong and well-disciplined; it was a formidable fighting unit by the standards of chaos-ridden Russia. Determined that the Legion should fight against the Central Powers, Masaryk rejected approaches by Whites for support in their civil war.

In May, 1918, near the western Siberian city of Chelyabinsk a detachment of Czechs encountered a trainload of Austrian and Hungarian prisoners of war who were being repatriated under the Treaty of Brest-Litovsk. The Austrians

By the early 1920's the Bolshevik victory was completely secured. Throughout the length and breadth of the Soviet Union crowds gathered to hail the new regime. This photograph depicts a parade in Vladivostok; the workers carry posters of Soviet Russia's new heroes. Stern images of Lenin, Marx, Trotsky, and other champions of Communism replace the traditional icons of saints and of "the Little Father," or tsar.

and Hungarians abused the Czechs as traitors, and the Czechs were provoked to lynch one of the Hungarians. When Soviet officials attempted to intervene, the Czechs on their own initiative went over to the White counter-revolutionaries. Trotsky sent orders that all eastward movements of these troop trains must be halted and the Czech Legion disarmed, but the Czechs broke into several groups, some of them fighting their way to the east. By the end of summer they had captured all the main towns and stations along the Trans-Siberian Railway except in the Irkutsk region.

The Soviet regime had not prepared for civil war, as Lenin later admitted to the Eighth Party Congress. The Bolsheviks had rejected building a regular army, an instrument of autocratic and imperialistic governments, but the workers' militia and the Red Guards proved incapable of suppressing even White troops. The first step toward creating a Red Army was a decree in January, 1918, coincident with the formation of the White Army. Sovnarkom envisaged a voluntary force, and within two months some hundred thousand men had offered their services, but they proved to be an undisciplined mob. Trotsky, who had predicted such a failure, called for conscription. He also insisted that an officer corps, able to impose stern discipline and technical efficiency, was essential. His most controversial proposal was that the technical knowledge and experience of tsarist officers be fully

employed, and lest such officers betray the Red Army and the revolution, he undertook to ensure their loyalty by a ruthless system of holding families under surveillance and placing each officer under the direct supervision of military commissars. Between 1918 and 1920, 48,409 former tsarist officers were recruited, and the Red Army strengthened from 331,000 soldiers to five million. Trotsky also issued a decree making it the first duty of commissars for military affairs to ensure that "the army does not become a thing apart from the entire Soviet system and that the various military establishments do not become foci of conspirators or instruments against workers and peasants."

Meanwhile, Communist leaders had been forced to resort to desperate expedients in preserving the economic life of the nation. Lenin recognized that the soviets and the workers were not yet competent to take over management of industry. He was prepared to move slowly toward nationalization; but the fact that industry was run by the traditional enemies of the socialist state thrust aside this commonsense approach. Under a system known as War Communism, all major industries were nationalized without compensation to the owners. In June, 1918, labor was put under rigorous controls, and a decree in October made it compulsory for all persons between the ages of sixteen and fifty to work.

The inevitable result of this centralization of government

and the nationalization of the economy was the rapid growth of a vast bureaucratic machine that wielded extensive powers, usually with gross inefficiency. One of the most powerful of the new institutions was the food commissariat. The government, now the sole producer and marketer of goods, took charge of food distribution. Ration cards were hurriedly issued to urban workers, and by 1920 some thirty-five million were in use. Peasants did not receive them, for they were expected to provide for themselves, as were people of upper- and middle-class origins. Nevertheless, malnutrition and starvation killed thousands of people in the cities and towns.

In the years 1916 to 1920 more than one third of the urban population in northern and central Russia moved to the country in search of food. Barter increasingly became the form of exchange. (Inflation had run unchecked with the result that in October, 1920, the ruble was worth only one per cent of its value in 1917.) The Soviet government was haunted by the specter of famine, intensified by the ceding of the Ukraine, the breadbasket of tsarist Russia, to Germany as part of the Treaty of Brest-Litovsk. The summer of 1918 brought the bread crisis to a head just as the regime was fighting for its existence against the White counter-revolutionaries. The peasants surrendered their grain to the government only under severe pressure. They had no interest in payment, since the industries in the cities produced few of

the goods they needed, and distributed less. By a decree of May 27, 1918, the food commissariat was vested with absolute powers to expedite the distribution of "articles of prime necessity and food supplies." Local food organizations and workers' detachments for collecting grain were established. Operated on military lines, each detachment was comprised of seventy-five or more men with two or three machine guns, led by a commander and often a political commissar.

Committees of the poor, known as *kombedy*, were charged with assisting local food organizations in extracting grain from the wealthier peasants. The whole country was soon engaged in a savage bread war. Countless villages were rent by struggles in which men were burned alive, cut up with scythes, or beaten to death. Lenin sent a circular to all provincial soviets and food committees seeking to stop this savagery; but once unleashed, it could not be easily halted. The wealthier peasants openly waged war against the armed workers' detachments, though they made no attempt to promote a counter-revolution. They believed still that the Communist Party was ultimately committed to peasant ownership of the land, whereas the Whites were characterized as advocating the return of all land to the landowners. (In fact, Communist policy was to merge small landholdings and to establish vast collective farms, though at this critical stage no attempt was made to implement this program.)

The famine that had threatened Russia since 1916 reached epidemic proportions in 1921. Under War Communism peasants were forced to surrender all surplus produce to the state instead of sending it to market. They reacted by raising no more than what they needed, thereby leaving city-dwellers without food. When government agents began seizing grain for the urban population, the peasantry found itself starving. Drought and a complete breakdown of transportation further aggravated the situation, and the government sought foreign aid. The American Relief Administration was set up under future president Herbert Hoover. With vehicles like those at top right, it distributed almost half a million tons of food, clothing, and medicine to famine victims who waited on bread lines (below right). Quakers and other service agencies also assisted: in the 1922 painting opposite, desperate Russians plunder sacks of wheat from a Red Cross train.

In the midst of all this strife the Fifth All-Russian Congress of Soviets met from July 4 to July 10, 1918. The Socialist Revolutionaries, the last surviving opposition party, accused Lenin of humiliating, oppressing, and betraying the peasants. Trotsky attempted to speak but was shouted down. The meeting seemed on the verge of dissolving until Lenin walked to the front of the stage and restored order.

But this congress was not to solve its conflicts by deliberation. The extremists among the Socialist Revolutionaries had already agreed on action. Their plan was to assassinate the German ambassador, hoping in this way to provoke the Germans to renew the war and perhaps ignite an uprising against the Bolshevik regime. The assassination took place on July 6, but it failed in its political objectives. The Germans, now hard-pressed on the Western Front, were unable to detach troops against the Soviets, and an attempt by the Socialist Revolutionaries to take over the city and arrest Bolshevik leaders was promptly suppressed. From this moment the leftist Socialist Revolutionaries were banned from the Congress of Soviets, and the regime was on its way to becoming a dictatorship of the Communist Party.

Only in Simbirsk and in central Russia did counter-revolutionary efforts have an impact. As the White Russian forces began to threaten Yekaterinburg (later Sverdlovsk), the Bolsheviks murdered Nicholas and the whole of his family with a brutality that epitomized the terror of the civil war. The imperial family had been arrested a few days after the tsar's abdication and held under close guard. The Bolsheviks feared that should White troops rescue the imperial family, they would establish a rallying point for all counter-revolutionary forces. Soon after midnight on July 16 Nicholas, his wife, children, and staff were led down to the cellar of the house where they had been held prisoners. Once in the cellar, the Bolshevik guard opened fire, shooting them down and bayoneting those who still showed signs of life. Their bodies were hurriedly taken to a nearby mine shaft, where they were destroyed. The public, barely informed of the event, seemed unaffected.

In the midst of these events the Fifth Congress of Soviets was still in session, and on July 10, 1918, it approved a new constitution that established the Russian Soviet Federated Socialist Republic (R.S.F.S.R.). The Declaration of the Rights of the Toiling and Exploited People, drafted earlier by Lenin and setting out in general terms the Communist ideals, formed the preamble to the constitution, and the second part defined the political organization of the regime.

The urban and rural soviets were described as the source of all authority, but the cities were given greater representation than the rural areas in that the urban proletariat had one delegate for 25,000 electors and the peasants were allowed

one delegate for 125,000 electors. This reflected the fact that the Bolsheviks had greater support in the cities and towns than among the peasantry. The local soviets were to be the foundations for the provincial congresses of soviets, which in turn sent delegates to the All-Russian Congress of Soviets. The Central Executive Committee exercised the functions of the All-Russian Congress when it was not in session (in these early years it met on an ad hoc basis) and appointed the Sovnarkom to direct the administration. But the real power was vested in the leadership of the Communist Party, notwithstanding these constitutional guarantees.

The summer of 1918 closed with two almost simultaneous acts of terrorism committed by fanatic Socialist Revolutionaries. On August 30 Mikhail Uritsky, head of the Petrograd Cheka, was assassinated. On the same day a young Jewish woman, Fanya Kaplan, shot and severely wounded Lenin as he was leaving a meeting of Moscow factory workers.

These acts were now taken as a pretext for reprisals and summary violence. The commissar for internal affairs issued instructions to all soviets that stated: "Chekas and militia departments should make special efforts to locate and arrest all those living under assumed names and to shoot without formality everyone mixed up with White Guards . . . and other dirty plotters against the government of the working class and the poorer peasantry. Show no hesitation whatso-

ever in carrying out mass terror. . . ." Terror was a means not only of destroying enemies of the regime but also of ruthlessly compelling obedience and active support. A senior Cheka official stated that during the first three years of its existence 12,733 people charged with counter-revolutionary activities were shot, but the true figure was probably around 50,000 for the whole civil war.

The late summer of 1918 was critical for the Soviet government. En route to the Pacific coast, the Czechoslovak Legion had divided into three groups and spread across Siberia. The Allied governments were now eager that the Czechs continue fighting with the Whites against the Red Army and that they return by land through the Ukraine to a Czechoslovakia liberated from the Austro-Hungarian empire.

The most serious threat to the regime at this stage was from the White forces. General Anton Denikin's volunteer army secured the support of the Kuban Cossacks, and General Peter Krasnov, hetman of the Cossacks, defeated the Red partisans in the Don region. He was planning to advance next to the middle Volga, but at Tsaritsyn the Red forces—under the joint command of Kliment Voroshilov, later the commissar for war and the navy, and of Stalin, who was requisitioning grain—repelled Krasnov's Cossacks.

Trotsky had traveled to the middle Volga front, where he was dismayed not only by the fall of Kazan but also by the

Education, a central aspect of the Bolshevik program, was carried out in the streets and the schools. The workers opposite are studying in one of the thousands of Centers for Liquidating Illiteracy set up in cities and rural areas. (By 1939 about eighty per cent of the population had been taught to read and write.) The agitation-propaganda train (right), carrying movies, recordings, pamphlets, and pageants to the countryside, represents one of the most successful means of outdoor instruction. "Agit-prop" shows were entrusted to leftist artists, writers, and actors who found a common cause in the political and artistic revolutions of the twentieth century.

demoralized condition of the Red troops. Lecturing and haranguing his men, he had revived morale, and on September 10 they recaptured Kazan. Trotsky loudly proclaimed this as a turning point in the civil war. Two days later Simbirsk was occupied, and the tide indeed began to turn in favor of the Red Army.

It was during this campaign that Trotsky and Stalin became involved in bitter conflict. Trotsky, then co-leader with Lenin of the Soviet regime, stood between Stalin and his ambitions. Stalin also felt himself frequently humiliated by Trotsky's arrogant behavior. When the antagonism between them reached a critical stage, Trotsky cabled to Lenin: "I insist on Stalin's recall." Although Lenin managed to keep a semblance of peace between them, the vendetta would erupt publicly after his death, leading to Trotsky's exile from Russia in 1929. (His murder in 1940 in Mexico was almost certainly carried out on the direct instigation of Stalin.)

Meanwhile, the collapse of Germany in the West had immediate repercussions in the Ukraine. The Germans had recognized the puppet leader Pavel Skoropadsky as hetman of the Ukraine. Violent strikes became commonplace, and peasant bands waged guerrilla warfare against both the hetman's government and occupation forces. In November the Ukrainian nationlists appointed a directory to rule over a Ukrainian People's Republic, but the new regime also failed

to gain support, for the peasants and workers continued to see their only salvation in the Communist Party. The Red forces advanced and on February 5, 1919, took Kiev. At this point the main anxiety of the Soviet leaders was the threat of Allied intervention.

In the last months of the war the Allies feared that the German divisions on the Eastern Front might be transferred to the Western Front, where they would tip the balance in Germany's favor. They were concerned also that the vast quantities of military supplies they had landed for use of the tsarist armies in Murmansk, Archangel, and Vladivostok might fall into German hands. Further, the Soviet regime represented a clear and present danger to vested interests in these nations: Soviet intentions to nationalize all industries meant sizable financial losses for foreign investors, and Soviet talk of awakening the working classes of the world seemed to threaten internal stability everywhere. After long debate Britain, France, the United States, Japan, and Italy landed troops in Soviet Russia.

The Allies were encouraged in their decision by the fact that in November, 1918, as a result of a coup, Admiral Alexander Kolchak had become "Supreme Ruler" and commander in chief of the White forces in Siberia. Kolchak was known and respected in the West for his brave record in the Russo-Japanese War, and subsequently for his work in re-

The 1922 photograph at left of Lenin and Stalin as a smiling duo was widely circulated in the Stalin era to publicize the allegedly close ties between the so-called Father of the Revolution and the new dictator; it was one of the last pictures taken of Lenin before his stroke. When he died in 1924 thousands of workers waited in line in front of the Moscow Trade Union House, as shown opposite, in 30-degrees-below-zero weather to pay their respects. Winston Churchill, who regarded Lenin's death as a great national tragedy, would later write: "He alone could have found the way back to the causeway. . . . The Russian people were left floundering in the bog. Their worst misfortune was his birth . . . their next worse, his death."

organizing the Russian navy. Early in 1919 he launched his offensive, and the troops advanced rapidly until they were on the point of retaking Kazan and Samara; Moscow seemed within reach. But when at the end of April the Red Army launched a counterattack, his army fell back in disorder. By mid-November Kolchak's force had been crushed, and many of his men had gone over to the Communists.

In May, 1919, Denikin had begun his drive, and within a few weeks he had occupied the whole of the Don region. In October he captured Orel. Only Tula, an important munitions center, stood between him and the capital. But he had overreached himself, and with hostile peasants harassing troops in the rear, he had to retreat.

Meanwhile, General Yudenich was threatening an attack on Petrograd, which was timed to coordinate with Denikin's attack on Moscow. Lenin was prepared to sacrifice Petrograd to save the new capital; but Trotsky hastened to Petrograd to take charge of its defenses, and Yudenich was beaten back.

By autumn, 1919, the Red Army had begun to advance on all fronts. In despair Kolchak nominated Denikin as his successor in January, 1920; but before he himself could escape to Vladivostok, he was executed by the Bolsheviks. The morale of Denikin's troops had collapsed, and his own officers were ranged against him. He appointed General Baron Peter Wrangel, who had been in command on the Caucasian front, to lead the White armies, and in July he left Russia.

Wrangel was far more of a statesman than were Kolchak or Denikin. He recognized that the Whites had to have peasant support, and he was prepared to give them full possession of the land. Among his flagging troops he imposed a new discipline and revived morale; but burdened in the Crimea by hordes of refugees seeking the protection of his troops and deprived suddenly of British help, he could not hope to succeed. He attempted, nevertheless, to advance against the Red Army. His forces broke through the lines in June and then turned into the Kuban and the Don in the hope of gaining Cossack reinforcements. He was now facing a seasoned Red Army of far superior strength. When he attempted to advance northwest across the Dnieper and into the western Ukraine he suffered a severe defeat. By the end of October he had been driven back to the Crimea. With this, the organized struggle of the White forces came to an end.

While Wrangel was marching northward, a small Polish army challenged the Reds from the west. Disappointed by the terms of the so-called Curzon Line—the Polish-Russian boundaries that the Allies had set at the Versailles peace negotiations in 1919—and believing that the Soviet regime was near to collapse, the Poles launched an offensive to annex the western Ukraine and western Belorussia. They were halted at Kiev and chased back as far as Warsaw, but a counteroffensive left

the Soviets in disarray. Anxious for peace, the Soviets signed a preliminary treaty at Riga in October, 1920, conceding to the Poles a frontier some one hundred twenty miles or more to the east of the Curzon Line and also direct access to the Baltic Sea by a corridor separating Russia from Lithuania.

Red forces met with greater success in the south, where they occupied Georgia, Armenia, and Azerbaidzhan; their grasp on Transcaucasia was secured in March, 1921, by a treaty signed with Turkey. In Central Asia and the Far East the regime extended its authority: in 1920 it set up the Far Eastern Republic and in 1922 recovered Vladivostok.

The wars at home and abroad had left the nation exhausted. More than twenty-six million Russians had died in the effort. Trotsky, elated by victory, argued furiously that the policy of War Communism must be continued as the only means of reviving the nation. Lenin approved his proposals for "the mobilization of the industrial proletariat, liability to labor service, militarization of economic life, and the use of military units for economic needs." Trotsky organized army units to serve in repairing railway lines, harvesting, and carrying out other essential labors; but neither the army nor the people were prepared to go on under this pressure. Troops deserted. Peasants burned their produce and obstructed the government in other ways. In Moscow and Petrograd work-

ers and even rank-and-file members of the Party demonstrated. In the Ukraine and in the Tambov region, notorious for its turbulence, rebellion broke out with as many as twenty thousand rebels defying the government. Order was restored by the autumn of 1921, but the discontent remained.

Lenin recognized now the urgent need to recover popular support and particularly to win over the peasantry or see the young revolutionary regime crushed. He made a strategic change in the economic direction of the country. At the Tenth All-Russian Congress of Soviets Lenin put foward his first measures of what was to become the New Economic Policy, or NEP. The measures gave peasants incentives to increase agricultural output and to trade their surplus products. Most significantly, perhaps, the NEP abolished the principle of collective responsibility, leaving peasants free to meet their own obligations and spend the rest of the time working for themselves. Private initiative was also encouraged in small industry (plants staffed by fewer than twenty men) and in retail trade. To the Bolsheviks the new policy meant reversion to the hated capitalist system; but Lenin was confident that so long as the state was in control of "the commanding heights" of heavy industry and foreign trade, true Communism could be eventually achieved. Bolshevik fears were intensified by the emergence of a class of enterprising and wealthy peasants known as kulaks, who flourished

The two bricklayers eating black bread and soup in a communal kitchen in this 1932 photograph enjoy their simple fare under a poster urging workers to accelerate production. The fact that Stalin's First Five-Year Plan ended in 1932, only four years and three months after it had been launched, attests to the control that the Soviet government exercised over its manpower. The main goal of the first, as well as of all subsequent plans, was the development of heavy industry. When the Second Five-Year Plan terminated in 1937, the Soviet Union had upgraded its industrial output from fifth to a position second only to that of the United States.

economically in the midst of the devastating famine of 1921.

Meanwhile, the Party, with a membership of some 705,000 by 1921, had been weakened by members who were careerists and lacked the dedication that Lenin demanded. A drive was begun to expel men of dubious loyalty, and membership was reduced to 472,000 by the end of 1922. At the same time the Soviet leaders had been building the constitutional basis of the regime. At the Tenth All-Russian Congress of Soviets of the R.S.F.S.R. Stalin had proposed a federal union with the three Soviet republics—the Ukrainian Soviet Socialist Republic, the Belorussian S.S.R., and the Transcaucasian S.S.R. The Treaty of Union was ratified by delegates of the republics who had been called to Moscow for the first All-Union Congress of Soviets of the Union of Soviet Socialist Republics. In July of the following year the constitution of the U.S.S.R. was approved and in January, 1924, the Second All-Union Congress of Soviets ratified it. It was modeled closely on the original Soviet constitution, with additional articles defining the division of powers within the union. The federal government was to have exclusive powers over foreign relations, trade, finance, the national economy, justice, education, and communications, while residual powers, which were extremely limited, were vested in the union republics. In theory supreme power belonged to the All-Union Congress of Soviets, comprising some two thousand deputies. In practice the All-Union Congress elected an All-Union Central Executive Committee of some five hundred members, which was the actual repository of power, and in turn it chose a Presidium of twenty-seven members who exercised full authority when the CEC was not in session. The CEC also appointed Sovnarkom, the chairman of which was the equivalent of Prime Minister. The constitution erected an imposing legal façade, behind which the Communist Party controlled all of the organs of government.

On May 26, 1922, Lenin suffered his first major stroke, which paralyzed his right side. Resting in his apartment, he was able to review the events since the revolution, and he became deeply concerned about the future of the Party. He made the trenchant comment: "Comrade Stalin, having become General Secretary, has concentrated enormous power in his hands, and I am not sure that he always knows how to use that power with sufficient caution." On Trotsky he commented that he was "distinguished not only by his exceptional abilities—personally he is to be sure the most able man in the present Central Committee—but also by his too far-reaching self-confidence and a disposition to be too much attracted by the administrative affairs." The fear that the Party would be irrevocably split preyed on Lenin's mind. On January 4, 1923, he dictated a postscript to his "Testament," in which he proposed that Stalin be replaced by another

The coming of the tractor to the kolkhoz, an event that brought the whole community out for inspection (above), began to transform Soviet agriculture in the 1920's. Equipment was leased from Machine and Tractor Stations, government agencies that oversaw the production quotas and political loyalties of district communes.

member who would be "more patient, more loyal, more polite, and more attentive to comrades . . . ." But Lenin was no longer able to act in the political arena. In March he had another stroke, which deprived him of the power of speech. At the Twelfth Party Congress in April, which he was unable to attend, members vied with each other in praising him.

The struggle for leadership of the Party was already developing. Trotsky and Grigory Zinoviev were the main contenders. Stalin at this stage was willing to work as a member with Zinoviev and Kamenev of the triumvirate that was to carry on during Lenin's absence. Zinoviev and Kamenev seemed to overshadow Stalin. Trotsky regarded him with contempt as "the outstanding mediocrity of our Party." The historian Nikolai Sukhanov wrote that he gave "the impression of a gray blur, floating dimly across the scene and leaving no trace. There is really nothing more to be said about him."

For some two years, however, Stalin had been virtually the unrecognized ruler of Russia. As commissar of nationalities, he had control over sixty-five million of the nation's population; as commissar of workers and peasants inspection until 1923, he had had almost unlimited control over the machinery of government; as a member of the Political Bureau (Politburo), the true center of Party power, he had been active in policy making; as a member of the Organization Bureau since 1919, he had been directly concerned with the posting of Party personnel throughout the country. Finally, his appointment on April 3, 1922, as General Secretary of the Central Committee had extended his authority even further. The other members of the Politburo, who were intent on watching that Trotsky did not emerge as a dictator, did not notice the real threat in their midst.

Lenin, reduced to impotence, was moved to a rest home at Gorky. As the winter wore on, his health deteriorated. On January 21, 1924, he died. The promotion of a cult of Lenin began immediately. He had requested that he should not be the subject of grandiose memorials and commemorations. However, Petrograd was renamed Leningrad, and he was lauded as the paragon of dedication, self-discipline, and simple and purposeful living. In his life he undoubtedly exemplified these qualities, but he was also a cold and dangerous fanatic, ruthless in his singleminded devotion to a cause. His immediate contribution to Russia's history was threefold. He fathered the October Revolution, for without his bold leadership it would probably not have succeeded. He created Marxism-Leninism by planting in Russia the Western ideology of Marxism, adapted to the particular circumstances of a peasant-dominated society; and through his insistence on the rule of a small, disciplined party, following one leader, he led the Bolsheviks to triumph over the Mensheviks in the creation of the socialist state. And he provided future genera-

357

According to Marx, Lenin, and their followers, religion is a means by which rulers can subjugate the poor and is thus inimical to socialist revolution. By a law of 1921 public religious instruction was forbidden to anyone under eighteen, and the following year the state began publishing an atheist propaganda journal. The Soviet regime was equally anxious to destroy churches and other visible symbols of Orthodoxy—the iconoclasts in this photograph are Red Army soldiers looting a convent. The government also expropriated ecclesiastical treasures, ostensibly to buy famine relief from abroad, and used the debris from fallen religious edifices to build what it deemed "useful constructions."

tions of Russian people with a hero to worship.

Competition for control within the Party became more intense after Lenin's death. Trotsky, with his international outlook, urged that the Bolsheviks give every support to revolutionary movements abroad, while maintaining a militant socialist policy at home. In this he was supported by Zinoviev and Kamenev. On the right, however, prominent members like Nikolai Bukharin urged that the New Economic Policy be continued in Russia; this would enable the country to develop its economic strength while awaiting the proletarian revolution in other countries. The centrist group, led by Stalin, maintained that Soviet Russia was a country so self-sufficient that socialism could be developed there without outside support. Stalin called on all citizens to devote themselves unsparingly to the transformation of the Soviet Union—and this was the policy finally adopted. At the Fourteenth Party Congress in December, 1925, Stalin received the overwhelming support of 559 votes to 65 for his policy of "socialism in one country."

At this time Stalin began to accelerate changes in the economic direction of the country. He had made up his mind that the NEP must be abandoned. Collectivization of agriculture and large-scale industrialization had long been important elements of Party policy. The debate had turned on the tempo of change. The general feeling was that it should

be gradual. Lenin himself had in 1919 denounced the "idea of compulsion with reference to economic relations with average peasants." Forcible collectivization of a peasantry numbering over one hundred million was a formidable undertaking. But Stalin had no sympathy for the peasants, and, indeed, resented the privileged position they enjoyed.

By June 1, 1928, the number of kolkhozes, or collective farms, had increased to 33,258. The system, which bore some resemblance to the pre-revolutionary communes, was not an immediate success, however, and only a fraction of the total peasant population was involved. The collectivization campaign gathered momentum during 1929. Special brigades of workers were dispatched from the towns to take militant action against peasants who fought to protect their property. They now found themselves being deprived of their hard-won land. In protest the peasants took such extreme action as slaughtering their livestock: of the thirty-four million horses in Russia in 1929, eighteen million were killed; 45 per cent of cattle and 60 per cent of sheep and goats were also destroyed. Collectivization continued inexorably. By March, 1930, more than half of the farmlands and half of the total peasant population had been affected, and by 1936, 91 per cent of all peasants were under some phase of the system.

The campaign for industrialization followed a similar pattern. By 1927 industry had attained the prewar levels of pro-

This 1926 antireligious cartoon, depicting the unholy saints of the capitalist system, satirizes the hier-archical convention of Orthodox icon paintings. Saint Capitalist, en-throned on a cannon and holding a bomb and a factory, dominates the group portrait while Saints Com-promise and President curry favor at either hand. Imperialist Saints United States, Britain, and France are ranged above businessmen saints —a snub-nosed American, bull-faced Englishman, and long-nosed Frenchman. Below them are law enforcers, policemen, and detectives, and singing the praises of the entire fraternity, the professional religion-ists of the Jewish, Orthodox, Cath-olic, Moslem, and Buddhist faiths.

duction; but at the Fifteenth Party Congress in December, 1927, Stalin set forth the first of a series of five-year plans outlining national growth objectives. Between 1928 and 1932 he demanded that production increase at the annual rate of fifteen per cent. Intensive propaganda was designed to make every worker think of himself as a partner in the ef-fort. Young people, and in particular the Komsomol (the Communist League of Youth), took up the plan enthusias-tically; but the mass of workers, weary from food shortages, the decline in living standards, and years of war and struggle, was not inspired. Increased absenteeism had to be curbed by severe disciplinary measures and punishments. In February, 1931, Stalin, addressing a workers' conference, spoke with passion about the need to reach the targets set.

"To retard the tempo—this means to drop behind. And those who are backward are beaten. We do not want to be beaten! No, we do not want that! The history of old Russia was, among other things, that she was constantly beaten be-cause of her backwardness. The Mongol khans beat her. The Turkish beys beat her. The Swedish feudal lords beat her. The Polish-Lithuanian nobles beat her. The Anglo-French capitalists beat her. The Japanese barons beat her. All beat her—for her backwardness, governmental back-wardness, industrial backwardness, agricultural backward-ness. They beat her because it was profitable and went un-

punished. Remember the words of the prerevolutionary poet: 'Thou art poor, Thou art abundant, Thou art power-ful, Thou art powerless, Mother Russia. . . .' We are fifty to a hundred years behind the advanced countries. We must make up this gap in ten years . . . or they crush us!"

The First Five-Year Plan, which began in 1928, was com-pressed into just over four years. The achievements were staggering, and many have described the first plan as the real Russian revolution. As much as 80 per cent of all in-dustrial investment was allocated to heavy industry in the period. More than one thousand five hundred new factories were built, and in the Urals and in western Siberia vast in-dustrial complexes were created. Almost half the machine tools in operation in 1932 had been put into production dur-ing the four-year period. A quarter of the total coal mined was from pits opened within the period, and there was a 25 per cent increase in the number of oil wells in production. The capacity of electric power stations was more than dou-bled. When the First Five-Year Plan was ended, it was claimed that it had been 93.7 per cent fulfilled. In the enthusiasm and shrill propaganda of the time many false assertions were made, but beyond dispute industrial production had multi-plied many times. In terms of world production Russia's out-put had increased from 2.6 per cent in 1913 to 3.7 per cent in 1929 and 13.7 per cent in 1937.

The Second Five-Year Plan, lasting from 1933 until 1937, and the Third, which started in 1938 and was broken off by the German invasion in 1941, continued the campaign of industrialization and collectivization. (To drive workers to still greater efforts, the government conceived the idea in 1935 of publicizing the real or fictional achievements of highly productive citizens. The Stakhanovites, named after a model coal miner, were generally regarded with cynicism.)

While directing these gigantic campaigns Stalin was constantly on the watch for signs of opposition. When in the summer of 1932 Mikhail Ryutin, a former Secretary of the Moscow Party Committee and a supporter of Bukharin, was found to have prepared a plan to slow down Stalin's policies and to overthrow him, Stalin demanded his execution. Lenin had warned the Party against applying the death penalty to its members, and among those men sitting in the Politburo there was reluctance to treat opposition as treason, punishable by death. Six members of the Politburo who opposed Stalin in this matter were all to die soon by assassination or in unexplained circumstances. But if there was conflict over the use of terror within the Party, there was none about terror against those outside the Party. In 1930 the first of the show trials that were to mark the Stalin era took place. The accused were denounced as wreckers and saboteurs, and all were sentenced to long prison terms, which they did not

survive. Stalin next instigated a thorough purge of the Party membership, and in the period 1931 to mid-1933 some 40,000 accused of political deviation were examined and 15,442 of them expelled.

The Seventeenth Party Congress, meeting early in 1934, was called the Congress of Victors. The harvest of 1933 had been exceptional. Stalin's position seemed beyond challenge, and each speaker at the congress heaped praise upon their great leader. But Stalin evidently suspected that there were potential rivals among the newly elected Central Committee. Within the next five years 98 of the committee's 139 members and candidates elected by this congress were executed.

In July, 1933, the OGPU was dissolved. It had succeeded the Cheka, which Feliks Dzerzhinsky had established. A fanatic Bolshevik, he had created a security police that was actively feared throughout Russia. He continued as the head of the OGPU until his death. Genrikh Yagoda succeeded him and in 1934 became leader of the NKVD, the commissariat for internal affairs, established to take over from the OGPU, but with wider powers, including responsibility for labor camps and frontier guards. Stalin soon became dissatisfied with Yagoda, and after a short time he was tried and shot. Nikolai Yezhov, one of Stalin's most trusted lieutenants, then became head of the NKVD, directing it during the worst of the Stalinist terror.

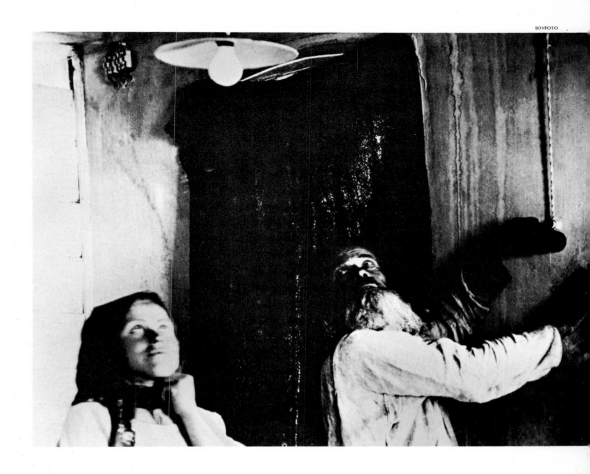

The peasants at right can hardly believe their eyes as they experiment with the first electric light in their village. Light bulbs were often called "Ilyich's lamps" in honor of Lenin, who coined the watchword "Electrification plus Soviet power equals Communism." The harnessing of the Soviet Union's mighty rivers to furnish hydroelectric power was a prime concern of the First Five-Year Plan. One of its major achievements was the completion in 1932 of the Dneprostroi Dam opposite on the Dnieper River in the Ukraine. Over half a mile long and two hundred feet high, it is Europe's largest dam and power station, supplying energy to run the Dnieper and Donets industrial centers.

The assassination of Sergei Kirov, a Central Committee member, on December 1, 1934, marked the beginning of the Great Purge that lasted until 1939, the darkest period of Stalin's reign. In three public trials sixteen of the most prominent members of the Party, in particular Zinoviev and Kamenev, Bukharin, and Alexei Rykov, were charged with sabotage and treason. All of them confessed to the charges, and all except four were condemned to death and executed. Under the direction of Yezhov, the NKVD arrested, interrogated, arbitrarily imprisoned, banished to labor camps, and shot an estimated ten million citizens.

Early in 1937 attentions of Stalin and of Yezhov turned to the Red Army. There was no evidence that the army had ever wavered in its loyalty, but in June, 1937, the newspaper *Pravda* disclosed that eight prominent Red Army generals had been secretly tried and shot for "espionage and treason to the fatherland." A widespread purge followed; according to reliable estimates, 35,000 officers, approximately half of all officers in the Red Army, were relieved of their rank.

The purge threatened to get out of hand. Stalin, with his instinct for halting short of disaster, directed the Central Committee plenum in January, 1938, to pass a resolution ending mass expulsions from the Party and even promoting a campaign to rehabilitate victimized Party leaders. With the appointment of Lavrenty Beria, like Stalin a Georgian, as

deputy to Yezhov the Great Purge closed in July, 1938. Soon afterward Beria became head of the NKVD, and Yezhov disappeared, himself a victim of political extermination.

Meanwhile, in 1936, in the midst of the terror, Stalin had launched his new constitution with great publicity, intended to impress world opinion. The charter legally defined the Soviet Union as a federal state of eleven republics, which were voluntarily united and each of which had the "right freely to secede." The highest authority was thenceforth constituted in the Supreme Soviet, composed of two chambers, the Soviet of the Union and the Soviet of Nationalities, the former directly elected on the basis of one deputy for every 300,000 persons, the latter also directly elected but on the basis of 25 deputies for each union republic, 11 deputies for each autonomous republic, 5 deputies for each autonomous region, and one deputy for each autonomous district. The Supreme Soviet appointed the Presidium, comprising the Chairman, 11 vice-chairmen, a secretary, and 24 members. In turn, the Presidium appointed the Soviet of Peoples' Commissars, which functioned as the executive and administrative authority of the Soviet Union. (Since 1936 the size of each of these bodies has been repeatedly altered.)

In addition to the new electoral system, Stalin's constitution also included a detailed statement of the fundamental rights and duties of citizens. Another innovation was the

reference in the constitution to the Communist Party, stating that "the most active and most politically conscious citizens in the ranks of the working class and other sections of the working people unite in the Communist Party of the Soviet Union (Bolsheviks), which is the vanguard of the working people, both public and state."

At the time of the revolution Lenin had not envisaged the need for an active foreign policy. He was awaiting the outbreak of world revolution that would unite all proletariats and eliminate the state system and its rivalries. But the world revolution had not come, and despite Communist efforts to cut all ties with the tsarist past, Russian interests asserted themselves and a Soviet foreign policy began to evolve. In many aspects it proved to be a nationalist policy concerned with the Soviet Union's security and with its economic and territorial aggrandizement. It was not unaffected, however, by Communist ideology, according to which the world was divided into "the army of capitalism" and "the army of socialism," between which permanent peace was impossible. It was therefore a function of Soviet policy to promote world revolution and to foment the internal contradictions, which Communists believed were destroying capitalist societies, before they could attack the Soviet Union. The Communist International, or Comintern, embracing the Communist parties of other countries, had been set up in 1919 for this purpose.

The immediate objectives of Soviet policy were to secure recognition of the nation's frontiers and to end its isolation from the world community. Their attainment was hindered by the desire to promote subversion and revolution in the very countries with which Russia was seeking understandings. Soviet policy therefore steered an uneasy course between ideological and national interests, with the latter becoming increasingly dominant.

From 1918 until 1930 the commissar for foreign affairs had been Yury Chicherin. He came of the old Russian gentry, had studied at St. Petersburg University, and for a time had served in the tsarist diplomatic service. As a leading Menshevik, he had gone abroad in 1904 and had been active in the labor movements of England, France, and Germany. Shortly after the revolution he was interned in England, but was released in January, 1918, and returned to Russia in exchange for British government officials who had been held as hostages. Chicherin was given responsibility for Soviet foreign policy, but was under the constant supervision of Lenin, Stalin, and the Politburo. His main task was to gain recognition of the Soviet regime.

The first international conference at which the Soviet government was represented was the World Economic Conference in Genoa in 1922. The European powers demanded payment of thirteen million dollars in debts and expropriated

Beneath a sinister glare of bright lights, one of the show trials of the Great Purge period, the Yezhovshchina, is underway in a hall of the Moscow Trade Union House. Under Nikolai Yezhov's direction, the NKVD eliminated over ten million alleged enemies, who were arbitrarily accused of being deviationists, Trotskyites, or foreign spies. The victims came from all ranks of society—the defendants shown are engineers and professors—and the arrest of anyone might mean the arrest of his associates, his family, and friends. However, the axe fell most heavily on Stalin's ideological enemies—those Party members who still supported world revolution.

investments in exchange for recognition, credits, and restoration of trade. The Soviets countered with a bill for sixty million dollars in damages incurred by European intervention in the civil war. Neither side yielded, but the conference provided Chicherin with the opportunity to hold clandestine discussions with the German foreign minister at nearby Rapallo. The resulting Treaty of Rapallo, signed on April 16, 1922, provided for friendly relations between Soviet Russia and Germany. It brought strong criticism, especially from Britain and France; but the treaty, which was to remain in force until Hitler came to power, ensured Russia with economic and technical assistance.

On February 1, 1924, Britain, then under her first Labor government with Ramsay MacDonald as Prime Minister, accorded de jure recognition of the Soviet regime. Italy, Austria, Sweden, Norway, Denmark, France, Mexico, and Japan followed, but the United States continued to refuse. Communism's assaults on capitalist societies were bitterly resented. Furthermore, the generous contributions made by the Hoover mission during the famine of 1922, and the pressure exerted by the United States in forcing the Japanese to withdraw from Siberia, had not been reciprocated. In particular, the United States demanded, unsuccessfully, that the Soviet government make some repayment of the loan of 188 million dollars, granted to Kerensky's Provisional Gov-

ernment, and of other private claims amounting in all to 400 million dollars. Only in 1933, after the American economy had been shaken by the crisis of Wall Street and by Germany's displacement of the United States in Soviet markets, was American recognition reluctantly extended.

In the Far East Chicherin had an even more difficult task in carrying out Stalin's involved policy. At first Stalin had supported the Kuomintang, the Chinese Nationalist movement led by Sun Yat-sen and his successor Chiang Kai-shek. He had sent hundreds of military experts to assist the Nationalists and had instructed the Chinese Communists to support the United Front policy. (This strategy, which was proposed as a means of combatting fascist governments in Europe as well, sought cooperation not only with socialist parties but also with bourgeois parties in the struggle.) In 1927, however, Chiang Kai-shek, having secured his authority throughout China, turned against the Communists— many of whom were killed—and expelled the Soviet advisers. In spite of these reverses, the Soviet government established its rule over Outer Mongolia, and it also retained control over the Chinese Eastern Railway.

In 1930 Maxim Litvinov succeeded Chicherin, who had been suffering from ill health. To Litvinov now fell the task of forging closer alliances with the Western powers in the interests of collective security. In September, 1934, Soviet

Russia joined the League of Nations. The Soviet leaders were disturbed by the policies of Japan and Germany, demonstrated by Japanese aggression in China in 1931 and the rise of Hitler to power in Germany in January, 1933.

A series of attempts to check Germany and Japan marked Soviet policy in the 1930's. In 1929 the Litvinov Protocol, based on the widely accepted Kellogg-Briand Pact of 1927, had sought to produce a regional pact to outlaw war. Latvia, Estonia, Lithuania, Poland, Romania, Turkey, Persia and the Free City of Danzig signed the Litvinov Protocol. In 1932 the Soviet government concluded nonaggression pacts with Poland, Estonia, Latvia, Finland, and France, and in 1934 it also made treaties with Czechoslovakia and Romania.

The Comintern at its Seventh Congress in 1935 strongly endorsed the policy of popular fronts. Communist parties were instructed to support political groups opposing fascism. Soviet activity in seeking to develop a system that would outlaw aggression was not matched, however, by the activity of other great powers or the League of Nations. Japan continued its aggression on the Chinese mainland, and Italy conquered Ethiopia without opposition. In 1936 civil war broke out in Spain, and the Soviet government immediately declared its opposition to Franco's Fascist militants. France and Great Britain, however, hesitated and finally adopted a policy of noninterference. Soviet advisers and military specialists aided the Loyalists, whereas Italian troops and German airmen actively helped Franco.

Russian fears were further aggravated in November, 1936, by the Anti-Comintern Pact, made by Germany and Japan and subsequently joined by Italy and Spain. Soviet-Japanese relations had long been strained, and during 1938 and 1939 fighting took place between Soviet and Japanese troops on the Manchuria and Mongolia borders. Meanwhile, Hitler declared his intention to destroy the Communist system and seize Lebensraum in Russian territory. Further, Nazi rearmament of the Rhineland in 1936 and the annexation of Austria in 1938 had failed to arouse the Western powers to positive action. Indeed, Britain and France, after timorous consultations, even pressured Czechoslovakia to surrender the Sudetenland to Germany in the interests of peace, followed by the British and French capitulation in September, 1938, at Munich.

Stalin and the Politburo were deeply disturbed by the evasive attitude of Britain and France—especially as Soviet Russia had not been invited to take part in the talks. It seemed that Soviet Russia was dangerously isolated, and its suspicion grew stronger that the Western powers were promising Hitler a free hand in the East provided that he left the West in peace.

In March, 1939, Hitler occupied the rest of Czechoslovakia and formed the German protectorates of Bohemia, Moravia, and Slovakia. He next turned to Poland, demanding the surrender of Danzig. By this time, however, Britain and France had recognized that the policy of appeasement had failed. Chamberlain announced the Polish-British Pact, committing Britain to fight if Poland were attacked.

On May 3, Vyacheslav Molotov replaced Litvinov as commissar for foreign affairs. It was a significant appointment, for Molotov was a hard-line member of the Politburo and likely to take a less friendly tack in relations with the West. At a May meeting of the Supreme Soviet, Molotov stated that the Soviet government was still eager to conclude a mutual assistance pact with Britain and France. Finally, after exchanges of notes, talks began. But Chamberlain still showed unwillingness to come to any real understanding. Stalin and Molotov, suspicious of British and French intentions, sought a new policy, and at this time Ribbentrop's secret proposal for a Soviet-German nonaggression pact was received. On August 23 the Molotov-Ribbentrop agreement of strict neutrality was announced. The Russian people were staggered by this sudden change in policy. The Western powers felt justified in their suspicions.

On September 1 Hitler crossed into Poland. The Anglo-French ultimatum, demanding the withdrawal of German troops, was ignored, and both countries were then at war with Germany. The Soviet government decreed partial mobilization, and soon afterward the Red Army began to occupy eastern Poland. As the Polish forces had already been crushed by the German advance, the Red Army met with little opposition. Ribbentrop paid a second visit to Moscow, and agreement was reached on the division of Poland. Lithuania was recognized as part of the Soviet sphere of interest, and the Soviet government imposed treaties of mutual assistance on Estonia, Latvia, and Lithuania.

In October, 1939, the Soviet government urgently requested in a note to the Finnish government the surrender of certain islands in the Gulf of Finland, a thirty-year lease on the Hango Peninsula, and concessions in the Petsamo area and the Karelian Isthmus in exchange for other territories. This request met with stubborn Finnish opposition, and on November 30, 1939 the massive Winter War with Finland was launched. Voroshilov was confident that the campaign would last no more than two weeks, but the Finns fought with outstanding courage and inflicted severe reverses on the Red Army. Only after 1,500,000 Soviet troops had been concentrated against the small Finnish army were the Finns compelled to concede to the Soviet demands in March, 1940.

In the summer of 1940 the Soviet government also exacted from Romania the disputed regions of Bessarabia and northern Bukovina, which were formed into the Moldavian Soviet Socialist Republic. In April, 1941, the Soviet government signed a nonaggression treaty with Japan, which gave some security in the East. The first priority of Stalin's policy now was to continue building up Soviet industrial and military strength, but time was too short.

Germany's massive, lightning-swift attack in June, 1941, caught the Soviets unprepared and carried the country to the brink of defeat. It was months before an effective defense was mounted. Here, enveloped in mist and smoke, a weary Russian crew fires a howitzer.

Nation at War

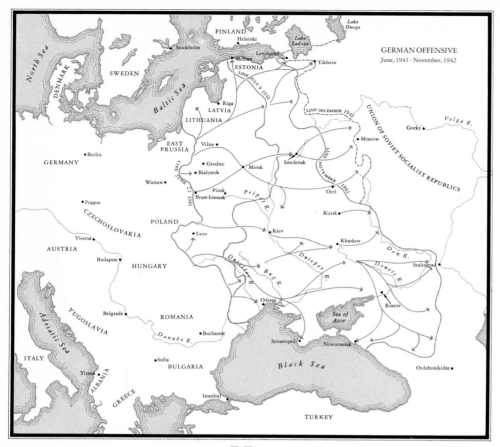

Hitler and his generals took six months to plan their Russian offensive. Code named Operation Barbarossa, its objectives were the rapid annihilation of the Red Army, the capture of Soviet political and industrial centers, and, finally, the occupation of the Ukraine and the Caucasus, major sources of coal, iron, oil, and grain. The three-pronged assault, launched at dawn on June 22, 1941, sent three million men—supported by 32,000 guns, 9,000 tanks, and 5,000 aircraft—across a 2,000-mile front stretching from the Baltic to the Black seas (see map above). Despite Allied warnings of impending attack, Stalin had continued to make declarations of friendship to Germany in an apparent attempt to buy time until Soviet defenses could be strengthened. The Nazi steamroller encountered little resistance from the incompetently led Red Army, killing thousands and taking more than two million prisoners, and within a few weeks enemy divisions had overrun the Ukraine and laid siege to Leningrad. By mid-October they had pushed to within fifty miles of Moscow. Government offices, and armament and other industries, were hastily evacuated to locations beyond the Urals. Thousands of panicked citizens fled with mounting reports of the enemy's invincibility and brutality —the Nazis had declared the Russian people *Untermenschen*, or "subhumans," and dealt with them accordingly. But many Russians responded magnificently in the crisis, forming partisan armies and civil defense units. (Typical are the factory workers, shown opposite, who turned out after grueling work days to dig antitank ditches on the capital's outskirts.) By November Russian resistance, mud, and Hitler's clumsy strategies had brought the German drive to a halt. On December 6 Marshal Georgy Zhukov, with "General Winter" as an ally, began a massive counteroffensive, relieving Moscow and driving the *Wehrmacht* back two hundred miles. Leningrad, too, held out despite starvation and constant bombardment. In the south and east, however, the German assault continued. By mid-1942 the invaders had reached the Caucasus. In early winter they gained the Crimea. Hitler's generals bungled again, failing to support the attack on Stalingrad, a key Volga river port, until it was too late. The battle, which marked the turning point of the war in Russia, left the city almost totally destroyed, but Soviet relief forces succeeded finally in surrounding and capturing most of the German Sixth Army in January, 1943. Rather than risk another encirclement, the Nazis retreated, and though they continued to launch attacks and counterattacks, the invaders were steadily pushed back. By September, 1944, the Red Army had driven the Germans off Russian soil.

Below, citizens of Leningrad, killed by a German shell, lie sprawled on Nevsky Prospekt as another shell explodes nearby. Nearly a third of the city's three million people died in the famine and fighting of the 900-day siege, but the "Hero City" held fast.

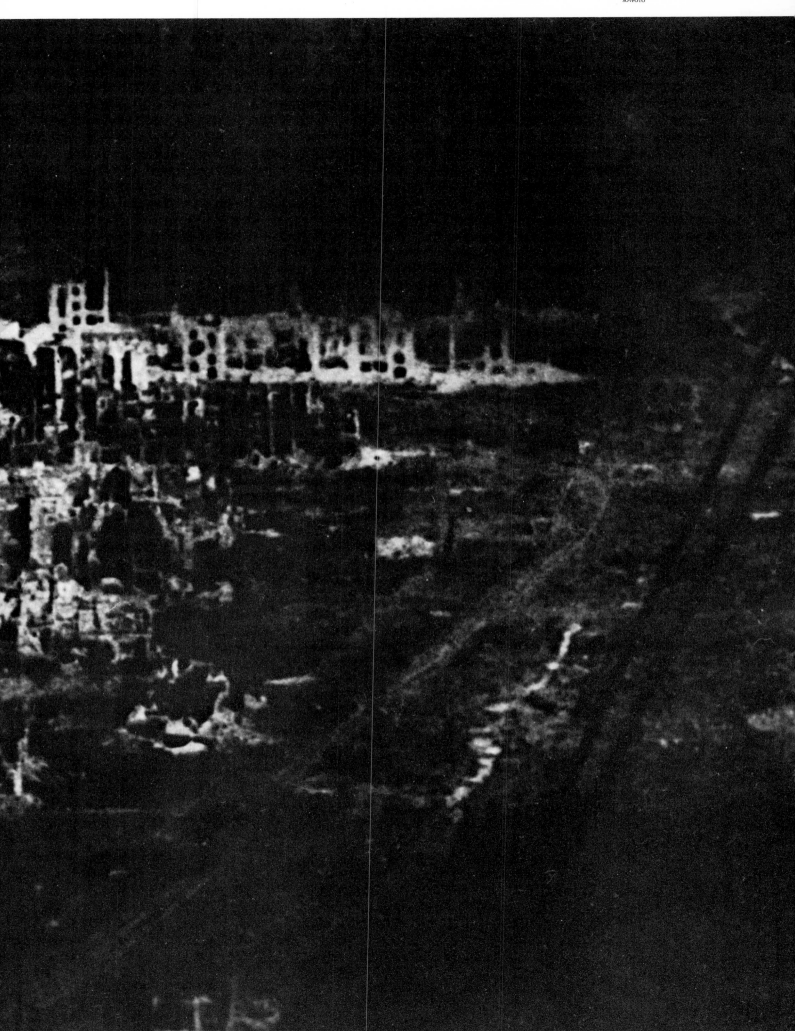

ruin. *"Animals flee this hell,"* wrote one German soldier. *"The hardest stones cannot bear it for long; only men endure."*

THE HOME FRONT

THE SIEGE OF LENINGRAD
by Alexander Werth

During the winter blockade of Leningrad in 1941–42, nearly 4,000 people died of starvation each day. A witness, a Russian-born British journalist, describes the struggle.

Most of the people pulled themselves together when they were given work. It was a great thing. But on the whole men collapsed more easily than women and at first the death-rate was highest among the men. However, those who survived the worst period of the famine finally survived. The women felt the after-effects more seriously than the men. Many died in the spring when the worst was already over. . . . so many people died that we had to bury most of them without coffins. People had their feelings blunted, and never seemed to weep at the burials. It was all done in complete silence without any display of emotion. When things began to improve the first signs were when women began to put rouge and lipstick on their pale skinny faces. Yes, we lived through hell right enough; but you should have been here the day the blockade was broken— people in the streets wept for joy . . .

One of the greatest examples of how Leningrad fought for its life was when in the spring 300,000 to 400,000 people came out into the street with shovels— people who could scarcely stand on their feet, so weak and hungry were they— and proceeded to clean up the town. All winter the drains and sewers had been out of action; there was a great danger of epidemics spreading with the coming of warm weather. And in a few days these 300,000 to 400,000 weak, hungry people —many of them were very old people who had never handled a shovel in their lives—had shovelled away and dumped into the river and the canals all those mountains of snow and filth which, had they remained there, would have poi-

soned Leningrad. And it was a joy to see the city streets a few days later all clean and tidy. It had a great moral effect.

ONE VILLAGE'S REVOLT
by Alexander Fadeyev

In this excerpt from his novel The Young Guards, *Fadeyev tells of the wartime devastation of the Ukrainian countryside and the people's resistance to the Nazi invaders.*

A person unfamiliar with the situation . . . happening upon a farming district in German-occupied territory would have been struck by the unusually dismal and strangely contrasting scenes befor his eyes. He would have seen hundreds of villages reduced to ashes, where in place of former villages and Cossack farmsteads nothing now remained but the frame of a stove here, a charred beam there, perhaps a lone cat sitting in the sun on a blackened doorstep overgrown with weeds. And he would also encounter Cossack farmsteads where no German had set foot, save for occasional, straggling marauding soldiers.

Then there were villages where German rule had been established in the way the Germans considered would be most profitable and convenient for the state, where downright military plunder, that is to say, pillaging by passing army units, and where every form of violence and bestiality was carried on . . .

Ivan Nikanorovich and his family had gone through experiences which were neither greater nor less than history recorded for the ordinary, everyday farming household during German domination. They had been robbed when the advancing German armies had passed through, robbed to the extent that their cattle, fowl and foodstuffs had been clearly evident; in a word they had been very thoroughly robbed, but not quite cleaned out. For nowhere in the world are there peasants so experienced in con-

cealing their possessions in lean times as are Russian peasants. . . .

As the German state was not at present in a position to estimate how much meat, milk and eggs it would need, it imposed on the hamlet of Nizhny Alexandrovsky an initial levy of one cow from every five households, and in addition, one pig, one hundredweight of potatoes, twenty eggs and seventy-five gallons of milk from every household. But! As more might be required—and more was for ever being required—Cossacks and peasants were not allowed to slaughter any cattle or fowl for their own use. . . .

. . . Ivan Nikanorovich and his fellow-villagers who daily felt on their backs the fruits of their activities, realized that German fascist rule was not only brute rule—that had been obvious from the start—but also an unimportant, stupid, robber state.

By that time Ivan Nikanorovich and his fellow-villagers and all the inhabitants of the neighbouring Cossack hamlets—Gundorovskaya, Davidov and Makarov Yar—began to behave towards the German authorities in the only way that self-respecting Cossacks could and should behave towards stupid authorities: they began to hoodwink them.

The chief way they deceived them was to make a show of working in the fields rather than actually doing so; to scatter to the four winds whatever they did grow, or if the opportunity presented itself, to pilfer it for their own use, and to conceal livestock, fowl and foodstuffs. To facilitate this process of deception, the Cossacks and peasants did their best to get the right people appointed as the Elders over ten households and the village and hamlet Elders. Like all brute forms of government the German authorities found sufficient brutes to appoint as Elders but, as the saying goes, man's life is not eternal. The Elders were here today and gone tomorrow. They just vanished into thin air.

In a muddy field grief-stricken villagers search for their dead among the bodies of civilians slain by the Germans.

Coexistence and Beyond

11

The official Soviet history of World War II, published in 1960, concluded that preparations for the nation's defense had been carried out "too slowly and too late," and that those efforts were jeopardized by the "unjustified repressions against the leading officers and political cadres of the army in the 1937–38 purge."

In the "Great Patriotic War," as the Soviets have called the defense of their homeland, the Red Army suffered seemingly irreversible defeats. During the first months it was poorly led and ill-equipped. There was a high incidence of surrender to the Nazis, especially in areas where the Communist regime was unpopular. Further, the government had been forced to evacuate to Kuibyshev (formerly Samara), a provincial town some 550 miles to the southeast of Moscow; over 1,500 industries, including 1,360 major armaments works, had been removed from the war zone, taxing the nation's defense capabilities to the breaking point.

Nevertheless, by January, 1943, the Soviet Union was fully mobilized, and the Red Army—with the help of a heroic partisan rear guard and of Allied war materiel—had

The spectacular Soviet offensive in the West, begun in January, 1945, culminated with the surrender of Berlin on May 2. In this photograph, taken on the eve of the city's capitulation, a Red Army soldier is seen atop the Reichstag waving the hammer and sickle.

gained the offensive. With the Nazi defeat at Stalingrad, Hitler's grandiose plans for the conquest of Russia, the Caucasus, and, ultimately, the whole of Middle East, were thwarted.

The Soviet war machine began to move steadily westward. Beginning in January, 1944, the Red Army launched ten separate counterattacks. Konstantin Rokossovsky's army, which succeeded in routing the Germans along the Belorussian front, continued to advance into Poland, capturing Lublin and Brest-Litovsk, and on July 31 it reached the suburb of Praga across the Vistula from Warsaw. Fearing that the Soviets would use liberation of the capital as a pretext for taking it over themselves, anti-Communist Poles began an uprising to free the city before the Red Army could reach it. When the German occupation forces showed that they were still capable of crushing the insurgents, Stalin did nothing to help the nationals, dismissing the Polish effort as an "adventuristic affair." Two hundred thousand Varsovians were killed. Washington and London interpreted the Soviet delay as part of a strategy to bring Poland under its rule.

In January, 1945, the Red Army opened its final drive on Germany, advancing across eastern Europe from the Baltic to the Danube. With Poland, Bulgaria, Romania, Hungary, and Czechoslovakia under Stalin's domination, the Red forces and the Yugoslav irregulars of Marshal Tito's Committee of

At left, two of Russia's wartime heroes, Marshals Semyon Timoshenko (with binoculars) and Georgy Zhukov, are seen on an inspection tour of Red Army exercises. Timoshenko, who commanded on several Soviet fronts, recaptured Rostov in November, 1941. Zhukov led the assault on Germany and accepted the surrender of its high command on May 8, 1945, in Berlin.

Opposite, the Big Three—Churchill, Roosevelt, and Stalin—pose for a photograph during the Yalta Conference held in February, 1945, at the Livadia Palace, a former tsarist winter retreat in the Crimea. Behind them, from left to right: British Foreign Minister Anthony Eden, Secretary of State Edward Stettinius, British Undersecretary Alexander Cadogan, Foreign Commissar Vyacheslav Molotov, and United States Ambassador W. Averell Harriman.

Liberation joined to smash Austria in early April. Racing toward Berlin, Marshal Zhukov reached the outskirts of the city on April 21. The battle for Berlin ended on May 2. Germany's formal surrender was submitted five days later.

The Soviet Union emerged from the second World War as one of the two most powerful countries on earth. Expectations that the nation would be able to enjoy the fruits of victory proved premature. The war had inflicted unparalleled casualties and devastation. It has been estimated that out of a population of 200 million, more than 25 million people perished. According to official Soviet calculations, approximately one quarter of all property was destroyed, including nearly 2,000 towns, 70,000 villages, 32,000 factories, and 84,000 schools; the damage to agriculture was equally severe, involving the loss of 137,000 tractors, 49,000 combine harvesters, as well as 17 million head of cattle, 7 million horses, and 27 million sheep and goats. Stalin was determined that no time should be lost in rebuilding the economy. The people, exhausted from years of overwork and privation, were now confronted with a massive job of reconstruction.

During the war the Allies had maintained close lines of communication, regarding themselves as partners in a joint effort against Nazi Germany. Stalin, Roosevelt, and Churchill met in Teheran in December, 1943, and again in Yalta in February, 1945. Stalin appeared anxious to strengthen the

alliance, and he valued the direct contacts with the two other Allied leaders. They reached agreement on a wide range of topics, including the dismemberment of Germany and the establishment of a United Nations organization.

Nevertheless, two problems had clouded the relations among the Big Three. The first involved the opening of a second front, which Soviet leaders believed was necessary to relieve the pressure of the Nazi attack on the Soviet Union. When the Allied invasion of western Europe did not take place in 1942 or 1943, Russians were convinced that the Allies were willing to let the U.S.S.R. bear the brunt of the war. (The evidence is inconclusive, but Western reluctance seems to have been based on Britain's continuing unpreparedness to enlarge the offensive while its own people were under siege.) The Soviets welcomed the Allied landing at Normandy in June, 1944, but they remained suspicious.

The second problem was the future of Poland. Stalin was determined to set up and maintain Communist regimes in the countries of eastern Europe. They would form a Communist bloc that would serve as a defense barrier. In particular, he was not prepared to tolerate an anti-Soviet regime in Poland. For this reason he broke off relations with the Polish government-in-exile in London. He also transferred to the British command in Iran the Polish army—it had been formed to fight alongside the Soviet army, but had shown it-

The Cold War reached a crisis point in June, 1948, when Soviet authorities halted all ground traffic between the western sectors of Berlin and the western occupation zones of Germany. Britain, France, and especially the United States countered by airlifting food and fuel to the stranded city through three narrow air corridors. In this photograph, the West Berliners watch C47 planes arriving at Tempelhof Airport; cargoes of flour, coal, dehydrated potatoes, and canned meat kept the people alive. Before the Red blockade was lifted in May, 1949, Allied aircraft had made 196,000 flights and delivered over a million and a half tons of vital supplies.

self to be of doubtful loyalty. (Eventually, upon Poland's liberation, a number of pro-Soviet Poles would serve as the nucleus of the Lublin government, which was to develop into the Polish Communist regime.) However, the Allies opposed the expansion of Soviet power in eastern Europe. Churchill and the British were especially anxious to ensure the freedom of the Poles, in defense of whom they had originally declared war on Germany.

The "Grand Alliance," as Churchill called the British, American, and Soviet cooperation, could not survive the Potsdam Conference, which took place in the summer of 1945, following the European armistice. Its purpose was to discuss the postwar settlement of Europe's disputed lands. Roosevelt was dead; Churchill had been defeated in a general election; and a new style of diplomacy was in evidence. President Harry S. Truman and Prime Minister Clement Attlee of Britain went to Potsdam prepared, in the words of one American general, "to be tough and indifferent."

An important reason for the change in attitude was the successful explosion of an American atom bomb in the New Mexican desert on July 16 of that year. The Allied leaders were quick to recognize that this new and terrible weapon greatly increased the strength of the Western powers in relation to that of Soviet Russia. The American success in the war against Japan had also eliminated the need for Soviet

action in the Far Eastern theater. Five months earlier, at Yalta, Roosevelt had been gratified when Stalin committed Russia to entering the war against Japan within three months of the defeat of Germany; and Truman had been eager after his assumption of the presidency, in April, to obtain confirmation of Russia's intention to participate. But by July Japan was on the point of surrender, and Great Britain and the United States were impatient to conclude the war and to cancel Allied concessions that had been exacted by Stalin in exchange for Soviet military support.

Acrimonious discussions on reparations and other matters marred the meetings at Potsdam. Stalin and Foreign Minister Vyacheslav Molotov were quick to notice the change. The Soviet leaders charged their allies with bad faith, especially in the efforts to deprive the U.S.S.R. of what it considered fair compensation for the sufferings the country had borne; the chief issue was ten billion dollars in German reparations. Also, Stalin would not be thwarted in obtaining from Japan the gains that had been agreed upon at Yalta.

On July 26 Japan was presented with an American ultimatum demanding immediate, unconditional surrender. Clearly, the purpose was to bring the war in the Far East to an end before Soviet forces could advance. The Russians complained that they had not been consulted, and when they asked that publication be delayed for two days, they

were told that the text had already been released. The Japanese reply was interpreted as rejecting the ultimatum, and on August 6 an atomic bomb was dropped on Hiroshima. Two days later Soviet Russia declared war on Japan, seeking to secure de facto title to everything that had been agreed to at the Yalta Conference.

The Soviet press briefly reported the devastation of Hiroshima. It was an event that disturbed many Russians, for it suggested that, although they had defeated Germany, they might now be confronted with a new and even more awesome threat. At the same time the declaration of war on Japan aroused no national enthusiasm. The people were weary, and their patriotic feelings were mixed with sympathy for the Japanese. Soviet troops, however, were massed in the Far East for this attack, and they now moved swiftly, occupying southern Sakhalin, the Kurile Islands, and Port Arthur before the Americans could reach the area. The Japanese declaration of surrender on August 14 was ignored, and the Russians continued to advance.

Relations between Soviet Russia and the Western powers deteriorated rapidly. The foreign ministers met successively in Paris, New York, Moscow, and London to draft peace treaties and to work out detailed solutions to a host of postwar problems. A conflict developed over Iran. British and Soviet forces had jointly occupied Iran early in the war to avert the danger of that country serving as a base for a German invasion of the U.S.S.R. The occupation forces were to withdraw within six months of the end of the war, but the Soviet units had remained. The United States, Great Britain, and the United Nations put increasing pressure on the Soviet Union to honor its agreement. Finally, Stalin yielded, pulling back his troops. At once the United States stepped in with an extensive economic and military aid program that brought Iran under American domination. The Western powers also rejected Soviet demands for access to the Black Sea and a share in the control of the Dardanelles.

On March 5, 1946, at Westminster College in Fulton, Missouri, Churchill delivered his militant "Iron Curtain" speech, in which he acknowledged openly: "A shadow has fallen upon the scenes so lately lighted by the Allied victory. . . . From Stettin in the Baltic to Trieste in the Adriatic, an 'iron curtain' has descended across the continent." Stalin was prompt to condemn the statement as "a dangerous act, calculated to sow seeds of dissent and hinder collaboration among the Allied nations. It has harmed the cause of peace and security. Mr. Churchill has now adopted the position of a warmonger." But the speech was no more than a recognition of the great gulf that had opened. Cooperation nevertheless continued long enough to bring about agreement on the division and control of Germany and Austria, and to try

the Nazi leaders at Nuremberg in 1946. Then, in 1947, peace treaties were signed by the victorious nations with Romania, Bulgaria, Hungary, Italy, and Finland.

Alarmed by the expansion of Soviet power in eastern Europe and by the establishment of a Communist regime in Greece, President Truman obtained funds from Congress to provide military and economic aid to countries threatened by Communist domination, thus enunciating the Truman Doctrine. In June, 1947, the Marshall Plan was announced as a vast program designed to revive the economies of Europe, but its political implications were clear. Stalin and Molotov viewed the capitalist aid program as deeply suspect, and they resolved that the U.S.S.R. and its satellites (Communist nations under Soviet influence) must restore their economies unaided. With Soviet pressure Poland and Czechoslovakia declined to participate. It also rankled Stalin that the United States had left unanswered tentative approaches for long-term credits made before the end of the war and that lend-lease supplies had abruptly stopped after the surrender of Germany. The North Atlantic Treaty Organization (NATO), guaranteeing mutual aid against aggression and signed in 1949 by twelve Western nations, was yet another instrument in further separating the Western and Communist blocs.

Offsetting these preparations in the West, the Cominform (Communist Information Bureau) had been established in 1947, reviving the Comintern (Communist International), which had been abolished in 1943. The Comintern had as its stated purpose the coordination of Communist parties throughout the world. It had always been dominated by Russian leaders, but now the Cominform openly championed central Kremlin control. The defection of Marshal Tito's Yugoslavia in 1948, primarily over this issue of centralization, was a setback Stalin was never to forgive; it was to serve as a precedent to other Communist countries eager to pursue their own national policies without Soviet supervision.

Meanwhile, the worsening in the relations of the wartime Allies was evident in Germany, where in March, 1948, the Allied Control Council broke up in dispute, and talks on the unification of Germany and on a peace treaty deadlocked. The Cold War reached a crisis in that summer when Soviet officials halted the overland transportation of supplies to the American, British, and French sectors of Berlin, which lay one hundred miles within the Soviet zone. The Soviet plan to force the Western powers to relinquish their hold on Berlin was, however, frustrated. A massive 324-day airlift by American and British planes carried supplies to West Berlin, and the Soviet government finally ended its blockade.

The Western powers, convinced that further four-power control of Germany was impossible, merged their three zones into the West German Federal Republic in May, 1949, with

On March 9, 1953, *amid typical bureaucratic pomp (as shown opposite) Stalin was buried alongside the mummified corpse of Lenin in the mausoleum outside the Kremlin walls. The pallbearers, from left to right: Bulganin (with white goatee), Molotov, Stalin's son Vasily, the new Chairman Malenkov, and chief of secret police Beria. Khrushchev spearheaded the "de-Stalinization" program in 1956; he is seen at right addressing a session of the United Nations General Assembly in New York City in October, 1960.*

its capital in Bonn. Five months later the East German Democratic Republic was established in the Soviet zone, with its capital in East Berlin.

Meanwhile, within the Asian sphere, attempts to seize power by native Communist parties in Indonesia, Burma, and Malaya were thwarted, but in China they were successful. Chiang Kai-shek withdrew the Nationalist government to Formosa (Taiwan), and the Communist Chinese People's Republic, led by Mao Tse-tung and occupying the whole of the Chinese mainland, was proclaimed in 1949. Russia had aided the Chinese Communists with supplies, and now it gave its full support to the People's Republic. Moscow was soon to find its authority challenged by the new partner.

The victory of the Chinese Communists encouraged the North Korean People's Republic to invade the South Korean Republic on June 25, 1950. Soon after, the Security Council of the United Nations met and agreed to extend military and other assistance, under American command, to the South Korean Republic. After nearly three years of fighting, an armistice was concluded in the summer of 1953, confirming the 38th parallel as the border between the two regimes.

Against the background of intransigence and hostility between the Soviet Union and the West, Stalin was giving priority to the great reconstruction of Soviet industry and the revival of the economy. The Fourth Five-Year Plan, approved by the Supreme Soviet in March, 1946, required that by 1950 industrial production be forty-eight per cent above the prewar level. This target appeared to be impossibly ambitious, especially after the exhaustion caused by the war years; but Stalin was driven by the vision of Soviet output exceeding that of western Europe—and ultimately of the United States.

The new five-year plan emphasized the development of heavy industry, to which almost eighty-five per cent of the total investment was allocated. The civilian working force was greatly strengthened by the more than twelve million men demobilized from the Red Army and repatriated from German labor camps. The plan went beyond restoring and increasing the output of existing industries; it gave special attention to creating and populating new industrial centers farther to the east—in the Urals and Siberia. According to Soviet authorities, the Fourth Five-Year Plan was overfulfilled in four years and three months. In many respects its achievements were outstanding. By 1948, two years after the plan's inauguration, industry had recouped the losses of wartime devastation, and overall productivity exceeded the 1940 level. In 1951, only a year after the Fifth Five-Year Plan had been launched, productivity was two and a half times greater than the prewar level.

In agriculture, however, the recovery was disastrously slow. In particular, the loss of livestock could not be made

The Hungarian revolution triumphed for one euphoric week beginning on October 23, 1956, when freedom fighters tore down Budapest's gigantic statue of Stalin and dragged it to the city's center. At left, crowds are seen inspecting the toppled colossus. On November 1, just as a newly formed government was proclaiming a "deSovietized," neutral Hungary, fifteen Red Army divisions, supported by 5,000 tanks, began penetrating the cities. Within days massive Soviet tanks, like those pictured opposite guarding a Budapest street intersection, had quashed the revolt, at the cost of some 25,000 Hungarian lives.

good so quickly. Moreover, efficiency and Party discipline on collective farms had declined sharply. On local initiative many farms had been divided up, and the land was being cultivated by individual peasants. In a drive to restore the collectives, some fourteen million acres of land were reportedly taken from the peasants and returned to the kolkhozes. In some cases two or more collectives were merged; in others they were converted into still larger state-owned farms (the sovkhoz, as this type of enterprise is known, generally specializes in a single crop and is run, like a factory, with a higher degree of mechanization than is practicable on a kolkhoz.)

Whatever shortcomings there were to be found in Stalin's postwar policies, they did not diminish the public stature of the man himself. At the Nineteenth Party Congress, held in Moscow in October, 1952, Stalin took no active part in the proceedings and merely delivered a short speech at the closing session, but he was still the supreme authority to whom every speaker paid fulsome tribute. For over thirty years he had borne up well under the strain of responsibility and of the long working hours, but now he was beginning to show the effects.

Stalin was increasingly convinced of internal subversion. He ordered high-level purges in Leningrad and then opened his campaign against Western influences, subjecting artists, writers, musicians, and scientists to harassment and persecution in a drive to repress all thought that might threaten the Communist Party. The anti-Semitic bias, evident in many of the attacks, appeared again in the "doctors' plot" in 1952, in which nine leading physicians, seven of them Jews, were charged with murder and conspiracy against the state. It was an attempt to explain away the mysterious death of Andrei Zhdanov, Stalin's former commissar in charge of ideological controls.

The Soviet people were stunned at the news of Stalin's death on March 5, 1953. The man whom Trotsky had dismissed as a mediocrity had dictated the fortunes of the whole nation of two hundred million people, often with extreme cruelty and ruthlessness. He had developed an extraordinary mastery of politics and economics, and even of industrial and military affairs. He had shown in his meetings with the Western leaders a shrewd, tough mind that pierced swiftly to the heart of the subject under discussion. The problem of assessing Joseph Stalin's greatness is like that which nineteenth-century Russians confronted in assessing Peter the Great's rule: though he achieved ends that few opposed, he did so by sinister means, putting the whole nation into a harness that left no room for personal freedom.

Stalin had observed, and even fostered, the rivalries among the men in authority below him, but he had not definitively

named a successor. Georgy Malenkov was prominent in the Communist hierarchy and had been close to Stalin since the time of the great purges of the 1930's. With Stalin's death, he at once became Chairman of the Council of Ministers and the First Secretary of the Central Committee. But Lavrenty Beria was strongly placed to seize power. As head of the police and security forces, he commanded a small army outside Party and government control. Nikita Khrushchev, who had served since 1949 in the Central Committee Secretariat, was also a contender, but at this stage he seemed satisfied to remain in the background. Nikolai Bulganin, although he held the position of minister of defense, apparently lacked the necessary support within the armed forces to enable him to bid for the leadership. Molotov, Lazar Kaganovich, and Kliment Voroshilov were highly regarded. Molotov in particular commanded respect for his sturdy dignity and his devotion to Party and Russian interests, but neither he nor Kaganovich nor Voroshilov had the broad support necessary to claim supreme power. For a time collective leadership ran the political life of the nation.

However, the first overt move toward a new takeover came only nine days after Malenkov assumed office. The Party Presidium (alternatively known as the Politburo) brought pressure to bear on Malenkov to relinquish the post of First Party Secretary while remaining Chairman of the Council of Ministers. Khrushchev became First Party Secretary in his place. He was to demonstrate, as Stalin had soon after the revolution, that this was the most influential political post in the U.S.S.R.

The new Presidium took prompt action, being clearly aware of the longing among the people for some respite from the pressures of five-year plans, for improvement in living conditions, and above all else for relief from terror and ceaseless persecution. A decree of March 27 released from forced labor camps thousands of prisoners, many of whom had been guilty only of surviving the war in enemy-occupied territory and many more who were the victims of Stalin's postwar purges. In addition, a review of conditions in all camps was started. In April the "doctors' plot" was declared to have been fraudulently created, and several of Beria's underlings were arrested. Two months later *Pravda* announced that Beria had been dismissed from all offices in the government and expelled from the Party as an "enemy of the people." In December a brief notice appeared in the Soviet press that Beria and six of his associates had been "tried" and summarily shot to death. A purge of the security police followed, and measures were introduced to ensure that the Party exercised control at every level. The Presidium was evidently unanimous in demanding that the security organs never again be in a position to challenge the Party and the state.

Soon the nationwide adulation of Stalin was stopped. The ubiquitous portraits began to disappear, and the grandiloquent tributes to his works of genius ceased. Indeed, *Pravda* even failed to mention his birthday on December 21, 1953, a day that had been marked by celebrations for two and a half decades. The emphasis on collective leadership had been proclaimed, and by implication the "cult of personality" and the dictatorship of one man condemned.

After Beria's removal Malenkov appeared to re-establish his title to power. He reported to the Central Committee on the crimes of Beria and made the main speech to the Supreme Soviet in August, 1953. In fact, however, he and his policies were increasingly under fire. He called for lessening the concentration on heavy industry and expanding the production of consumer goods. In foreign affairs he favored a reduction of Cold War tensions and the cultivation of more friendly relations with the West.

Khrushchev, in his struggle for leadership, repeatedly raised opposition to Malenkov's policies. As First Secretary he took advantage of his control over the Party apparatus to appoint his own supporters to influential posts in Moscow, Leningrad, and regional centers.

A peasant's cunning, combined with an ability to lead, were operative in this experienced Party functionary. He had become First Secretary of the Ukrainian Central Committee in 1938, and during the war he had served as a senior military commissar. He had retreated with the Red Army to Stalingrad, and then in the westward advance had taken part in the liberation of his native Ukraine. But during the years from 1944 until 1947, when drought and failure of the harvest plagued the Ukraine, Khrushchev had drawn criticism from Moscow. Kaganovich had been sent to the Ukraine to take over as First Party Secretary, leaving Khrushchev as Chairman of the Council of Ministers. Having survived this crisis, Khrushchev was summoned to Moscow late in 1949 to serve in the Central Committee Secretariat. (Stalin's purpose in engaging this ebullient Ukrainian in a key position may well have been to offset the growing influence of Malenkov.)

Khrushchev's reputation as an expert on agriculture had made him the leading spokesman on reform during the late Stalin years—a position that exposed him to attack from Malenkov and Beria. Under Stalin he had directed the policy of amalgamating collective farms and was responsible for reducing the number of kolkhozes from 252,000 to 95,000 by the end of 1952.

The harvest in 1953 had been very poor and the grain shortage was acute. Now Khrushchev was in a strong position to promote his radical ideas, and agriculture came under urgent review. In February, 1954, Khrushchev presented further reforms to the Central Committee. The chief proposal

Since the war, vast segments of the Soviet society have been mobilized in construction projects all over the Soviet Union, especially in formerly uninhabited regions. The workers opposite belong to the Young Communist League (Komsomol). Neftyanie Kamni (right) is a new oil town built on piles in the Caspian Sea, not far from Baku; it has over 1,000 oil wells, plus all the attributes of a settlement on land—schools, shops, a newspaper, and a military post. Its labor force of 5,000 young men and women alternates fifteen work days with fifteen days shore leave.

OVERLEAF: *The men and women in this 1957 photograph are construction workers (in Russia it is common for women to do heavy labor) taking a break at a club they have set up in the apartment house they are building. Union bulletins, honor lists of the best workers, and posters urging increased productivity decorate the club's walls.*

HENRI CARTIER-BRESSON-MAGNUM

was nothing less than to plow and sow in 1954–55 some 32 million acres of virgin land in Siberia, Kazakh, the Volga region, northern Caucasia, and beyond. This mammoth undertaking, which involved resettlement of more than one hundred thousand laborers, was to be continued until 1960, by which time some 101 million acres would be under cultivation. The vast project depended, however, on climatic conditions and, in particular, on adequate rainfall. Much of the land lay in regions of long and harsh winters. In 1954 the rainfall was good and the harvest excellent, but in the following years droughts led to poor results. In 1956, however, a record harvest was brought in, and gradually the grain yield from these virgin lands improved, except in Kazakh, where dust storms were a severe setback.

Khrushchev's other proposal was to sow more productive crops. The acreage of corn was greatly expanded, since the cereal was an excellent feed for livestock. His plan was that the output of meat, milk, and butter would improve considerably with better-fed livestock. Despite a disappointing corn harvest, the number of pigs increased from 31 million in 1955 to 59 million six years later. He also ordered that the Machine and Tractor Stations (MTS), which had formerly played a major part in transmitting Party policies at the kolkhoz level, sell their equipment to the collectives. As a result, the once powerful MTS agents were reduced to little

more than repairmen of their district's many farm implements.

Khrushchev exhibited the same bold approach in developing industry, and in this he came more directly into conflict with Malenkov and what was left of the collective leadership. Malenkov's de-emphasis of heavy industry had resulted in allocations for defense being cut from 110 billion rubles in 1953 to 100.3 billion in 1954. *Pravda*, speaking for Khrushchev, denounced Malenkov's consumer-oriented policies as "utterly alien to Marxist-Leninist political economy" and proclaimed that "heavy industry was, is, and will be the granite foundation . . . of the might of the Soviet country and of its people's well-being." Khrushchev attacked his opponent's policy in more threatening terms in a speech to the Central Committee in January, 1955. A few days later Malenkov "resigned" as Chairman of the Council of Ministers. Bulganin was elected Chairman in his place, and Georgy Zhukov, who had replaced Beria on the Central Committee, now succeeded Bulganin as minister of defense. In undertaking to restore the priority of heavy industry and armaments, and also to bring the popular Zhukov into the Presidium, Khrushchev obtained the support of the majority of Party leaders. He also demoted Molotov and Kaganovich. The era of collective leadership was closed.

In February, 1956, the Twentieth Party Congress took place, and its proceedings were to stagger the Russian people

387

The vast majority of Soviet farmers are either hired wage earners on a state-owned sovkhoz—operated like a "factory in the field"—or members of a kolkhoz, such as the Irkutsk dairy collective pictured here. Movement to cities or from one farm to another is permitted, but is confined principally to the young. In theory, peasants voluntarily pool their resources and are paid from the collective profit—in kind or money—according to the quantity and quality of the work they do. In practice, kolkhozes are subject to intensive government control, and the only free enterprise permitted the farmers is the cultivation of diminutive household plots, a very controversial prerogative.

ARNOLD MICHAELIS

and to shock the Communist parties of the world. Anastas Mikoyan, Khrushchev's chief trouble-shooter, launched the attack on Stalin and the cult of personality. Khrushchev followed with a detailed and sensational denunciation. He reminded the congress of Lenin's fears about Stalin, and while paying brief formal tribute to his leadership against Trotskyites, bourgeois nationalists, and others, he indicted him for "glaring violations of revolutionary legality" and for causing the deaths of thousands of devoted Communists. In particular Khrushchev condemned Stalin's purge of the army —including several outstanding officers. He also charged Stalin with failing to make the necessary preparations against the German invasion, of which he had had early warning, and criticized his military leadership during the war. He then described Stalin's persecution mania and referred to the unfounded accusations in the "doctors' plot."

Khrushchev's attack was a strong bid for supreme power. The text of the speech was not published in the Soviet Union —it was not intended for public consumption—but its essence was disseminated discreetly within the Party. Abroad the full text became available through the United States Department of State, which had obtained a copy bearing every mark of authenticity; the "secret speech" was released to the world in June, 1956.

The speech was anxiously debated by Communist parties everywhere, and the overall result was a marked diminution in the prestige and authority of the Soviet Communist Party. It was to prove an important step in the disintegration of international Communist solidarity, which Stalin had created and which, with the exception of Yugoslavia's independent stance, had prevailed. Palmiero Togliatti, the leader of the Italian Communist Party, was later to express the new questioning attitude of European Communists: "Formerly, all that was good was attributed to the superhuman, positive qualities of one man; now all that is evil is attributed to his equally exceptional and astonishing faults. In the one case as well as in the other we are outside the criterion of judgment intrinsic in Marxism. The true problems are . . . how and why Soviet society could reach and did reach certain forms alien to the democratic way and to the legality that it set for itself, even to the point of degeneration. . . ."

Khrushchev's bold gamble was successful within the Soviet party structure. Five of his special protégés—Georgy Zhukov, Leonid Brezhnev, First Secretary of the Kazakh Party, Yekaterina Furtseva, First Secretary of the Moscow City Organization, Dmitry Shepilov, editor of *Pravda*, and Nuritdin Mukhitdinov, First Secretary of the Uzbek Party— were appointed to the Presidium. Also, the congress elected to the Central Committee fifty-three new members and seventy-six new candidate members, nearly all of whom were

known to be strong supporters of Khrushchev.

A few months later, however, unrest erupted in Poland and then, more seriously, in Hungary. Both rebellions were inspired by bitter antagonism toward the Soviet Union and by demands for independence. On October 9, 1956, Wladislaw Gomulka replaced the Stalinist puppet as Polish leader, but only with the express understanding that Poland would remain within the Soviet bloc. The partial success of the Polish revolt gave rise to intensified hopes for Hungarian independence. In late October Prime Minister Imre Nagy of Hungary demanded that his nation be allowed its freedom within the Communist bloc; and the Red Army was brought into action to crush the insurgents. The violent intervention, lasting several weeks, left thousands of Hungarians dead or wounded and Soviet Russia's reputation severely damaged.

Khrushchev suffered further setbacks that December in the Central Committee, which adopted policies modifying many of his proposals. At the session of the Supreme Soviet in February, 1957, he fought back. Since inefficiency and duplication of effort were seen as major factors in industry's failure to meet its production targets, a sweeping reorganization was undertaken. The nation's priorities were no longer as clearly discernible as they had been in the twenties and thirties, when the task of Soviet planners had been to effect fundamental changes and to create a socialist state where

none had existed before; it was now becoming evident that more sophisticated direction and greater flexibility were needed to continue the growth process.

Khrushchev proposed a massive decentralization of industry in which the 140 all-union ministries (each of which was responsible for a branch of industrial management, such as textiles, coal, and motor vehicles) would be replaced by 105 regional economic councils (each of which was to oversee and coordinate the specific implementation and management of all industries in a region). Broad national guidelines were to be set by the U.S.S.R. State Planning Commission, or Gosplan. Khrushchev argued that a policy of decentralization would enable more direct and effective control of industrial development. The Supreme Soviet approved his new plan in May, 1957.

Despite the rapid growth in industry and a record harvest in 1958, the leadership's optimism was ill-founded. The Twenty-first Party Congress, convened in Moscow in January, 1959, approved a seven-year plan, which was to supersede the five-year plan slated to end in 1960. The new plan for 1959–65, ostensibly introduced to take into account late discoveries in natural resources, was in reality an attempt to disguise the miscalculations of the earlier plan and the nation's continuing failure to meet its objectives.

The Twenty-second Party Congress, held in October,

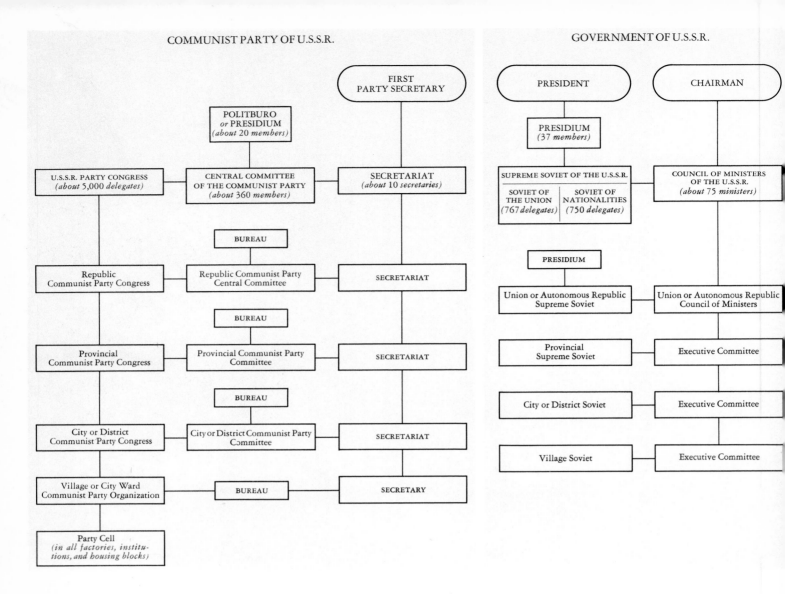

COMMUNIST PARTY OF U.S.S.R.

GOVERNMENT OF U.S.S.R.

1961, approved a twenty-year forecast, which anticipated that by 1970 per capita production in the Soviet Union would exceed that of the United States. At the same time it was asserted that the stepped-up provision of housing units and consumer goods, the expansion of welfare services, and the reduction in the working week would move Russia yet further along the socialist road to the Communist millennium. The published program then declared, "under the tried and tested leadership of the Communist Party, under the banner of Marxism-Leninism, the Soviet people have built Socialism. . . . The Party solemnly proclaims: the present generation of Soviet people shall live in Communism."

Despite these brave promises, Khrushchev's ambitious schemes continued to have difficulties in the sixties. Reorganization and kindred changes failed to solve the central problems of incentives and productivity. Household plots, ranging in size from six tenths of an acre up to one and a quarter acres (variations provided by law and predicated on the nature of the local economy), continued to be a major source of food for the nation. In 1959 this private sector produced over 80 per cent of the eggs, 46 per cent of the vegetables, and 60 per cent of the potatoes consumed in the Soviet Union. In 1963 45.6 per cent of meat and milk products came from private husbandry, which occupied a scant 3.1 per cent of the total land under cultivation. Khrushchev

and others in the Soviet hierarchy disapproved strongly of these holdings, charging that they encouraged bourgeois tendencies among the farm workers, who clearly gave them priority over their work on the collective farms. (The First Party Secretary noted that even private cows were calving at a faster rate than socialist cows.) The Party wanted to abolish private plots, but as no formula had been found to produce adequate food supplies through the kolkhoz and sovkhoz farms alone, such drastic action could not be taken.

The Communist Party had failed to come to terms with the peasants. The collective farm and the state farms seemed to the majority of them to perpetuate the worst features of serfdom and the village communes, and they resented the intrusion of the Party bureaucrats, who interfered in their lives, as much as they had hated the domination of tsarist landlords. They met the incessant exhortations to work harder with indifference and even passive resistance.

Meanwhile, Khrushchev had also begun a drive to increase and diversify membership of the Party, in particular by reducing the proportion of white-collar workers and increasing membership among workers in agriculture and forestry. His reforms were designed both to expand the Party's influence and also to tighten his own control. He was, nevertheless, in a dangerous position, especially as seven of the eleven-member Presidium—including Molotov, Malenkov, Ka-

The Communist Party of the Soviet Union exercises its rule through an intricate administrative and bureaucratic system, and the government (whose structure, as well as that of the CPSU, is diagrammed opposite) merely administers party directives. Candidates for all political bodies—from village soviet to the Supreme Soviet—are freely nominated by "public organizations and societies of the working people." After the nominations have been made, informal, extra-legal "primaries," supervised by the Party, determine which candidates (one for each seat) will remain on the ballot. The rest withdraw, and the electorate ultimately votes its concurrence. Party policy is formulated at the top by the Politburo and passed downward through the secretariats to some 330,000 primary units, or cells, whose rolls include roughly four per cent of the population. Members, such as the kolkhoz farmer at right, usually voice approval of the Party line.

ganovich, Bulganin, and Voroshilov—continued to oppose his radical ideas. Indeed, in June, 1957, a crisis came about in the Presidium. Meeting almost continuously from June 18 to 21, a majority of the members called for Khrushchev's resignation. The First Party Secretary demanded that the matter be referred to the Central Committee, where he could be assured of support. The Presidium placed every obstacle in his way. Actively assisted by Zhukov and others in the high command, who even provided military aircraft to bring Central Committee members to Moscow, Khrushchev won a special meeting, which began on June 22. Khrushchev's enemies in the Presidium found themselves isolated when a clear majority of the Central Committee expressed support for the First Secretary. Molotov maintained his opposition, but Voroshilov wavered and then went over to Khrushchev's side. In the final resolution his opponents were condemned as the "anti-Party" faction. Khrushchev at once increased the size of the Presidium to fifteen, the four new members being his supporters. At the Twenty-first Party Congress, which met in January, 1959, Khrushchev's men seized the opportunity to make fervent tributes to Khrushchev's "Leninist firmness" and dedication, and delivered still more savage criticism of his opponents, especially Molotov, Malenkov, and Kaganovich. (Unlike victims of Stalin's purges, however, they were demoted or dismissed, not executed.)

The nation was undergoing a thaw, and a new mood was noticeable in the conduct of foreign policy. As Chairman of the Council of Ministers, Malenkov had acknowledged in March, 1954, that use of the hydrogen bomb would result in "the destruction of world civilization." His statement was so furiously attacked by Khrushchev, Molotov, and others that he was compelled to amend it and to assert that nuclear war would destroy capitalism, but not world civilization. Soviet foreign policy nevertheless displayed a more fundamentally conciliatory attitude. An armistice in the Korean War was signed in July, 1953, and shortly after, the Soviet government announced that no further reparations would be exacted from Germany after January 1, 1954. In the Far East the transfer of all rights in Manchuria to the Chinese People's Republic was negotiated. However, where the essential interests of the U.S.S.R. were concerned, there continued to be no signs of yielding.

At this time John Foster Dulles was the spokesman for United States foreign policy. A staunch anti-Communist, he had no sooner been appointed in 1953 than he proclaimed United States' intention to liberate all countries under Soviet domination, and threatened "massive retaliation," predicated on America's monopoly of thermonuclear weapons. (The monopoly came to an end in August, 1953, when the Soviets exploded their own hydrogen bomb.) The following

January Dulles participated in a four-power conference of foreign ministers in Berlin, and he proved as intractable as Molotov on the issues surrounding German unification. The Russian minister made it clear that the Soviet Union would not accept free elections in Germany, for they might result in an all-German government aligned with the West.

Two other problems that were closely discussed at the foreign ministers' conference convened in Geneva in April were peace in Korea (the existing armistice agreement was merely confirmed) and in Indochina. Ho Chi Minh, the Vietnamese leader who had been trained in Communist Party ideology in Moscow, was advancing southward against the French, and after the storming of Dien Bien Phu in May, the whole of Indochina seemed about to fall under Communist domination. The French had appealed for American help. Dulles was eager to halt the Communist advance, but only in some collective action with the Western allies; Britain in particular was unwilling to be committed. Dulles withdrew from the Geneva Conference, and the British and French representatives managed to negotiate an armistice in July, 1954, whereby Vietnam was divided at the 17th parallel.

Soviet leaders were disturbed by the subsequent creation of the Southeast Asia Treaty Organization (SEATO) in September, 1954. The entry of Western Germany into NATO in May, 1955, seemed more threatening, despite West Ger-

man guarantees not to produce atomic weapons, long-range missiles, or strategic bombers. The Baghdad Pact, originally concluded in February, 1955, between Turkey and Iraq—and later joined by Iran, Britain, and Pakistan—was taken by the Russians as further proof of the aggressive policies of the Western powers and their allies. The Soviets responded to these pressures with the Eastern Security Treaty, or Warsaw Pact, providing for joint military organization within the Communist bloc.

Nevertheless, 1955 was marked by a number of important Soviet concessions, and a general atmosphere of optimism prevailed. In May the Austrian State Treaty was signed by Soviet Russia, the United States, Great Britain, and France, thus ending the ten-year occupation of that nation by the four powers in return for guarantees of Austrian neutrality. In July the Soviets entered into discussions on disarmament, trade, and further talks on the German problem at a Geneva summit conference. And in September they returned to Finland the important naval base of Porkkala Peninsula.

The change to a more conciliatory approach was stated in February at the historic Twentieth Party Congress of 1956. In addition to denouncing Stalin, Khrushchev revised the fundamentals of Soviet foreign policy. The proposals made by Malenkov for reducing tensions in relations with the Western powers had earlier been opposed by his colleagues in the

*Fizkultura—physical fitness and sports
activities—is a dominating factor in Soviet
life. Mass media produce a continual
barage of propaganda, urging citizens of
all ages to participate in government
health programs. The Young Pioneers
pictured opposite are taking part in the
massive Sports Day exercises held throughout the U.S.S.R. each spring. Factory,
office, and farm workers have their physical culture organizations as well: in the
photograph at right, draftsmen of the
Leningrad hydroelectric works are seen
taking their morning* zaryadki *at their
posts. Instruction is by government radio.*

Presidium; they were now reintroduced. Khrushchev declared that "war is not a fatalistic inevitability. Today there are mighty social and political forces possessing formidable means to prevent the imperialists from unleashing war"; Soviet policy was to pursue "peaceful coexistence." At the same time emphasis was laid on overtaking the West in economic and military strength.

In the spring of 1955 the first Russian intermediate range ballistic missile (IRBM) had been successfully tested. This weapon was already part of the American armory, and in August, 1957, the Russians announced the firing of their first intercontinental ballistic missile (ICBM), which meant that they had the unique capacity to dispatch thermonuclear missiles across the oceans. A few weeks later Soviet technological ascendancy was dramatically demonstrated by the orbiting of *Sputnik*, the first earth satellite. Khrushchev was prompt to claim the superiority of Soviet science over capitalist science, but less than three months later, in December, 1957, the United States officially launched its first ICBM and announced its intention to equip NATO with missiles and to install IRBMs in Turkey and Greece.

In November, 1957, soon after the *Sputnik* spectacular, a conference of world Communist leaders was held in Moscow. Elated by these technological successes, Khrushchev and his colleagues were intent on launching a diplomatic offensive to gather the uncommitted nations of the "third world" into the Communist bloc, opposed to the capitalist West. Mao Tse-tung attended the Moscow conference, and much was made of Sino-Soviet solidarity. However, discord between Moscow and Peking had actually sharpened after Stalin's death. Mao Tse-tung had established his regime with little help from Russia, and while acknowledging the historic role of the Soviet Communist Party, he regarded his party as independent and equal. He had respected Stalin as a strong leader and had always showed restraint in expressing views that might disturb Communist unity.

Since the Twentieth Party Congress, however, Mao and his comrades had become openly critical. They had been angered by Khrushchev's attack on Stalin, and indeed, Mao evidently regarded Khrushchev as a crude opportunist, falling far short of the dedication and discipline expected of a Communist leader. The Chinese Communists were fundamentalists in their interpretation of Communism. Mao maintained, in accordance with orthodox doctrine, that military conflict with the capitalist world was inevitable. At the November, 1957, Moscow conference of world Communists he declared that a nuclear war would destroy capitalism but not Communism, and he put pressure on the Soviet leaders to make use of their nuclear power. Khrushchev and his colleagues recognized that nuclear war would cause a holocaust

in which all countries would suffer fearfully, and regarded their arsenal as a means to negotiate from strength.

In March, 1958, when Khrushchev became Chairman of the Council of Ministers, he made it clear that he would welcome another summit conference. His main purpose was to advance his campaign for the dismantling of NATO and to reach an acceptable arrangement over Germany. Fear of German rearmament remained strong even after the U.S.S.R. had developed its own nuclear weapons. In November, 1958, Khrushchev delivered an ultimatum to the Soviet Union's war-time allies demanding their evacuation of Berlin within six months, posing what appeared to be a real threat to world peace. The Western powers refused to capitulate, and Khrushchev put off pursuing the matter. Berlin nevertheless remained a crisis point. In the following year, still seeking a summit conference, Chairman Khrushchev visited the United States and had cordial meetings at Camp David, Maryland, with President Dwight D. Eisenhower. In December the Western powers agreed to attend a summit conference. The meeting, held in Paris in May, 1960, was broken up by Khrushchev, ostensibly because an American U-2 reconnaissance plane was discovered over Sverdlovsk.

A further conference of world Communist parties was held in Moscow in November, 1960; it sought to demonstrate once more the solidarity of world Communism. Again, communiqués and appearances were deceptive, for at this conference the schism within the movement, resulting from the Chinese challenge to Moscow's leadership, became an acknowledged fact. In particular, Peking formally denounced the Soviet rapprochement with revisionist Yugoslavia and expressed the resentment of the Soviet Union's refusal to share nuclear weapons. The final breakdown was marked by the recall in August, 1960, of all Russian technicians who had been assisting in the development of Chinese industry. Peking began a campaign to build its own Communist bloc, taking Albania into its camp almost immediately, working to secure Afro-Asian support, and denouncing the U.S.S.R. as a European power with an imperialist past.

Khrushchev, preoccupied with Berlin and the problem of Germany, attempted now to wring agreement from John F. Kennedy, the new American President. Soon after taking office in January, 1961, Kennedy's position had been weakened by an ill-conceived attempt to land anti-Communist Cubans on the island's Bay of Pigs. American prestige suffered another blow when in April, 1961, Russia won world acclaim by putting Yury Gagarin into space in the first manned satellite. These two events encouraged Khrushchev to think that the United States would be more amenable to his proposals. When in late May President Kennedy made an official visit to Europe, Khrushchev met him in Vienna and

personally presented him with a note demanding the evacuation of West Berlin. Khrushchev was at his most truculent, but he was given a firm refusal by Kennedy, supported by the other Western powers. In July Kennedy announced that the American armed forces would be further strengthened, and once again Khrushchev was compelled to retreat from what had sounded like an ultimatum.

A more dramatic and dangerous crisis arose over Cuba in 1962 when Khrushchev gravely miscalculated the temper of Kennedy and the American people. The Cuban leader, Fidel Castro, had turned to Soviet Russia for technical and military aid, and at the beginning of 1962 the two countries signed a security pact. Khrushchev then installed Soviet missiles on launching sites in Cuba. In this the First Secretary probably had several objectives: not only was it a demonstration of the U.S.S.R.'s new standing as thermonuclear power, but also a means to gain an advantage in German negotiations. Further, Soviet presence off the United States mainland provided a dramatic attempt to seize the initiative in the ideological war with China by threatening the most powerful symbol of capitalism. He evidently did not believe that the United States would be prepared to embark on a war. President Kennedy's speech to the nation on October 22, in which he stated that America would take whatever steps were necessary to secure removal of the missiles, brought a hurried exchange

of notes between Washington and Moscow, and on October 28 the Kremlin agreed to a withdrawal, subject to United States promises not to invade Cuba.

Soviet American relations were further shaken by sudden changes in leadership. Khrushchev was deposed in October, 1964, less than a year after President Kennedy's assassination. There was a feeling of mutual relief, for in provoking three serious crises—twice over Berlin and once over Cuba— he had shown himself to be dangerously volatile.

On Khrushchev's removal from office, the Presidium at once announced that collective leadership would again be restored. Leonid Brezhnev became First Party Secretary, and Alexei Kosygin was appointed Chairman of the Council of Ministers. Nikolai Podgorny took over the somewhat less influential post of President of the Presidium. All three were men of broad experience and had served in industry, economic planning, as well as administration.

Brezhnev and Kosygin were at once faced with the disorders in the economy, in foreign relations, and within the Communist bloc. The growth rate of the economy had fallen from 12 to 15 per cent annually in the late 1950's to 2.5 per cent, according to some estimates. The stagnation in agriculture was an important element in this decline. A seven-year plan had set the target of a 70 per cent increase in productivity, but by 1964 the growth had been no more than 10 per

397

The 1960's witnessed growing tensions within the Soviet bloc. The Berlin Wall, erected in 1961 on Khrushchev's orders, halted a daily exodus of about 700 refugees from East to West Berlin. At left, East German guards are seen through a portion of the cement and barbed wire barrier. In August, 1968, when Czechs were exulting in the liberalizing policies of Alexander Dubcek's newly formed regime, some 200,000 Russian soldiers, accompanied by token contingents from other Warsaw Pact powers, descended on Czechoslovakia by plane, armored car, and truck. The nation offered no organized military resistance to the Soviet tanks that appeared in the streets of Prague (opposite) and other Czech cities, and government policies reverted to the Kremlin line.

cent. Failure of the harvest in 1963-64 had required urgent action, and the U.S.S.R. had imported over ten million tons of grain at the cost of one billion dollars, which the nation could ill-afford. The Twenty-third Party Congress instituted a five-year plan to run from 1966 to 1970, in which the total investment in agriculture was to be increased to 70 billion dollars, equivalent to the total capital investment for the previous nineteen years. Tractors were to be produced at the rate of 625,000 a year, with a forecast of 1,790,000 tractors in service by 1970. Other changes, aimed at stimulating a 25 per cent increase in productivity, were instituted in the price system and the levies on collective farms. Improved results were reported in 1966, when the grain harvest was 170.8 million tons compared with 130.3 million tons in the previous year. Brezhnev told the Central Committee plenum on October 30, 1968, that agricultural production in the two years since the new five-year plan had been implemented had risen 15 per cent over the preceding three-year averages. (Many Western economists dispute these claims.)

In industry, too, the last years under Khrushchev's supreme authority recorded a decline. Official Soviet figures show that the rate of growth of industrial output had fallen from 10.6 per cent in the period 1950-58 to an estimated 7.3 per cent in 1964. Kosygin backed a limited experiment in free-market economy, including incentive bonuses, prices re-

flecting supply and demand, and encouragements toward greater local initiative on the part of management in the manufacture of goods. Libermanism, as the new approach was called after the chief proponent Professor Yevsei Liberman, was regarded with some hostility. Conservative Communists detected capitalist tendencies in the plan. Nevertheless, 400 consumer-goods factories were on the incentive plan by 1965, and by 1967 fully half of Soviet industry had come under some parts of Liberman's system.

In October, 1968, Brezhnev made the claim that Soviet industrial output would rise by nearly 30 per cent in the period from 1966 to 1968. But subsequent official figures showed that industrial growth rates continued to fall short of goals. At the end of December, 1969, Brezhnev reported that the Russian economy was faced with a recession. *Pravda*, on January 13, 1970, noted with concern the "lag of development rates in a number of industries, the slow growth of labor productivity and production efficiency." A few days later *Trud*, the official paper of the Central Council of Trade Unions, called for severe punishments to be applied by local union organizations to "strengthen the struggle . . . against absenteeism, loafing, and drunkenness."

In foreign policy Brezhnev and Kosygin have been cautious and conservative. In March, 1966, Brezhnev, in his speech to the Twenty-third Party Congress, enunciated no

basic changes. The dangers of a revived Germany were still in the forefront of Soviet minds, but there now appeared to be no intention of provoking a crisis over Berlin or elsewhere. The escalation of the war in Vietnam troubled Soviet leaders. They were anxious to maintain the improved relations with the United States. However, Communist China put the Soviets on the defensive by claiming to be the real champion of the world Communist cause in the "war of national liberation" in South Vietnam and against the United States policy of "containment."

The threat of Communist China, with a population of over seven hundred fifty million, was intensified by the successful explosion of its first atomic bomb in October, 1964. Relations continued to deteriorate sharply as the Chinese promoted Mao Tse-tung as the true spokesman on Marxism-Leninism. Soviet attempts to rally all Communist parties behind Moscow met with limited success. Leaders of eighty-six Communist parties attended the 1966 conference in Moscow, but only sixty-five parties could be counted on to support Moscow's leadership in its disputes with China.

The militant attitudes of the Soviet and Western governments of the early Cold War period have moderated, and the Soviet leaders assert their intention to develop "peaceful coexistence" in the midst of competition between the socialist and the capitalist camps. But Chinese hostility, fears of Ger-

man resurgence, and even the possibility of a rapprochement between Washington and Peking have caused the leadership to feel that their policies cannot be relaxed. They have shown anxious concern to maintain the defense barrier provided by their Communist allies in eastern Europe. The Hungarian revolution of 1956 alerted them to the antagonism that Soviet domination aroused. Moscow is compelled to allow some measure of independence, with the result that the Communist nations of eastern Europe have tended to become junior allies rather than satellites.

Romania was able to strike out on a surprisingly independent course without suffering direct Soviet intervention, no doubt partly because it was surrounded by other Communist allies. In Czechoslovakia, however, Alexander Dubcek's liberal politics and proposals for modification of the Warsaw Pact were seen as a threat to the security and the stability of the Communist regimes in the Soviet Union and throughout the Eastern bloc. The leaders of the U.S.S.R., East Germany, Poland, Bulgaria, and Hungary made strong protests, and then in August, 1968, sent troops to put an end to Czech ambitions. Gradually the liberal regime has been replaced. But the aspirations of the Czechoslovak people, although suppressed, have not been extinguished.

In many other ways the U.S.S.R. seems frustrated by disappointments. Since the death of Stalin the nation has stood

Politburo members are pictured here at a December, 1969, meeting of the Supreme Soviet. Front row, from left to right: Gennady Voronov, Mikhail Suslov, and the current collective leadership—Nikolai Podgorny, Presidium President and titular head of state, Alexei Kosygin, Chairman of the Council of Ministers and real chief of state, and Leonid Brezhnev, First Secretary of the Communist Party.

hesitantly on the threshold of a new era into which it has been unable to advance. Its leaders face certain intractable problems, which in essense have always confronted Russia's rulers. Nor has the unresponsive nature of authority changed greatly. After the collapse of the tsarist regime the Soviet Communist Party continued to produce autocrats in Lenin, Stalin, and, to a limited extent, in Khrushchev. With the opening of the second half of the twentieth century it seemed possible that this historical pattern might be broken under the aegis of collective leadership. But Brezhnev, Kosygin, and Podgorny are undistinguished, and among the younger members in the upper strata of the Party none has so far emerged to challenge their position. In these circumstances collective leadership may once again become the convention, but the potential for a strong and ambitious man to emerge as autocrat remains.

Problems of agriculture have always burdened the nation, contributing significantly to its low standard of living and its backwardness. Only in the brief period of Peter Stolypin's ministry, after the revolution of 1905, were there real signs of a new spirit among the peasantry; but war and then revolution destroyed Stolypin's work and choked the spirit of initiative that had begun to stir. Stalin's enforced collectivization bore heavily upon the Russian peasants, who were subjected to unending exhortations and severe discipline.

Agriculture, for so long the stepchild of the Russian economy, had in the late 1960's received injections of capital on a massive scale, but productivity has remained at a very low level. Some thirty per cent of the population continues to be tied to farming. Extension of modern methods and greater incentives, such as have been applied so effectively in many countries of the West, would lead to a marked growth in efficiency. It would then be possible for as much as two thirds of the labor force to be moved from agriculture to far more productive work in industry. But the Soviet regime has proved unable to enlist the cooperation of the peasants—necessary to achieve this revolution.

Industry has made tremendous strides forward since the beginning of the century, and especially during the first three five-year plans. The war caused widescale dislocation of plants and destroyed many of its industrial centers. Immediately after the war, however, there was a substantial revival. (The 1970 Soviet census shows 56 per cent of the population, 136 million people, living in urban areas. Of these, ten have at their center cities of over one million population.) Moreover, during the 1950's Russia demonstrated a mastery of the most advanced technology. But by the end of the 1960's industry, too, was stagnating. Inefficiency and wastefulness pervade the whole of the Soviet economy, and because productivity is so low and national priorities so high,

The rifle-brandishing Red Chinese soldiers shown in this January, 1969, photograph skirmish with Soviet forces near Damansky, a small, uninhabited island in the icebound Ussuri River—part of the Russian-Chinese Far Eastern border. Claimed by both sides, the island was the scene that winter of continued fierce Sino-Soviet clashes, which were widely exploited by both sides for propaganda purposes.

the standard of living has failed to reach anticipated levels; popular discontent is an attendant problem.

The nation, now numbering nearly 242 million, remains confined within Marxism-Leninism, as formerly it was enchained by autocracy and the Orthodox Church. The Communist hierarchy is evidently incapable of adopting flexible and pragmatic policies for fear of sacrificing the broad aims of socialism. But this rigid outlook, of which Nicholas was the most depressing exponent, has been a constant factor in Russia's history.

Considerations of national security have been an important ingredient in this fear of experiment and change and in the general acceptance by Russians of their centralized system with power vested in the hands of the autocrat. The Soviets continue to see threats on an even greater scale. Relations with Communist China deteriorated to the point that localized hostilities occurred in March, 1969, on the Ussuri River. Chinese territorial claims, including Outer Mongolia, amount to an area of nearly two million square miles. Indeed, the Sino-Russian crisis arises more from the conflict of vital national interests than from ideological rivalry. Nor can Moscow any longer take for granted, as it did during Stalin's rule, the reliability of the Communist allies on the Soviet Union's western borders. There is also a continuing fear of Germany, which could, in the future, be armed by the Western powers with nuclear weapons. Bearing in mind that the Russian nation suffered some twenty million dead as a result of German aggression in the second World War, this anxiety is unlikely to diminish.

Soviet leaders have given indications of seeking closer relations and understanding with the United States and with western Europe. But here, too, political rivalry with the United States hinders such a policy, and Soviet apprehensions, bolstered during the height of the Cold War, have lingered. The fear of being isolated in international affairs is nevertheless strong, and although actively cultivating allies in the Middle East and elsewhere, the Soviet leaders can have no illusions about the value of such friendships in the event of a major outbreak of war.

The Russians are a people of stamina, rich in talent in every field of human endeavor. They are capable of incredible feats of endurance, of long patience, and of outbreaks of fury. Indeed, like their climate, they are a people of extremes. They have usually advanced in great spurts, as in the reign of Peter the Great and under Stalin, and then have settled down in periods of stagnation. As Russia enters the 1970's the economy is sluggish and the leadership is aging. The hope, for which there is but slight evidence, must be that the coming generations, more broadly educated than their fathers, will promote the liberal evolution of the Soviet system.

Acknowledgments

The editors gratefully acknowledge the valuable editorial assistance of Claire de Forbin, Paris; Sandra N. Humphrey and Gretchen Maynes, Moscow; Elena Whiteside, New York; and Christine Sutherland, London. They are also grateful to Cal Sacks for the original maps; and to the following individuals and institutions for providing pictorial material and supplying information.

Virginia Bennett, Princeton, N.J.
William L. Blackwell, New York
Count Alexis Bobrinskoy, London
Bodleian Library, Oxford University
Margaret Bourke-White, Darien, Conn.
British Museum, London
    Department of Oriental Manuscripts
    Department of Prints and Drawings
    Department of Western Manuscripts
Edmée Busch, New York
Geoffrey Clements, New York
Nathaniel Floyd, New York
Galerie Charpentier, Paris
Perihan and Ara Güler, Istanbul
Imperial War Museum, London
Malcolm C. Johnson Jr., New York
Koninklijke Bibliotheek, The Hague
    H.P. de Soeten
Norman Kotker, New York
Library of Congress, Washington, D.C.
    Virginia Daiker
Metropolitan Museum of Art, New York
    Colta Ives
Museum der Stadt Wien, Vienna
National Maritime Museum,
  Greenwich, England
New York Public Library,
  Slavonic Division
    John L. Mish, Viktor Koressaar,
    Abraham Jaeger
Novosti Press Agency, Moscow
    Guenrikh A. Borovik, New York
Osterreichische National Bibliothek,
  Vienna
    Walter Wiesser
Yale Richmond, Counselor for Cultural
  Affairs, U.S. Embassy, Moscow
Max Steinbook, New York
George S. Yaney, Cambridge,
  Massachusetts

RECOMMENDED READING

Billington, James H., *The Icon and the Axe*, New York, Alfred A. Knopf, Inc., 1966.

Blackwell, William, *Beginnings of Russian Industrialization*, 1800–1860, Princeton, Princeton University Press, 1968.

Blum, Jerome, *Lord and Peasant in Russia from the Ninth to the Nineteenth Century*, Princeton, Princeton University Press, 1961. Also paperback, Atheneum.

Carr, Edward Hallett, *The Bolshevik Revolution*, 1917–1923, New York, Macmillan & Co., 1952. Also paperback, Penguin.

Dmytryshyn, Basil, *U.S.S.R: A Concise History*, New York, Charles Scribner's Sons, 1965. Also paperback.

Dvornik, Francis, *The Slavs in European History and Civilization*, New Brunswick, Rutgers Univesity Press, 1962.

Fainsod, Merle, *How Russia is Ruled*, Cambridge, Harvard University Press, revised ed., 1963.

Florinsky, Michael T., *Russia, A History and an Interpretation*, 2 vols., New York, The Macmillan Company, 1954.

Gregory, James S., *Russian Land—Soviet People: A Geographical Approach to the U.S.S.R.*, Racine, Western Publishing Co., Inc. 1968.

Grey, Ian, *The First Fifty Years: Soviet Russia 1917–1967*, New York, Coward-McCann, Inc. 1967

Marsden, Christopher, *Palmyra of the North: The First Days of St. Petersburg*, London, Faber and Faber, 1942.

Mazour, Anatole G., *The First Russian Revolution*, 1925, Stanford, Stanford University Press, 1964. Also paperback.

Medieval Russia's Epics, Chronicles, and Tales, Serge A. Zenkovsky, ed., New York, E.P. Dutton & Co., Inc., 1963. Paperback.

Miliukov, Paul, *Religion and the Church in Russia*, Philadelphia, University of Pennsylvania Press, 1942. Also paperback, A.S. Barnes.

Prospects for Soviet Society, Allen Kassof, ed., New York, Frederick A. Praeger, Inc., 1968. Also paperback.

Readings in Russian Civilization, Thomas Riha, ed., 3 vols., Chicago, University of Chicago Press, revised ed., 1969. Also paperback.

Revolutionary Russia: A Symposium, Richard Pipes, ed., Cambridge, Harvard University Press, 1968. Also paperback, Anchor.

Riasanovsky, Nicholas V. *A History of Russia*, New York, Oxford University Press, 1963. Also paperback.

Nicholas I *and Official Nationality in Russia, 1825–1855.* Berkeley, University of California Press, 1967. Also paperback.

Robinson, Geroid Tanquary, *Rural Russia Under the Old Régime,* New York, The Macmillan Company, 1967. Also paperback, University of California Press.

Rude & Barbarous Kingdom, Russia in the Accounts of Sixteenth Century English Voyagers, Lloyd E. Berry and Robert O. Crummey, eds., Madison, The University of Wisconsin Press, 1968.

Russia's Eastward Expansion, George Alexander Lensen, ed., Englewood Cliffs, N.J., 1964. Paperback.

Seton-Watson, Hugh, *The Russian Empire, 1801–1917,* Oxford, Oxford University Press, 1967.

Seven Britons in Imperial Russia (1698–1812), Peter Putnam, ed., Princeton, Princeton University Press, 1952.

Tupper, Harmon, *To the Great Ocean: Siberia and the Trans-Siberian Railway,* Boston, Little, Brown & Co., 1965.

The Moscow Kremlin, Berkeley, University of California Press, 1954.

Vernadsky, George, *A History of Russia,* New Haven, Yale University Press, revised ed., 1961. Also paperback.

Voyce, Arthur, *The Art and Architecture of Medieval Russia,* Norman, University of Oklahoma Press, 1966.

Vucinich, Alexander, *Science in Russian Culture, A History to 1860,* Stanford, Stanford University Press, 1963.

Ware, Timothy, *The Orthodox Church,* Baltimore, Penguin Books, 1964. Paperback.

Werth, Alexander, *Russia at War, 1941–1945,* New York, E. P. Dutton & Co., Inc., 1964.

Wolfe, Bertram D., *Three Who Made A Revolution,* New York, The Dial Press, Inc., 1964. Also paperback, Dell.

PERMISSIONS

Where not otherwise noted, excerpts from Russian works have been translated by the author. The editors have generally transliterated Russian names according to Thomas Shaw's *The Transliteration of Modern Russian for English-Language Publications,* with the exception of certain names for which a familiar English version exists. In the anthology selections, however, the spellings are those of the translator. Grateful acknowledgment is also made for permission to quote from the following works.

CHAPTER I: 21, 24, 25, 26, 28, 29, 30, 32, 34, from *The Russian Primary Chronicle Laurentian Text,* translated and edited by Samual H. Cross and Olgerd P. Sherbowitz-Wetzor. Reprinted by permission of the Mediaeval Academy of America, Cambridge, Mass. 32, from *Medieval Russian Laws,* translated by George Vernadsky. Copyright © 1947. Reprinted by permission of Columbia University Press, New York. 34, from *Anthology of Russian Literature,* vol. I, by Leo Wiener. Copyright © 1902. Reprinted by permission of G. P. Putnam's Sons, New York.

THE DIVINE CITY: 40, from *The Itinerary of Benjamin of Tudela,* translated by Marcus Nathan Adler. Reprinted by permission of Philipp Feldheim, Inc, New York. / *Medieval Russia's Epics, Chronicles and Tales,* edited by Serge A. Zenkovsky. Copyright © 1963. Reprinted by permission of E. P. Dutton Co., Inc., New York.

CHAPTER II: 45, 46, from *Medieval Russia's Epics, Chronicles and Tales,* edited by Serge A. Zenkovsky. Copyright © 1963. Reprinted by permission of E. P. Dutton Co., Inc., New York. / *A Literary History of Persia,* vol. III, by E. G. Browne. Reprinted by permission of Cambridge University Press, England.

CHAPTER III: 93–94, from *Russia at the Close of the Sixteenth Century,* by E. A. Bond. Reprinted by permission of Burt Franklin Publishing, New York.

CHURCH AND STATE: 106, from *The Travels of Macarius, Patriarch of Antioch,* by Archdeacon Paul of Aleppo. / *A Popular History of Russia from the Earliest Times to 1880,* by Alfred Rimbaud. / *Readings in Russian Civilization,* vol. I, edited by Thomas Riha. Copyright © 1964. Reprinted by permission of The University of Chicago Press, Ill. 114, from *Russia at the Close of the Sixteenth Century,* by E. A. Bond. Reprinted by permission of Burt Franklin Publishing, New York. / *Medieval Russia's Epics, Chronicles and Tales,* edited by Serge A. Zenkovsky. Copyright © 1963. Reprinted by permission of E. P. Dutton Co., Inc., New York. / *A Description of Moscow and Muscovy,* by Sigmund von Herberstein, translated by J. B. C. Grundy. Copyright © 1969. Reprinted by permission of J. M. Dent & Sons, Ltd., London.

CHAPTER IV: 117, 119, from *Russia at the Close of the Sixteenth Century,* by E. A. Bond. Reprinted by permission of Burt Franklin Publishing, New York.

THE SIBERIAN FRONTIER: 144, from *A Journey from St. Petersburg to Pekin 1719–1722,* by John Bell, edited by J. L. Stevenson. Copyright © 1966. Reprinted by permission of the Edinburgh University Press, Ltd., Scotland. / *Russia's Eastward Expansion,* edited by George Alexander Lensen. Copyright © 1964. Reprinted by permission of Prentice-Hall, Inc., Englewood Cliffs, N.J. / *The Travels of Macarius, Patriarch of Antioch,* by Archdeacon Paul of Aleppo.

PETER'S GLORY: 184–85, from *Splendours of Leningrad,* by Abraam Kaganovich, translated by James Hogarth. Copyright © 1969. Reprinted by permission of the Cowles Book Company, Inc., New York, and Nagel Publishers, Geneva. 178, from *A New Royal and Authentic System of Universal Geography* by Rev. Thomas Bankes.

SOUL OF RUSSIA: 219, from *A Journey from St. Petersburg to Moscow,* by Alexander Radishchev, translated by Leo Wiener, edited by Roderick Page Thaler. Copyright © 1958. Reprinted by permission of Harvard University Press, Cambridge, Mass.

THE INTELLIGENTSIA: 264, from *My Past and Thoughts—The Memoirs of Alexander Herzen,* Vol. II, translated by Constance Garnett, revised by Humphrey Higgens. Copyright © 1968. Reprinted by permission of Random House, Inc., New York; David Garnett; and Chatto & Windus Ltd., London.

1917: THE ONSLAUGHT: 331, from *Russia and History's Turning Point,* by Alexander Kerensky. Copyright © 1965. Reprinted by permission of Hawthorn Books, Inc. / *The History of the Russian Revolution,* Vol. III, *The Triumph of the Soviets,* translated by Max Eastman.

NATION AT WAR: 374, from *Leningrad: Eyewitness History of World War* II, vol. III. Reprinted by permission of Hamish Hamilton Ltd., London. / *The Young Guards,* by Alexander Fadeyev.

Index

NOTE: *Page numbers in boldface type refer to illustrations.*